OCÉANO ATLÁNTICO

Las Bahamas
…echo de Florida
…tanzas
…ienfuegos
CUBA
Camagüey
Guantánamo
Santiago de Cuba
REPÚBLICA DOMINICANA
PUERTO RICO
HAITÍ
Mayagüez
Ponce
San Juan
Islas Vírgenes
Antigua
Santo Domingo
Port-au-Prince
Kingston
JAMAICA
Guadalupe
Dominica
Martinique
Santa Lucía
San Vicente
Barbados
Antillas Menores
Granada
MAR DEL CARIBE
Aruba
Bonaire
Curaçao
Isla de Margarita
Trinidad
Tobago
Port-of-Spain
Caracas
Canal de Panamá
Colón
Panamá
PANAMÁ
R. Orinoco
VENEZUELA
GUYANA
GUA… FRAN…
SURINAM
R. Magdalena
Golfo de Panamá
AMÉRICA DEL SUR
Bogotá
COLOMBIA
BRASIL

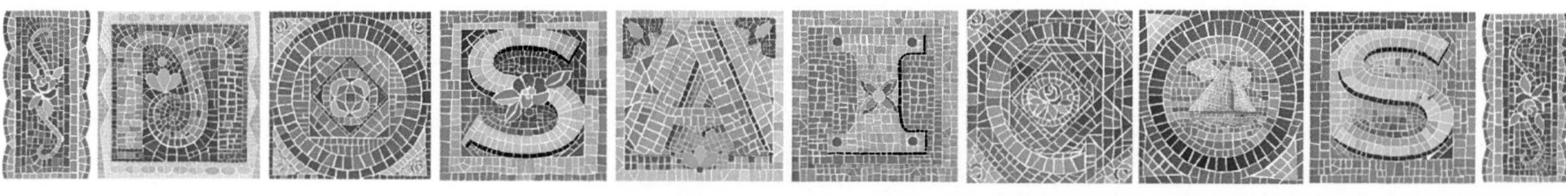

SPANISH I

CUSTOM EDITION FOR PENN STATE UNIVERSITY

Taken from:
Mosaicos: Spanish as a World Language, Third Edition
by Matilde Olivella de Castells, Elizabeth Guzmán,
Paloma Lapuerta, and Carmen García

Taken from:

Mosaicos: Spanish as a World Language, Third Edition
by Matilde Olivella de Castells, Elizabeth Guzmán, Paloma Lapuerta, and Carmen García

Published by Prentice Hall
Upper Saddle River, New Jersey 07458

This special edition published in cooperation with Pearson Custom Publishing.

Printed in the United States of America

10 9 8 7 6 5 4 3 2

ISBN 0-536-83648-5

2004320037

KK

Please visit our web site at *www.pearsoncustom.com*

PEARSON CUSTOM PUBLISHING
501 Boylston Street, Suite 900, Boston, MA 02116
A Pearson Education Company

Contents

Preface

About the *Mosaicos* Program

Welcome to the third edition of ***Mosaicos***! With this text, the beginning classroom becomes a setting for true communication and cultural exchange. ***Mosaicos*** combines the best elements of language instruction in a highly interactive approach. An emphasis on frequently used vocabulary, practical applications of grammar, illustrated language contexts, and engaging activities help to successfully develop good communication skills.

Mosaicos is built on a foundation of interaction, communication, and culture. Its functional grammatical syllabus provides an understanding of the language in a clear, concise format. Structures are presented as a means to effective communication and valuable class time can be spent interacting as well as developing and improving language skills in Spanish.

Highlights of the Program

The third edition of ***Mosaicos*** continues the successful tradition of the first and second, retaining and enhancing the core features, and presenting an all-new integrated video, CD-ROM, and Website that are unique to the ***Mosaicos*** program.

Focus on communication

The ***Mosaicos*** program features a lively and visual communicative format for presenting and practicing new language. Abundant activities in the *A primera vista* section of each chapter foster use of newly-acquired and previously-learned words and expressions in a variety of contexts. These contexts provide a natural environment for learning and practicing new vocabulary, as well as for recycling previously-taught language and previewing new structures.

Mosaicos presents grammar as a means to communicate effectively. The scope and sequence of grammatical topics in ***Mosaicos, Third Edition***, is dictated by the communicative needs of beginning students. Activities in the *Explicación y expansión* section of each chapter develop the ability to use linguistic structures for direct communicative purposes.

Opportunities for previewing and recycling. The *Algo más* section is designed to introduce structural points needed for communication in increments, which facilitates students' internalization of these linguistic structures. Throughout the text, annotations suggest opportunities for instructors to review and reinforce recycled structures and vocabulary clusters.

A closer integration of culture and language

In the third edition, the integration of culture and language has been further enriched and developed. Each chapter focuses closely on a country or region, and numerous examples from that country or region are used consistently throughout the chapter in language samples, photos, maps, and realia. Related cultural content is interwoven throughout the text in activities and readings.

Integrated media program

Mosaicos, Third Edition offers a robust and truly integrated technology program featuring a new *Fortunas* Video, an Activity CD-ROM bound into every new copy of the text, and a Website. Each of the 15 chapters now concludes with the newly developed *Enfoque interactivo*, which integrates the ***Mosaicos*** media program —Video, Activity CD-ROM, and Website— into the course. The *Enfoque interactivo* highlights the activities that are available in the media program, indicates when the activities can be completed, and provides guidance to the instructor and student for when and how to use the media components and for the amount of time required by the task. Also new to this edition are the E-Workbook and E-Lab Manual, which are on-line versions of the print Workbook/Lab Manual.

From skill building to skill using

The unique culture-based ***Mosaicos*** sections of each chapter provide skill-building and skill-using activities in each area: listening, speaking, reading, and writing. These sections also provide ample opportunities for skill-chaining.

Listening strategy work. Many *A escuchar* sections include pre-listening activities that provide general listening strategies. In many cases, students are asked to fill in charts, comment on, or otherwise process the information they hear after completing the specific listening task, integrating listening with productive skills.

Personalized speaking activities. More open-ended activities in every chapter provide opportunities for individuals, pairs and groups of students to gather, process and share information in Spanish, stimulating real communication in the classroom. Conversation activities in the *A conversar* section of each chapter encourage interaction on a personal level combining newly acquired structures and vocabulary in discussions on chapter topics.

Increased attention to reading skills. Pre- and post-reading activities provide opportunities and strategies for developing reading skills. Reading selections include a greater number of authentic texts and reflect a variety of discourse types and styles ranging from journalistic to literary. Texts become longer and more challenging as the book progresses.

Process writing apparatus. Carefully-crafted process writing activities conclude each *Mosaicos* section. Pre- and post-writing activities are a guide through critical steps in the writing process. Throughout, extensive annotations guide instructors to teach writing as a recursive —rather than linear— process.

Scope and Sequence of the Third Edition

In response to helpful feedback from users of the second edition, the following adjustments have been made to the scope and sequence:

- To quickly facilitate learners' ability to communicate in Spanish, a number of linguistic structures needed for conversation are now presented earlier in the text. For example: question words are now in lesson 1, possessive adjectives are in lesson 2, adverbs and some reflexive verbs appear in lesson 4.
- Key structural points were moved. In the third edition, the presentation and practice of the preterit has been divided between lessons 6 and 7. Lesson 6 covers the preterit tense of regular verbs and the preterit of **ir** and **ser.** Lesson 7 addresses the irregular forms of the preterit, the preterit of *-er* and *-ir* verbs whose stem ends in a vowel and the preterit of stem-changing *-ir* verbs: (*e* → *i*) (*o* → *u*).

- Indirect commands were moved to lesson 10, and informal commands to lesson 11; the conditional was moved to lesson 13 to be presented immediately after the future; the past perfect and the infinitive as subject of a sentence and object of a preposition were moved to lesson 14; the imperfect subjunctive was moved to lesson 15.
- The present perfect subjunctive, the past perfect subjunctive, *if* clauses using the perfect tenses, and the passive voice were moved to the *Expansión gramatical.* Instructors who wish to include these structures may incorporate them in the core lessons of the program.

Other features of the third edition that should prove beneficial for both students and instructors are:

- **Expanded *Enfoque cultural* sections.** These sections in each chapter provide practical knowledge of specific cultural topics of the Spanish-speaking world as well as an orientation to the countries that make up that world. Activities in each *Enfoque cultural* encourage the exploration of Spanish-language Websites to gather information on the cultural topic presented. A new, interactive version of the *Enfoque cultural* on the ***Mosaicos*** Website provides hotlinks to related Spanish language Websites that extend the range of cultural examples to which the student is introduced. The new ***Mosaicos*** Website also provides numerous activities based on — and hotlinked to — Websites all over Spain and Latin America.
- **Revised *situaciones* sections** offer students guided, semi-guided, and open-ended role plays. These *situaciones* foster the use of the various patterns of oral exchanges in Spanish, allows for personalization of information and/or the filling of a communication gap, and aim at specific student output.
- **More extensive and consistent use of *Cultura* boxes.** The range of the *Cultura* boxes has been expanded in the third edition and they now appear in each chapter to ensure students gain an understanding and appreciation of people and cultures while building linguistic skills.
- ***Acentos* boxes.** Syllable stress and accent rules in Spanish often overlooked in introductory texts appear in new concept boxes called *Acentos.*
- ***Lengua* boxes,** which inform learners of socio-linguistic distinctions in the Spanish language, appeared at strategic intervals throughout the second edition. In the third edition, they appear in every chapter.
- ***A investigar boxes*** as well as *A investigar* activities appear in every lesson of the text to make the acquisition of cultural knowledge an active process by guiding students to gather information in the library or on the World Wide Web, which they then use to examine the cultural content embedded in the chapter materials.

Organization of the Text

Mosaicos consists of a preliminary chapter (*Bienvenidos*) and fifteen regular chapters. Through a variety of visual stimuli, the *Bienvenidos* chapter allows instructors to conduct classes in Spanish from the very first day. Each regular chapter maintains the following consistent structure:

Goals. Succinct, easy-to-understand objectives in each chapter opener provide realistic, communicative, structural, and cultural goals.

A primera vista. This opening section of each chapter provides a richly contextualized, cultural framework for learning and practicing new language. New material is presented within two or three thematic groupings, which make use of photos, illustrations, and authentic documents.

Comprehensible input is provided through a wide variety of language samples (dialogs, brief narratives, brochures, comic strips, captions, etc.). Within each thematic grouping, activities provide opportunities to practice the new vocabulary and in some cases preview grammar points which are formally presented later in the chapter. Following the thematic presentations, the *A escuchar* listening activity recycles vocabulary in an authentic conversational framework while providing practice in global listening skills. Previously-taught material is consistently recycled and reinforced.

Explicación y expansión. The *Explicación y expansión* sections consist of concise grammar explanations focused on usage followed by immediate practice of each new structural item within a contextualized framework. The exercises and activities in this section develop students' abilities to use linguistic structures for direct communicative purposes. Contextualized and personalized, the exercises focus student attention on a variety of useful tasks and provide practice for communicating effectively in pairs or small groups in a variety of real-life situations. These activities reinforce both vocabulary introduced in the *A primera vista* section of the chapter and vocabulary presented in previous chapters.

Mosaicos. Skills and topics are interwoven at the end of each chapter into a series of skill-building and skill-chaining activities that bring together the chapter vocabulary, structures, and cultural content:

- *A escuchar* develops students' ability to understand spoken Spanish in a variety of authentic contexts: brief exchanges and longer conversations between two or more speakers, telephone messages, radio broadcasts, literary texts, etc.
- *A conversar* includes open-ended speaking activities based on naturally-occurring discourse situations and authentic written texts. Students learn to express and discuss their own needs and interests. This section provides many opportunities for personalized expression.
- *A leer* teaches students how to become independent readers by introducing basic strategies for understanding the general meaning of a text as well as for extracting specific information from it. A complete apparatus of pre-, during-, and post-reading activities guides students to develop their ability to read a variety of high-interest, authentic Spanish texts, from simple documents such as advertisements to the extended discourse of brochures, newspaper and magazine articles, letters, literary texts, etc.
- *A escribir* provides step-by-step activities in which students learn to compose messages and memos, postcards and letters, journals, simple expository paragraphs and brief essays. Pre- and post-writing activities guide students through critical steps in the writing process, including: brainstorming (to develop ideas for topics); defining one's purpose, means of communication, tone, and reader; making an outline; revising; and conferencing and peer editing. Additionally, useful tips in *A leer* provide students with specific lexicon, structures, and points of syntax relevant to the writing task at hand.

Vocabulario. The vocabulary list includes all new, active vocabulary words and expressions presented in the chapter in clear, semantically-organized groups. All words included in the list are practiced and recycled throughout the chapter and in subsequent chapters in a variety of contexts. Written vocabulary practice appears in the *A primera vista* sections and in the accompanying Workbook/Lab Manual, and a recording of all active vocabulary words is included in the lab program and on the CD-ROM.

Enfoque cultural. This entertaining and informative section focuses on contemporary cultural issues related to the chapter theme. *Enfoque cultural* sections use a graphic layout, combining visual and textual elements—photos, maps, brief essays—to capture students' interest and expose them to key information. Additionally, every *Enfoque cultural* includes activities that encourage students to explore the issues at hand. A broad variety of contemporary topics is featured, ranging from distinctive and changing aspects of daily life, such as family, housing, shopping, and travel, to broader social, political, and economic issues in Hispanic countries. Students can explore the topics presented in the *Enfoque cultural* on the Web via an interactive version presented on the *Mosaicos* Website.

Enfoque interactivo. The *Enfoque interactivo* highlights the numerous resources and activities available on the *Mosaicos Fortunas* Video, Activity CD-ROM, and Website, and provides guidance to the instructor for how to integrate those components into his or her course. Media activities in the *Enfoque interactivo* can be done during classroom media lab sessions, or can be assigned as homework. Time estimates indicate the approximate time necessary to complete the activity, and teacher's annotations provide suggestions for using the activities in the classroom.

The Complete Program

Mosaicos is a complete learning and teaching program that includes the following components:

- Student text with Activity CD-ROM
- Annotated Instructor's Edition with Activity CD-ROM
- Instructor's Resource Manual
- *Fortunas* Video
- *Mosaicos* Activity CD-ROM
- *Mosaicos* Website
- Testing Program
- Computerized Testing Program
- Transparencies
- Student Audio CDs/Cassettes
- Workbook/Lab Manual
- Workbook Answer Key
- Audioprogram (Lab CDs/Cassettes)
- E-Workbook
- E-Lab Manual

Student Text with Activity CD-ROM

A copy of the *Mosaicos* Activity CD-ROM is included in each copy of the student text and instructor's edition. Also, ***Mosaicos*** is available for purchase with or without two sixty-minute audio CDs or cassettes that contain recordings of the *A escuchar* sections in the textbook. The *A escuchar* sections are also recorded for departmental language labs free of charge and are included in the audioprogram.

Annotated Instructor's Edition

Marginal annotations in the Annotated Instructor's Edition include extensive strategies, activities, expansion exercises, and a selected answer key for all sections of the text, and a printed Tapescript for the *A escuchar* section. Additional tips and hints offer effective classroom techniques.

Instructor's Resource Manual

The Instructor's Resource Manual is designed to aid instructors in using the text. It addresses theoretical and pedagogical concerns such as classroom atmosphere and the communicative oriented classroom. In addition, it provides course syllabi, suggestions for lesson plans, suggestions for using the media components of the program, a complete Tapescript for the Audioprogram, and tips for using video successfully.

Fortunas Video

Written and filmed specifically for the ***Mosaicos, Third Edition*** program, the new *Fortunas* video is an ongoing drama that features four contestants competing to solve cultural mysteries and locate three fortunes within Mexico. The three fortunes correspond to three cultural periods of Mexican history (Aztec, Colonial, and Contemporary). Clues highlight and teach students about these cultural periods while the contest atmosphere provides students with a dynamic, interesting environment in which to learn the target grammar and vocabulary. The *Fortunas* contest becomes interactive as activities presented in the in-text *Enfoque interactivo*, Activity CD-ROM, and Website allow students to try to solve the mysteries themselves, interact with the video characters by writing and voice-recording on the Activity CD-ROM, and influence the outcome of the contest by awarding the contestants points through viewer polls on the Website.

Mosaicos Activity CD-ROM

Packaged FREE with each copy of ***Mosaicos, Third Edition,*** the *Mosaicos* Activity CD-ROM includes the entire *Fortunas* Video with a series of activities designed to involve students in the video story-line. Students work with the information presented in order to follow clues, gather information, and draw conclusions. These activities engage students and offer practice of the four skills (reading, writing, listening, and speaking). In addition, the *Mosaicos* Activity CD-ROM also includes numerous grammar and vocabulary practice exercises, cultural e-mails for the development of reading and writing skills, and fun review games.

Mosaicos Website

The *Mosaicos* Website offers abundant vocabulary and grammar practice exercises and opportunities to explore Spanish language Websites. The entire *Enfoque cultural* section from the text is now available online with hotlinks to authentic Spanish Websites enabling students to further explore the themes and topics presented and to complete the *Para investigar* activities which accompany each *Enfoque cultural.* The *Mosaicos* Website also features a *Fortunas* section based on the video where students can work with clues and weblinks to solve the video mysteries, read contestant biographies and diaries, and cast their vote for different characters to influence the outcome of the contest through viewer polls.

Testing Program

The Testing Program consists of vocabulary quizzes for each *A primera vista* and three alternate versions of tests for each chapter: a more open-ended test, a structured test, and a multiple choice test. Each test is organized by skill, and uses a variety of techniques and activity formats to complement the text. The Testing Program is available in paper or computerized formats.

Computerized Testing Program

The Testing Program is available electronically for Macintosh and IBM. With the electronic version, instructors can mix and match testing materials according to their own needs.

Transparencies

Created specifically for the *Mosaicos* program, this set of fifty-three full-color transparencies of illustrations, realia, and maps, offers the instructor visual classroom support for presenting vocabulary, creating activities, and reviewing chapter materials.

Student Audio CDs or Cassettes

The Student Audio CDs/Cassettes contain the recordings for the in-text *A escuchar* listening activities. These recordings help students acquire and review vocabulary, become more accustomed to hearing spoken Spanish, and understand it better.

Workbook

The organization of the Workbook parallels that of the main text. The Workbook provides further practice of each chapter's vocabulary and grammar structures through sentence building and completion exercises, fill-ins, and art- and realia-cued activities. Reading and writing activities include strategies for improving reading and writing skills. Two new sections have been added to the third edition: a section to assess comprehension of the *Enfoque Cultural* and a section to practice accentuation, which correlates with the stress and written accent in the Lab Manual and the Acentos boxes in the text.

Workbook Answer Key. An answer key for the Workbook is available for instructors who want students to check their own work.

Lab Manual

The Lab Manual is to be used in conjunction with the Audioprogram recordings of listening-comprehension passages such as conversations, descriptions, interviews, and public announcements. The listening-comprehension passages are followed by various comprehension check activities such as true-or-false, multiple choice, completion, and writing responses. Answers to the activities are included at the end of the Lab Manual.

Audioprogram

The Audioprogram is available in either CD or cassette format and consists of the following three components: listening segments to accompany the Lab Manual; chapter-by-chapter text vocabulary; and in-text *A escuchar* listening selections. The listening CDs/Cassettes and the Lab Manual activities help students move beyond the in-text activities towards guided, more realistic, listening contexts.

E-Workbook

This on-line, passcode protected version of the print Workbook allows students to complete activities and receive instant feedback on close-ended Workbook activities. The results for graded activities and students' answers to open-ended activities can be e-mailed to instructors.

E-Lab Manual

The E-Lab Manual offers an on-line version of the print Lab Manual, with streaming audio. The passcode protected E-Lab Manual offers flexibility and convenience to students for accessing listening materials and completing the Lab Manual activities.

National Standards

The National Standards in Foreign Language Education Project published *Standards for Foreign*

Language Learning: Preparing for the 21st Century which identified five goal areas for programs of foreign language instruction: Communication, Cultures, Connections, Comparisons, and Communities. These goal areas inform the pedagogy of the Third Edition of ***Mosaicos***.

Communication. Throughout the text, students engage in meaningful conversations, providing and obtaining information, expressing their opinions and feelings, and sharing their experiences. Students also listen to, read, and interpret language on a variety of topics. Through *informes* as part of many activities and in compositions in *A escribir*, students present information and ideas in both written and oral communication.

Cultures. *Cultura* boxes and the *Enfoque cultural* sections of each chapter give students an understanding of the relationship between culture and language throughout the Spanish-speaking world.

Connections. Realia, readings, and conversation activities throughout the text provide opportunities for making connections with other discipline areas. Students gain information and insight into the distinctive viewpoints of Spanish speakers and their cultures.

Comparisons. *Lengua* boxes often provide students with points of comparison between English and Spanish. *Para pensar* activities in the *Enfoque cultural* sections encourage students to reflect on aspects of daily life in their own culture before reading about and investigating similar aspects of daily life in Spanish-speaking countries.

Communities. The text encourages students to go beyond the classroom through Internet activities, and the *Mosaicos* Website provides abundant opportunities for exploration, personal enjoyment, and enrichment. Instructors are reminded to encourage students to explore and become a part of Spanish-speaking communities in their areas.

Acknowledgments

The Third Edition of ***Mosaicos*** is the result of a collaborative effort between ourselves, our publisher, and you, our colleagues. We are sincerely appreciative of all the comments and suggestions from First and Second Edition users, and we look forward to continuing the dialog and having your input on this edition. We are especially indebted to the many members of the Spanish teaching community whose reviews and comments at various stages throughout the preparation of the First, Second, and Third Editions have made ***Mosaicos*** the solid program that it is. We especially acknowledge and thank:

Mercedes Arissó-Thompson, El Camino College
Lucrecia Artalejo, Northeastern Illinois University
José Bahamonde, Miami Dade Community College
Linda Jane C. Barnette, Ball State University
Debra L. Barrett, University of Minnesota
Margarita Batlle, Miami Dade Community College
Kathleen Boykin, Slippery Rock University
Rodney Lee Bransdorfer, Gustavus Adolphus College
J. Dianne Broyles, Oklahoma City Community College
Morris E. Carson, J. Sargent Reynolds Community College
John Chaston, University of New Hampshire
María Cooks, Purdue University
Rafael Correa, California State University, San Bernardino

Debora Cristo, Arizona State University
Jorge H. Cubillos, University of Delaware
Harry J. Dennis, California State University, Sacramento
Anthony F. DiSalvo, Frederick Community College
Martin Durrant, Mesa Community College
Raymond Elliott, University of Texas-Arlington
Herbert O. Espinoza, College of Charleston
José Feliciano-Butler, University of South Florida
José B. Fernández, University of Central Florida
Rosa Fernández, University of New Mexico
Marcella Fierro, Mesa Community College
Mary Beth Floyd, Northern Illinois University
Herschel Frey, University of Pittsburgh
Robert K. Fritz, Ball State University
Dulce M. García, City College of New York
Ricardo García, San Jacinto College, South Campus
Marta Garza, Oxnard College
Barbara González-Pino, University of Texas-San Antonio
Ronni Gordon, Harvard University
Lynn Carbón Gorrell, University of Michigan, Ann Arbor
James A. Grabowska, Minnesota State University-Mankato
John W. Griggs, Glendale Community College
Terry Hansen, Pellissippi State Technical Community College
Mark Harpring, University of Kansas
Juana Amelia Hernández, Hood College
Sonja G. Hokanson, Washington State University
Ed Hopper, UNC-Charlotte
Hildegart Hoquee, San Jacinto College, Central Campus
Michael Horswell, University of Maryland-College Park
René Izquierdo, Miami-Dade Community College
María C. Jiménez, Sam Houston State University
Teresa Johnson, St. Louis University
Marilyn Kiss, Wagner College
Barbara A. Lafford, Arizona State University
Roberta Levine, University of Maryland-College Park
Lucia Lombardi, University of Illinois-Chicago
Timothy McGovern, University of California Santa Barbara
Marcelino Marcos, Lakeland Community College
Marina Martin, College of Saint Benedict, St. John's University
Hope Maxwell-Snyder, Shepherd College
Cynthia Medina, York College of Pennsylvania
Niurka Medina-Valin, Cerritos Community College
Robert M. Mee, Delta College
Karen-Jean Muñoz, Florida Community College at Jacksonville
Raúl Neira, Buffalo State College
Carmen Pena-Eblen, Oxnard College
M. Mercedes Rahilly, Lansing Community College
Ana M. Rambaldo, Montclair State College
Richard Raschio, University of St. Thomas

Elaine Rees, Cosumnes River College
Arsenio Rey, University of Alaska
Teresa Roig-Torres, Miami University
Marcia H. Rosenbusch, Iowa State University
Hildebrando Ruiz, University of Georgia
Cecilia Ryan, McNeese University
Carmen Salazar, Los Angeles Valley College
Kimberley Sallee, University of Missouri-Columbia
David Shook, Georgia Institute of Technology
Jay Siskin, Brandeis University
Karen L. Smith, University of Arizona
R. Roger Smith, Indiana University of Pennsylvania
Lourdes Torres, University of Kentucky
Joanna Vargas, Columbia College
Irma Velez, City College of New York
Carmen Vigo-Acosta, Mesa Community College
Montserrat Vilarrubla, Illinois State University
Helga Winkler, Eastern Montana College
Bill Woodard, Hampden-Sydney College
Janice Wright, University of Kansas

We would like to thank Professors Juan Felipe García Santos and Jesús Fernández González, University of Salamanca, Spain, for their collaboration. Thanks are also due to Blanca and César Gómez Villegas, Ana María and Juan Jorge Sanz, Gloria Toriello de Herrera, Johanna Herrera, Miguel Ordóñez, Benjamín Guzmán, and Raúl Salas for their help in obtaining authentic materials, and their advice regarding elements of current Spanish usage in their respective countries.

We would also like to thank all the editorial, production, and marketing staff at Prentice Hall who have contributed to the ***Mosaicos*** program. Special thanks to Charlyce Jones Owen, Editorial Director, and Rosemary Bradley, former Editor-in-Chief, for their support, direction and organization; Mariam Rohlfing, Development Editor, for her dedication, creative ideas and meticulous work on the manuscript and page proofs; Claudia Dukeshire, Production Editor, for her careful and resourceful attention to every detail during the book production; Ximena de la Piedra Tamvakopoulos, Art Director, who worked endless hours to create the beautiful design of the text; and Ann Marie McCarthy, Executive Managing Editor, who supervised the book's production; Heather Finstuen, Media Editor, for her creativity, dedication, and many hours of hard work on the exciting *Fortunas* Video, Website, *Mosaicos* Activity CD-ROM, and *Enfoque interactivo* sections; Julia Caballero, Development Editor, for her hard work and commitment to quality in creating the *Fortunas* video; Rob Reynolds, University of Oklahoma, creator of the *Fortunas* concept, for his inspired work in writing the Mosaicos video, *Enfoque interactivo* sections, and *Fortunas* Website and CD-ROM activities; José Juan Colín, University of Oklahoma, for his excellent CD-ROM activities; Kate Ramunda, Media Project Editor, for her commitment to the success of the Website and CD-ROM projects, and all the hard work it took to make that happen; Meriel Martínez, Assistant Editor, for her calm efficiency and good humor in managing the audio supplements, the Workbook and Lab Manual; Mark Harpring, University of Kansas, for his cooperative, thoughtful work on the testing program; Frank Morris, Development Editor, who came in on the final stages of the preparation of the manuscript, for his support and enthusiasm for the project; Meghan Barnes, Editorial Assistant, for her willing assistance; Stacy Best, Marketing Manager, for her inspiration and many excellent ideas; Andrew Lange, Illustrator, for his excellent illustrations and cooperation throughout; Wanda España for composing the pages, and Mirella Signoretto for creating the realia.

Lección preliminar

Bienvenidos

COMUNICACION

- Introducing oneself and others
- Greetings and good-byes
- Expressions of courtesy
- Spelling in Spanish
- Identifying people and classroom objects
- Locating people and objects
- Using numbers from 0 to 99
- Expressing dates
- Telling time
- Using classroom expressions

Un primer paso

Las presentaciones

ANTONIO: Me llamo Antonio Mendoza. Y tú, ¿cómo te llamas?
BENITO: Benito Sánchez.
ANTONIO: Mucho gusto.
BENITO: Igualmente.

PROFESOR: ¿Cómo se llama usted?
ISABEL: Me llamo Isabel Mendoza.
PROFESOR: Mucho gusto.
ISABEL: Encantada.

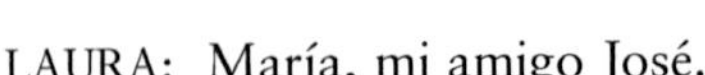

LAURA: María, mi amigo José.
MARIA: Mucho gusto.
JOSE: Encantado.

- Spanish has more than one word meaning *you*. Use **tú** when talking to someone on a first-name basis (close friend, relative, child). Use **usted** when talking to someone you address in a respectful or formal manner, as **doctor, profesor, señora, don, doña**, and so on. Use it also to address individuals you do not know well.
- Young people normally use **tú** when speaking to each other.
- **Mucho gusto** is used by both men and women when meeting someone for the first time. A man may also say **encantado** and a woman **encantada.**
- When responding to **mucho gusto**, you may use either **encantado/a** or **igualmente.**

¿Qué dice usted?

B-1 Presentaciones. With a classmate, complete the following conversation with the appropriate expressions from the column on the right. Then move around the classroom introducing yourself to several classmates, and introducing classmates to each other.

ALICIA:	Me llamo Alicia. Y tú, ¿cómo te llamas?	Igualmente
ISABEL:	Isabel Pérez. ________.	Mucho gusto
ALICIA:	________.	
ALICIA:	Isabel, ________.	Encantado
ISABEL:	Mucho gusto.	mi amigo Pedro
PEDRO:	________.	

Los saludos

SENOR: Buenos días, señorita Mena.
SENORITA: Buenos días. ¿Cómo está usted, señor Gómez?
SENOR: Bien, gracias. ¿Y usted?
SENORITA: Muy bien, gracias.

MARTA: ¡Hola, Inés! ¿Qué tal? ¿Cómo estás?
INES: Regular, ¿y tú?
MARTA: Bastante bien, gracias.

SENORA: Buenas tardes, Felipe. ¿Cómo estás?
FELIPE: Bien, gracias. Y usted, ¿cómo está, señora?
SENORA: Mal, Felipe, mal.
FELIPE: Lo siento.

- Use **buenas tardes** from noon until nightfall. After nightfall, use **buenas noches** (*good evening, good night*).
- **¿Qué tal?**, is a more informal greeting. It is normally used with **tú**, but it may also be used with **usted.**
- Use **está** with **usted**, and **estás** with **tú.**

Cultura

When saying *hello* or *good-bye* and when being introduced, Spanish-speaking men and women almost always shake hands. When greeting each other, young girls and women often kiss each other on the cheek. This is also the custom for men and women who are close friends. In Spain this kissing is done on both cheeks. Men who are close friends normally embrace and pat each other on the back. Native Spanish speakers also tend to get physically closer to the person with whom they are talking than do Americans. In Spain, people normally use **buenos días** until lunch time, which is around 2:00 P.M.

¿Qué dice usted?

B-2 Saludos. You work as a receptionist in a hotel. Which of the following greetings is appropriate at the following times: **buenos días, buenas tardes, buenas noches**?

a. 9:00 a.m
b. 11:00 p.m.
c. 4:00 p.m.
d. 8:00 a.m
e. 1:00 p.m.
f. 10:00 p.m.

Las despedidas

adiós	*good-bye*
hasta luego	*see you later*
hasta mañana	*see you tomorrow*
hasta pronto	*see you soon*

- **Adiós** is generally used when you do not expect to see the other person for a while. It is also used as a greeting when people pass each other, but have no time to stop and talk.
- **Chao** (also spelled **chau**) is an informal way of saying good-bye, which is very popular in South America.

Expresiones de cortesía

con permiso	*pardon me, excuse me*
de nada	*you're welcome*
gracias	*thanks, thank you*
lo siento	*I'm sorry*
perdón	*pardon me, excuse me*
por favor	*please*

Con permiso and **perdón** may be used "before the fact," as when asking a person to allow you to go by or when trying to get someone's attention. Only **perdón** is used "after the fact," as when you have stepped on someone's foot or need to interrupt a conversation.

¿Qué dice usted?

B-3 ¿Perdón o con permiso? Would you use **perdón** or **con permiso** in these situations?

a. b. c. d. e.

B-4 Expresiones de cortesía y despedidas. Which expression(s) would you use in the following situations?

gracias	de nada	por favor
adiós	hasta luego	lo siento

1. Someone thanks you.
2. You are saying good-bye to a friend whom you will see later that evening.
3. You are asking a classmate for his/her notes.
4. You hear that your friend is sick.
5. You receive a present from a friend.
6. Your friend is leaving for a vacation in Spain.

B-5 Encuentros. You meet the following people on the street. Greet them, ask them how they are, and then say good-bye. A classmate will play the other role.

1. su amigo Miguel
2. su profesor/a
3. su amiga Isabel
4. su doctor/a

A ESCUCHAR

Saludos. You will hear four brief conversations. Mark the appropriate column to indicate whether the greetings are formal (with **usted**) or informal (with **tú**). Do not worry if you do not understand every word.

	FORMAL	INFORMAL
1.	_____	_____
2.	_____	_____
3.	_____	_____
4.	_____	_____

El alfabeto

a	a	**o**	o
b	be	**p**	pe
c	ce	**q**	cu
d	de	**r**	ere
e	e	**s**	ese
f	efe	**t**	te
g	ge	**u**	u
h	hache	**v**	ve, uve
i	i	**w**	doble ve, doble uve, uve doble
j	jota		
k	ka		
l	ele	**x**	equis
m	eme	**y**	i griega, ye
n	ene	**z**	zeta
ñ	eñe		

- The letter **ñ** does not exist in English.
- The letters **k** and **w** appear mainly in words of foreign origin.

¿Qué dice usted?

B-6 ¿Cómo se escribe? Ask your classmate how to spell these Spanish last names.

MODELO: Zamora
E1: ¿Cómo se escribe Zamora?
E2: Con z.

1. Celaya
2. Montalvo
3. Salas
4. Bolaños
5. Henares
6. Velázquez

B-7 Los nombres. Ask three of your classmates their names. Write down their names as they spell them.

MODELO: E1: ¿Cómo te llamas?
E2: Me llamo David Montoya.
E1: ¿Cómo se escribe Montoya?
E2: M-o-n-t-o-y-a

Identificación y descripción de personas

CARLOS: ¿Quién es ese chico?
SANDRA: Es Julio.
CARLOS: ¿Cómo es Julio?
SANDRA: Es romántico y sentimental.

LUIS: ¿Quién es esa chica?
ENRIQUE: Es Carmen.
LUIS: ¿Cómo es Carmen?
ENRIQUE: Es activa y muy seria.

SER (*to be*)			
yo	soy	*I*	*am*
tú	eres	*you*	*are*
usted	es	*you*	*are*
él, ella	es	*he, she*	*is*

- Use **ser** to describe what someone is like.
- To make a sentence negative, place the word **no** before the appropriate form of **ser**. When answering a question with a negative statement, say **no** twice.

Ella es inteligente.	→	Ella **no** es inteligente.
¿Es rebelde?	→	**No, no** es rebelde.

Cognados

Cognates are words from two languages that have the same origin and are similar in form and meaning. Since English shares many words with Spanish, you will discover that you already recognize many Spanish words. Here are some that are used to describe people.

The cognates in this first group use the same form to describe a man or a woman.

arrogante	**importante**	**optimista**	**rebelde**
competente	**independiente**	**paciente**	**responsable**
eficiente	**inteligente**	**parcial**	**sentimental**
elegante	**interesante**	**perfeccionista**	**terrible**
idealista	**liberal**	**pesimista**	**tradicional**
imparcial	**materialista**	**popular**	**valiente**

The cognates in the second group have two forms. The **-o** form is used to describe a male and the **-a** form to describe a female.

atlético/a	**creativo/a**	**introvertido/a**	**romántico/a**
atractivo/a	**dinámico/a**	**lógico/a**	**serio/a**
agresivo/a	**extrovertido/a**	**moderno/a**	**sincero/a**
ambicioso/a	**generoso/a**	**pasivo/a**	**tímido/a**
cómico/a	**impulsivo/a**	**religioso/a**	**tranquilo/a**

There are also some words that appear to be cognates, but do not have the same meaning in both languages. These are called false cognates. **Lectura** (*reading*) and **éxito** (*success*) are examples of this kind. You will find more examples in future lessons.

¿Qué dice usted?

B-8 Conversación. With a partner, ask each other about your classmates. Describe them using cognates from the lists above.

MODELO: E1: ¿Cómo es... ?
E2: Es...

B-9 ¿Cómo es mi compañero/a? Choose words from the cognates list on page 10 to ask the person next to you about his/her personality traits.

MODELO: E1: ¿Eres pesimista?
E2: No, no soy pesimista. *o*
Sí, soy (muy) pesimista.

Then find out what he/she is really like.

MODELO: E1: ¿Cómo eres (tú)?
E2: Soy activo, rebelde y creativo.

¿Qué hay en el salón de clase?

¿Qué dice usted?

B-10 Identificación. With a partner, identify the items on this table.

B-11 Para la clase de español. Write down a list of the things you need for this class. Compare your list with that of your partner.

¿Dónde está?

To ask about the location of a person or an object, use **dónde + está**.

¿Dónde está la profesora?	Está en la clase.
¿Dónde está el libro?	Está sobre el escritorio.

¿Qué dice usted?

B-12 Para completar. With a classmate, complete the following sentences based on the relative position of people or objects in the drawing on the previous page.

1. La pizarra está ________ la profesora.
2. El libro está ________ el escritorio.
3. María está ________ de la profesora.
4. Mercedes está ________ Juan y María.
5. Juan está ________ Mercedes.
6. El cesto está ________ la pizarra.
7. María está ________ de la ventana.
8. El televisor está ________ la pizarra y la puerta.

B-13 La clase de español. The X marks your location on the seating chart below.

María	Juan	Ester	Susana	Pedro
Carlos	Cristina	Ángeles	Alberto	Anita (ventana)
(puerta) Mercedes	X	Roberto	Rocío	Pablo
		Profesor Gallegos		

1. Tell where Juan, Ángeles, Cristina, and Pedro are seated.
2. Ask questions about the location of other students.

B-14 ¿Dónde está? Your partner will ask where several items in your classroom are. Answer by giving their position in relation to a person or another object.

MODELO: E1: ¿Dónde está el libro?
E2: Está sobre el escritorio.

B-15 ¿Quién es? Based on what your partner says regarding the location of another student, guess who he/she is.

MODELO: E1: Está al lado de Juan. ¿Quién es?
E2: Es María.

A ESCUCHAR

¿Dónde está? Look at the drawing of the classroom on the previous page. You will hear statements about the location of several people and objects. Mark the appropriate column to indicate whether each of the statements is true (**sí**) or false (**no**).

	SI	NO		SI	NO
1.	____	____	4.	____	____
2.	____	____	5.	____	____
3.	____	____	6.	____	____

ACENTOS

You may have noticed that the word **tú** (meaning *you*) has an accent, and that the word **tu** (meaning *your*) does not. Beginning with **Lección 1**, you will learn and practice the rules for accentuation step by step in the **Pronunciación** section of the Lab Manual. Additional practice is presented in the Workbook. In your text, boxes similar to this will help you focus your attention on when to use accents. You will find a complete set of the rules of accentuation in the appendix.

Los números 0–99

¿Cuál es tu dirección?
Calle Colón, número 10

¿Y cuál es tu teléfono?
234-19-05

0	**cero**	11	**once**	21	**veintiuno**
1	**uno**	12	**doce**	22	**veintidós**
2	**dos**	13	**trece**	30	**treinta**
3	**tres**	14	**catorce**	31	**treinta y uno**
4	**cuatro**	15	**quince**	40	**cuarenta**
5	**cinco**	16	**dieciséis**	50	**cincuenta**
6	**seis**	17	**diecisiete**	60	**sesenta**
7	**siete**	18	**dieciocho**	70	**setenta**
8	**ocho**	19	**diecinueve**	80	**ochenta**
9	**nueve**	20	**veinte**	90	**noventa**
10	**diez**				

- Numbers from 16 through 29 are usually written as one word. Note the spelling changes and the written accent on some forms.

  18 dieciocho **22 veintidós**

- Beginning with 31, numbers are written as three words.

  31 treinta y uno **45 cuarenta y cinco**

- The number one has three forms in Spanish: **uno, un,** and **una.** Use **uno** when counting: **uno, dos, tres...** Use **un** or **una** before nouns: **un borrador, una mochila, veintiún libros, veintiuna mochilas.**

- Use **hay** for both *there is* and *there are.*

  Hay un libro sobre la mesa. *There is a book on the table.*
  Hay dos libros sobre la mesa. *There are two books on the table.*

¿Qué dice usted?

B-16 ¿Qué número es? Your instructor will read a number from each group. Circle the number.

a.	8	4	3	5	d.	54	38	76	95
b.	12	9	16	6	e.	83	62	72	49
c.	37	59	41	26	f.	47	14	91	56

B-17 Una lista. This is a list of items you might need for your new office. The numbers next to each item indicate the quantity you can order. Choose five items and tell your partner (the acquisitions manager) how many of each you want. Exchange roles.

MODELO: Necesito cuatro mesas.

1. 6–10 teléfonos
2. 8–12 escritorios
3. 4–8 mesas
4. 10–13 sillas
5. 40–60 disquetes
6. 6–12 calculadoras
7. 10–20 cestos
8. 24–48 bolígrafos
9. 9–15 computadoras
10. 1–2 computadora(s) portátil(es)
11. 1–3 reloj(es)
12. ....

B-18 Problemas. With a classmate, take turns in solving the following problems. Use **y** (+), **menos** (-), and **son** (=).

MODELO: 2 + 4 =
dos y cuatro son seis

12 - 5 =
doce menos cinco son siete

a. 11 + 4 =
b. 8 + 2 =
c. 13 + 3 =
d. 20 - 6 =
e. 39 + 50 =
f. 80 - 1 =
g. 50 - 25 =
h. 26 + 40 =
i. 90 - 12 =

B-19 Los números de teléfono y las direcciones. With a classmate, ask each other the addresses and phone numbers of some of these people.

MODELO: Castellanos Rey, Carlos Colón 62 654-6416
E1: ¿Cuál es la dirección de Carlos Castellanos?
E2: Calle Colón, número 62.
E1: ¿Cuál es su teléfono?
E2: (El) 6-54-64-16

Cárdenas Alfaro, Joaquín	General Páez 40	423-4837
Cárdenas Villanueva, Sara	Avenida Bolívar 7	956-1709
Castellanos Rey, Carlos	Colón 62	654-6416
Castelli Rivero, Victoria	Chamberí 3	615-7359
Castillo Montoya, Rafael	Santa Cruz 73	956-3382

Cultura

In Spanish-speaking countries, the name of the street precedes the house or building number. At times, a comma is placed before the number.

Calle Bolívar 132
132 Bolívar Street

Telephone numbers are generally not stated as individual numbers, but in groups of two whenever possible. This also depends on how the numbers are written, or the number of digits, which varies from country to country.

12-24-67 =
doce - veinticuatro - sesenta y siete

243-89-07 =
dos - cuarenta y tres - ochenta y nueve - cero siete

Los meses del año y los días de la semana

enero	*January*	**mayo**	*May*	**septiembre**	*September*
febrero	*February*	**junio**	*June*	**octubre**	*October*
marzo	*March*	**julio**	*July*	**noviembre**	*November*
abril	*April*	**agosto**	*August*	**diciembre**	*December*

LENGUA

Days of the week and months of the year are not generally capitalized in Spanish, but sometimes they are capitalized in advertisements and invitations.

- Monday (**lunes**) is normally the first day of the week on Hispanic calendars.
- To ask what day it is, use **¿Qué día es hoy?** Answer with **Hoy es. . .**
- To ask about the date, use **¿Cuál es la fecha?** Respond with **Es el (14) de (octubre).**
- Express *on + a day* of the week as follows:

el lunes	*on Monday*	**los lunes**	*on Mondays*
el domingo	*on Sunday*	**los domingos**	*on Sundays*

- Cardinal numbers are used with dates (e.g., **el dos, el tres**) except for the first day of the month, which is **el primero.** In Spain, the first day could be **el uno.**
- When dates are given in numbers, the day precedes the month: *11/10* = **el 11 de octubre.**

¿Qué dice usted?

B-20 ¿Qué día de la semana es? With a classmate, take turns asking and answering the following questions. Use the calendar on the previous page.

1. ¿Qué día de la semana es el 2?
2. ¿Qué día de la semana es el 5?
3. ¿Qué día de la semana es el 22?
4. ¿Qué día de la semana es el 18?
5. ¿Qué día de la semana es el 10?
6. ¿Qué día de la semana es el 13?
7. ¿Qué día de la semana es el 28?
8. ...

B-21 Preguntas. Now, take turns with your partner asking and answering these questions.

1. ¿Qué día es hoy?
2. Hoy es martes, ¿qué día es mañana?
3. Hoy es jueves, ¿qué día es mañana?
4. ¿Hay clase de español los domingos? ¿Y los sábados?
5. ¿Qué días hay clase de español?

B-22 Fechas importantes. With a classmate, tell each other the dates on which these events take place.

MODELO: la reunión de estudiantes (10/9)
E1: ¿Cuándo es la reunión de estudiantes?
E2: (Es) el 10 de septiembre.

1. el concierto de Gloria Estefan (9/11)
2. el aniversario de Carlos y María (14/5)
3. el banquete (18/3)
4. la graduación (22/5)
5. la fiesta de bienvenida (24/8)

B-23 El cumpleaños. Find out when your classmates' birthdays are. Write your classmates' names and birthdays in the appropriate space in the chart.

MODELO: E1: ¿Cuándo es tu cumpleaños?
E2: (Es) el 3 de mayo.

CUMPLEANOS			
enero	febrero	marzo	abril
mayo	junio	julio	agosto
septiembre	octubre	noviembre	diciembre

Cultura

In Spanish-speaking countries, events such as concerts, bullfights, and religious services begin on time. Normally, business meetings and medical appointments are also kept at the scheduled hour. However, informal social functions such as parties and private gatherings do not usually begin on time. In fact, guests are expected to arrive from one half to one full hour after the time indicated. When in doubt, you may ask either **¿hora latina?** or **¿hora americana/inglesa?** (*precise time?*) to find out whether or not you should be punctual.

La hora

- Use **¿Qué hora es?** to inquire about the hour. To tell time, use **Es la...** from one o'clock to one thirty and **Son las...** with the other hours.

Es la una.	*It's one o'clock.*
Son las tres.	*It's three o'clock.*

- To express the quarter hour use **y cuarto** or **y quince**. To express the half hour use **y media** or **y treinta**.

Son las dos **y cuarto**.	*It's two fifteen.*
Son las dos **y quince**.	
Es la una **y media**.	*It's one thirty.*
Es la una **y treinta**.	

- To express time after the half hour subtract minutes from the next hour using **menos**.

Son las cuatro **menos** diez.	*It's ten to four.*

- Add **en punto** for the exact time and **más o menos** for approximate time.

Es la una **en punto**.	*It's one o'clock sharp.*
Son las cinco menos cuarto **más o menos**.	*It's about quarter to five.*

- Use **mediodía** for noon and **medianoche** for midnight.

- For **A.M.** and **P.M.**, use the following:

de la mañana	(from midnight to noon)
de la tarde	(from noon to approximately 7:00 P.M.)
de la noche	(from nightfall to midnight)

- Use **¿A qué hora es... ?** to ask the hour at which something happens.

¿A qué hora es la clase?	*At what time is (the) class?*
Es a las nueve y media.	*It's at 9:30.*

¿Qué dice usted?

B-24 ¿Qué hora es en… ? What time is it in the following cities?

Los Ángeles, a.m.

México, p.m.

San Juan, p.m.

Buenos Aires, p.m.

Madrid, p.m.

B-25 El horario de María. Take turns with a classmate asking and answering questions about María's schedule.

MODELO: E1: ¿A qué hora es la clase de español?
E2: Es a las nueve.

LUNES	
9:00	clase de español
10:15	receso
10:30	clase de matemáticas
11:45	laboratorio
1:00	almuerzo
2:00	clase de física
5:00	partido de tenis

B-26 Mi horario. Write down your Monday schedule omitting the time each class meets. Exchange schedules with your partner and find out what time each of his/her classes starts.

A LEER

Reading is an important skill that you will develop as you study Spanish. You should not expect to be able to read proficiently at first, however, it is important to begin developing this ability early in the language learning process. Here you'll find some helpful tips that you should keep in mind as you begin to read in Spanish.

- Draw on your experience and knowledge of the world to comprehend an unfamiliar text. Use what you know about the topic as you read; this will help you predict and/or discover new meanings.
- Underline cognates, that is, words that are spelled similarly in Spanish and English and that bear the same meaning. Such words will help tremendously with comprehension of the text. Beware that there are also false cognates—words with the same or almost the same spelling—, which may hinder your interpretation of meaning. When in doubt, guess meaning from context.
- Avoid doing a word-by-word reading of a text. Instead, read holistically—that is, try to get the gist of what you're reading. As you begin to read in Spanish, understanding key concepts or words such as simple nouns and verbs will be sufficient.
- Pay close attention to visual cues like photographs, illustrations and charts that may accompany the reading, or to the size of type used for headings, etc. These visual cues will help you make educated guesses about the content and meaning of the text.
- Read the title and subtitles or headings in the text, and pay attention to the format. This is a strategy called skimming that helps you get a general overview of the text you are going to read.
- Do not consult your dictionary every time you come across an unfamiliar word. Guess meanings using contextual clues. You will be surprised how much you can hypothesize about as you infer the meanings of new words and phrases.
- As you expand your knowledge of Spanish grammar and structure, use it to comprehend new words and unfamiliar structures.
- Get used to reading a text at least twice. First, read the text to get the general sense and main ideas. When you read the second time, underline or jot down unfamiliar expressions or structures that block your comprehension of the text. Then, use some of the techniques explained above as well as grammatical and contextual clues to help you clarify obscured meanings. Make hypotheses about possible meanings and read the text a third time. This last reading should serve as a confirmation of your guesses.

Now look at the following text and consider the following questions: 1. What type of text is it? 2. How do you know? 3. Do you see any cognates? If so, which one/s?

TELEVISIÓN

LUNES 10

CANAL 3

6:00	Buenos días
7:00	Encuentros extraterrestres
8:00	Panorama
9:00	Barrio Sésamo
10:00	Pepe y sus amigos
10:30	El reino animal
11:00	Documental
12:00	Escuela de deportes
13.00	El arte de la cocina
13.30	Conversaciones
14:00	Exploradores del universo
15:00	Telenoticias
15:35	El tiempo
15:40	Tardes de cine: "El Santo"
17:40	El mundo de hoy
18:00	★Harry, detective privado
19:00	Zona M
19:30	El precio justo
20:30	Telenoticias
21:00	El tiempo
21:15	Mesa redonda
23:00	★La familia de enfrente
23:30	★Documentos TV
0:30	Cine: "Pasión oculta"
3:30	Teledeporte

Most likely, you immediately recognized this text as a TV listing even before you read it. The size and color of the title **Televisión** made it stand out. The format and the times provided additional information to corroborate your guess. You also found some cognates: **detective, privado, justo, documentos.**

As you read the listing a second time, look for the following specific information. This strategy is called scanning.

1. Day and date of programs
2. Time of the morning shows
3. Names of recommended shows*
4. Titles of the first and last shows
5. Name of a program for children
6. Number of newscasts during the day

Programas interesantes. Review the TV listing and select the programs that seem most interesting to you. Then, in small groups, compare your lists to determine the two most popular programs.

Expresiones útiles en la clase

Siéntese.
Levántese.
Abra el libro.
Cierre el libro.
Escuche.
Pregúntele a su compañero.
?
Manuel Arias
Josefina Barrios

Vaya a la pizarra.

Voy a pasar (la) lista: Manuel Arias, Josefina Barrios.

La tarea, por favor.

Conteste.

Repita.

Levante la mano.

Lea.

Escriba.

- When asking two or more people to do something, the verb form ends in **-n: vaya → vayan, conteste → contesten, repita → repitan.**
- Although you may not have to use all these expressions, you should be able to recognize them and respond accordingly. Other expressions that you may hear or say in the classroom are:

Abra/n el libro en la página...	*Open the book to page...*
Más alto, por favor.	*Louder, please.*
Otra vez.	*Again.*
¿Comprende/n?	*Do you understand?*
¿Tiene/n alguna pregunta?	*Do you have any questions?*
Repita/n por favor.	*Repeat please.*
No comprendo.	*I don't understand.*
No sé.	*I don't know.*
Tengo una pregunta.	*I have a question.*
Más despacio, por favor.	*More slowly, please.*
¿En qué página?	*On what page?*
¿Cómo se dice... en español?	*How do you say... in Spanish?*
¿Cómo se escribe... ?	*How do you spell. . .?*
Presente	*Here, present*
Ausente	*Absent*
Cambien de papel.	*Switch roles.*

Vocabulario*

Presentaciones

¿Cómo se llama usted? | *What's your name?* (formal)
¿Cómo te llamas? | *What's your name?* (familiar)
encantado/a | *delighted*
igualmente | *likewise*
me llamo... | *my name is...*
mucho gusto | *pleased/nice to meet you*

Saludos y contestaciones

bien | *well*
bastante bien | *pretty well, rather well*
muy bien | *very well*
buenos días | *good morning*
buenas noches | *good evening, good night*
buenas tardes | *good afternoon*
¿Cómo está usted? | *How are you?* (formal)
¿Cómo estás? | *How are you?* (familiar)
hola | *hello, hi*
mal | *not well*
¿Qué tal? | *How's it going?*
regular | *so-so*

Despedidas

adiós | *good-bye*
chao/chau | *good-bye* (informal)
hasta luego | *see you later*
hasta mañana | *see you tomorrow*
hasta pronto | *see you soon*

Expresiones de cortesía

con permiso | *excuse me*
de nada | *you're welcome*
gracias | *thanks, thank you*
lo siento | *I'm sorry*
perdón | *excuse me*
por favor | *please*

En el salón de clase

el bolígrafo | *ball-point pen*
el borrador | *eraser*
la calculadora | *calculator*
el cesto | *wastepaper basket*
la computadora | *computer*
el cuaderno | *notebook*
el escritorio | *desk*
la grabadora | *tape recorder, cassette player*
el lápiz | *pencil*
el libro | *book*
la mesa | *table*
la mochila | *backpack*
la pizarra | *chalkboard*
la puerta | *door*
el pupitre | *student's desk*
el reloj | *clock*
la silla | *chair*
la tarea | *homework*
el televisor | *TV set*
la tiza | *chalk*
la ventana | *window*
la videocasetera | *VCR*

La dirección

la calle | *street*
el número | *number*

Posición

al lado (de) | *next to*
debajo (de) | *under*
detrás (de) | *behind*
enfrente (de) | *in front of*
entre | *between, among*
sobre | *on, above*

Personas

el/la amigo/a	*friend*
la chica	*girl*
el chico	*boy*
don[1]	*Mr.*
doña	*Mrs.*
él	*he*
ella	*she*
el/la estudiante	*student*
el/la profesor/a	*professor*
señor (Sr.)	*Mr.*
señora (Sra.)	*Mrs.*
señorita (Srta.)	*Miss*
tú	*you* (familiar)
usted	*you* (formal)
yo	*I*

Tiempo, hora y fecha

el año	*year*
cuarto	*quarter*
el día	*day*
en punto	*sharp*
la fecha	*date*
la hora	*hour*
hoy	*today*
mañana	*tomorrow*
la mañana	*morning*
de la mañana	*A.M.*
media	*half*
mediodía	*noon*
medianoche	*midnight*
menos	*minus, to* (for telling time)
el mes	*month*
la noche	*night*
de la noche	*P.M.*
la semana	*week*
la tarde	*afternoon*
de la tarde	*P.M.*

[1]**Don** and **doña** are titles roughly equivalent to *Mr.* and *Miss/Mrs.* They are used with a person's first name, for example, **don Pedro, doña Inés.**

Verbos

eres	*you are* (familiar)
es	*you are* (formal), *he/she is*
está	*he/she is, you are* (formal)
estás	*you are* (familiar)
hay	*there is, there are*
son	*they, you* (familiar) *are*
soy	*I am*

Palabras útiles

a	*at, to*
con	*with*
¿cuándo?	*when?*
¿dónde?	*where?*
en	*in*
ese/a	*that* (adjective)
mi	*my*
sí	*yes*
su (formal)	*his, her, their, your*
tu	*your* (familiar)
un/una	*a, an*
y	*and*

Expresiones útiles

¿A qué hora es... ?	*At what time is... ?*
¿Cómo es... ?	*What is he/she/it like?*
¿Cuál es la fecha?	*What is the date?*
Es el... de...	*It is the ... of...*
Es la... /Son las...	*It's ...* (for telling time)
Es a las...	*It's at...*
Hoy es...	*Today is...*
más o menos	*more or less*
¿Qué día es hoy?	*What day is it today?*
¿Qué hora es?	*What time is it?*

*See page 10 for cognates.
**See pages 14 and 16 for numbers, days of the week, and months of the year.

Lección 1

Los estudiantes y la universidad

COMUNICACION

- Asking for and providing information
- Expressing needs
- Asking for prices
- Talking about daily activities
- Asking about and expressing location

ESTRUCTURAS

- Subject pronouns
- Present tense of regular **-ar** verbs
- Articles and nouns: gender and number
- Present tense of the verb **estar**
- Question words
- ALGO MAS: Some regular **-er** and **-ir** verbs

MOSAICOS

A ESCUCHAR

A CONVERSAR

A LEER

- Identifying cognates to improve reading comprehension
- Guessing content of specific texts

A ESCRIBIR

- Identifying basic aspects of writing
- Revising content and form to improve communication

ENFOQUE CULTURAL

- Las universidades hispanas
- España

ENFOQUE INTERACTIVO

WWW

VIDEO

CD ROM

A primera vista

Los estudiantes y los cursos

Practice activities for each vocabulary section are provided on the CD-ROM and website (www.prenhall.com/mosaicos)

Me llamo Carmen Granados. Soy estudiante de la Universidad de Salamanca. Voy a clase todos los días. Llego a la universidad a las ocho y media. Trabajo en una oficina por las tardes. Este semestre estudio psicología, economía, sociología y antropología. La clase de economía es mi favorita. La clase de antropología es difícil, pero el profesor es muy bueno. La clase de psicología es fácil y muy interesante.

Este chico es mi amigo. Se llama David Thomas. Es norteamericano y estudia español. También estudia literatura, historia y geografía. David es un chico muy responsable y estudioso. Llega a la universidad a las diez. Habla español y practica todos los días con sus compañeros de clase. Por la tarde él escucha los casetes en el laboratorio de lenguas.

¿Qué dice usted?

1-1 ¿Qué sabe usted de Carmen? Complete the following information about Carmen with a classmate.

Nombre completo:
Universidad:
Clases:
Clase favorita:
Clase difícil:
Clase fácil:

1-2 ¿Y qué sabe usted de David? Answer the following questions about David.

1. ¿Es norteamericano David?
2. ¿Habla español?
3. ¿Qué estudia David?
4. ¿A qué hora llega a la universidad?
5. ¿Con quién practica español?
6. ¿Dónde escucha los casetes?

David y Carmen hablan de sus clases

DAVID: Hola, Carmen. ¿Cómo estás?

CARMEN: Hola, David. ¿Cómo te va?

DAVID: Bueno... bastante bien, pero mi clase de historia es muy difícil.

CARMEN: ¿Quién es tu profesor?

DAVID: Se llama Pedro Hernández. Es inteligente, pero la clase es aburrida.

CARMEN: ¡Vaya! Lo siento. ¿Estudias bastante?

DAVID: Estudio mucho, pero saco malas notas.

CARMEN: ¡Qué lástima! Mis cuatro clases son excelentes. Y tú, ¿cuántas clases tienes?

DAVID: Tengo cuatro también.

CARMEN: ¡Uy! Son las once. Tengo un examen de economía ahora. Hasta luego.

DAVID: Hasta la vista. ¡Buena suerte!

¿Qué dice usted?

1-3 ¿En qué clase... ? Match the words on the left with the appropriate class.

1. _______ casetes
2. _______ números
3. _______ mapa
4. _______ animales
5. _______ Freud
6. _______ Napoleón

a. geografía
b. biología
c. español
d. historia
e. matemáticas
f. psicología

1-4 Mis clases. Make a list of your classes. Next to each one, indicate the days and times it meets. Also say whether the class is easy, difficult, interesting or boring. Compare your list with those of your classmates.

CLASE	DIAS	HORA	¿COMO ES?

Look up **Universidad de Salamanca** on the Internet (www.usal.es).

1. Go to **Centros y Departamentos** and write down six of the departments listed.
2. Find out the name of one professor in each of the departments you listed. Share your findings with those of other classmates.

1-5 Las clases de mis compañeros/as. Use the following questions to interview one of your classmates. Then, change roles.

1. ¿Qué estudias tú este semestre?
2. ¿Cuántas clases tienes?
3. ¿Cuál es tu clase favorita?
4. Tu clase de español, ¿es fácil o difícil? ¿interesante o aburrida?
5. ¿Trabajas con computadoras/ordenadores?
6. ¿Escuchas casetes en el laboratorio?
7. ¿Sacas buenas notas?
8. ¿Tienes muchos exámenes?

La vida estudiantil

En la biblioteca

Unos alumnos estudian en la biblioteca. No conversan porque está prohibido. Estudian, toman apuntes y revisan sus tareas. A veces buscan palabras en el diccionario.

¿Y qué hacen los fines de semana?

Los estudiantes toman algo en un café.

Miran televisión en casa.

Bailan en una discoteca.

Caminan en la playa.

Montan en bicicleta.

¿Qué dice usted?

1-6 Para escoger. Look at the illustrations above and on the previous page. Then, with a classmate, choose the word or phrase that makes sense.

1. Los estudiantes _______ en la biblioteca.
   a. toman café
   b. estudian
   c. hablan
2. Buscan palabras en _______.
   a. el reloj
   b. el diccionario
   c. el laboratorio
3. Miran televisión en _______.
   a. la biblioteca
   b. la playa
   c. casa
4. Montan en bicicleta _______.
   a. los fines de semana
   b. en el café
   c. los jueves

En la librería

ESTUDIANTE: Buenos días. Necesito comprar un diccionario de español.
DEPENDIENTE: ¿Grande o pequeño?
ESTUDIANTE: Grande. Es para mi clase de español.
DEPENDIENTE: Este diccionario es muy bueno.
ESTUDIANTE: ¿Cuánto cuesta?
DEPENDIENTE: Cuarenta y ocho euros.

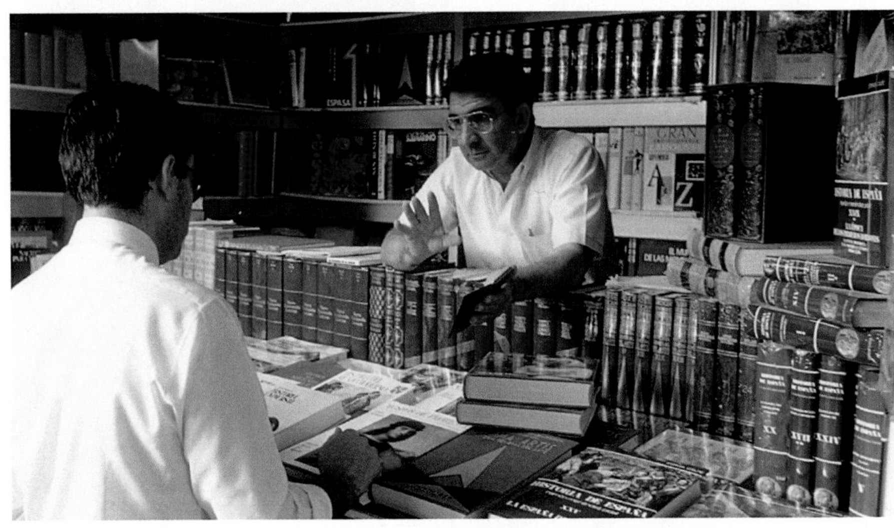

Cultura

Although many Spanish-speaking countries (Argentina, Chile, Colombia, Cuba, México, República Dominicana, and Uruguay) use the **peso** as the basic currency, a significant number do not. Note the following countries and their currencies: Bolivia – **boliviano**; Costa Rica – **colón**; Ecuador – **sucre**; El Salvador – **colón**; Guatemala – **quetzal**; Honduras – **lempira**; Nicaragua – **córdoba**; Panamá – **balboa**; Paraguay – **guaraní**; Perú – **nuevo sol**; Puerto Rico – **dólar (U.S.)**; España – **peseta** until 2002, **euro** after 2002; and Venezuela – **bolívar**.

¿Qué dice usted?

1-7 Para completar. With a classmate, complete the following statements.

1. El estudiante necesita _________.
2. Es un diccionario _________.
3. Es para su clase de _________.
4. El diccionario cuesta _________.

1-8 ¿Cuánto cuesta? You are at the university bookstore. Ask the salesclerk how much each of the following items costs.

MODELO:

ESTUDIANTE:
¿Cuánto cuesta la grabadora?
DEPENDIENTE/A:
Cuesta cincuenta dólares.

En la universidad

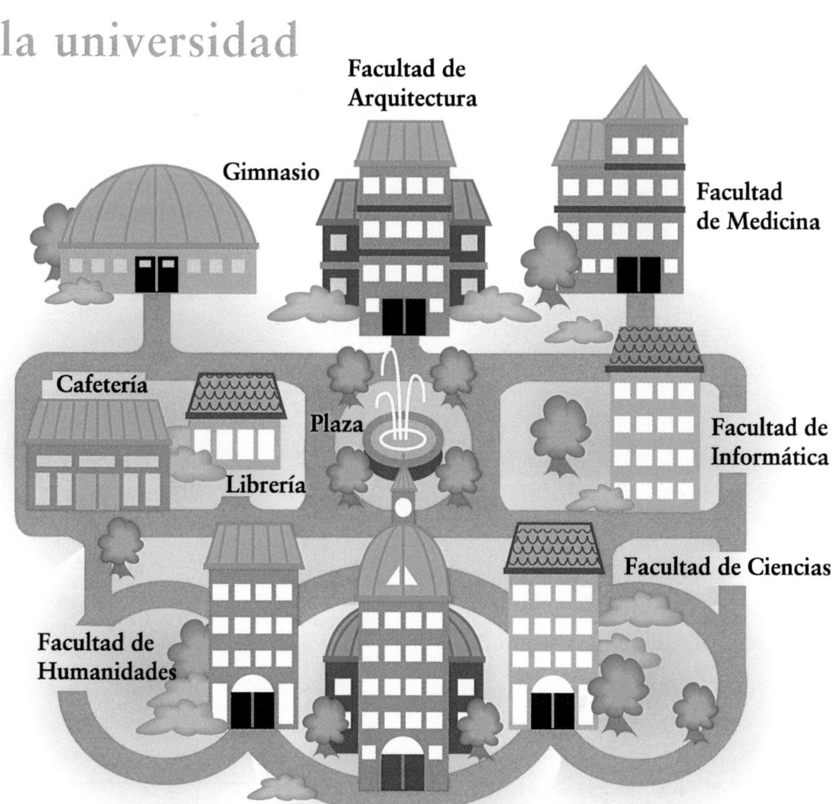

¿Qué dice usted?

1-9 Encuesta. Ask a classmate where and when he/she does each of the following activities.

MODELO: practicar frisbi
E1: ¿Dónde practicas frisbi?
E2: Practico frisbi en la plaza.
E1: ¿Cuándo practicas?
E2: Practico por las tardes.

ACTIVIDAD	DONDE	CUANDO
1. ESTUDIAR PARA UN EXAMEN DIFICIL		
2. MIRAR TELEVISION EN ESPANOL		
3. TOMAR CAFE		
4. BAILAR		
5. ESCUCHAR MUSICA		
6 COMPRAR UN DICCIONARIO		

1-10 En la universidad. Tell your partner about your classes. Take turns to complete the following sentences.

1. Llego a la universidad a la(s)...
2. Mi clase favorita es...
3. El/La profesor/a se llama...
4. La clase es muy...
5. Practico español en...
6. Para mi clase de composición en español, yo necesito...

1-11 Busco una escuela. With a classmate, read the following brochure and look for the following specific information:

a) name of the school,
b) classes offered,
c) school's address, and
d) school's telephone number

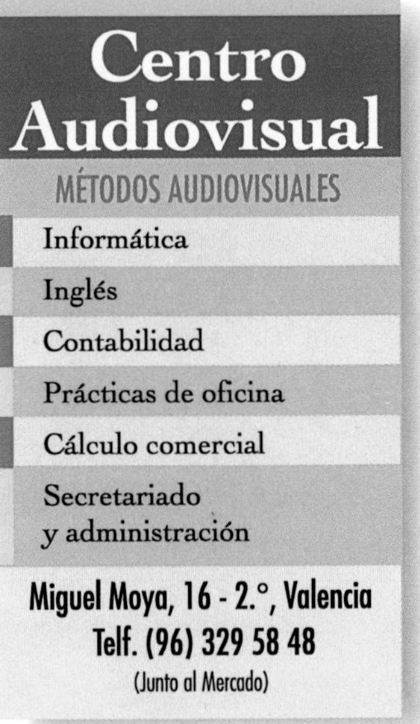

Centro Audiovisual
MÉTODOS AUDIOVISUALES
Informática
Inglés
Contabilidad
Prácticas de oficina
Cálculo comercial
Secretariado y administración
Miguel Moya, 16 - 2.°, Valencia
Telf. (96) 329 58 48
(Junto al Mercado)

A ESCUCHAR

A. ¿Qué hacen estas personas? You will hear three people talking about work, studies, and free time. As you listen, determine what the main topic is. Then write the number of the description under the appropriate heading.

_____ estudios
_____ trabajo
_____ tiempo libre

B. ¿Cómo es Alicia? Listen to the following description to determine if it refers to the activities of a student or a professor.

_____ estudiante
_____ profesor

Now read the statements below and listen to the description again. Then indicate whether each of the statements is correct (**sí**) or incorrect (**no**).

	SI	NO
1. Alicia es muy inteligente y activa.	_____	_____
2. Ella estudia matemáticas en la universidad.	_____	_____
3. Alicia estudia mucho y saca buenas notas.	_____	_____
4. Ella llega a la universidad a las tres de la tarde.	_____	_____

Explicación y expansión

1. Subject pronouns

SINGULAR		PLURAL	
yo	*I*	nosotros, nosotras	*we*
tú	*you*	vosotros, vosotras	*you* (familiar)
usted	*you* (formal)	ustedes	*you* (formal/familiar)
él	*he*	ellos	*they* (masculine)
ella	*she*	ellas	*they* (feminine)

- In Spain, the plural of **tú** is **vosotros** or **vosotras**. In other Spanish-speaking countries, the plural of both **tú** and **usted** is **ustedes**.
- Except for **ustedes**, the plural pronouns have masculine and feminine endings. Use **-as** for a group composed only of females; use **-os** for a mixed group or one composed only of males.
- Because the endings of Spanish verbs indicate the subject (the doer of the action), subject pronouns are generally used only for emphasis, clarification, or contrast.

Practice activities for each numbered grammar point are provided on the CD-ROM and website (www.prenhall.com/mosaicos)

¿Qué dice usted?

1-12 ¿Qué pronombre usa usted? Indicate which pronoun you would use in these situations:

1. You're talking about the following people:
   a. el Sr. Martínez
   b. la Sra. Gómez
   c. Alicia y Susana
   d. Alfredo y Juana
   e. usted (*yourself*)
   f. Ana y usted
2. You're talking with the following people:
   a. su profesor de historia
   b. su amigo íntimo
   c. dos doctores
   d. una senadora
   e. dos compañeros
   f. una niña (*a child*)

1-13 Mis compañeros. Working with a small group, ask questions to find out what your classmates are like. One student will take notes and share answers with the class.

MODELO: E1: ¿Quién es optimista?
E2: Yo (or él, ella, etc.)
RESULTADO FINAL: Hay tres estudiantes optimistas, *o*
No hay estudiantes optimistas en el grupo.

hiperactivo/a	responsable	pesimista	hipocondríaco/a
estudioso/a	perfeccionista	tolerante	...

RESULTADO FINAL: ______________

2. Present tense of regular *-ar* verbs

HABLAR			
yo	habl**o**	nosotros/as	habl**amos**
tú	habl**as**	vosotros/as	habl**áis**
Ud., él, ella	habl**a**	Uds., ellos, ellas	habl**an**

- Use the present tense to express what you and others generally or habitually do or do not do. You may also use the present tense to express an ongoing action. Context will tell you which meaning is intended.

Ana trabaja en la oficina.	*Ana works in the office.* *Ana is working in the office.*

- Here are some expressions you may find useful when talking about what you and others habitually do or do not do.

siempre	*always*	**muchas veces**	*often*
todos los días/meses	*every day/month*	**a veces**	*sometimes*
todas las semanas	*every week*	**nunca**	*never*

¿Qué dice usted?

1-14 Preferencias. Rank the following activities from 1 to 8, according to your preferences (1=more interesting, 8= the least interesting). Compare your answers with those of your classmates.

_____ bailar en una discoteca
_____ mirar televisión en casa
_____ conversar con amigos en los cafés
_____ caminar en la playa
_____ montar en bicicleta los fines de semana
_____ escuchar música rock
_____ comprar casetes y videos
_____ hablar por teléfono con amigos

1-15 Intercambio. Ask a classmate about the following people and activities.

MODELOS: E1: ¿Quién estudia por la tarde? *o* ¿Cuándo estudia Marta?
E2: Marta (estudia por la tarde). Estudia por la tarde.

PERSONA	ACTIVIDAD	CUANDO/DONDE
Marta	estudia español	por la tarde
	mira televisión	por la noche
Asunción	llega a la universidad	a las 9:30 a.m.
	escucha música clásica	en su casa los domingos
David y Andrea	practican español con sus amigos	en la universidad
	trabajan en una oficina	los martes y jueves

1-16 Mis actividades. Indicate with a check mark which of the following activities are part of your routine at the university. Then compare your answers with those of a classmate, and report your findings to the class.

MODELO: David y yo somos (muy) similares. Él y yo miramos programas cómicos en la televisión.
David y yo somos (muy) diferentes. Yo estudio por las mañanas; él estudia por las tardes.

1. Llego a la universidad a las nueve de la mañana.
2. Tomo notas en todas las clases.
3. Hablo con mis amigos en la plaza.
4. Reviso las tareas con mis compañeros.
5. Estudio por las mañanas.
6. Practico español con el CD-ROM en el laboratorio de computadoras.
7. Miro programas cómicos en la televisión.
8. A veces camino en el parque con un amigo.

1-17 Unos estudiantes muy buenos. Both you and a classmate are good students. Make a list of things you do and not do to get good grades. Then, compare your list with those of other classmates.

MODELO: Siempre tomamos apuntes.
No conversamos en las clases.

1-18 Firmas: las actividades de mis compañeros/as. Walk around the classroom and ask classmates if they do the activities listed on the chart, below. Your classmates should write their names in the space that indicates the frequency with which they do the activity.

MODELO: estudiar psicología
E1: ¿Estudias psicología?
E2: Sí.
E1: Firma aquí, por favor.
E2: (firma)
E1: Gracias.

ACTIVIDADES	A VECES	MUCHAS VECES	SIEMPRE	NUNCA
estudiar con amigos				
sacar buenas notas				
llegar tarde a la facultad				
mirar televisión por la noche				
bailar los sábados				

1-19 Tengo mucha curiosidad. You are really curious about how busy or quiet Friday evenings/nights are for one of your classmates. Write down four questions and ask him/her. Be prepared to answer his/her questions as well.

MODELO: ¿Estudias los viernes por la noche?

1-20 Un día típico en la vida de Asunción. Primera fase. With a classmate, describe what Asunción does on a typical day.

MODELO: Asunción llega a la oficina a las nueve menos diez.

1.

2.

3.

4.

5.

6.

Segunda fase. Tell each other what you normally do on a regular workday.

1. Greet your partner and ask a) how he/she is, b) what subjects he/she is studying this semester, c) the time of his/her first class (**primera clase**), and d) what the professor is like.
2. You would like to know more about your partner's job. Ask your partner a) where he/she works, b) what days of the week and which hours, and c) how interesting/boring/difficult/easy the job is.
3. Tell your partner at least four activities you do on Saturdays. Ask what he/she does (**¿Qué haces?**).

3. Articles and nouns: gender and number

Nouns are words that name a person, place, or thing. In English all nouns use the same definite article, *the*, and the indefinite articles *a* and *an*. In Spanish, however, masculine nouns use **el** or **un** and feminine nouns use **la** or **una**. The terms masculine and feminine are used in a grammatical sense and have nothing to do with biological gender.

Gender

	MASCULINE	FEMININE	
SINGULAR DEFINITE ARTICLES	el	la	*the*
SINGULAR INDEFINITE ARTICLES	un	una	*a/an*

- Generally, nouns that end in **-o** are masculine and require **el** or **un**, and those that end in **-a** are feminine and require **la** or **una**.

  el/un libro — **el/un** cuaderno — **el/un** diccionario
  la/una mesa — **la/una** silla — **la/una** ventana

- Nouns that end in **-d**, **-ción**, **-sión** are feminine and require **la** or **una**.

  la/una universidad — **la/una** lección — **la/una** televisión

- Some nouns that end in **-a** and **-ma** are masculine.

  el/un día — **el/un** mapa
  el/un programa — **el/un** problema

- In general, nouns that refer to males are masculine and require **el/un** while nouns that refer to females are feminine and require **la/una**. Masculine nouns ending in **-o** change the **-o** to **-a** for the feminine; those ending in a consonant add **-a** for the feminine.

  el/un amigo — **la/una** amiga
  el/un profesor — **la/una** profesora

- Nouns ending in **-e** normally share the same form (**el/la estudiante**), but sometimes they have a feminine form ending in **-a** (**el dependiente, la dependienta**).

- Use definite articles with titles (except **don** and **doña**) when you are talking about someone. Do not use definite articles when addressing someone directly.

La señorita Andrade trabaja en el Departamento de Lenguas Extranjeras.	*Miss Andrade works in the Department of Foreign Languages.*
Cuando **el** profesor Jones llega por la mañana, ella dice: "Buenos días, profesor Jones", y él contesta: "Buenos días, señorita Andrade".	*When Professor Jones arrives in the morning, she says, "Good morning, Professor Jones," and he answers, "Good morning, Miss Andrade."*

Number

	MASCULINE	FEMININE	
PLURAL DEFINITE ARTICLES	**los**	**las**	*the*
PLURAL INDEFINITE ARTICLES	**unos**	**unas**	*some*

- Add -s to form the plural of nouns that end in a vowel. Add **-es** to nouns ending in a consonant.

  la silla　　las sillas　　el cuaderno　　los cuadernos
  la actividad　　las actividades　　el señor　　los señores

- Nouns that end in **-z** change the **z** to **c** before **-es**.

  el lápiz　　los lápi**ces**

- To refer to a mixed group, use masculine plural forms.

  los chicos　　*the boys and girls*

¿Qué dice usted?

1-21 Conversaciones incompletas. Complete the following dialogs as indicated.

A. Supply the appropriate definite articles (**el, la, los, las**).

E1: ¿Dónde está María?
E2: Está en _______ clase de _______ profesora Sánchez.
E1: ¡Qué lástima! Necesito hablar con ella. Es urgente.
E2: Bueno, ella está en _______ salón de clase hasta _______ una, y por _______ tarde trabaja en _______ laboratorio.
E1: ¿Y a qué hora llega?
E2: Llega a _______ dos, más o menos.

B. Supply the appropriate indefinite articles (**un, una, unos, unas**).

E1: Necesito comprar _______ grabadora y _______ lápices.
E2: Y yo necesito _______ bolígrafo y _______ diccionario, pero no sé qué diccionario comprar.
E1: Para el primer curso, _______ profesores usan _______ diccionario pequeño y otros usan _______ diccionario grande. Habla con tu profesor.

C. Supply the appropriate definite or indefinite articles.

E1: Tengo _______ examen de matemáticas mañana y necesito sacar _______ buena nota en esa clase.
E2: ¿Quién es _______ profesor?
E1: Es _______ doctora Solís.
E2: ¡Ah! Es _______ profesora excelente.
E1: Sí, pero _______ clase es muy difícil. Estudio y reviso _______ tareas todos _______ días, pero no saco buenas notas.
E2: ¡Vaya! Lo siento mucho.

1-22 ¿Qué necesitan? With your partner, take turns to say what these students need, according to each situation.

MODELO: Alicia tiene que escuchar unos casetes.
Necesita una grabadora.

1. Mónica tiene que tomar apuntes en la clase de historia.
2. Blanca y Lucía tienen que buscar dónde está Salamanca.
3. Carlos y Ana tienen que hacer (*to do*) la tarea de matemáticas.
4. Alfredo tiene que estudiar para el examen de geografía.
5. Isabel tiene que escribir una composición para su clase de inglés.
6. David tiene que copiar un programa de su computadora para un compañero.

1. **Role A.** You have missed the first day of class. Ask one of your classmates a) at what time the class is, b) who the professor is, and c) what you need for the class.

   Role B. Tell your classmate a) the time of the class, and if the class is in the morning, afternoon or evening, b) the name of the professor and what he/she is like, and c) at least three items that your classmate will need for the class.

2. **Role A.** You work for the student newspaper at your college/university and you have been asked to interview students to find out what they typically do on weekends. After introducing yourself, find out if the person interviewed a) works, b) what he/she studies, and c) what he/she does on Saturdays and Sundays.

   Role B. Tell the interviewer a) if you work and where you work, b) the classes you take, and c) the things you do on weekends, where you do them, and with whom you do them.

4. Present tense of the verb *estar*

ESTAR			
yo	**estoy**	*I*	*am*
tú	**estás**	*you*	*are*
Ud., él, ella	**está**	*you are, he/she*	*is*
nosotros/as	**estamos**	*we*	*are*
vosotros/as	**estáis**	*you*	*are*
Uds., ellos, ellas	**están**	*you are, they*	*are*

- Use **estar** to express the location of persons or objects.

¿Dónde **está** el gimnasio?	*Where is the gym?*
Está al lado de la cafetería.	*It is next to the cafeteria.*

- Use **estar** to talk about states of health.

¿Cómo **está** el señor Mora?	*How is Mr. Mora?*
Está muy bien.	*He is very well.*

¿Qué dice usted?

1-23 ¿Dónde está...? Ask a classmate where various buildings on campus are. He/she will answer as specifically as possible.

MODELO: E1: ¿Dónde está la biblioteca?
E2: Está ________.

1-24 Horas y lugares. Ask a classmate where he/she usually is at the following times and days. Take turns asking and answering the questions.

MODELO: 8:00 a.m. /los lunes
E1: ¿Dónde estás a las ocho de la mañana los lunes?
E2: Estoy en la clase de física.

a. 9:00 a.m / los martes
b. 11:00 a.m. / los miércoles
c. 1:00 p.m / los viernes
d. 3:00 p.m. / los domingos
e. 9:00 p.m. / los lunes
f. ...

Ask two classmates where they usually are a) in the morning, b) in the afternoon, and c) in the evening on weekends.

1-25 Conversación. Look at the following drawings. Ask a classmate where these people are, how they feel, and what they're doing.

MODELO: E1: ¿Dónde está la chica?
E2: Está en la biblioteca.
E1: ¿Cómo está?
E2: Está regular.
E1: ¿Qué hace?
E2: Estudia.

1.

2.

3.

SITUACIONES

1. **Role A.** You are the university representative who has to give directions to a graphic designer for the new students' handbook. Explain to him/her the location of the various buildings below, according to a campus map that you have previously drawn.

cafetería	librería
Facultad de Ciencias	Facultad de Humanidades
biblioteca	gimnasio

   Role B. You are the graphic designer for the campus map. Ask questions, clarification, etc. as you draw the new map. When you have finished, compare your map with that of the university representative to verify that they are alike.

2. **Role A.** You are a new student at the university and you don't know where the bookstore is. Introduce yourself to one of your classmates. Then, a) tell him/her that you need to go (**ir**) to the bookstore and b) ask where it is.

   Role B. A new student will greet you and ask you questions. Your answers should be as complete and specific as possible.

5. Question words

cómo	*how/what*	**cuál(es)**	*which*
dónde	*where*	**quién(es)**	*who*
qué	*what*	**cuánto/a**	*how much*
cuándo	*when*	**cuántos/as**	*how many*

ACENTOS

All question words have a written accent over the stressed syllable: **cómo, dónde.**

- If a subject is used in a question, it normally follows the verb.

  ¿Dónde trabaja Elsa? — *Where does Elsa work?*

- Use **por qué** to ask *why*. The equivalent of *because* is **porque.**

  ¿**Por qué** está Pepe en la biblioteca? — *Why is Pepe at the library?*
  Porque necesita estudiar. — *Because he needs to study.*

- Use **qué + ser** when you want to ask for a definition or an explanation.

  ¿**Qué** es la sardana? — *What is the sardana?*
  Es un baile típico de Cataluña. — *It's a typical dance of Catalonia.*

- Use **cuál(es) + ser** when you want to ask which one(s).

  ¿**Cuál** es tu mochila? — *Which (one) is your backpack?*
  ¿**Cuáles** son tus papeles? — *Which (ones) are your papers?*

- Questions that may be answered with **sí** or **no** do not use a question word.

  ¿Trabajan ustedes los sábados? — *Do you work on Saturdays?*
  No, no trabajamos. — *No, we don't.*

- Another way to ask a question is to place an interrogative tag after a declarative statement.

  Tú hablas inglés, **¿verdad?** — *You speak English, don't you?*
  David es norteamericano, **¿no?** — *David is an American, isn't he?*

¿Qué dice usted?

LENGUA

To request repetition or clarification use **¿Cómo?** or ***Perdón.*** The use of **¿Qué?,** the equivalent of English *what?,* is generally considered rude by some native speakers.

1-26 Entrevista. Look at the cues in the right column before completing the questions using **quién, cuándo, cuántos/as, cuál, por qué,** as needed. Then, working with a classmate, take turns to interview each other.

1. ¿_____ clases tomas?	Tomo...
2. ¿_____ son tus clases?	Por la...
3. ¿_____ es tu clase favorita?	La clase de...
4. ¿_____ es tu profesor favorito?	El/La profesor/a...
5. ¿_____ estudias español?	Porque...
6. ¿_____ estudiantes hay en tu clase de español?	Hay...

1-27 Firmas. What are your classmates like? What do they do? Walk around the room and ask the questions below. Have classmates who answer these questions affirmatively sign their names.

1. ¿Eres una persona optimista? ______
2. ¿Estudias y trabajas? ______
3. ¿Eres muy activo/a? ______
4. ¿Trabajas por las tardes? ______

1-28 Entrevista. Ask a classmate the following questions; then tell the rest of the class about him/her.

1. ¿Cuántas clases tomas este semestre?
2. ¿Cuál es tu clase favorita? ¿Por qué?
3. ¿Cuántos alumnos hay en la clase?
4. ¿Quién es el profesor?
5. ¿Cuándo estudias?
6. ¿Dónde trabajas?
7. ¿Quién es tu mejor (*best*) amigo/a?
8. ¿Cómo es él/ella?

1-29 Encuesta. You are conducting a survey for a Spanish TV station. Ask your partner the appropriate questions to find out the information requested below.

1. Dirección y teléfono ____________
2. Número de personas en la casa/el apartamento ____________
3. Número de televisores en la casa/el apartamento ____________
4. Programas favoritos ____________
5. Número de horas que miran televisión durante la semana ____________
6. Número de horas que miran televisión los fines de semana ____________

SITUACIONES

1. You have just run across a Spanish-speaking friend that you have not seen for a long time. Tell him/her about a) your university (location and size), b) your courses, and c) your activities. Ask him/her questions to get the same information.
2. **Role A.** It is the beginning of the term, and you missed yesterday's class. As usual, you expect some minor changes in the course schedule and syllabus. Ask your partner a) if there is homework, b) at what time the class is tomorrow, c) if there is an exam soon, and d) when the exam is.

   Role B. Answer your classmate's questions being as specific as possible. You may add that the exam will take place in a different classroom and give him/her the classroom location.

ALGO MÁS

Some regular *-er* and *-ir* verbs

The verb form found in dictionaries and in most vocabulary lists is the infinitive: **hablar**, **estudiar**, etc. Its equivalent in English is the verb preceded by *to: to speak, to study*. In Spanish, most infinitives end in **-ar**; other infinitives end in **-er** and **-ir**.
So far you have practiced the present tense of regular **-ar** verbs. Now you will practice the **yo**, **tú**, and **usted/él/ella** forms of some **-er** and **-ir** verbs: **leer**–*to read*, **comer**–*to eat*, **aprender**–*to learn*, **escribir**–*to write*, **vivir**–*to live*.

- As you did with **-ar** verbs, use the ending **-o** when talking about your daily activities.

Leo y **escribo** en la clase todos los días.	*I read and I write in class everyday.*

- For the **tú** form, use the ending **-es**.

¿**Comes** en la cafetería o en tu casa?	*Do you eat in the cafeteria or at home?*

- For the **usted/él/ella** form, delete the final **-s** of the **tú** form.

Ella **vive** en la calle Salud.	*She lives on Salud Street.*

¿Qué dice usted?

1-30 **¿Conoce usted a su profesor/a?** With a classmate, discuss whether the following information about your instructor is true (**cierta**) or false (**falsa**). Then ask your instructor to verify the information.

1. _____ Escribe poemas.
2. _____ Come en restaurantes los fines de semana.
3. _____ Enseña cuatro clases todos los días.
4. _____ Vive en un condominio.
5. _____ Toma mucho café.
6. _____ Consulta la Internet para sus clases.

1-31 ¿Con qué frecuencia? With a classmate, decide who is going to be **Estudiante 1** and who will be **Estudiante 2.** After filling out the chart corresponding to your number, ask your classmate when he/she does each activity listed under his/her number.

MODELO: Comer pizza
E1: Yo como pizza los domingos. Y tú, ¿cuándo comes pizza?
E2: Yo nunca como pizza.

ACTIVIDAD	TODOS LOS DIAS	A VECES	LOS DOMINGOS	NUNCA
ESTUDIANTE 1				
comer hamburguesas				
mirar televisión por la noche				
leer novelas de detectives				
escribir composiciones				
ESTUDIANTE 2				
comer pasta				
escuchar música rock				
leer novelas de misterio				
aprender palabras en español				

mosaicos

A ESCUCHAR

A. ¿Cierto o falso? You will hear two students talking about their classes. Before listening to the recording, think about the kinds of things they may say and make a list of what you might expect to hear. Your experience and previous knowledge will help you anticipate some of the things they may say. Then listen to the conversation between Ana and Mario and indicate whether each statement is **Cierto** or **Falso**. Read the statements before listening to the tape.

	CIERTO	FALSO
1. Ana y Mario están muy bien.	______	______
2. Mario toma clases de ciencias y de humanidades.	______	______
3. Ana toma sólo *(only)* clases de ciencias.	______	______
4. Los estudiantes trabajan mucho en la clase de literatura.	______	______
5. La clase favorita de Mario es historia.	______	______

B. ¿Qué clases toman? First, as you listen to the description, circle the words you hear. Then read the passage and complete the chart on page 48, based on the information you obtained.

Cristina y Ester estudian (**biología / lenguas**) y no estudian (**psicología / economía**). Ester tiene clases de (**inglés / portugués**) y de (**historia / geografía**) los lunes, miércoles y viernes. Los martes y jueves ella toma (**informática / física**) y (**filosofía / psicología**). Geografía es su clase favorita. Cristina estudia (**contabilidad / matemáticas**) y (**química / biología**) los lunes, miércoles y viernes. Los martes y jueves ella toma (**química / biología**) y (**portugués / inglés**). Ella no toma (**psicología / filosofía**) este año, pero sí estudia física. Las clases de (**física / química, contabilidad / cálculo**) y economía de Jorge son los lunes, miércoles y viernes. Los martes y jueves son sus clases de psicología y biología.

NOMBRE	LUNES, MIERCOLES Y VIERNES	MARTES Y JUEVES
	economía	biología
	química	psicología
	contabilidad	
	matemáticas	biología
	química	física
		portugués
	portugués	psicología
	geografía	informática

A CONVERSAR

1-32 Buscando una librería. You and a friend are visiting Málaga, Spain. Your friend finds the following ad in the local newspaper. Ask him/her the following questions about the ad.

a. the name of the bookstore
b. the address of the bookstore
c. the bookstore's phone number

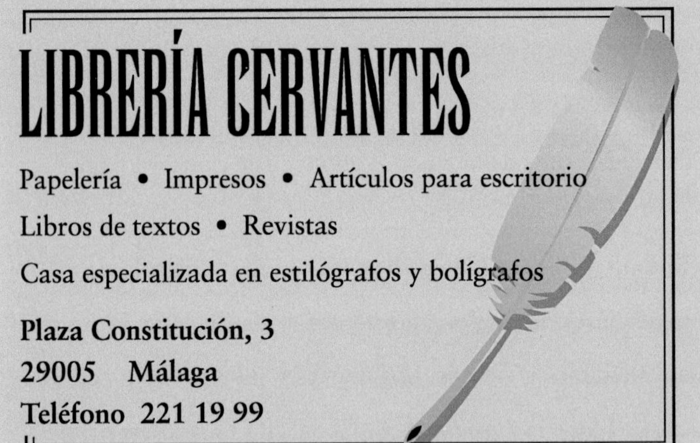

LIBRERÍA CERVANTES
Papelería • Impresos • Artículos para escritorio
Libros de textos • Revistas
Casa especializada en estilógrafos y bolígrafos
Plaza Constitución, 3
29005 Málaga
Teléfono 221 19 99

1-33 Encuesta: las clases. Primera fase. In small groups, ask all members of your group what courses they're taking and what their classes are like. Complete the chart on the next page with the results of your poll.

MODELO: E1: ¿Estudias biología?
E2: Sí, estudio biología
E1: ¿Es una clase difícil?
E2: No, es (una clase) fácil.

MATERIAS	COMPANEROS/AS	DIFICIL	FACIL
biología			
inglés			
economía			
física			
español			
literatura inglesa			
matemáticas			
historia			

Segunda fase. Now, summarize the results of your poll and share them with the class.

1. ¿Cuántos/as compañeros/as estudian biología, economía, etc.?
2. Según la opinión del grupo, ¿qué clases son fáciles?
3. ¿Qué clases son difíciles?

A LEER

An important skill that must be developed to become proficient in another language is accurate, fluent reading. Of course this comes with exposure to the language over time, but it is vital to develop this skill from the earliest stages of learning a new language.

Reading proficiently means more than just knowing words. It represents an active process in which linguistic and non-linguistic variables intervene while you are trying to make sense of a written text. Before proceeding with the following activities, look at some of the reading tips you learned on p. 20 of **Bienvenidos.** What is the format of the following texts? Can you recognize some cognates? Underline them.

1-34 Preparación. In your opinion, which of the following classes are more interesting for a North American student planning to study in Spain? Write a check mark in front of the numbers. Then compare your responses with those of a classmate

1. ____ Diseño gráfico
2. ____ Guitarra clásica
3. ____ Historia precolombina
4. ____ Cocina de Andalucía
5. ____ Ritmos árabes
6. ____ Matemática avanzada
7. ____ Folclor catalán
8. ____ Historia norteamericana contemporánea

1-35 Primera mirada. Read the following text from a brochure by **Universidad de Salamanca,** Spain, and underline the correct response in each statement.

a. Según este texto, la Universidad de Salamanca ofrece como cursos complementarios clases de ciencia / arte / historia.
b. Los alumnos que desean aprender guitarra tienen la posibilidad de tomar una clase / dos clases.
c. En la clase de danza, los profesores enseñan baile clásico / bailes de varias regiones de España.
d. Las clases de danza y las clases de guitarra cuestan igual / tienen precios diferentes.
e. Las clases que ofrecen son a las 12:00 / tienen una duración de 12 horas.
f. Las clases son principalmente para estudiantes españoles / extranjeros.

CURSOS CULTURALES COMPLEMENTARIOS

Usted puede completar su formación con alguno de los siguientes cursos de nuestro programa. Nuestro objetivo fundamental es que su inmersión en lo español se enriquezca por el contacto con actividades muy relacionadas con lo hispánico.

No hay preinscripción para estos cursos. Si usted está interesado, puede matricularse en Madrid.

• Curso de guitarra

Se ofrece en dos niveles:

1. Primeros pasos en el manejo de la guitarra.
2. Las raíces de lo folclórico y su proyección en Hispanoamérica. Práctica de los ritmos básicos.

Duración: 12 horas
Precio: 50 euros

• Curso de danza española

Usted conocerá y practicará los bailes de Andalucía, Castilla y León, Aragón, Galicia, etc.

Duración: 12 horas
Precio: 45 euros

20 ....Cursos Internacionales

1-36 Ampliación. Find the answer to the following questions in the brochure and underline them.

1. ¿Cuál es el objetivo principal de estos cursos de la universidad?
2. ¿Es necesario inscribirse en los cursos antes (*before*) del primer día de clases?
3. ¿Qué hace el/la estudiante que toma la clase de Danza española?
4. ¿Qué nivel toma un/a estudiante que no sabe (*knows*) tocar la guitarra?

A ESCRIBIR

Writing is an act of communication in every language. In order for your writing to be effective, you need to consider the following questions before you begin:

1. **Purpose:** Why am I writing? To communicate with a friend? To request something in a business situation? To complain? To inform?
2. **Means of communication:** What channel am I using to communicate? Is it a letter, a postcard, an essay? Am I filling out a form, writing a report?
3. **Reader:** Who will be the recipient of my message? Someone I know or someone unknown to me? If it is someone I know, is it an acquaintance, a friend, a relative? Is the reader my age, younger or older? Is this person someone who holds authority over me?
4. **Topic:** What is the content of my writing? Am I writing about my personal experience or about a broader, more general topic? Am I reporting a scientific experiment I made or read about, or am I recounting a funny story?
5. **Language:** What vocabulary and structures will I potentially need to develop my topic? When writing in a language other than your own, you'll find it helpful to list these before you begin. For example, if you are interviewing a classmate about his or her background, you'll find it useful to make a list of the questions for requesting personal information: **¿Dónde vives? ¿Qué estudias?**, etc.

1-37 Preparación. Before doing Activity 1-38, specify the following:

1. Purpose:
2. Means of communication:
3. Reader:
4. Topic:
5. Language:

1-38 Manos a la obra. This is the first time you are away from home and would like to send a postcard to your parents, telling them about your life at the university. Cover the following points in your postcard:

- How things are going for you.
- Your university or college, the number and names of your classes, when you are taking them, how interesting (or not) your classes and professors are.
- What your daily routine is like, what you do after (*después de*) class, on weekends, etc

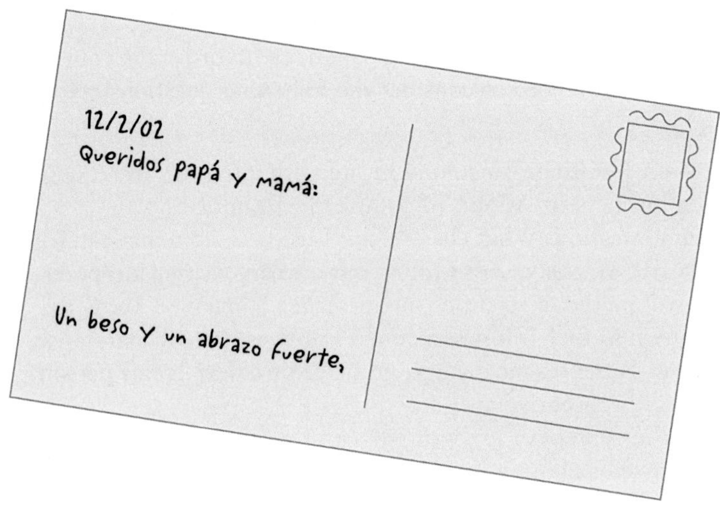

12/2/02
Queridos papá y mamá:
Un beso y un abrazo fuerte,

1-39 Revisión. After writing your postcard, discuss it with a classmate. Then, make any necessary changes.

- Make sure you've covered all the information requested in Activity 1–38.
- Revise any possible inaccuracies you may find regarding language use, spelling, punctuation, accentuation, etc.
- Finally, make any necessary changes that will make your text clear and comprehensible to your reader.

Vocabulario*

En la clase

el casete	*cassette*
el diccionario	*dictionary*
el mapa	*map*
la nota	*note, grade*
la tarea	*homework*

Materias

la antropología	*anthropology*
la biología	*biology*
la economía	*economics*
el español	*Spanish*
la geografía	*geography*
la historia	*history*
la informática	*computer science*
la literatura	*literature*
las matemáticas	*mathematics*
la (p)sicología	*psychology*
la sociología	*sociology*

Lugares

la biblioteca	*library*
el café	*coffee house*
la cafetería	*cafeteria*
la casa	*house, home*
la discoteca	*dance club*
el gimnasio	*gymnasium*
el laboratorio	*laboratory*
el laboratorio de lenguas	*language lab*
la librería	*bookstore*
la oficina	*office*
la playa	*beach*
la plaza	*plaza*
la universidad	*university*

Facultades

arquitectura	*architecture*
ciencias	*sciences*
humanidades	*humanities*
medicina	*medicine*

Personas

el/la alumno/a	*student*
el/la compañero/a	*partner, classmate*
el/la dependiente/a	*salesperson*
ellos/ellas	*they*
nosotros/nosotras	*we*
ustedes	*you* (plural)

Descripciones

aburrido/a	*boring*
bueno/a	*good*
difícil	*difficult*
estudioso/a	*studious*
excelente	*excellent*
fácil	*easy*
favorito/a	*favorite*
grande	*big*
malo/a	*bad*
norteamericano/a	*American/North American*
pequeño/a	*small*
prohibido/a	*forbidden, not allowed*
responsable	*responsible*

Verbos

bailar	*to dance*
buscar	*to look for*
caminar	*to walk*
comprar	*to buy*
conversar	*to talk, to converse*
escuchar	*to listen (to)*
estar	*to be*
estudiar	*to study*
hablar	*to speak*
llegar	*to arrive*
mirar	*to look (at)*
montar	*to ride*
montar en bicicleta	*to ride a bicycle*
necesitar	*to need*
practicar	*to practice*
revisar	*to revise, to go over*
sacar	*to get, to take (out)*
tomar	*to take, to drink*
tomar apuntes	*to take notes*
trabajar	*to work*

yo estoy

Expresiones de tiempo y frecuencia

a veces	*sometimes*
el fin de semana	*weekend*
muchas veces	*often, many times*
nunca	*never*
por la tarde	*in the afternoon*
siempre	*always*
todos los días	*everyday*

Palabras y expresiones útiles

algo	*something*
buena suerte	*good luck*
¿Cómo te va?	*How is it going?*
¿Cuánto cuesta?	*How much is it?*
el dólar	*dollar*
este/a	*this*
Hasta la vista.	*See you later.*
para	*for, to*
pero	*but*
porque	*because*
¿Qué haces?	*What do you do? What are you doing?*
¡Qué lástima!	*What a pity!*
también	*also*
¿Verdad?	*Right?*

*See page 43 for question words.

Las universidades hispanas

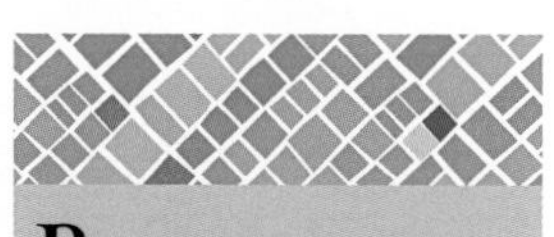

Para pensar

¿Cómo se llama su universidad? ¿Es grande o pequeña? ¿nueva o antigua? ¿privada o pública? ¿Es difícil ingresar (*be admitted*) a la universidad en los Estados Unidos? ¿Qué examen tienen que tomar los estudiantes de secundaria para ingresar a la universidad?

En los países hispanos hay muchas universidades muy buenas, pero ingresar a la universidad no es fácil. En muchos países, los estudiantes tienen que tomar un examen de admisión y solamente los mejores son admitidos. En algunos países, la nota que un estudiante saca en este examen determina qué carrera puede estudiar o no estudiar. Es por eso que las personas que quieren ingresar a la universidad se preparan con muchos meses de anticipación.

Algunas universidades son muy grandes, como por ejemplo la Universidad Complutense de Madrid (vaya a la página de Mosaicos en la Internet *www.prenhall.com/mosaicos*), en la que estudian más de 120.000 estudiantes; otras son más pequeñas y tienen sólo unos cuantos cientos de estudiantes. Algunas universidades son privadas y el costo es alto. Otras son públicas y no cuestan tanto, y por eso tienen muchos estudiantes. Una desventaja de estas universidades es que las clases son muy grandes y muchas veces los estudiantes no tienen lugar en el salón para sentarse. Algunas universidades son modernas, pero también hay otras que son muy antiguas. Entre las universidades más antiguas está la Universidad de Salamanca (vaya a *www.prenhall.com/mosaicos*) en España fundada en el siglo XIII. Esta universidad es famosa no sólo por la belleza de su arquitectura, sino también por las personas importantes que han enseñado ahí.

La educación universitaria dura un promedio de cinco años. Muchos estudiantes permanecen más tiempo en la universidad porque trabajan y en general, hay clases por las mañanas, tardes y noches. En la mayor parte de las universidades hispanas no hay residencias estudiantiles y los estudiantes viven con sus familias o en casas de huéspedes.

En las universidades hispanas, igual que en las norteamericanas, se practican deportes y hay competencias entre ellas. Sin embargo, estas competencias no son tan populares entre los estudiantes como en las universidades norteamericanas. Hay otras cosas que son más interesantes para los estudiantes universitarios en los países hispanos. Por ejemplo, ellos participan activamente en la vida política del país y frecuentemente organizan marchas y protestas en reacción a algún acontecimiento político nacional o internacional.

La universidad de Salamanca

Muchas universidades del mundo hispano tienen programas de español para estudiantes extranjeros. Así por ejemplo, hay programas especiales en la Universidad de Salamanca y en la Universidad de Valencia (vaya a *www.prenhall.com/mosaicos)* en España. ¡Estudiar en una universidad hispana es una experiencia inolvidable!

The *Enfoque cultural* is available in an interactive online format at *www.prenhall.com/mosaicos*

Para contestar

A. Las universidades. Trabajando con su compañero/a responda a las siguientes preguntas:

1. ¿Cómo son las universidades en el mundo hispano? Describa por lo menos tres características según la información anterior.
2. ¿Hay muchas universidades antiguas en los países hispanos? Dé un ejemplo.
3. Si un estudiante quiere ir a la universidad en un país hispano, ¿qué tiene que hacer?

B. Riqueza cultural. En grupos de tres, mencionen dos cosas que los estudiantes de los Estados Unidos y de los países hispanos tienen que hacer para ingresar a la universidad.

 Para investigar en la WWW

1. Busque información acerca de la Universidad de Salamanca, la Universidad Complutense de Madrid o cualquier otra universidad española. Averigüe (*find out*): ¿Cómo es su arquitectura? ¿Qué especialidades se pueden estudiar en esta universidad? ¿Cuándo son los exámenes de admisión? Luego, comparta con la clase la información que encontró y lo que le pareció interesante.
2. Busque información acerca de programas de español para estudiantes extranjeros en la Universidad de Salamanca o en otras universidades del mundo hispano. Averigüe qué cursos ofrecen, el costo, etc. Seleccione una universidad adonde Ud. quiera ir y explique a la clase por qué seleccionó esta universidad.
3. Busque información acerca de la vida del estudiante universitario hispano (eventos deportivos, bibliotecas, cafés, exposiciones de arte, charlas/conferencias, etc.). ¿Qué actividades son interesantes? ¿Desea usted participar en este tipo de actividades o prefiere las actividades de su universidad?

España

Ciudades importantes y lugares de interés: Madrid, la capital, es una ciudad de gran vitalidad y energía, como pocas ciudades en el mundo (vaya a *www.prenhall.com/mosaicos*). Vivir en Madrid significa poder disfrutar de una intensa vida intelectual y social. Durante el día, los madrileños se reúnen en los cafés y terrazas, y por la noche, hasta la madrugada, en los bares y discotecas. Madrid es una ciudad en constante movimiento. Madrid tiene además importantes museos (El Prado), palacios (Palacio Real), iglesias (Iglesia de San Francisco el Grande), impresionantes plazas (Plaza Mayor), bellísimas fuentes (La Cibeles), hermosos parques (Parque El Retiro), avenidas amplias (La Gran Vía) y universidades importantes.

Otra ciudad de interés es Salamanca, situada en la parte occidental de España. Allí se encuentra una de las universidades más antiguas de Europa. Además, Salamanca cuenta con plazas, monumentos y edificios importantes como sus dos catedrales y la Plaza Mayor, donde se reúnen estudiantes y turistas para conversar en los cafés o pasear alrededor de la Plaza. También es común que las tunas (*group of student minstrels*) lleguen a la plaza y ofrezcan serenatas.

En el sur de España se encuentra Sevilla, ciudad de encanto y alegría sin par. Sevilla es famosa no sólo por su catedral, la Torre de Oro y el Alcázar, palacio real construido por los moros en el siglo XII, sino también por sus famosas celebraciones de Semana Santa y la Feria de Abril. En la Feria, las corridas de toros y el baile flamenco llenan de alegría la ciudad.

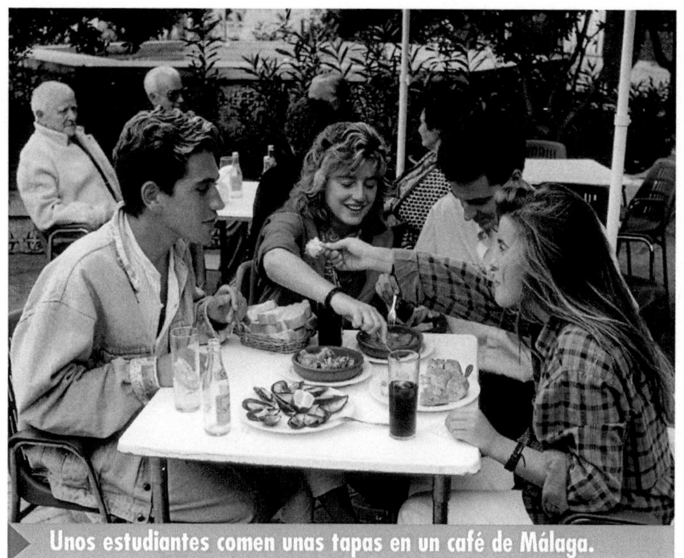

Unos estudiantes comen unas tapas en un café de Málaga.

Además del español o castellano que es el idioma oficial, en algunas regiones de España se hablan otras lenguas y/o dialectos. En Galicia, al noroeste, se habla el gallego. En Cataluña, al noreste, se habla el catalán. La capital de Cataluña es Barcelona, que es además la segunda ciudad más importante del país, después de Madrid. En el norte está el País Vasco y allí se habla vascuence o euskera; en las islas Baleares se habla el mallorquín, y finalmente, en la región valenciana, en la costa este de la península, se habla el valenciano.

¡Visitar España es visitar un mundo de alegría y de estímulo intelectual!

Expresiones españolas:

Ir de copas:	¡Vamos de copas!	*Let's go have a drink!*
Catear:	¡Me han cateado!	*They've flunked me!*
Majo/a:	Ella es muy maja.	*She's a very nice person.*
Vale:	Te llamo luego, ¿vale?	*I'll call you later, ok?*
Chaval:	¿Dónde está ese chaval?	*Where is that kid?*

ENFOQUE INTERACTIVO

A MIRAR EL VIDEO 5:00

Watch the *Fortunas* video segment for *Lección 1* in class or on your CD-ROM. Learn about this year's *Fortunas* treasure hunt and find out who are the four contestants who have been chosen to compete in the current edition of this exciting contest.

Now complete the accompanying video activities on the CD-ROM. This is your chance to interact with the video characters! **25:00**

Katie

Comienza el concurso

The *Fortunas* contest requires participants to use *pistas* (clues) to solve seven *misterios* and find three *fortunas*. All the *misterios* and *fortunas* are located within Mexico City and are related to the history of Mexico and the New World. Players earn points by solving *misterios*, locating *fortunas*, and winning viewer polls.

PARA GANAR

Puntos

- 7 misterios = 300 puntos cada uno
- 3 fortunas = 1000 puntos cada una
- 13 encuestas = 150 puntos cada una
- Encuesta final = 500 puntos

Premios

Ganador: ❶ Viaje a las Islas Canarias
Segundo: ❷ Viaje a Nueva York
Tercero: ❸ Viaje a Puerto Rico
Cuarto: ❹ Viaje a Acapulco

¡COMENCEMOS LA BÚSQUEDA! 5:00

The *Fortunas* contest is interactive. It allows you to match your skills with those of the contestants and to vote in viewer polls. Go to the *Mosaicos Website* (*www.prenhall.com/mosaicos*) and click on the *Fortunas* module to learn more about the contest. See if you can solve the first *misterio* before the contestants do.

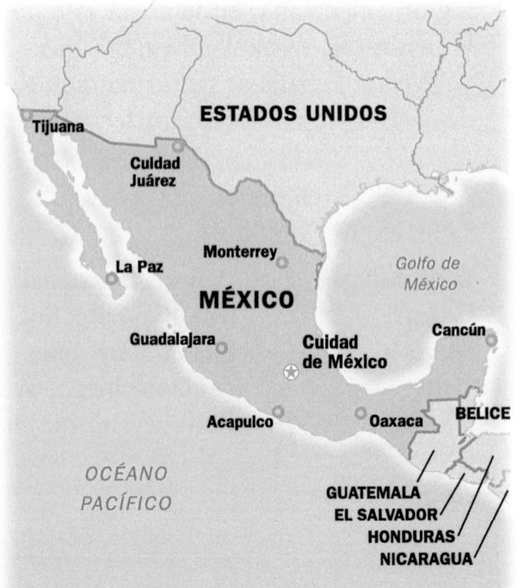

¿QUÉ OPINA USTED? 5:00

Fortunas contestants can earn valuable points by winning viewer polls on the Internet. After each episode you can vote in the *Fortunas* viewer poll and help determine the winner of the contest. Please go to the *Fortunas* module on the *Mosaicos Website* and click on *¿Qué opina usted?* to cast your vote. Before voting in this episode's viewer poll, read the biographies of the four contestants on the website to learn more about them.

PARA NAVEGAR 10:00

UNA ESTUDIANTE ESPAÑOLA

Sabrina Medina es una estudiante de España. Estudia derecho en la Universidad de Salamanca. Las universidades del mundo hispáno son similares a las de los Estados Unidos, pero hay ciertas diferencias también. ¿Sabe usted dónde está Salamanca?

Universidad de Salamanca

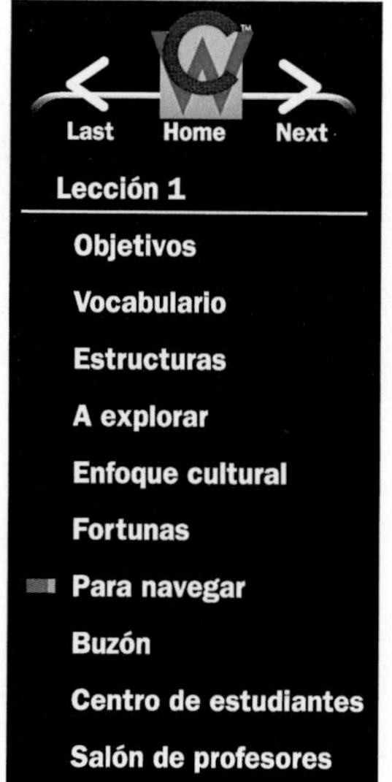

Go to the *Mosaicos Website* and click on the *Para navegar* module to explore links to Spain and Spanish universities. Look at course schedules and descriptions and complete the related activities. Read about the country's rich artistic tradition and history, and explore some of its exciting dimensions.

Lección 2

Los amigos hispanos

COMUNICACION

- Asking about and describing persons, animals, places, and things
- Expressing nationality and place of origin
- Expressing where and when events take place
- Expressing possession
- Expressing likes and dislikes

ESTRUCTURAS

- Adjectives
- Present tense and some uses of the verb **ser**
- **Ser** and **estar** with adjectives
- Possessive adjectives
- ALGO MAS: Expressions with **gustar**

MOSAICOS

A ESCUCHAR

A CONVERSAR

A LEER

- Scanning a text
- Inferring meaning

A ESCRIBIR

- Responding to an ad
- Addressing an unknown reader formally

ENFOQUE CULTURAL

- La diversidad étnica
- Argentina

ENFOQUE INTERACTIVO

WWW

VIDEO

CD ROM

A primera vista

Mis amigos y yo

Me llamo Luis López. Soy de Argentina y tengo veintidós años. Me gusta escuchar música y mirar televisión. Estudio en la Universidad de Buenos Aires y deseo ser profesor de historia. Los chicos en estas fotografías también estudian en la universidad y somos muy buenos amigos.

Practice Activities for each vocabulary section are provided on the CD-ROM and website (www.prenhall.com/mosaicos)

Esta chica es Amanda Martone. Es alta, delgada, tiene los ojos de color café y el pelo castaño y muy largo. Amanda es una chica muy agradable. Estudia en la universidad conmigo y desea ser economista.

Este chico se llama Ernesto Fernández. Ernesto es moreno, bajo, fuerte, muy hablador y simpático. Le gusta usar la computadora para conversar con sus amigos.

Mi amiga se llama Ana Villegas. No es alta ni baja, es mediana y usa lentes de contacto. Es pelirroja y tiene ojos negros. Ana es callada, trabajadora y muy inteligente.

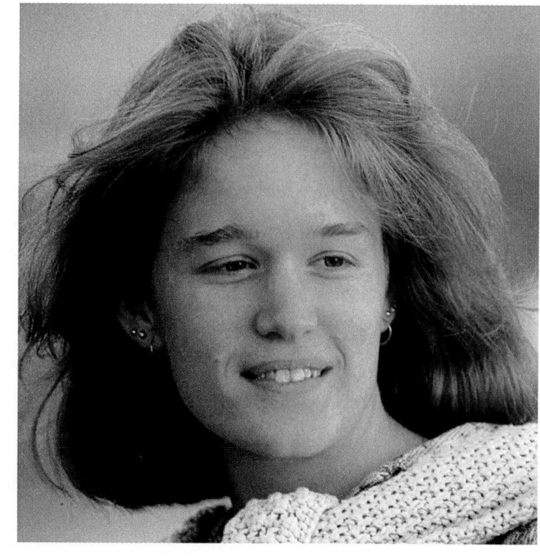

Cultura

In some Spanish-speaking countries, such as Spain and Cuba, the hand gesture used to express height when referring to people, animals, or objects is the same as in the United States—hand extended horizontally with the palm down. In other Hispanic countries, this gesture is used to express the height of only animals or objects. When referring to people in these countries, the hand is held straight up with palm facing out, sometimes with fingers slightly curved; still in other countries, the palm is placed sideways with fingers extended.

ESPAÑA
NOMBRE
MARTA
PRIMER APELLIDO
CHÁVEZ
SEGUNDO APELLIDO
CONDE
16533103-J
EXPED. 03-06-1997 VAL 02-06-2002
MINISTERIO DEL INTERIOR
16533103-J
NACIÓ EN SANTA CRUZ DE TENERIFE
PROVINCIA STA C TENERIFE 24-07-1977
HIJA DE INOCENCIO Y ROSARIO SEXO F
DIRECCIÓN C CÓRCEGA 397 11
LOCALIDAD BARCELONA
PROVINCIA BARCELONA EQUIPO 08055A606
ID<ESP<<<<<<<<<<<<<<<<<<<<<<<<<<<<
16533103-J<<<<<<<<<<<<<<<<<<<<<<<<

Esta chica es Marta Chávez Conde. Es española y tiene veintiún años. Es rubia, tiene pelo corto y ojos azules. Marta es soltera y muy divertida. Este año está en Buenos Aires con su familia.

¿Qué dice usted?

2-1 Asociaciones. To whom do the descriptions on the left refer?

1. ____ Tiene el pelo largo.
2. ____ Tiene veintidós años.
3. ____ Es de España.
4. ____ Es bajo y fuerte.
5. ____ Es callada y muy inteligente.
6. ____ Habla mucho.
7. ____ Tiene los ojos de color café.
8. ____ Es rubia.
9. ____ Es soltera y divertida.
10. ____ Desea ser profesor de historia.

a. Luis López
b. Amanda Martone
c. Ernesto Fernández
d. Ana Villegas
e. Marta Chávez

2-2 Adivine quién es. Primera fase. With a classmate, read again the texts on pages 62 and 63. Then make a list of expressions that you may use to describe people in regards to: a) their physical appearance and b) their personality traits. Use at least 6 expressions per column.

Segunda fase. Now, working in a group, think of a classmate and describe him/her in at least three sentences, using the vocabulary from **Primera fase** or any other that you may need. The rest of the group will have to guess who is being described.

MODELO: E1: Es alto y delgado. Tiene pelo negro. Es fuerte y callado.
E2: Es...

2-3 ¿Qué me gusta y qué no me gusta? Indicate whether you like or dislike each of the following activities. Then, ask a classmate and compare your answers.

MODELO: estar en casa por las noches
E1: ¿Te gusta estar en casa por las noches?
E2: Sí, me gusta. *o* No, no me gusta.

ACTIVIDADES	USTED		COMPANERO/A	
	SI	NO	SI	NO
1. mirar televisión por la tarde				
2. estudiar español				
3. practicar tenis/fútbol/béisbol				
4. escribir en la computadora				
5. trabajar los sábados y los domingos				
6. tomar café por la noche				
7. bailar los fines de semana				
8. hablar con los amigos en los cafés				

¿De qué color son estos autos?

Es rojo. Es amarillo.

Otros colores

blanco
verde
marrón
gris
rosado
morado
anaranjado

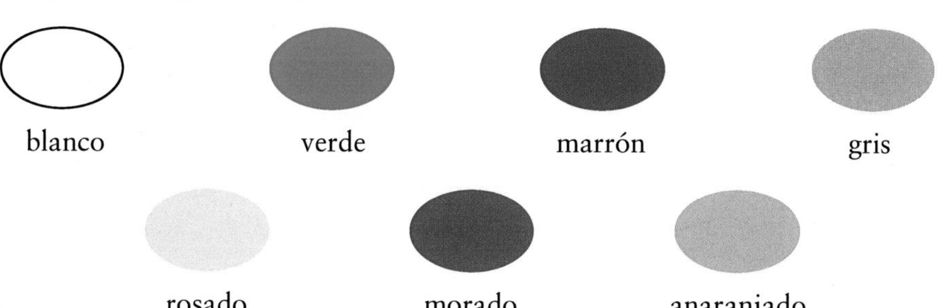

LENGUA

There are several Spanish words, depending on the country, to express the color brown: **café**, **marrón**, **carmelita**, **castaño**, and **pardo/a**. The words **naranja** and **rosa** are also used instead of **anaranjado** and **rosado**.

¿Cómo son estas personas?

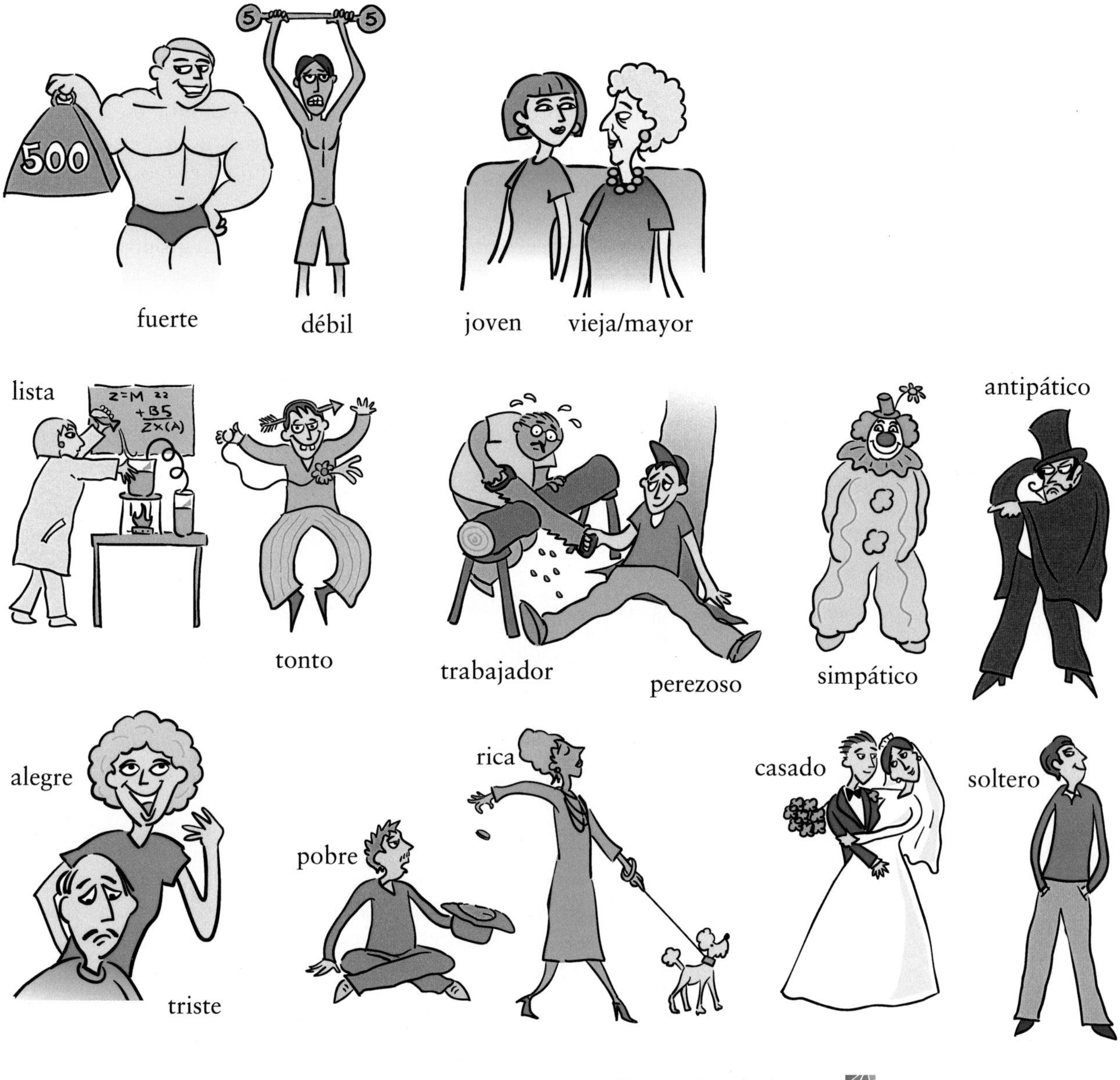

500
5
5
fuerte
débil
joven
vieja/mayor
lista
Z=M 22
+B5
ZX(A)
tonto
trabajador
perezoso
simpático
antipático
alegre
triste
pobre
rica
casado
soltero

¿Y cómo son estos animales?

Es feo. Es muy bonita/guapa. Es delgada. Es gordo.

¿Qué dice usted?

2-4 Opuestos. Complete the following statements.

MODELO: Leonardo Di Caprio no es viejo, es joven.

1. Julia Roberts no es gorda, es...
2. El presidente no es perezoso, es...
3. Jennifer López no es antipática, es...
4. Madonna no es tonta, es...
5. Bill Gates no es pobre, es...
6. Ricky Martin no es feo, es...

2-5 Los ojos y los lentes de contacto. Primera fase. In groups of four, gather the following information.

1. ¿Cuántos estudiantes tienen ojos verdes? ¿azules? ¿café? ¿negros?
2. ¿Cuál es el color de ojos más común?
3. ¿Cuántas personas usan lentes (*eyeglasses*)? ¿lentes de contacto? ¿lentes de contacto de color? ¿no usan lentes?
4. ¿Hay más estudiantes con o sin lentes de contacto?

Segunda fase. Now, read the ad for **Multicolor** contact lenses and ask your partner questions based on it.

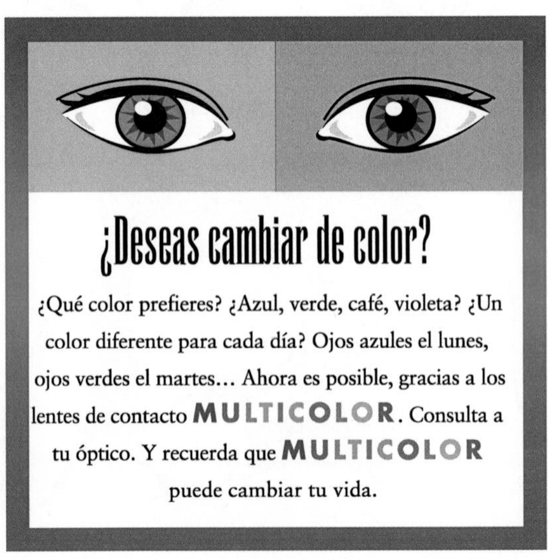

¿Deseas cambiar de color?
¿Qué color prefieres? ¿Azul, verde, café, violeta? ¿Un color diferente para cada día? Ojos azules el lunes, ojos verdes el martes... Ahora es posible, gracias a los lentes de contacto MULTICOLOR. Consulta a tu óptico. Y recuerda que MULTICOLOR puede cambiar tu vida.

2-6 Autodescripción. You're appearing on the TV program **Cita a ciegas** (*Blind Date*). Describe yourself to make a good first impression.

1. Me llamo...
2. Soy... No soy...
3. Tengo...
4. Estudio...
5. Trabajo...
6. Me gusta...

2-7 ¿Quién soy? In a small piece of paper, write a brief description of yourself (physical and personality wise); DO NOT include your name. Fold the piece of paper and give it to your instructor. He/She will ask each one of you to draw a description, read it, and match the description with the name of the classmate who wrote it.

MODELO: Soy alta y morena; uso lentes, tengo el pelo corto; soy (muy) trabajadora.

¿De dónde son?

LENGUA

In Argentina, as well as in other countries in South and Central America, close friends address each other using the pronoun **vos**. Most verb forms used with **vos** are slightly different from those used with **tú**.

Vos estás muy bien.
Vos comés mucho.
¿Vos vivís en la calle Libertador?

¿Qué dice usted?

2-8 ¿Quiénes son? Identify the following people.

1. cantante (*singer*), actor y político panameño	a. Bill Gates
2. diseñadora (*designer*) famosa	b. Mario Vargas Llosa
3. escritor de Perú, *La ciudad y los perros*	c. Rigoberta Menchú
4. poeta de México, Premio Nobel, 1990	d. Rubén Blades
5. Premio Nobel de la Paz, 1992	e. Carolina Herrera
6. bailarín de ballet argentino	f. Julio Bocca
7. cofundador de Microsoft	g. Octavio Paz
8. ex-presidenta de Nicaragua	h. Violeta Chamorro

2-9 Adivinanzas. Think of a well-known person. A classmate will try to guess his or her identity by asking you questions.

MODELO: E1: ¿De dónde es?
E2: Es cubanoamericana.
E1: ¿En qué trabaja?
E2: Es cantante y trabaja con su esposo en Miami.
E1: ¿Es Gloria Estefan?
E2: ¡Sí!

A ESCUCHAR

¿Cómo son estas personas? You will hear a student talk about himself. Before listening to the recording, think about the things he may say and go over the information below. Then listen carefully to determine if this information is mentioned or not. Mark the appropriate column.

	SI	NO
1. name	_____	_____
2. age	_____	_____
3. address	_____	_____
4. physical description	_____	_____
5. preferences	_____	_____
6. place of work	_____	_____

Now you will hear a young woman describe herself. Mark the appropriate column on the chart according to the information that you hear.

NACIONALIDAD:	____ salvadoreña	____ norteamericana	____ argentina
EDAD:	____ 15 años	____ 21 años	____ 30 años
DESCRIPCION:	____ alta y rubia	____ baja y morena	____ fea y lista
ESTUDIOS:	____ lenguas	____ ciencias	____ psicología

Explicación y expansión

1. Adjectives

- Adjectives are words that describe people, places, and things. Like articles (**el, la, un, una**) and nouns (**chico, chica**), they generally have more than one form. In Spanish an adjective must agree in gender (masculine or feminine) and number (singular or plural) with the noun or pronoun it describes. Adjectives that describe characteristics of a noun usually follow the noun.

Practice activities for each numbered grammar point are provided on the CD-ROM and website (www.prenhall.com/mosaicos)

- Many adjectives end in **-o** when used with masculine words and in **-a** when used with feminine words. To form the plural these adjectives add **-s**.

	MASCULINE	FEMININE
SINGULAR	chico alto	chica alta
PLURAL	chicos altos	chicas altas

- Adjectives that end in **-e** and some adjectives that end in a consonant have only two forms, singular and plural. To form the plural, adjectives that end in **-e** add **-s**; adjectives that end in a consonant add **-es**.

	MASCULINE	FEMININE
SINGULAR	amigo interesante	amiga interesante
	chico popular	chica popular
PLURAL	amigos interesantes	amigas interesantes
	chicos populares	chicas populares

- Other adjectives that end in a consonant have four forms. This group includes some adjectives of nationality.

	MASCULINE	FEMININE
SINGULAR	alumno español	alumna española
	alumno trabajador	alumna trabajadora
PLURAL	alumnos españoles	alumnas españolas
	alumnos trabajadores	alumnas trabajadoras

- Adjectives that end in **-ista** have only two forms, singular and plural.

Pedro es muy optim**ista**, pero Alicia es pesim**ista**.	*Pedro is very optimistic, but Alicia is pessimistic.*
Ellos no son material**istas**.	*They are not materialistic.*

¿Qué dice usted?

2-10 Descripciones. You're the head of a growing company and need to hire more staff. Tell your classmate (the personnel manager) what qualities you're looking for in the job candidates. Answer the questions the personnel manager may have.

1. Necesito un/a director/a de relaciones públicas...

activo	competente	agradable
bilingüe	callado	antipático
extrovertido	pasivo	...

2. Necesito un/a subdirector/a...

inteligente	perezoso	débil
imparcial	trabajador	guapo
simpático	tonto	...

3. Necesito unos/as empleados/as...

arrogante	perfeccionista	divertido
atractivo	hablador	eficiente
agradable	responsable	...

2-11 Personas importantes. Primera fase. With a classmate, describe the people below, using at least three of the following adjectives or expressions for each one. Compare your description with those of other classmates.

serio	trabajador	cómico
inteligente	simpático	atlético
guapo	extrovertido	liberal
tiene ojos...	tiene pelo...	...

1. Gloria Estefan
2. Whoopi Goldberg
3. Peter Jennings
4. Christina Aguilera
5. Antonio Banderas
6. Plácido Domingo

Segunda fase. Now, take turns describing someone important in your life. Your partner will ask questions to get more information about him/her and to find out why he/she is important to you.

SITUACIONES

1. **Role A.** You are the personnel manager who is interviewing one of the job applicants in 2-10. Verify his/her name and ask him/her a) where he/she is from, b) what his/her personality traits are, c) if he/she currently works; if so, where, and d) what he/she likes to do in his/her free time **(tiempo libre)**.

   Role B. You are one of the job applicants in activity 2-10. Answer the personnel manager's questions in detail and ask any questions you may have.

2. **Role A.** You finally got your first job, but you don't like the office that you have been assigned (it is small, has an old computer, etc.). Describe it in detail to your partner. Then, describe to him/her your ideal office.

   Role B. Sketch each item of your classmate's description. Interrupt him/her as necessary to get the information you need. At the end, show him/her your drawing to see if it matches the description. You may need some additional vocabulary: **archivo** (*filing cabinet*), **impresora** (*printer*).

2. Present tense and some uses of the verb *ser*

SER (*to be*)			
yo	**soy**	nosotros/as	**somos**
tú	**eres**	vosotros/as	**sois**
Ud., él, ella	**es**	Uds., ellos/as	**son**

You have practiced some forms of the verb **ser** and have used them for identification (**Ese señor es el dependiente**) and to tell time. (**Son las cuatro**). Below you will learn other uses of the verb **ser.**

- **Ser** is used with adjectives to describe what a person, a place, or a thing is like.

¿Cómo **es** ella?	*What is she like?*
Es inteligente y simpática.	*She's intelligent and nice.*
¿Cómo **es** la casa?	*What is the house like?*
La casa **es** grande y muy bonita.	*The house is big and very beautiful.*

- **Ser** is used to express the nationality of a person; **ser + de** is used to express the origin of a person.

NATIONALITY

Luis **es** chileno.	*Luis is Chilean.*
Rosa **es** argentina.	*Ana is Argentinean.*

ORIGIN

Luis **es de** Chile.	*Luis is from Chile.*
Ana **es de** Argentina.	*Ana is from Argentina.*

- **Ser + de** is also used to express possession. The equivalent of the English word *whose* is **¿de quién?**

¿**De quién** es la casa?	*Whose house is it?*
La casa **es de** Marta.	*The house is Marta's.*

- **De + el** contracts to **del. De + la**(s) or **los** does not contract.

El diccionario **es del** profesor, no **es de la** estudiante.	*The dictionary is the professor's, not the student's.*

- **Ser** is used to express the location or time of an event.

El baile **es** en la universidad.	*The dance is (takes place) at the university.*
El examen **es** a las tres.	*The test is (takes place) at three.*

3. *Ser* and *estar* with adjectives

- **Ser** and **estar** are often used with the same adjectives. However, the choice of verb determines the meaning of the sentence.
- As you already know, **ser** + *adjective* states the norm, what someone or something is like.

Manolo **es** delgado.	*Manolo is thin. (He is a thin boy.)*
Sara **es** muy nerviosa.	*Sara is very nervous. (She is a nervous person.)*
El libro **es** nuevo.	*The book is new. (It's a new book.)*

- **Estar** + *adjective* comments on something. It expresses a change from the norm, a condition, and/or how one feels about the person or object being discussed.

Manolo **está** delgado.	*Manolo is thin. (He lost weight recently.)*
Sara **está** muy nerviosa.	*Sara is very nervous. (She has been nervous lately.)*
El libro **está** nuevo.	*The book is new. (It seems like a brand new book.)*

- The adjectives **contento/a, cansado/a, enojado/a** are always used with **estar.**

Ella **está contenta** ahora.	*She is happy now.*
El niño **está cansado.**	*The boy is tired.*
Carlos **está enojado.**	*Carlos is angry.*

- Some adjectives have one meaning with **ser** and another with **estar.**

Ese señor **es** malo.	*That man is bad/evil.*
Ese señor **está** malo.	*That man is ill.*
El chico **es** listo.	*The boy is clever.*
El chico **está** listo.	*The boy is ready.*
La manzana **es** verde.	*The apple is green.*
La manzana **está** verde.	*The apple is not ripe.*
Ella **es** aburrida.	*She is boring.*
Ella **está** aburrida.	*She is bored.*

¿Qué dice usted?

2-12 ¿Cómo somos? Read the following descriptions and write an X under the appropriate heading. Then, compare your answers with those of a classmate. You may ask each other questions to expand the conversation.

	SI	NO
1. Soy muy responsable y trabajador/a.	_____	_____
2. A veces soy un poco rebelde.	_____	_____
3. Mi familia es muy religiosa y tradicional.	_____	_____
4. Mi mejor amigo es muy creativo y dinámico.	_____	_____
5. Él y yo somos agradables.	_____	_____
6. Las clases de este semestre son interesantes.	_____	_____

2-13 Descripciones. Ask a classmate what the following people and places are like.

MODELO: tu profesor/a de inglés
E1: ¿Cómo es tu profesor de inglés?
E2: Es alto, moreno y muy simpático.

1. la oficina del Departamento de Lenguas
2. tu cuarto (*bedroom*)
3. tu compañero/a de cuarto
4. tu auto/bicicleta
5. los chicos/las chicas de la clase
6. el laboratorio de computadoras

2-14 ¿De quién es/son...? You walk into your room and find several objects that don't belong to you. Ask your classmate whose they are. He/she will ask you at least two questions to help you identify the owner.

MODELO: computadora portátil
E1: ¿De quién es la computadora?
E2: No sé. ¿De qué color es?
E1: Es negra.
E2: ¿Es grande o pequeña?
E1: Es pequeña.
E2: Entonces es la computadora de Luis.

1.

2.

3.

4.

5.

6.

2-15 Una persona diferente. A classmate will use the adjectives in the following list to describe several people you both know. However, you know those people have changed. Tell him/her what they're like now.

MODELO: Arturo/gordo
E1: Arturo es gordo.
E2: Pero ahora está muy delgado.

1. Ramón/optimista
2. Ana y Gustavo/habladores
3. Catalina/tranquila
4. Julián/fuerte
5. Berta y Luisa/activas
6. Carmen/alegre

2-16 ¿Quiénes son estas personas? You're at a gathering where there are several foreign students. Ask a friend about the following people, as in the model.

MODELO: Olga Mendoza / Bolivia
E1: ¿Quién es esa chica?
E2: ¿Qué chica?
E1: La chica alta y rubia.
E2: ¡Ah! Es Olga Mendoza.
E1: ¿De dónde es?
E2: Es boliviana, es de La Paz.

1. Elda Capetillo / México
2. Fernando y Eduardo Arenas / Argentina
3. María Juana Herrera / Nicaragua
4. Ernesto Gutiérrez / Colombia
5. Alberto Díaz / Puerto Rico
6. Carmen Cisneros / Venezuela

2-17 Termómetro emocional. Primera fase. Write an X under the words that indicate how you feel in these places and situations. Then, write two more words, one under **yo** and the other under **compañero/a**, to show how you feel and how you guess your classmate feels.

LUGARES	ABURRIDO/A	CONTENTO/A	TRANQUILO/A	NERVIOSO/A	YO	COMPANERO/A
en la cafetería con mis amigos						
en los exámenes finales						
en el trabajo						
en una entrevista de trabajo						
en una fiesta formal						
en mi casa por la noche						

Segunda fase. Now compare your responses with those of a classmate and expand the conversation as necessary. You may find below, some helpful expressions for your conversation.

MODELO: en la clase de español
E1: Yo estoy contento/a en la clase de español y tú estás contento también.
E2: Sí, yo estoy contento/a. *o* Sí, nosotros/as estamos contentos/as. *o* No, yo estoy aburrido/a.

USEFUL EXPRESSIONS		
TO DISAGREE	TO AGREE	TO EXPRESS SURPRISE
Estás equivocado/a.	Tienes razón.	¡Qué increíble!
No, no es verdad.	Es verdad.	¡Qué buen/a observador/a (eres)!

ACENTOS

All words that are stressed on the third syllable from the end must have a written accent:

examen → **exámenes** (3 2 1)

joven → **jóvenes** (3 2 1)

2-18 Eventos y lugares. You're working at the university's information booth and your classmate (a visitor) stops by. Answer his/her questions. Then reverse roles.

MODELO:
VISITANTE: ¿Dónde es la exposición del club de fotografía?
EMPLEADO/A: Es en la biblioteca.
VISITANTE: ¿Y dónde está la biblioteca?
EMPLEADO/A: Está al lado de la cafetería.

1. el concierto
2. la conferencia
3. el banquete
4. la reunión de profesores
5. la función del club de español
6. la graduación

1. **Role A.** A new student from Argentina has joined your class. Introduce yourself and find out the following information from him/her: a) name; b) country and city of origin; c) size and location of city/town; d) characteristics of people from his country (what they are like, what they do, etc.).

   Role B. You are a foreign student from Buenos Aires, Argentina, who has recently joined this class. Answer your classmate's questions with as much detail as possible. Then ask him/her questions in order to get the same information he/she obtained from you.

2. **Role A.** You are trying to set up your classmate on a blind date with a friend. Answer your classmate's questions trying to tailor your answers to what you think he/she would like in a person since you want them to meet.

   Role B. Your classmate is trying to set you up on a blind date. Ask as many questions as possible to get the information you would like to know before deciding what to do.

4. Possessive adjectives

mi(s)	*my*
tu(s)	*your* (familiar)
su(s)	*your* (formal), *his, her, its, their*
nuestro(s), nuestra(s)	*our*
vuestro(s), vuestra(s)	*your* (familiar plural)

- These possessive adjectives always precede the noun they modify.

  mi casa　　　　**tu** bicicleta

- Possessive adjectives change number (and gender for **nosotros** and **vosotros**) to agree with the thing possessed, not with the possessor.

  mi casa, **mis** casas
  nuestro profesor, **nuestros** amigos; **nuestra** profesora, **nuestras** amigas

- **Su** and **sus** have multiple meanings. To ensure clarity, you may use **de** + the name of the possessor or the appropriate pronoun.

  su compañera = la compañera
  de ella (la compañera de Elena)
  de él (la compañera de Jorge)
  de usted
  de ustedes
  de ellos (la compañera de Elena y Jorge)
  de ellas (la compañera de Elena y Olga)

¿Qué dice usted?

2-19 Mi mundo. With a classmate, take turns describing the following things and people in your life. How different/similar are they for both of you?

MODELO: bicicleta
E1: Mi bicicleta es negra y fea. ¿Cómo es tu bicicleta?
E2: Es azul y bastante vieja.

1. familia
2. novio/a *(boy friend/girlfriend)*
3. casa/apartamento
4. restaurante favorito
5. clases
6. auto

2-20 Mi familia. First, mark your answers in the appropriate column. Then interview a classmate and compare your answers.

	YO		MI COMPANERO/A	
	SI	NO	SI	NO
1. Vivo en una ciudad grande.	____	____	____	____
2. Otros miembros de la familia viven con nosotros.	____	____	____	____
3. Siempre pasamos las vacaciones juntos *(together)*.	____	____	____	____
4. Siempre conversamos sobre temas políticos.	____	____	____	____
5. A veces no estamos de acuerdo y discutimos.	____	____	____	____
6. Nuestros amigos visitan la casa frecuentemente.	____	____	____	____

2-21 Nuestra universidad. Prepare a short oral presentation about your university, using the correct forms of **nuestro**. Some of the topics you may address are your professors, your classes, the students, the football/basketball teams (**equipo de fútbol/basquetbol**).

1. You are looking for an apartment to move into with another student. Two of your classmates need roommates and are each trying to talk you into picking their apartment. Before making a decision, ask them questions to get information about their apartments regarding a) size, b) location, and c) cost. You may find the following vocabulary useful: **cocina** (*kitchen*), **baño** (*bath*), **oscuro** (*dark*), **claro** (*light*).
2. **Role A.** You are planning to give your best friend a surprise birthday party (**una fiesta sorpresa**) and would like to invite one of your classmates. Tell your classmate a) that your friend's birthday is on Sunday, and b) where the party will take place.

   Role B. Your classmate invites you to a party. Find out a) the exact address, b) the time, and c) who else is going (**va**) to the party. At the end, thank your classmate for the invitation (**por la invitación**).

ALGO MÁS

Expressions with *gustar*

- To express what you like to do, use **me gusta** + *infinitive.* To express what you don't like to do, say **No me gusta** + *infinitive.*

Me gusta bailar.	*I like to dance.*
No me gusta mirar la televisión.	*I don't like to watch television.*

- To express that you like something, use **me gusta** + *singular noun* or **me gustan** + *plural noun.*

Me gusta la música clásica.	*I like classical music.*
Me gustan las fiestas.	*I like parties.*

- To ask a classmate what he/she likes, use **¿Te gusta/n...?** To ask your instructor, use **¿Le gusta/n...?**

¿Te gusta/Le gusta tomar mate?	*Do you like to drink mate?*
¿Te gustan/Le gustan los chocolates?	*Do you like chocolates?*

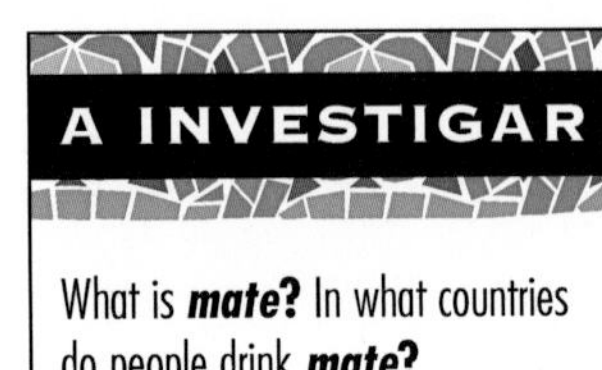

A INVESTIGAR

What is ***mate?*** In what countries do people drink ***mate?***

¿Qué dice usted?

2-22 Mis preferencias. Fill in the following chart based on your preferences. Compare your answers with those of a classmate.

ACTIVIDAD	ME GUSTA MUCHO	ME GUSTA	NO ME GUSTA
escribir en español			
hablar por teléfono			
bailar tango			
leer libros de ciencia-ficción			
...			

2-23 ¿Te gusta...? Ask a classmate if he/she likes the following things.

1. la biblioteca de la universidad
2. las discotecas
3. la informática
4. los autos de este año

2-24 ¿Qué te gusta hacer? Interview two classmates and ask each of them what he/she likes to do a) on a weekday morning/afternoon/evening, b) on Saturday afternoons, and c) on Sunday mornings. Compare their responses and be prepared to share your conclusions with the rest of the class or another group.

mosaicos

A ESCUCHAR

A. ¿Quiénes son? First, as you listen to the description of these students, circle the words that you hear. Then read the sentences and complete the chart, based on the information you have obtained.

1. (Amanda y César/Amanda y Rafael) estudian en la Facultad de Arquitectura de la Universidad de Belgrano.
2. (César y Rafael/Laura y Rafael) estudian en la Universidad de Buenos Aires.
3. Laura tiene (21/23) años y es una chica muy (trabajadora/tranquila).
4. La pasión de Laura es la (arquitectura/medicina).
5. Amanda y César tienen (22/24) años, pero Rafael es más joven, sólo tiene 20 años.
6. César es muy (hablador/perezoso), pero su compañera es callada.
7. Rafael es muy inteligente y desea ser profesor de (literatura/matemáticas).

NOMBRE	EDAD	DESCRIPCION	FACULTAD	UNIVERSIDAD
	20		Humanidades	
		callada		de Belgrano
		hablador	Arquitectura	
	23			de Buenos Aires

B. Dos personas diferentes. You will hear Amanda describe herself and her classmate Mónica. Mark the appropriate column(s) to indicate whether the following statements describe Amanda, Mónica, or both. Read the statements before listening to the passage.

	AMANDA	MONICA
1. Estudia arquitectura.	_____	_____
2. Le gusta la arquitectura colonial.	_____	_____
3. Le gusta la arquitectura moderna.	_____	_____
4. Es alta y morena.	_____	_____
5. Tiene el pelo corto y los ojos azules.	_____	_____
6. Le gusta la salsa.	_____	_____
7. Es tranquila y callada.	_____	_____
8. Le gusta bailar el tango.	_____	_____

A CONVERSAR

2-25 **Mis compañeros/as.** Working in a group, describe and give additional information about a student from another group. The class will guess who the student is.

2-26 **¿Cómo son?** Look at the Mafalda comic strip and ask a classmate what the various characters are like. He/she will answer according to the chart.

MODELO: E1: ¿Cómo es Mafalda?
E2: Mafalda es agradable, divertida, inteligente, habladora y simpática.

	AGRADABLE	BAJO/A	DIVERTIDO/A	FEO/A	INTELIGENTE	HABLADOR/A	PEREZOSO/A	SIMPATICO/A
Mafalda	X		X		X	X		X
Felipe	X		X	X	X	X	X	X
Miguelito	X	X	X		X			X
Manolito			X	X		X		
Susanita			X	X	X		X	

2-27 **La persona famosa que más admiro.** With a classmate, take turns asking each other questions about the person each of you most admire. Gather the following information; **nombre, nacionalidad, descripción, motivo de admiración.**

2-28 Entrevista: mi mejor amigo/a. Take turns with a classmate to gather information about his/her best friend.

1. Nombre
2. Lugar de origen
3. Características físicas
4. Personalidad
5. Estudios
6. Lenguas que habla
7. Lugar donde trabaja
8. ...

A LEER

2-29 Preparación. Interview a classmate about the qualities that his/her ideal mate should have. Mark his/her choices with an X.

MODELO: E1: Tu pareja ideal, ¿es morena?
E2: Sí, es morena. *o* No, es rubia.

1. ____ moreno/a
2. ____ rubio/a
3. ____ simpático/a
4. ____ conservador/a
5. ____ liberal
6. ____ rico/a
7. ____ alegre
8. ____ extranjero/a
9. ____ trabajador/a
10. ____ ....

2-30 Primera mirada. Read the first ad and find two people compatible with Susana Hardman. Fill in the form below the ad. In some cases, it may not be possible to provide all the information requested.

HACER AMIGOS

* Soy soltera, sin hijos y sin compromiso. Tengo 30 años de edad. Busco al hombre de mis sueños. Puede ser extranjero, argentino, soltero, separado o divorciado, joven o mayor. Soy amable, cariñosa y super trabajadora. Por mi trabajo, viajo mucho sola, pero prefiero la compañía de otras personas. ¡Ah! Si les interesa, también hablo varias lenguas. Escriban a Susana Hardman, Avenida José Martí 312, Mar del Plata, República Argentina.

* Soy Ricardo Biaggini. Tengo 38 años y en este momento no tengo pareja. Deseo conocer a una dama no mayor de 40 años. Prefiero una mujer inteligente e independiente económicamente. También es importante que le guste bailar y explorar lugares nuevos. Escríbanme a Avenida Florida 134, Buenos Aires, República Argentina.

Continúa en la próxima página

Cultura

There are many popular comic strips in the Hispanic world. One of the best known is Mafalda, created by the Argentinian cartoonist Quino. Mafalda's philosophy and ideas about life are among the many reasons for her popularity. Other very funny and well-known cartoon characters are Condorito, from Chile, and Mortadelo y Filemón, from Spain. You may get more information about them on the Web.

LENGUA

Y *(and)* changes to **e** when it precedes a word beginning with **i** or **hi.**

inteligente y agradable, but **agradable e inteligente**
inglés y español, but **español e inglés**

✻ El verano es una excelente época para hacer amigos. Por esta razón, quiero conocer a jóvenes de ambos sexos para intercambiar ideas sobre política internacional y deportes. Los interesados pueden escribir a Claudio R. Nuñez, calle Baquedano S/N, San Juan, República Argentina.

✻ Me llamo Paulo Sabatini, tengo 35 años y soy de Santa Fe. Soy amigable y romántico. Mis amigos dicen que soy guapo e inteligente. Una de mis pasiones es la música, por eso me gustaría mantener correspondencia con personas del extranjero para intercambiar discos compactos de música clásica y popular. Dirijan su correspondencia a: Avenida 5 de Mayo 5439, Depto. 101, Salta, República Argentina.

✻ Mi nombre es Ángel Ferdman. Soy joven de espíritu, aunque tengo 45 años. El optimismo, un poco de ambición y la responsabilidad son características intrínsecas de mi personalidad. También me gusta hacer todo muy bien. Por mi trabajo, en este momento vivo en Mendoza, lejos de mi familia. Por eso, quiero conocer a una mujer argentina o extranjera que hable español o hebreo para comenzar mi nueva vida en esta ciudad. Favor de escribirme a Circunvalación Oriente 98, Depto. 1A, Mendoza, República Argentina.

✻ Quiero mantener correspondencia con damas y caballeros del país o del extranjero. Siento una gran fascinación por la historia, el arte y también por la cocina internacional. Aparte del castellano, hablo francés, italiano y un poco de hebreo. Soy habladora, pero interesante. Prometo responder a toda la correspondencia con prontitud. Dirijan sus cartas a Paseo del Gaucho 482, Bariloche, República Argentina.

✻ Mi nombre es Victor Stravinsky y no soy muy viejo. Soy cocinero especialista en platos rusos. Mi familia es muy importante para mí. Soy agradable, pero tengo pocos amigos porque paso muchas horas en mi trabajo. Quiero un cambio en mi vida. Deseo tener nuevos amigos que vivan en la ciudad de Buenos Aires. Mi dirección es Calle Gardel 78, La Boca, Buenos Aires, República Argentina.

	SOLICITANTE	CANDIDATO	CANDIDATO
Nombre:			
Edad:			
Dirección:			
Estado civil:			
Preferencias:			

2-31 Ampliación. ¿What qualities do you associate with Paulo (**P**), Ángel (**A**), and Susana (**S**)? Why? With a classmate, write the initial(s) next to each quality, and discuss your opinions with another group.

1. ____ sociable
2. ____ simpático/a
3. ____ modesto/a
4. ____ perfeccionista
5. ____ viejo/a
6. ____ flexible
7. ____ ambicioso/a

2-32 Preparación. What information does a passport contain?

	SI	NO
1. apellido materno y paterno	____	____
2. fecha y lugar de nacimiento	____	____
3. nacionalidad	____	____
4. edad	____	____
5. profesión	____	____
6. estado civil	____	____
7. fotografía en colores	____	____
8. fotografía de la pareja	____	____
9. número de hijos	____	____
10. dirección de trabajo	____	____

2-33 Primera mirada. With a classmate, look at the passport on page 84 and answer the following questions.

1. ¿Cuál es el nombre de la persona en este pasaporte?
2. ¿De dónde es?
3. ¿Cuál es la fecha de su nacimiento (*birth*)?
4. ¿Cuántos años tiene?
5. ¿Es casada?
6. ¿Cuál es su profesión?
7. ¿Dónde vive?
8. ¿Qué lengua habla?
9. ¿Son iguales o diferentes el número del pasaporte y el de la cédula nacional de identidad (documento nacional de identificación)?

MERCOSUR
REPÚBLICA ARGENTINA
MINISTERIO DEL INTERIOR
POLICÍA FEDERAL

PASAPORTE ARGENTINO

Este documento carece de validez si tiene raspaduras, enmiendas o agregados entre líneas

06477329

MERCOSUR
REPÚBLICA ARGENTINA
MINISTERIO DEL INTERIOR
POLICÍA FEDERAL

OSORIO
MARÍA ALICIA
06477329N

La foto del titular se corresponde con la del reverso.
The bearer's photograph corresponds with the one on the reverse.

06477329

MERCOSUR
REPÚBLICA ARGENTINA
MINISTERIO DEL INTERIOR
POLICÍA FEDERAL

NO. 06477329
DATOS PERSONALES
NOMBRE DEL TITULAR: María Alicia Osorio
CÉDULA NACIONAL DE IDENTIDAD: 06.477.329-N
NACIONALIDAD: argentina
FECHA DE NACIMIENTO: 29-4-67
ESTADO CIVIL: soltera
PROFESIÓN: empleada
DOMICILIO: Av. España PB-5, 5500 Mendoza, Mza., Argentina

A escribir

As you gain more experience with the language, you will be discussing ways to approach the writing task more effectively with your peers and your instructor. The following expressions will be very useful in discussing your writing:

- To state the purpose (**propósito**) of your writing: **narrar, contestar, reclamar** (*complain*), **explicar, completar, solicitar** (*request*)
- To describe the means of communication (**medio de comunicación**): **carta, tarjeta postal, formulario, informe** (*report*), **correo electrónico**
- To describe the reader (**lector/a**): **amigo/a, conocido/a** (*acquaintance*), **familiar, presidente/a de una compañía**
- To describe the tone (**tono**) of your writing: **formal, informal, cómico, satírico**

2-34 Lluvia de ideas. Mark with an X the information that a company looking for a bilingual secretary would normally request of a candidate in a want ad. Then, compare your answers with those of a classmate.

1. ____ edad
2. ____ apariencia física
3. ____ lenguas que la persona habla
4. ____ estado civil
5. ____ país de origen
6. ____ raza
7. ____ experiencia
8. ____ fecha de nacimiento

2-35 Preparación. Before doing activity 2-36, specify the following:

1. Propósito:
2. Medio de comunicación:
3. Lector:
4. Tema:
5. Uso de la lengua:

2-36 Manos a la obra. The Argentinean Consulate in Miami is looking to hire a person of United States citizenship. Read the following want ad, then complete the letter of application with the necessary information.

Consulado de la República Argentina

Oficina de Relaciones Públicas busca profesional con experiencia en diplomacia.
Requisitos:
norteamericano/a
buen español (oral y escrito)
buena presencia
entre 25-45 años
con estudios de diplomacia
disponible para trabajar inmediatamente
mínimo 1 año de experiencia en trabajo diplomático

Enviar carta autobiográfica a:

Jefe de Personal
Consulado de la República Argentina
1200 SE Flagler St.
Miami, FL 33143
Candidatos seleccionados tendrán una entrevista con el Cónsul.

_____ de _____ de 200_

Estimad__ ____________:

Acabo de leer en *El Nuevo Herald* sobre el puesto en la oficina de Relaciones Públicas del Consulado Argentino. Deseo informarle que estoy muy interesad__ en participar como candidat___.

Tengo__________ años y soy de ________, Estados Unidos. Tengo cinco años de experiencia en consulados hispanos en Chicago y Los Ángeles. En este momento _________ como secretari___ del Cónsul de Guatemala en la ciudad de Washington D.C.

Entre otras calificaciones, soy bilingüe; es decir, ________ y ________inglés y español muy bien. También______________________________________ ________________.

A la espera de su respuesta, queda de usted
Muy atentamente,
(Firma)
____
(Nombre)

2-37 Revisión. After completing your letter of application, discuss it with a classmate. First concentrate on the effectiveness of the letter, and then edit any errors you may have (grammar, spelling, accent marks, etc.)

Vocabulario*

Descripciones

agradable	*nice*
alegre	*happy, glad*
alto/a	*tall*
antipático/a	*unpleasant*
bajo/a	*short* (in stature)
bonito/a	*pretty*
callado/a	*quiet*
cansado/a	*tired*
casado/a	*married*
contento/a	*happy, glad*
corto/a	*short* (in length)
débil	*weak*
delgado/a	*thin*
divertido/a	*funny, amusing*
enojado/a	*angry*
feliz	*happy*
feo/a	*ugly*
fuerte	*strong*
gordo/a	*fat*
guapo/a	*good-looking, handsome*
hablador/a	*talkative*
joven	*young*
largo/a	*long*
listo/a	*smart, ready*
mayor	*old*
mediano/a	*average, medium*
moreno/a	*brunet, brunette*
nervioso/a	*nervous*
nuevo/a	*new*
pelirrojo/a	*redhead*
perezoso/a	*lazy*
pobre	*poor*
rico/a	*rich, wealthy*
rubio/a	*blond*
simpático/a	*nice, charming*
soltero/a	*single*
tonto/a	*silly, foolish*
trabajador/a	*hard working*
tranquilo/a	*calm, tranquil*
triste	*sad*
viejo/a	*old*

Verbos

desear	*to wish, to want*
ser	*to be*
usar	*to use*

El cuerpo

los ojos	*eyes*
ojos azules	*blue eyes*
ojos verdes	*green eyes*
ojos (de color) café	*brown eyes*
el pelo	*hair*
pelo castaño	*brown hair*
pelo negro	*black hair*

Nacionalidades**

argentino/a	*Argentinean*
chileno/a	*Chilean*
colombiano/a	*Colombian*
cubano/a	*Cuban*
español/a	*Spanish*
guatemalteco/a	*Guatemalan*
mexicano/a	*Mexican*
nicaragüense	*Nicaraguan*
panameño/a	*Panamanian*
peruano/a	*Peruvian*
puertorriqueño/a	*Puerto Rican*
venezolano/a	*Venezuelan*

Palabras y expresiones útiles

ahora	*now*
de	*of, from*
del	*of the* (contraction of *de* + *el*)
le gusta(n)	*you* (formal) *like*
los lentes	*glasses*
me gusta(n)	*I like*
mucho/a	*much, a lot*
no (ni)... ni	*neither... nor*
pero	*but*
que	*that*
te gusta(n)	*you* (familiar) *like*
Tengo... años.	*I am... years old*
tiene	*he/she has, you* (formal) *have*

*See pages 64-66 for animals and additional colors.
**Other adjectives of nationality can be found in the English-Spanish and Spanish-English glossaries at the end of the book.
***See page 76 for possessive adjectives.

La diversidad étnica

Para pensar

¿A qué grupo étnico pertenece Ud.? ¿Es de origen europeo, indígena, asiático, africano? ¿Y sus compañeros/as de clase? ¿Pertenecen todos al mismo grupo étnico o hay una diversidad étnica?

En los países hispanoamericanos, al igual que en los Estados Unidos, hay una gran diversidad étnica: hay personas de origen indígena, así como también personas de origen europeo, africano y asiático. La diversidad étnica, sin embargo, es diferente de un país a otro, y en muchos países los diferentes grupos étnicos se han unido y forman una población mestiza (personas que tienen sangre europea e indígena, asiática o africana). Por ejemplo, en la zona del Caribe, gran parte de la población tiene sangre europea y africana, mientras que en México y otros países centroamericanos y suramericanos, el mestizaje que predomina es el de sangre europea e indígena. Además, en muchos países, especialmente en Perú, existe una importante inmigración asiática, lo que contribuye también a la diversidad étnica de Hispanoamérica. Esta diversidad étnica se refleja en la variedad de características físicas de su población. En España también hay diversidad. Aunque (*although*) es un país relativamente pequeño, los habitantes de cada región tienen sus propias características, con orígenes, en parte, en las culturas celta, romana, árabe y hebrea.

En la Argentina, la ascendencia europea es evidente. El 85% de la población es de origen europeo, principalmente italiano, pero también alemán, yugoslavo, inglés, francés y judío de Europa Oriental (vaya a la página de *Mosaicos* en la Internet *www.prenhall.com/mosaicos*); el otro 15% es de origen indígena o de otros grupos étnicos. Como consecuencia, hay más personas con apellidos de origen italiano que español. Un ejemplo es el apellido de Gabriela Sabatini, la famosa tenista argentina, que es de origen italiano.

Estudiantes de la Universidad de Buenos Aires

ENFOQUE CULTURAL

The *Enfoque cultural* is available in an interactive online format at *www.prenhall.com/mosaicos*

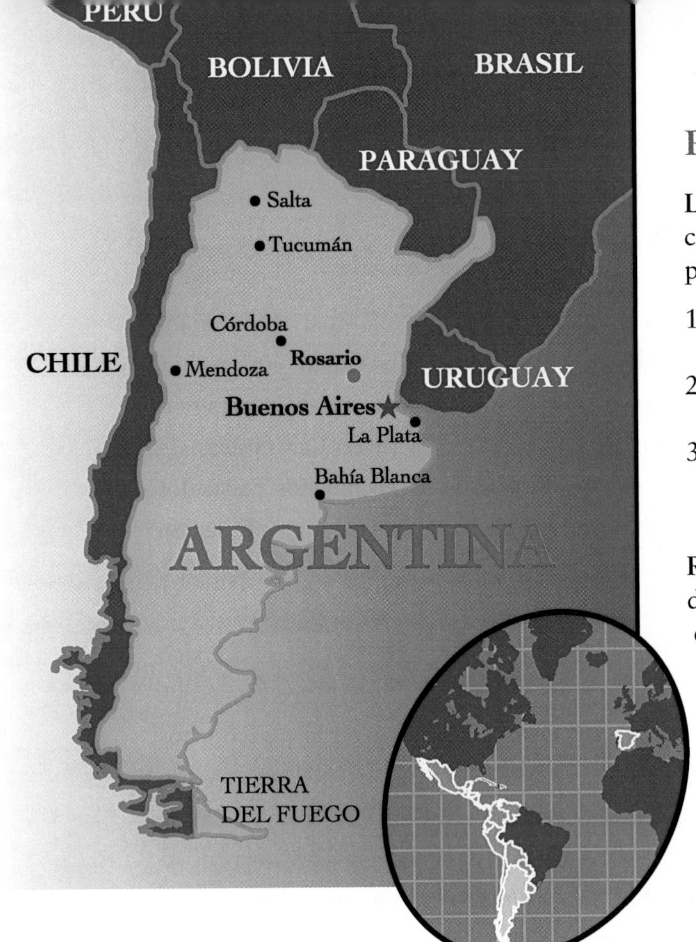

Para contestar

Los grupos étnicos. Trabajando con su compañero/a responda a las siguientes preguntas:

1. ¿Es la población hispanoamericana étnicamente homogénea? Explique.
2. ¿Qué es un mestizo? ¿Hay muchos mestizos en Argentina? ¿Y en otros países?
3. ¿Qué grupo étnico predomina en Argentina? ¿De qué países son estas personas?

Riqueza cultural. En grupos de tres, indiquen dos ventajas (*advantages*) de vivir en un país con gran diversidad étnica. ¿Hay mucha diversidad étnica en su país? ¿Hay más o menos diversidad en su país que en Argentina?

 Para investigar en la WWW

1. Averigüe cuál es el origen étnico y las ocupaciones de tres o cuatro de las siguientes personalidades argentinas. Luego, informe a la clase lo que Ud. encontró.
   Fernando de la Rúa, Alfonsina Storni, Carlos Gardel, Eva Perón, Jorge Luis Borges, José Luis Chilavert, Julio Cortázar, Luisa Futoransky, José de San Martín, Angélica Gorodischer, Cristina Civale.
2. Averigüe qué son "los desaparecidos" (vaya a *www.prenhall.com/mosaicos*). Luego, informe a sus compañeros sobre lo que encontró. ¿Qué le impresionó más?
3. Consiga información acerca del tango (vaya a *www.prenhall.com/mosaicos*). Luego, informe a sus compañeros/as sobre algunos aspectos que son interesantes para usted (historia, bailarines famosos, escuelas, canciones, etc.).

Argentina

Ciudades importantes y lugares de interés: Buenos Aires, la capital, con 11.500.000 habitantes, es una ciudad de intensa vida comercial e intelectual. Tiene un aire muy europeo con amplios parques, bulevares, avenidas y altos rascacielos. La amistad y las relaciones familiares tienen gran importancia en la vida de los porteños (*Buenos Aires' residents*); por eso los numerosos cafés de la ciudad están siempre llenos de personas que se reúnen a conversar mientras toman un delicioso cortado (*coffee with cream*) acompañado de una medialuna (*type of croissant*). Los fines de semana, muchos porteños van a los parques de la ciudad a pasear y conversar con sus amigos, a admirar las obras de los artesanos (*craftsmen/craftswomen*) que exhiben sus productos, o a ver las presentaciones de algunos artistas. Entre los lugares más visitados están el Parque Palermo y el Centro Cultural Recoleta.

Bariloche, Argentina

Hay muchos otros sitios de interés en Argentina: Mar del Plata, en la costa atlántica, es un balneario (*resort area*) famoso en toda Latinoamérica; Córdoba, una ciudad en el centro del país, es conocida por su bella arquitectura colonial. Para esquiar, un lugar ideal es Bariloche, a orillas del lago Nahuel Huapi. Las cataratas de Iguazú, en la frontera con Paraguay y Brasil, son consideradas una de las maravillas naturales del mundo, igual que el Glaciar Perito Moreno, cerca de la frontera con Chile.

Una de las características geográficas más distintivas de Argentina es la pampa. Estas enormes extensiones de tierra (*land*) llana y fértil constituyen una de las bases de la economía argentina.

Expresiones argentinas:

Ché:	**Ché, Martita, ¿dónde está mi camisa?**	*Hey, Martita, where is my shirt?*
Mandarse la parte:	**¡No te mandes la parte!**	*Don't exaggerate!*
Laburo:	**Siempre salgo temprano para el laburo.**	*I always leave early to go to my job.*
Bárbaro:	**¡Bárbaro! Ganamos el partido.**	*Great! We won the game.*
Morocho/a:	**Isabel es morocha.**	*Isabel is a brunette.*

ENFOQUE INTERACTIVO

A MIRAR EL VIDEO 5:00

Watch the *Fortunas* video segment for *Lección 2* in class or on your CD-ROM. Where will Efraín and Sabrina begin their search to solve the first *misterio*? Will they form an alliance for the contest?

Now complete the accompanying video activities on the CD-ROM. This is your chance to interact with the video characters! **25:00**

Efraín y Sabrina

El concurso

In this episode of *Fortunas* we learn the first *misterio* in this year's treasure hunt. We also gain insight into the personalities of two of the players. Which of the two seems more likely to succeed in the contest? Remember, the contestants' goal is to locate three *fortunas*, each hidden in a different place within Mexico City. The *pistas* and *misterios* that reveal the location of these *fortunas* relate to the history of Mexico and the New World.

LA BÚSQUEDA 5:00

Sabrina seems eager to get started but Efraín looks unsure. Although all the contestants know the theme for the first *misterio*, each of them has only one *pista*. You, on the other hand, have all four *pistas*. What do the clues have in common? Go to the *Mosaicos Website* (*www.prenhall.com/mosaicos*) and click on the *Fortunas* module to explore the first *misterio* and the various places where the contestants might begin their searches. Where would you go to solve the *misterio*?

Misterio Nº 1: Cinco es suficiente

Pistas

1. *Destrucción de los gigantes por el viento (monos)*
2. *Destrucción por la lluvia (pájaros)*
3. *Destrucción por el diluvio (peces)*
4. *Destrucción por el jaguar*

¿QUÉ OPINA USTED? 5:00

In each episode, study the contestants carefully before voting in the *Fortunas* viewer poll. What you see on the surface does not always represent everything that's happening behind the scenes, so you should also read the contestants' diaries. Now go to the *Fortunas* module on the *Mosaicos Website* and click on *¿Qué opina usted?* to vote in this episode's viewer poll. Remember, your vote counts.

PARA NAVEGAR 10:00

LA MÚSICA ARGENTINA

En la Argentina, como en los Estados Unidos, hay muchos tipos de música popular. Hay grupos de rock, jazz, tango y de música folclórica. Desde Carlos Gardel y Astor Piazzola (tango), a Charly García (rock) y el Cuarteto Zupay (música folclórica), la música argentina tiene una tradición rica y variada.

Los fabulosos cadillacs

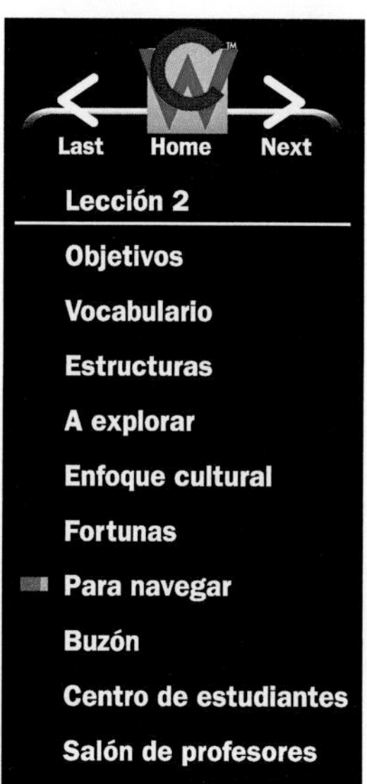

Go to the *Mosaicos Website* and click on the *Para navegar* module to explore links to Argentine music. Listen to Argentine artists perform and then complete the related activities.

Lección 3

Las actividades y los planes

COMUNICACION

- Asking about and discussing leisure activities
- Communicating by phone
- Ordering food in a restaurant
- Making suggestions and future plans
- Using numbers above 100

ESTRUCTURAS

- Present tense of regular **-er** and **-ir** verbs
- Present tense of **ir**
- **Ir** + **a** + infinitive to express future action
- The present tense to express future action
- Numbers 100 to 2,000,000
- ALGO MAS: Some uses of **por** and **para**

MOSAICOS

A ESCUCHAR

A CONVERSAR

A LEER

- Locating specific information in a text
- Identifying synonyms

A ESCRIBIR

- Writing questions to elicit information and opinions
- Using appropriate form of address
- Reporting information

ENFOQUE CULTURAL

- El cine, el teatro, las peñas
- El Perú

ENFOQUE INTERACTIVO

 WWW

 VIDEO

 CD ROM

A primera vista

Diversiones populares

En las fiestas y reuniones los muchachos jóvenes bailan, escuchan música o conversan. A veces tocan la guitarra y cantan canciones populares.

Practice activities for each vocabulary section are provided on the CD-ROM and website (www.prenhall.com/mosaicos)

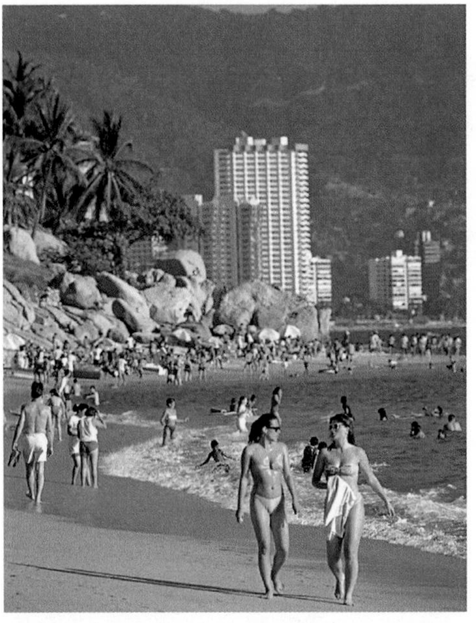

Estas chicas van a la playa en su tiempo libre y también durante las vacaciones. Allí, caminan y conversan mientras otras personas toman el sol, nadan en el mar y descansan.

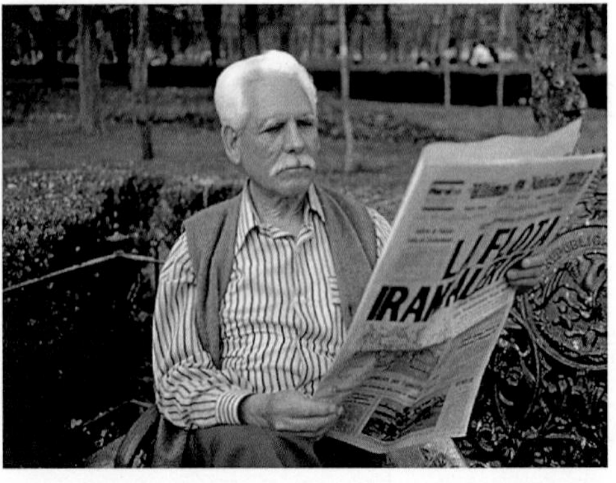

El señor López del Río lee el periódico al aire libre. Y usted, ¿lee el periódico? ¿Qué periódicos o revistas lee?

Muchos jóvenes van al cine, especialmente los fines de semana. También es común alquilar películas en videocasetes para ver en casa.

Una conversación por teléfono

TERESA: ¿Aló?

JAVIER: Hola, Teresa, ¿qué te parece si vamos al cine esta tarde y después vamos a cenar fuera para celebrar tu cumpleaños?

TERESA: ¡Ay, Javier, qué bien! ¿Y qué vamos a ver?

JAVIER: Tú decides, mi amor, es tu cumpleaños.

TERESA: Pues, la película nueva de Pedro Almodóvar.

JAVIER: Fabuloso. Voy para la casa ahora. Hasta pronto.

TERESA: Chao.

¿Qué dice usted?

3-1 Asociaciones. What activities do you associate with the following places?

1. ____ la playa
2. ____ la fiesta
3. ____ el cine
4. ____ la biblioteca
5. ____ la casa

a. ver una película
b. leer el periódico
c. tomar el sol
d. mirar televisión
e. bailar y conversar

3-2 Mis actividades. What do you do in the following places? Working with a classmate, take turns asking each other questions.

MODELO: ... las fiestas
E1: ¿Qué haces en las fiestas?
E2: En las fiestas yo bailo mucho. ¿Y tú?
E1: Yo bailo y hablo con mis amigos.
E2: Y tú, ¿qué haces en...?

1. ... la universidad por las mañanas
2. ... la biblioteca pública de tu ciudad
3. ... casa el fin de semana
4. ... un parque de tu ciudad
5. ... la playa durante las vacaciones
6. ... la discoteca con tus amigos

Cultura

There have been significant improvements in television broadcasting in many Spanish-speaking countries. Satellite dishes for worldwide reception are becoming a common sight, in both rural and urban areas. Nevertheless, going to the movies, as well as renting films, is a popular form of entertainment in Spanish-speaking countries.

3-3 ¿Adónde vamos? Primera fase. Look at the cultural section of the Peruvian newspaper below and underline three activities that you would like to do on the weekend. Then fill in the information in the following chart, including the day and the time you are planning to do them.

El Diario

Exposiciones

"El vestido de la mujer en la historia del Perú" En el Museo de Sitio, Parque Reducto cuadra 9 de la avenida Benavides, Miraflores. 6:30 pm.

"Hechos de barro" Primera Trienal de Cerámica. En el C.C. Peruano Británico. Galería John Harriman, Jr., Bellavista 531, Miraflores.

"Muestra internacional de escultura en pequeño formato" En la galería de Arte Praxis, Av. San Martín 689, Barranco. De 9:30 a 1:30 pm y de 5 a 9 pm.

"Primer simposium internacional de escultura moderna" Se exhiben 23 esculturas en pequeño formato. En el restaurante Rosa Náutica.

Música

"Orquesta juvenil de música nueva" con la participación de la solista Gabriela Ezeta, bajo la dirección de Gabriel Alegría y Simon Porter. En el ICPNA de Miraflores, Av. Angamos 160. 7:30 pm.

"Jam Sessions" en el C.C. La Noche, Av. Bolognesi 307, Barranco. 10:30 pm

"Jazz" en el C.C. La Noche, Av. Bolognesi 307, Barranco. 11 pm.

Cine

"El acorazado Potemkin" (URSS, 1925) de S.M. Eisentein. En la Filmoteca de Lima, Museo de Arte 125: Lima. 4 y 8 pm.

"Belleza americana" de Sam Mendes. En el C.C. de PUCP, Camino Real 1975, San Isidro. 3:30, 5:45, 8:00 y 10:15 pm.

Teatro

"Por siempre jamás" bajo la dirección de Nicolás Fantinato. En el auditorio de la Alianza Francesa, Av. Arequipa 2595, Miraflores. 8:45 pm.

¿ADONDE VAMOS?	¿QUE VAMOS A VER / HACER / ESCUCHAR?	¿CUANDO?

Segunda fase. Phone a classmate and invite him/her to one of the events you chose in **Primera fase.** He/She will give you an excuse as in the model.

MODELO: E1: ¿Aló?
E2: Hola, Pedro. Soy María, ¿Vamos el viernes a ver la exposición "El vestido" en el museo?
E1: Lo siento, el viernes Carlos y yo vamos al cine. Vamos a ver "El acorazado Potemkin" en la filmoteca (a las cuatro).

Expresiones útiles

Para invitar a un/a amigo/a:

Te llamo para ver si quieres...
Tengo una idea. ¿Por qué no.... ?

La comida

En el restaurante. Ahora Javier y Teresa están en el restaurante para celebrar el cumpleaños de Teresa.

CAMARERO: Buenas noches. ¿Qué desean los señores?
JAVIER: Teresa, ¿qué vas a comer?
TERESA: Para mí, una ensalada primero y después pollo con verduras.
JAVIER: Yo, para empezar, ceviche de camarones. Y luego un bistec con papas.
CAMARERO: ¿Y para beber?
JAVIER: Vamos a beber vino. Y también agua con gas, por favor.

Cultura

Peruvian cooking uses mainly regional ingredients, and preparation follows the traditional ways inherited from various indigenous cultures. A very typical dish of Peru and other countries in Latin America is **ceviche**. It is generally made with seafood, which is not cooked, but cured in lemon and spices. For more information about this dish and its variations see: **www.prenhall.com/mosaicos**

ESPECIALIDADES DE LA CASA

ENTRADAS	
Ceviche de pescado	S/.15
Papa a la huancaína	S/.10
Causa a la limeña	S/.12
PLATO PRINCIPAL	
Chupe de camarones	S/.25
Ají de gallina	S/.18
Lomo saltado	S/.17
POSTRES	
Suspiro de limeña	S/.8
Alfajor	S/.8
Mazamorra morada	S/.6
BEBIDAS	
Chicha morada	S/.4
Jugo de maracuyá	S/.4
Inca-Kola	S/.3

A INVESTIGAR

S/. or NS/ is the abbreviation for the monetary unit in Perú. What is the name of the monetary unit? What is the current rate of exchange?

La comida rápida

La comida rápida es muy popular entre los jóvenes y las "hamburgueserías" de tipo americano existen en muchas ciudades del mundo hispano. Estos restaurantes de comida rápida frecuentemente combinan comida de los Estados Unidos con comidas típicas de cada país. Por ejemplo, usted puede comer una hamburguesa con papas fritas o con arroz y frijoles negros. En muchos países, usted puede tomar vino o cerveza en estos restaurantes.

Más comidas y bebidas

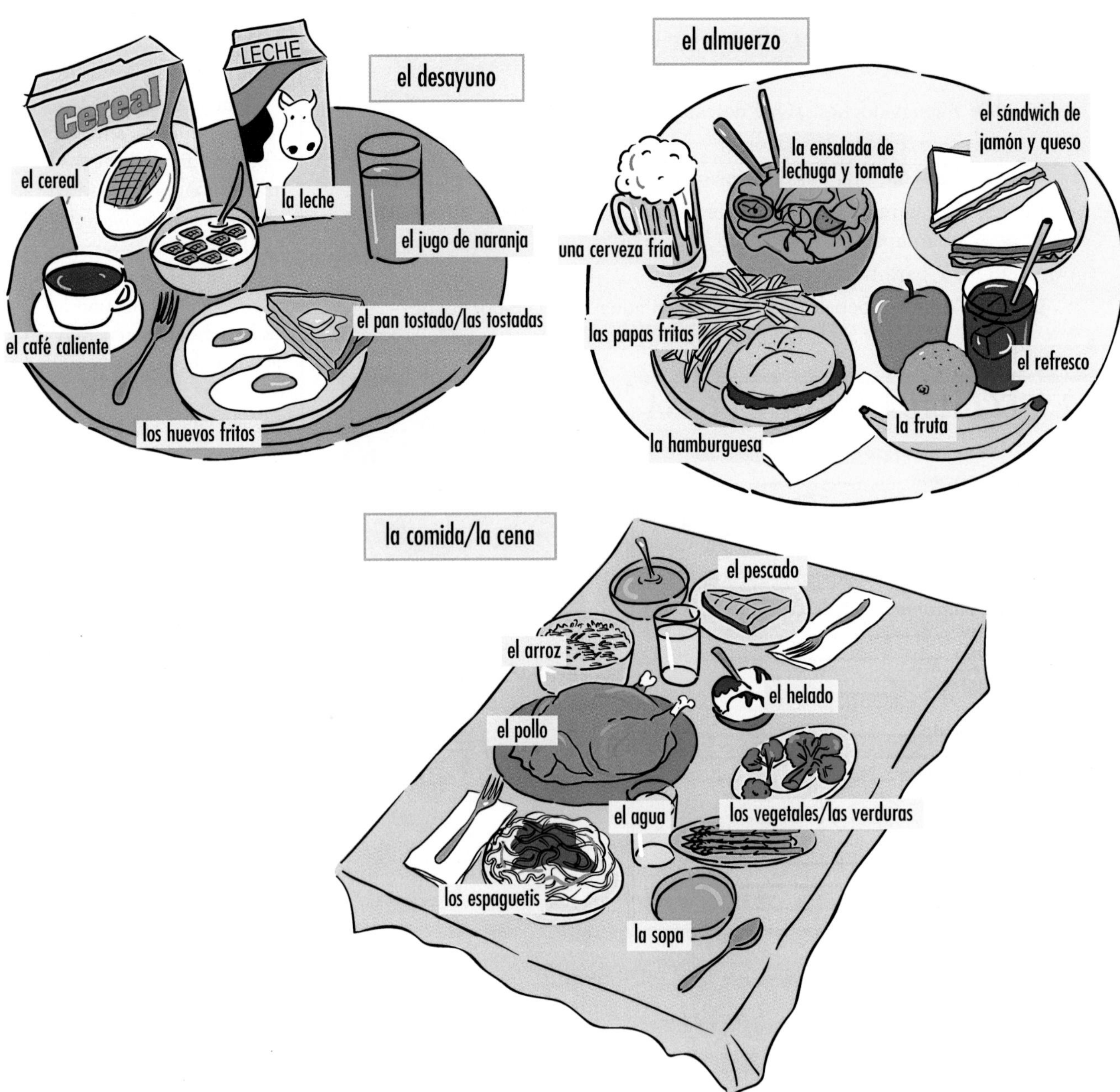

¿Qué dice usted?

3-4 La dieta. Which of the following contains more calories?

1. la sopa de tomate, las hamburguesas, la sopa de pollo
2. el pollo frito, el pescado, la ensalada
3. los vegetales, la fruta, las papas fritas
4. la cerveza, la leche, el café
5. el helado de chocolate, el cereal, el arroz

3-5 Las comidas. Tell a classmate what you have for breakfast, lunch and dinner, then find out what he/she has.

MODELO: En el desayuno, yo como tostadas y bebo café. ¿Y tú?

3-6 Dietas especiales. With a classmate, look at the menu below and provide a solution for each of the following problems.

1. Su padre y usted son un poco delgados y desean subir de peso (*gain weight*) ¿Qué van a comer de este menú?
2. Su mamá tiene alergia a los productos del mar. ¿Cuál de las ensaladas va a comer?
3. Su mejor amigo/a está un poco gordo/a y quiere bajar (*lose*) de peso. ¿Cuál de los platos principales no debe tomar?
4. El/La profesor/a de español está enfermo/a (*sick*) del estómago hoy. ¿Qué debe comer?

SOPAS

Sopa de pollo	S/. 12
Sopa de tomate	S/. 10
Sopa de vegetales	S/. 10
Sopa de pescado	S/. 14

ENSALADAS

Ensalada de lechuga y tomate	S/. 8
Ensalada de pollo	S/. 14
Ensalada de atún	S/. 12

PLATOS PRINCIPALES

Bistec con papas y vegetales	S/. 20
Hamburguesa con papas fritas	S/. 16
Pescado con papas fritas	S/. 18
Arroz con vegetales	S/. 15

3-7 ¿Qué te gusta más? Using the words below, ask a classmate what he/she prefers to drink: **por las mañanas, al mediodía, por las noches.** Alternate asking questions and taking notes. Then in small groups decide which are the most popular drinks.

MODELO: E1: ¿Qué te gusta más por las mañanas, el té o el café?
E2: Me gusta más el café.

el té	un vaso (*a glass*) de leche	una cerveza	un chocolate caliente
el café	el agua mineral con gas	un refresco	un batido (*shake*) de fruta
el jugo de naranja	el agua mineral sin gas	un vaso de vino	un té de hierbas

3-8 En el café. It's 8:00 a.m. on a Saturday morning, and you are in your favorite café with a classmate. Ask him/her what he or she would like to order. Then say what you would like to order.

MODELO: E1: El desayuno es muy bueno aquí. ¿Qué deseas comer?
E2: _____ ¿Y tú?
E1: _____ ¿Y qué vas a tomar?
E2: _____

café	4
té	4
café con leche	6
jugo de naranja	5
chocolate	7
tostadas	5
pan con mantequilla	5
pan dulce	6
cereal	8
huevos fritos	10

3-9 Nuestro menú. Your roommate (a classmate) and you want to have guests for dinner tonight. First, decide whom each of you is going to invite; then ask each other the guests' phone numbers so one of you can make the calls later. Decide what you're going to serve. Finally, compare your menu with that of another pair of classmates.

3-10 **Una excursión.** In small groups, plan a trip to one of the restaurants along the coast of Lima, Peru.

a. Find out when everyone is free (*está libre*).
b. Decide what meal you will have there.
c. Discuss what you will eat and drink.
d. Decide how you will go there.

A ESCUCHAR

Una semana en la vida de Rafael. You will hear a young man talk about himself and his activities. Complete the statements by marking the appropriate answer according to the information you hear.

1. Rafael es...
   ___ profesor
   ___ camarero
   ___ estudiante
2. Rafael es de...
   ___ Perú
   ___ México
   ___ San Diego
3. Este fin de semana Rafael y su amigo van a ir...
   ___ al cine
   ___ a la playa
   ___ a una fiesta
4. Este fin de semana Rafael va a...
   ___ estudiar
   ___ trabajar
   ___ descansar
5. La especialidad del restaurante que Rafael describe es...
   ___ el pollo
   ___ la comida peruana
   ___ el pescado

Explicación y expansión

1. Present tense of regular *-er* and *-ir* verbs

COMER *(to eat)*			
yo	como	nosotros/as	com**emos**
tú	com**es**	vosotros/as	com**éis**
Ud., él, ella	com**e**	Uds., ellos/as	com**en**

Practice activities for each numbered grammar point are provided on the CD-ROM and website (www.prenhall.com/mosaicos)

VIVIR *(to live)*			
yo	viv**o**	nosotros/as	viv**imos**
tú	viv**es**	vosotros/as	viv**ís**
Ud., él, ella	viv**e**	Uds., ellos/as	viv**en**

- The endings for **-er** and **-ir** verbs are the same, except for the **nosotros** and **vosotros** forms.
- The verb **ver** has an irregular **yo** form.

  ver: veo, ves, ve, vemos, veis, ven
- Use **deber** + *infinitive* to express what you *should* or *ought* to do.

  Debes beber mucha agua. *You should (must) drink lots of water.*

¿Qué dice usted?

3-11 Mi profesor/a modelo. Primera fase. Indicate which of the following activities are or are not part of an ideal instructor's routine.

	SI	NO
1. Lee el periódico en la clase.	_____	_____
2. Nunca está en su oficina.	_____	_____
3. Siempre prepara sus clases.	_____	_____
4. Saca libros de la biblioteca y lee mucho.	_____	_____
5. Comprende los problemas de los estudiantes.	_____	_____
6. Bebe café en la clase todo el tiempo.	_____	_____

Segunda fase. Compare your answers with those of a classmate. Do both of you agree? Finally, write two more activities/features of an ideal instructor's academic life and ask your instructor if they are part of his/her real routine.

3-12 Intercambio. Primera fase. Working with a classmate, find out the following information about the Mencía family and Julia Arango:

1. What they do to have fun (*pasarlo bien*).
2. When they do it.

NOMBRE	LOS SABADOS	LOS DOMINGOS
Julia Arango	estudia en la biblioteca	trabaja en la casa
	va al cine con unos amigos	come fuera con unos amigos
Los Sres. Mencía	caminan por la playa	leen el periódico
	ven programas de televisión	alquilan películas en español
Dora Sánchez	descansa en la casa	va a un café con su amigo
	ve películas viejas en la televisión	canta y toca la guitarra con unos compañeros

Segunda fase. Now your classmate will ask you about Dora Sánchez:

1. What she does with friends over the weekend.
2. How different is her weekend from Julia's.

3-13 Lugares y actividades. Ask a classmate what he/she does in the following places. He/She will respond with one of the activities listed. Then ask your classmate what he/she doesn't do in each place.

MODELO: en la clase/ver videos
E1: ¿Qué haces en la clase?
E2: Veo videos en español.
E1: ¿Y qué no haces en la clase?
E2: No bailo salsa (ni leo el periódico).

LUGARES	ACTIVIDADES
en la playa	beber cerveza
en un café	tomar el sol y descansar
en una discoteca	bailar salsa
en una fiesta	mirar televisión
en el cine	leer el periódico
en la casa	comer un sándwich y tomar algo
en un restaurante	ver películas españolas y argentinas
en la biblioteca	escuchar música clásica

ACENTOS

You have probably noticed that the words **examen, casas, fruta** do not have a written accent, while **débil, sándwich, López** do. In Spanish, words stressed on the next-to-last syllable do not have a written accent if they end in **n**, **s**, or a *vowel* (**examen**, **casas**, **fruta**). If they end in any other letter, they carry an accent mark (**débil**, **sándwich**, **López**).

3-14 Las diversiones estudiantiles. Primera fase. Working in a small group, appoint a secretary to tally responses. Then, find out which of you do the following things. When you finish, get together with another group, compare your findings, and tally responses once again.

MODELO: nadar en la playa
E1: ¿Nadas en la playa los fines de semana?
E2: Sí, nado (en la playa) los fines de semana.

	SI	NO
1. beber café y conversar con amigos	_____	_____
2. tocar la guitarra	_____	_____
3. comer en restaurantes peruanos	_____	_____
4. ver programas cómicos en la televisión	_____	_____
5. tomar cerveza con amigos	_____	_____
6. leer libros de ciencia-ficción	_____	_____

Segunda fase. Finally, as a class, discuss the following:

a. Which item on the list got the most affirmative responses?
b. Which got the most negative responses?
c. How can you, as a class, explain the most affirmative and negative responses?

3-15 Sugerencias. What should or shouldn't the following people do?

MODELO: Luis está muy enfermo.
E1: ¿Qué debe hacer Luis?
E2: Debe descansar. *o* No debe comer mucho.

1. Juan tiene un examen el lunes.
2. Francisco está débil y muy delgado.
3. Marta ve televisión todos los días y saca malas notas.
4. Luis y Emilia desean aprender español.

3-16 Un/a compañero/a nuevo/a. Get together with a classmate you don't know very well and ask him/her questions to find out more about him/her.

1. Lugar donde vive
2. Si ese lugar le gusta o no le gusta
3. Lugar donde come fuera de casa
4. Si le gusta la comida de ese lugar
5. Comida favorita
6. Bebida favorita
7. ...
8. ...

SITUACIONES

1. Find out a) if your partner likes to read, b) when he/she reads, c) what newspapers and magazines he/she reads, and d) what books or magazines in Spanish he/she likes to read.
2. You are a waiter/waitress at a café. Two of your classmates will play the part of the customers. Greet your customers and ask them what they would like to eat and drink. Be prepared to answer any questions they may have.

2. Present tense of *ir*

IR *(to go)*			
yo	**voy**	nosotros/as	**vamos**
tú	**vas**	vosotros/as	**vais**
Ud., él, ella	**va**	Uds., ellos/as	**van**

- Use **a** to introduce a noun after the verb **ir**. When **a** is followed by the article **el**, they contract to form **al**.

Voy **a la** fiesta de María.	*I'm going to María's party.*
Vamos **al** gimnasio.	*We're going to the gymnasium.*

- Use **adónde** when asking *where to* with the verb **ir**.

¿**Adónde** vas ahora?	*Where are you going now?*

3. *Ir* + *a* + infinitive to express future action

- To express future action, use the present tense of **ir** + **a** + the *infinitive* form of the verb.

Ellos **van a nadar** después.	*They're going to swim later.*
¿**Vas a ir** a la fiesta?	*Are you going to go to the party?*

4. The present tense to express future action

- You may also express future action with the present tense of the verb. The context shows whether you are referring to the present or the future.

Ellos **nadan** después.	*They'll swim later.*
¿**Vas** a la fiesta esta noche?	*Are you going to the party tonight?*

- The following expressions denote future time:

después	*afterwards, later*
más tarde	*later*
esta noche	*tonight*
mañana	*tomorrow*
pasado mañana	*the day after tomorrow*
la próxima semana	*next week*
el próximo mes/año	*next month/year*

¿Qué dice usted?

3-17 Lugares y actividades. With a classmate talk about where the following people are going. Say what they are going to do there.

MODELO: María / cine
María va al cine. Va a ver una película española.

1. Victoria / hamburguesería
2. Elena y Alberto / biblioteca
3. Rodrigo / playa
4. yo / casa
5. nosotros / café
6. Alina / librería hispana

3-18 La agenda de Laura. Ask a classmate questions about Laura's activities this week based on her schedule below.

MODELO: E1: ¿Cuándo va a ir Laura al laboratorio?
E2: El viernes a las once de la mañana.
E1: ¿Qué va a hacer el lunes por la tarde?
E2: Va a caminar.

LAURA GARCIA PRADO						
LUNES	**MARTES**	**MIERCOLES**	**JUEVES**	**VIERNES**	**SABADO**	**DOMINGO**
6	7	8	9	10	11	12
biblioteca 8:30 a.m.	llamar a María 9:00 a.m.	terminar proyecto 10:00 a.m.	estudiar en casa de Teté 9:30 a.m.	laboratorio 11:00 a.m.	playa 11:00 a.m.	ir a la iglesia 12:00 a.m.
caminar 5:30 p.m.	trabajar librería 4:00 p.m.					restaurante 1:00 p.m.
casa de Ana 8:00 p.m.		programa T.V. 7:00 p.m.	película televisión 10:00 p.m.	fiesta de Pablo 9:00 p.m.	café 9:00 p.m.	cine 7:00 p.m.

3-19 Vamos a comer fuera. A friend and you are planning to eat out tonight. Your friend is a very finicky eater, so you will have to talk him/her into going to your favorite restaurant, by mentioning some of the dishes they prepare, the good prices (**precios**), etc. Decide on the time and where you will go. Finally, tell other classmates about your plans.

3-20 Los planes de Maribel para el viernes. With a classmate, take turns to tell what Maribel is going to do. Ask questions to get additional information from your partner regarding Maribel.

3-21 Este fin de semana. With a classmate, discuss what each of you is going to do this weekend. Expand the conversation by asking questions of each other to get more details, if necessary. Take notes about each other's plans. Then share your findings about your partner with another classmate.

3-22 ¡Vivan los feriados! Working with another classmate, share information about your plans for the next holiday, for example **Navidad, Januká, Ramadán, el Año Nuevo, el Día de la Independencia,** etc. Get as much information as possible about each other's plans.

1. Your friend is planning to go to a concert (**un concierto**). Find out a) where and when the concert is, b) who is going to sing, c) who is going to play an instrument, and d) how much the ticket is (**el boleto/billete, la entrada**).
2. Tell your partner about your plans for tonight. Tell him/her a) what you are planning to do, b) with whom, and) how much money (**cuánto dinero**) you are going to need. Inquire about his/her plans too.

5. Numbers 100 to 2.000.000

100	**cien/ciento**	1.000	**mil**
200	**doscientos/as**	1.100	**mil cien**
300	**trescientos/as**	2.000	**dos mil**
400	**cuatrocientos/as**	10.000	**diez mil**
500	**quinientos/as**	100.000	**cien mil**
600	**seiscientos/as**	150.000	**ciento cincuenta mil**
700	**setecientos/as**	500.000	**quinientos mil**
800	**ochocientos/as**	1.000.000	**un millón (de)**
900	**novecientos/as**	2.000.000	**dos millones (de)**

- Use **cien** to say 100 used alone or followed by a noun, and **ciento** for numbers from 101 to 199.

100	**cien**
100 chicos	**cien chicos**
120 profesoras	**ciento veinte profesoras**

- Multiples of 100 agree in gender with the noun they modify.

200 periódicos	**doscientos** periódicos
1.400 revistas	**mil cuatrocientas** revistas

- Use **mil** for *one thousand*.

1.000	**mil alumnos, mil alumnas**

- Use **un millón** to say *one million*. Use **un millón de** when a noun follows.

1.000.000	**un millón, un millón de personas**

- Spanish normally uses a period to separate thousands, and a comma to separate decimals.

$1.000	$19,50

LENGUA

In Spanish, numbers higher than one thousand are not stated in pairs as they often are in English. For example, 1942 must be expressed as **mil novecientos cuarenta y dos**, whereas in English it is often given as nineteen forty-two.

¿Qué dice usted?

3-23 Para identificar. Your instructor will say a number from each of the following series. Identify each one.

a. 114	360	850	524
b. 213	330	490	919
c. 818	625	723	513
d. 667	777	984	534
e. 1.310	1.420	3.640	6.860
f. 10.467	50.312	100.000	2.000.000

3-24 ¿Cuándo va a ocurrir? Exchange opinions with a classmate about when each of the following events will occur.

MODELO: Todos los libros van a ser electrónicos.
E1: En el año 2010.
E2: Estoy de acuerdo. *o* No estoy de acuerdo.
Va a ser en el año 2020.

1. Las personas sólo van a trabajar 20 horas a la semana.
2. Los estudiantes no van a ir a clase. Van a estudiar en universidades virtuales.
3. Todos vamos a tener autos eléctricos muy rápidos.
4. Los turistas van a ir de un país a otro sin pasaporte.
5. La comida va a estar contaminada, por eso muchas personas van a consumir comida en pastillas (*pills*).
6. Los robots, no los camareros, van a servir la comida en los restaurantes.
7. Las personas van a comunicarse por telepatía.

3-25 Unas vacaciones. Primera fase. Your classmate has chosen one of the destinations in the ad below for his/her next vacation. To find out where he/she is going and why, ask him/her the following questions.

1. ¿Adónde vas?
2. ¿Con quién vas?
3. ¿Qué lugares vas a ver?
4. ¿Cuándo vas?
5. ¿Cuántos días vas a estar allí?
6. ¿Por qué vas a ir a ese lugar?
7. ¿Cuánto cuesta la excursión?
8. ...

AGENCIA MUNDIAL

A SU SERVICIO SIEMPRE *20 años de experiencia, responsabilidad y profesionalismo*

TODOS LOS PRECIOS INCLUYEN PASAJES AÉREOS Y SERVICIOS TERRESTRES POR PERSONA

PERÚ Y BOLIVIA

LIMA, AREQUIPA, CUZCO, MACHU PICCHU, PUNO, LA PAZ, 15 días. La Ruta del Inca. Hoteles de 3 y 4 estrellas. Desayuno incluido.
$1.960

PERÚ

LIMA, CUZCO, MACHU PICCHU, NAZCA, 12 días. Visite fortalezas incas. Vea las misteriosas líneas de Nazca desde el aire. Hoteles de primera. Desayuno y cena incluidos.
$2.250

LIMA, NAZCA, AREQUIPA, LAGO TITICACA, 10 días. Admire la arquitectura colonial de Lima y Arequipa. Vea las líneas de Nazca desde el aire. Navegue en el lago más alto del mundo. Hoteles de primera.
$1.650

ARGENTINA

BUENOS AIRES, BARILOCHE, MENDOZA, 12 días. Disfrute de una gran metrópoli. Esquíe en uno de los lugares más bellos del mundo. Hoteles de 4 y 5 estrellas. Desayuno y cena.
$2.990

CHILE Y ARGENTINA

SANTIAGO, PUERTO MONTT, BARILOCHE, BUENOS AIRES, 12 días. Excursión a Viña del Mar y Valparaíso. Cruce de los Andes en minibus y barco. Hoteles de 3 y 4 estrellas.
$3.190

CARIBE

JAMAICA, 7 días, Happy Inn, todo incluido. Exclusivo para parejas.
$1.750

PUERTO RICO

SAN JUAN, 5 días. Hotel de 5 estrellas. Excursión a Ponce. Visita con guía al Viejo San Juan. Desayuno incluido.
$1.250

MÉXICO

MÉXICO, TAXCO, ACAPULCO, 7 días. Hoteles de 3 y 4 estrellas. Excursión a Teotihuacán. Desayuno buffet incluido.
$1.450

CANCÚN, 5 días. Hotel de 4 estrellas. Excursión a Cozumel. Visita a ruinas mayas. Las mejores playas.
$1.150

Solicite los programas detallados con variantes de hoteles e itinerarios a su agente de viajes.

Tel. 312-785-4455 Fax: 312-785-4456

Segunda fase. Based on your classmate's answers for the **Primera fase**, fill in the information requested below and share it with another classmate.

1. Su compañero/a necesita...
   a. __________ sacar un pasaporte
   b. __________ obtener una visa
   c. __________ hacer reservaciones
2. Lugar que va a visitar __________
3. Tiempo que va a estar allí __________
4. Costo de la excursión __________
5. Dinero extra que usted cree que su compañero/a va a necesitar __________
6. ¿Algo inusual?

SITUACIONES

1. **Role A:** You have received a very generous check from your rich aunt. Answer your classmate's questions in detail. If necessary, ask for advice as to what to do with the money, what to buy, where to go shopping **(ir de compras)**, etc.

   Role B: Your classmate has received a great sum of money from his/her wealthy aunt. Find out how much money he/she has now. Ask him/her how he/she is planning to spend the money; ask for specific amounts each time he/she talks about expenditure. Give him/her reasonable advice on prices of things and on what he/she should do with the money.

2. **Role A:** A friend and you are making plans for Saturday. Your friend is going to tell you what he/she plans to do. Tell your friend that you need to rest and want to spend **(pasar)** the day at the beach. He/She will try to convince you to change your mind. Inquire about specifics of his/her plan such as: where, with whom, how much, when, etc. Politely, be firm about your original plans.

   Role B: Your friend and you are making plans for Saturday. Tell him/her that you want to go to a fancy restaurant and to a discotheque afterwards. Try to convince your friend to change plans. Answer his/her questions. Finally tell him/her that you're going to go along with his/her plans, but that next weekend he/she must go along with your plans.

3. **Role A:** You would like to order some CDs **(discos compactos)** of your favorite singer **(cantante)** over the phone. Tell the salesperson the names of the CDs you want and ask him/her when they'll arrive. Answer the salesperson's questions and provide him/her with the information requested.

   Role B: A customer calls you to order some CDs **(discos compactos)** of his/her favorite singer. Answer the customer's questions and ask for the following information: a) name, b) address, c) zip code **(código postal)**, and d) the credit card **(tarjeta de crédito)** number and expiration date **(fecha de vencimiento)**.

ALGO MÁS

Some uses of *por* and *para*

In previous activities, you used **para** as an equivalent of *for*, with the meaning *intended* or *to be used for:* **Necesito un diccionario para la clase.** *I need a dictionary for the class.* You used **por** in expressions such as **por favor, por teléfono,** and **por la mañana/tarde/noche.** Other fixed expressions with **por** that you will find useful when communicating in Spanish follow:

por ejemplo	*for example*	**por lo menos**	*at least*
por eso	*that's why*	**por supuesto**	*of course*
por fin	*finally, at last*	**por ciento**	*per cent*

Por and **para** can also be used to express movement in space and time.

- Use **para** to indicate movement toward a destination.

  Caminan **para** la playa. — *They walk toward the beach.*
  Vamos **para** el túnel. — *We are going toward the tunnel.*

- Use **por** to indicate movement through or by a place.

  Caminan **por** la playa. — *They walk along the beach.*
  Vamos **por** el túnel. — *We are going through the tunnel.*

- You may also use **por** to indicate length of time or duration of an action/event. Many Spanish speakers omit **por** in this case, or use **durante.**

  Necesito el auto (**por**) tres días. — *I need the car for three days.*

¿Qué dice usted?

3-26 ¿Para dónde van? Read the following and guess where these persons are going. Compare your guesses with those of your classmate. Are they similar? Then, find out where your classmate is going after class, and why.

MODELO: Jorge busca su uniforme de fútbol.
Va para el estadio.

1. Es la una de la tarde y Pedro desea comer.
2. Sebastián lleva una mochila con sus libros de química y una calculadora.
3. Magdalena y Roberto van a consultar unos libros porque tienen un examen.
4. Gregorio está muy enfermo y necesita ver al doctor.
5. Ana María va a ver una película de su actor favorito.
6. Amanda y Clara están muy elegantes y contentas. En este momento llegan Arturo y Felipe.

3-27 Caminante. Your classmate likes to walk. Ask him/her where, when, with whom, and why he/she enjoys walking. Reverse roles.

mosaicos

A ESCUCHAR

A. Las grabaciones telefónicas. You are calling several museums to find their hours of operation and where they are located. Write the information you hear on the chart below.

	HORAS	DIRECCION	
Museo de Arte	________	Ave. Ponce de León	_____
Museo de Historia	________	San Martín	_____
Museo de Antropología	________	Calle Mercaderes	_____
Museo de Ciencias Naturales	________	Ave. Bolívar	_____

B. ¿Quiénes van? ¿Adónde van? ¿Cuánto pagan? First, as you listen to the following statements, circle the words you hear. Then complete the chart, based on the information you obtain (point of reference: U.S.).

1. Agustina va a estar en (**Perú / México**). Ella va a pagar (**2.255 / 1.155**) dólares.
2. Tomás paga (**657 / 756**) euros y él (**no va / va**) a Latinoamérica.
3. El vuelo 332 (**no va / va**) a España.
4. El vuelo 900 (**no es / es**) internacional.
5. Adriana (**no va / va**) a un país de Norteamérica en el vuelo 201.
6. El vuelo a Lima (**es / no es**) el 606.
7. La persona que va a México paga 2.240 pesos y (**no toma / toma**) el vuelo 201.
8. Pablo (**va / no va**) a viajar por Estados Unidos y paga 564 dólares.

NOMBRE	DESTINO	VUELO	PRECIO
	Miami		
	Madrid		
	México		
	Lima		

3-28 Una encuesta. Working in small groups, tell each other what time you eat breakfast, lunch, and dinner. Then, with other groups, calculate the average times of meals for the class and compare them to the average times in Perú.

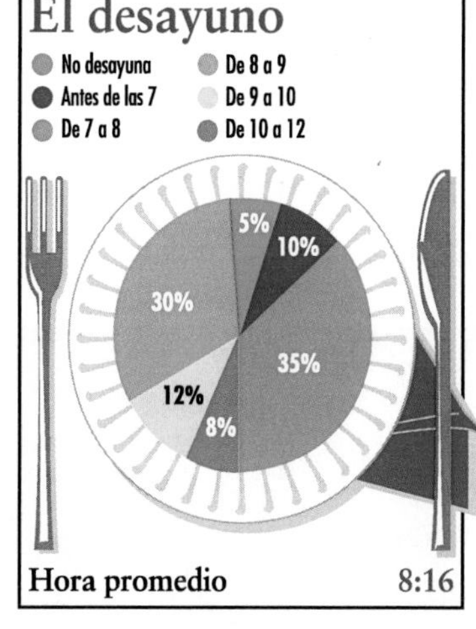

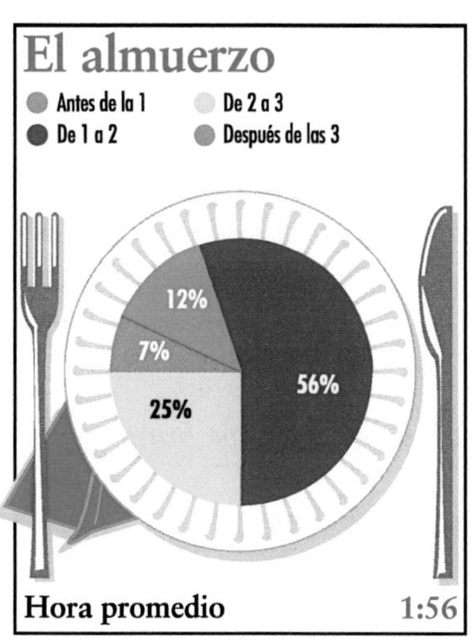

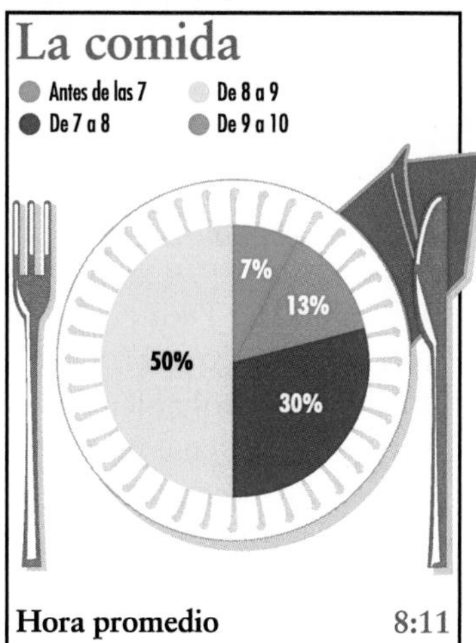

3-29 ¿Qué comen sus compañeros? In small groups, first find out what all of you eat and drink at different meals on campus. Then, take a vote on who, in your group, eats the most healthy of all. Be prepared to share your results with the rest of the class.

MODELO: E1: Susana, ¿comes cereal en el desayuno?
E2: Sí, como cereal en el desayuno.

	DESAYUNO	ALMUERZO	CENA
cereal con leche			
café			
jugo de naranja			
hamburguesa			
ensalada de frutas			
vino			
papas asadas (*baked*)			

Cultura

Mealtimes in Hispanic countries differ from those in the United States. Although there are differences among Hispanic countries, people typically eat breakfast at around 7:00 or 8:00 a.m. Breakfast normally consists of **café con leche** (*hot milk with strong coffee*), **té**, or **chocolate caliente** with bread, a sweet roll, and sometimes juice or fruit. This is a light breakfast, so people sometimes have a snack in the late morning. Cereals are becoming more popular, especially among the younger generation. The main meal of the day is lunch (**el almuerzo** or **la comida**), eaten between 12:30 and 3:00 p.m., depending on the country. Supper (**la cena** or **la comida**) is served after 7:00 or 8:00 p.m., and sometimes as late as 10:00 or 11:00 in Spain.

A LEER

3-30 Preparación. Look at the picture and answer the questions.

1. ¿Qué ciudad de Perú piensa usted que muestra esta fotografía?
2. En su opinión, ¿qué lugares de diversión hay en esta ciudad?
3. ¿Qué hora es probablemente?
4. En su opinión, ¿cuál es la mejor hora para divertirse (*to have fun*)?
5. ¿Adónde va usted para divertirse?
6. Manejar un auto por la noche, ¿es una diversión para usted?

3-31 Primera mirada. Read the ads from a Peruvian newspaper, and offer a solution for each of the problems on the following page.

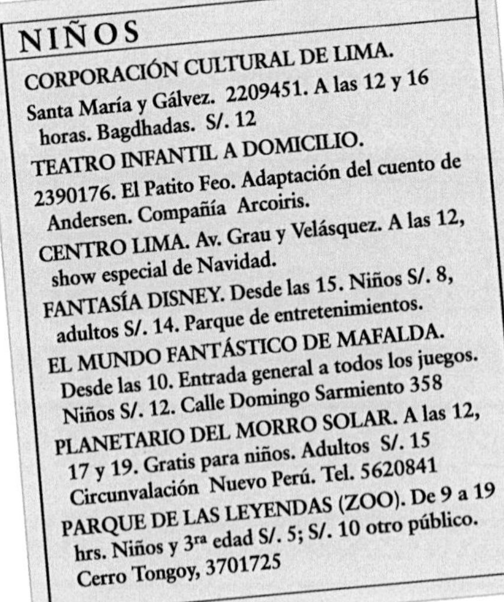

NIÑOS

CORPORACIÓN CULTURAL DE LIMA. Santa María y Gálvez. 2209451. A las 12 y 16 horas. Bagdhadas. S/. 12

TEATRO INFANTIL A DOMICILIO. 2390176. El Patito Feo. Adaptación del cuento de Andersen. Compañía Arcoiris.

CENTRO LIMA. Av. Grau y Velásquez. A las 12, show especial de Navidad.

FANTASÍA DISNEY. Desde las 15. Niños S/. 8, adultos S/. 14. Parque de entretenimientos.

EL MUNDO FANTÁSTICO DE MAFALDA. Desde las 10. Entrada general a todos los juegos. Niños S/. 12. Calle Domingo Sarmiento 358

PLANETARIO DEL MORRO SOLAR. A las 12, 17 y 19. Gratis para niños. Adultos S/. 15 Circunvalación Nuevo Perú. Tel. 5620841

PARQUE DE LAS LEYENDAS (ZOO). De 9 a 19 hrs. Niños y 3ra edad S/. 5; S/. 10 otro público. Cerro Tongoy, 3701725

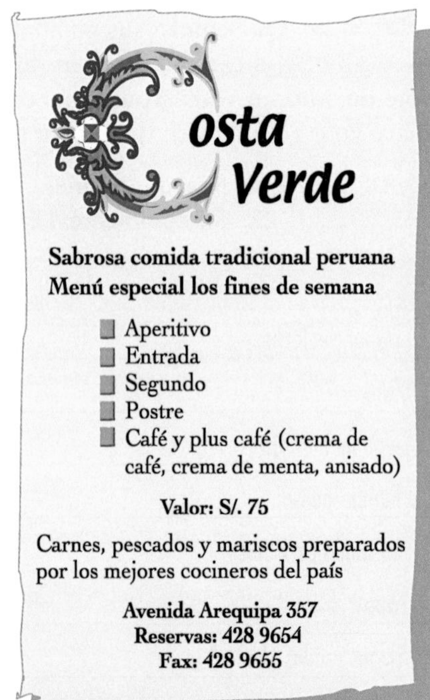

Costa Verde

Sabrosa comida tradicional peruana
Menú especial los fines de semana

- Aperitivo
- Entrada
- Segundo
- Postre
- Café y plus café (crema de café, crema de menta, anisado)

Valor: S/. 75

Carnes, pescados y mariscos preparados por los mejores cocineros del país

Avenida Arequipa 357
Reservas: 428 9654
Fax: 428 9655

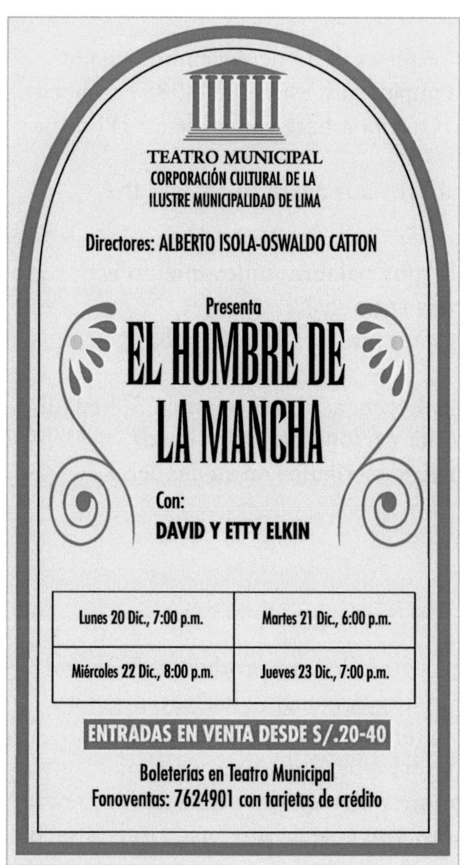

PROBLEMAS

1. El señor y la señora Molina tienen cuatro hijos entre tres y ocho años de edad. A los niños les fascinan los animales, en particular las especies no existentes en Perú, por ejemplo los leones africanos, los elefantes, los tigres, los osos panda, etc. También les gustan mucho todos los entretenimientos de Disney. Toda la familia desea salir este fin de semana, pero tiene poco dinero. ¿Adónde van a ir ellos probablemente? ¿Por qué?

2. El señor Liskin, un turista norteamericano, visita Lima por primera vez. Él piensa que es una buena idea ver todo lo típico de Perú. Este fin de semana no va a trabajar y va a tener suficiente tiempo para otras actividades. Al señor Liskin le gusta mucho escuchar música clásica, ver obras de teatro y comer bien. ¿Qué debe hacer durante el fin de semana?

3. Hoy es el cumpleaños de Carlitos, el hijo de Paloma. ¡Ya tiene cinco años! A diferencia de otros años en esta fecha, hoy el niño está en casa. El doctor dice que no debe caminar porque se fracturó una pierna. Carlitos está muy triste porque no va a celebrar su fiesta de cumpleaños con sus amigos, pero su mamá tiene una sorpresa para él. ¿Qué va a hacer Paloma?

4. Cuatro médicos alemanes visitan el Centro de Investigaciones del Cáncer del Hospital Central. El Dr. Moreira, director del Centro, desea invitar a sus colegas a un buen lugar esta noche para comer productos del mar peruanos. Él desea un restaurante cómodo, con buena comida y excelente

atención. Hoy va a ser muy difícil porque es el 23 de diciembre, cuando mucha gente cena fuera de casa, la temperatura está a 35° (98° Farenheit). ¿A qué restaurante va a invitarlos? ¿Qué va a hacer antes de ir? ¿Por qué?

3-32 Segunda mirada. Go back and read the ads again to answer the following questions.

1. En el anuncio del Teatro Municipal, ¿qué palabra indica que no es necesario ir al teatro para comprar las entradas?
2. ¿Qué expresión en el anuncio del restaurante El Chifa Lungfung es un sinónimo de "reservación"?
3. En la sección de niños, Parque de las Leyendas, ¿qué significa 3ra edad? ¿Cuántos años tiene como mínimo una persona de la 3ra edad?
4. Busque dos cognados en cada anuncio y escríbalos en su cuaderno.

A ESCRIBIR

The writing process—the series of steps you follow to produce a clear and effective piece of writing—is the same in any language. First you organize your thoughts, perhaps by writing an outline. Then you write a first draft. As you write, or once you finish, you may revise to find better ways of expressing your ideas. For example you may change the organization, rewrite sentences or choose better words. Finally, you correct any inaccuracies such as errors in spelling, punctuation, accent marks, etc.

Questions, asked orally or in writing, play an important role in our daily life. We read and/or write questions at school or at home, in letters, memos, and notes. Questions may reflect our inquisitive nature, our quest for needed information, or simply our need to fill a communication gap. The manner in which we ask questions is determined by the person whom we ask, and affects the way that person responds. Thus, we need to take special care with our word choice and register. (Shall we address the person as **usted** or **tú**?)

3-33 Manos a la obra: Fase preliminar. As a journalist working for the **Universidad de San Marcos** newspaper, you're looking to identify the "Student of the Year." With a classmate, develop two questionnaires: one for a potential candidate, and another for the student's parents. What information will you need? Probably ...

- información personal básica del candidato
- los rasgos (características) excepcionales de su personalidad
- su rutina diaria, especialmente aquellas actividades que diferencian a esta persona del estudiante promedio
- sus planes académicos y personales
- otra información...

After preparing the questionnaires, interview two classmates: one will act as the candidate, and the other one as the candidate's mother/father. You should verify the information from both parties and take notes, or record your conversation for the next phase of the activity.

3-34 Manos a la obra. Now write a report (*un informe*) to the editor of the newspaper about the candidate you identified. Use the following guidelines.

- datos generales del/de la candidato/a: nombre completo, edad, rasgos de personalidad, etc.
- actividades diarias y planes del/de la candidato/a que indican que es un/a estudiante modelo
- opinión que el padre/la madre tiene de su hijo/a
- su opinión personal del/de la candidato/a

_____de_________de ___

Estimad__ Sr./Sra./Srta.________:

Acabo de entrevistar al/a la alumn___ ____________________ y a su madre/padre, el/la señor/a ___________. Nuestra conversación fue muy ___________________ [describa el tono de la conversación].

Según (*according to*) la opinión de su ________________________
____
____
____
_____________________________________ [describa por qué el/la candidato/a es un/a estudiante modelo, según el padre/la madre.]

En mi opinión, el/la candidat____
____
_______________________________________ [exprese su opinión sobre el candidato].

Sin otro particular, me despido de usted

Atte.,

_____________ (Firma)

_____________ (Nombre)

3-35 Revisión. After completing your report, discuss the content and style of your writing with your peer editor/reader. Then make any necessary changes.

EXPRESIONES ÚTILES

The following expressions may come in handy:

- To discuss content:

  No comprendo la/esta palabra/expresión.
  Necesito más información.
  No hay suficiente información sobre...
  ¿Qué significa...? (*What does ... mean?*)
  ¿Por qué dices...? (*Why do you say...?*)

- To discuss grammar and mechanics:

Necesitas conjugar el verbo...	**necesitas un punto (.)**
La palabra 'también' necesita acento	**una coma (,)**
el verbo... es mejor en este contexto	**punto y coma (;)**

Vocabulario*

Comunicación

el periódico	*newspaper*
la revista	*magazine*
el teléfono	*telephone*

Diversiones

la canción	*song*
el cumpleaños	*birthday*
la fiesta	*party*
la guitarra	*guitar*
la música	*music*
la película	*film*
la reunión	*meeting, gathering*
la sorpresa	*surprise*
las vacaciones	*vacation*

Personas

la camarera	*waitress*
el camarero	*waiter*
el/la joven	*young man/woman*
el muchacho	*boy, young man*
la muchacha	*girl, young woman*

En un café o restaurante

el agua	*water*
agua con gas	*carbonated water*
el almuerzo	*lunch*
el arroz	*rice*
la bebida	*drink*
el bistec	*steak*
el café	*coffee*
el camarón	*shrimp*
la cena	*dinner, supper*
el cereal	*cereal*
la cerveza	*beer*
el ceviche	*raw fish dish*
la comida	*dinner, supper*
el desayuno	*breakfast*
la ensalada	*salad*
los espaguetis	*spaghetti*
la fruta	*fruit*
la hamburguesa	*hamburger*
el helado	*ice cream*
el huevo	*egg*
el jamón	*ham*
el jugo	*juice*
la leche	*milk*
la lechuga	*lettuce*
la naranja	*orange*
el pan	*bread*
la papa	*potato*
las papas fritas	*French fries*
el pescado	*fish*
el plato principal	*main course*
el pollo	*chicken*
el queso	*cheese*
el refresco	*soda*
el sándwich	*sandwich*
la sopa	*soup*
el té	*tea*
el tomate	*tomato*
la tostada	*toast*
el vegetal/ la verdura	*vegetable*
el vino	*wine*

Lugares

el cine	*movies*
la ciudad	*city*
el mar	*sea*
el país	*country, nation*

Descripciones

caliente	*hot*
fabuloso/a	*fabulous, great*
frío/a	*cold*
frito/a	*fried*
rápido/a	*fast*
típico/a	*typical*

Verbos

alquilar	*to rent*
beber	*to drink*
cantar	*to sing*
celebrar	*to celebrate*
cenar	*to have dinner*
comer	*to eat*
deber	*ought to, should*
decidir	*to decide*
descansar	*to rest*
escribir	*to write*

ir	*to go*
leer	*to read*
nadar	*to swim*
terminar	*to finish*
tocar (un instrumento)	*to play* (an instrument), *to touch*
tomar el sol	*to sunbathe*
ver	*to see*
vivir	*to live*

Tiempo

después	*after, afterwards*
durante	*during*
esta noche	*tonight*
más tarde	*later*
mientras	*meanwhile*
pasado mañana	*the day after*
el próximo año	*next year*
el próximo mes	*next month*
la próxima semana	*next week*

Palabras y expresiones útiles

¿Aló?	*Hello*
¿Adónde?	*Where (to)?*
al	*to the* (contraction of **a** + **el**)
al aire libre	*outdoors*
estar a dieta	*to be on a diet*
estar de acuerdo	*to agree*
fuera	*out, outside*
mi amor	*dear, my love*
otro/a	*other, another*
para mí	*for me*
pues	*well*
¡Qué bien!	*That's great!*
si	*if*
sólo	*only*
tiempo libre	*free time*

* For expressions with *por* see page 111

El cine, el teatro, las peñas

Para pensar

¿Qué hace Ud. cuando quiere pasar un rato agradable? ¿Adónde va? ¿A la playa, al cine, al teatro, a la discoteca, al parque? ¿Con quién va a estos lugares?

En los países hispanos hay muchos lugares adonde se puede ir y muchas actividades que se pueden hacer cuando se quiere pasar un rato agradable. Como el clima es cálido en muchos países, se puede ir a la playa durante todo el año a bañarse, tomar el sol, navegar en velero, etc. Sin embargo, también hay muchas otras cosas que se pueden hacer además de ir a la playa. A muchas personas les gustan las corridas de toros (*bullfights*) o las carreras de caballos (*horse races*) y por eso van a la Plaza de toros o al Hipódromo. Otras personas prefieren ir a un cine y disfrutar de una película americana, francesa, italiana, sueca, o alemana. Hay muchos cines y las películas extranjeras están dobladas (*dubbed*) o tienen subtítulos en español. Para los que prefieren el ballet, la ópera o la zarzuela (*Spanish operetta*) hay numerosos teatros que presentan gran variedad de obras. Por otra parte, hay personas que prefieren sentarse tranquilamente con sus amigos y conversar con ellos. Estas personas disfrutan en los muchos cafés que hay en todas las ciudades y pueblos. Si quieren conversar pero también disfrutar de una obra de teatro, pueden ir a los café-teatros donde se presentan comedias cortas, y donde además se puede comer y tomar un café o una copa (*cocktail*).

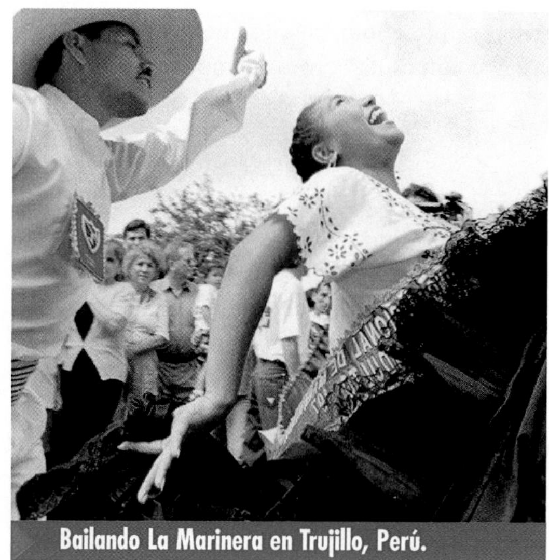

Bailando La Marinera en Trujillo, Perú.

En algunos países, como en el Perú por ejemplo, además de las playas, cines, teatros, plaza de toros, hipódromo, discotecas, café-teatros, etc., hay muchas peñas. Las peñas son lugares donde se presentan cantantes de música criolla y conjuntos de bailes folclóricos. Mucha gente va a las peñas no solamente a disfrutar del espectáculo que ofrecen, sino también a bailar, a cantar, a comer comida criolla, y sobre todo a pasar un rato muy, pero muy agradable. En resumen, ¡en el mundo hispano hay muchas cosas que hacer para divertirse!

Si quiere conseguir más información sobre la cultura peruana, puede visitar (*www.prenhall.com/mosaicos*)

Para contestar

Las diversiones. Con su compañero/a responda a las siguientes preguntas:

1. Si ustedes son personas muy activas y visitan un país hispano, ¿a qué lugares pueden ir? ¿Qué pueden hacer allí?
2. Si prefieren actividades más relajantes, ¿qué pueden hacer en un país hispano?
3. Si quieren aprender algo más de la cultura de un país hispano, ¿adónde pueden ir? ¿Qué pueden aprender allí?

Riqueza cultural. En grupos de tres discutan qué actividades pueden hacer en los países hispanos que no pueden hacer en los Estados Unidos.

Para investigar en la WWW

1. Busque el nombre de algunas playas y balnearios *(resorts)* famosos en el Perú. Diga dónde quedan, qué actividades se pueden hacer allí, cuánto cuesta ir desde su ciudad por avión, etc.
2. Con su compañero/a, planifiquen un viaje al Perú. Decidan adónde van a ir, qué van a hacer, cuánto van a gastar, etc.
3. Busque información acerca de los bailes folclóricos de Bolivia, Perú y México. ¿Cómo son? ¿Cómo es la música? ¿Qué instrumentos usan? ¿Cómo son los trajes *(costumes)* que usan los bailarines? Comparta la información con el resto de la clase. Traiga fotos y si es posible, una grabación de la música que escuchó para compartirla con sus compañeros/as. Ellos/as le darán sus comentarios.
4. En un periódico peruano busque un anuncio que presente información sobre los espectáculos que hay en una peña esta semana. Averigüe el nombre de la peña, dónde está, a qué hora abre, qué artistas se presentan, cuánto cuesta el espectáculo, etc. Traiga la información que consiga a la clase y compártala con sus compañeros/as. Dígales por qué prefiere Ud. ir a un lugar y no al otro.

Perú

Ciudades importantes y lugares de interés: Lima, la capital, tiene cerca de siete millones de habitantes. Es una ciudad que tiene zonas antiguas de gran belleza y valor histórico y también zonas modernas. Hay muchos museos de importancia como el Museo de Oro y el Museo de la Nación. El Museo de Oro tiene una excelente colección de joyería (*jewelry*) y objetos precolombinos; el Museo de la Nación exhibe joyería, artesanía y gran variedad de objetos de las civilizaciones que se desarrollaron en el Perú. Si está interesado en saber más de Lima, llamada también la Ciudad de los Reyes, puede visitar *www.prenhall.com/mosaicos*.

Palacio del Arzobispado, Lima.

Otro lugar de gran interés en la costa del Perú es Nazca, más o menos a 300 kilómetros al sur de Lima. Nazca es muy conocida por sus famosas líneas en el desierto. Visite *www.prenhall.com/mosaicos* y aprenda más sobre estas intrigantes líneas. Al norte de Lima está Trujillo, ciudad de gran encanto colonial. Cerca de Trujillo se encuentran las ruinas de las antiguas civilizaciones Mochica y Chimú. Si visita www.prenhall/mosaicos podrá conocer Chan-Chan, centro de la cultura Chimú y considerada la ciudad de barro más grande del mundo. Otra ciudad importante es Cuzco, la antigua capital del imperio de los Incas. Cerca de Cuzco se encuentran las ruinas de la ciudad inca de Machu Picchu y la fortaleza de Sacsayhuaman (vaya a *www.prenhall.com/mosaicos*).

Como Ud. puede ver, el Perú es un país muy rico y variado en su cultura y geografía.

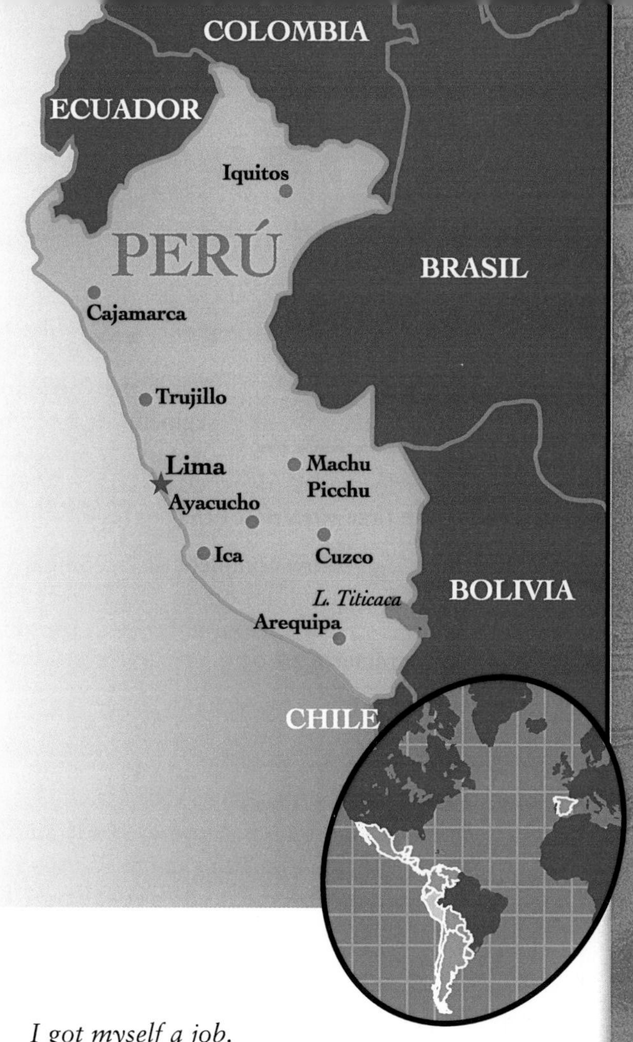

Expresiones peruanas:

Chamba	**Me conseguí una chamba.**	*I got myself a job.*
Maldita	**¡La película estuvo maldita!**	*The movie was great!*
Bacán	**¡Ella es bacán!**	*She is great/a lot of fun!*
Chancón	**¡Él es un chancón!**	*He studies all the time.*

Chan Chan, Peru

ENFOQUE INTERACTIVO

A MIRAR EL VIDEO **5:00**

Watch the *Fortunas* video segment for *Lección 3* in class or on your CD-ROM. Will Carlos and Katie work together? Who will solve the first *misterio* of the contest?

Now complete the accompanying video activities on the CD-ROM. This is your chance to interact with the video characters! **25:00**

Carlos y Katie

El concurso

In this episode of *Fortunas*, Katie and Carlos consider forming an alliance. Carlos is convinced that he and Katie need to collaborate but she is not so sure. How does this encounter differ from the one in the last episode between Sabrina and Efraín? What strategy would you use to form alliances? Or would you rather solve the *misterios* alone?

PUNTOS

Las alianzas

Contestants are allowed to form open and secret alliances throughout the course of the contest in order to solve the different *misterios* and locate the *fortunas.* If a *misterio* is solved or a *fortuna* is located through an alliance, all points awarded are to be shared equally among the allied contestants.

LA BÚSQUEDA! **5:00**

Katie and Carlos have only *pistas 1* and *4*. These are enough, however, to trigger a possible solution for Carlos. If they solve the first *misterio* by working together, they will share equally the points awarded for the discovery. Are you forming an idea of what the first *misterio* means? Go to the *Fortunas* module to gather more information about the first *misterio*. Can you can solve the *misterio* before the contestants do?

Misterio Nº 1: Cinco es suficiente

Pistas

1. *Destrucción de los gigantes por el viento (monos)*
2. *Destrucción por la lluvia (pájaros)*
3. *Destrucción por el diluvio (peces)*
4. *Destrucción por el jaguar*

¿QUÉ OPINA USTED? 5:00

This week we see a different side of Efraín. Instead of the aloof musician, we find a young man with all-too-familiar family problems. Do you identify with Efraín? Remember, each week you have the opportunity to vote in the *Fortunas* viewer poll. Go to the *Fortunas* module now and click on *¿Qué opina usted?* to participate in this episode's poll.

PARA NAVEGAR 10:00

EL CINE HISPANO

El cine es un fenómeno cultural en todo el mundo. Pero no todas las producciones cinematográficas se originan en Hollywood. También hay cine importante en otras partes del mundo, específicamente en España y en algunos países de Latinoamérica.

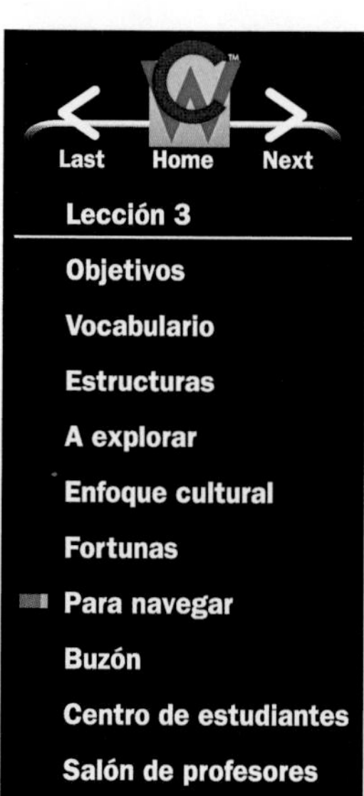

Go to the *Mosaicos Website* and click on the *Para navegar* module to explore links to Hispanic cinema. Read movie reviews and learn about well-known actors from Spain and Latin America.

Como agua para chocolate

Mujeres al borde de un ataque de nervios

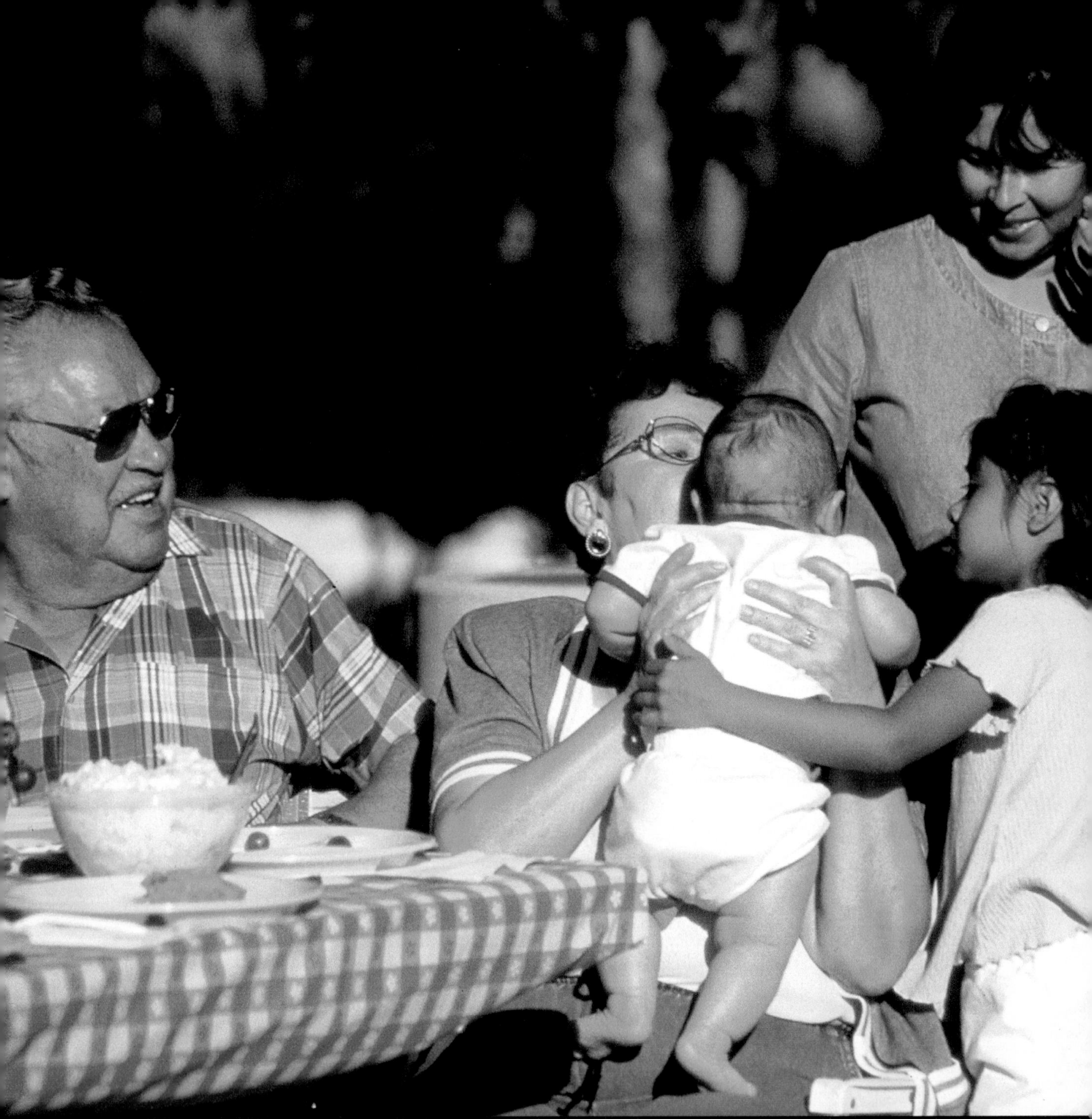

Lección 4

La familia

COMUNICACION

- Identifying and describing family members
- Describing routine activities
- Expressing preferences, desires, and feelings
- Asking and giving permission
- Expressing when, where, or how an action is done
- Expressing how long events and states have been going on

ESTRUCTURAS

- Present tense of stem-changing verbs: **e → ie**, **o → ue**, **e → i**
- Adverbs
- Present tense of **hacer**, **poner**, **salir**, **traer**, and **oír**
- **Hace** with expressions of time
- ALGO MÁS: Some reflexive verbs and pronouns

MOSAICOS

A ESCUCHAR

A CONVERSAR

A LEER

- Anticipating and inferring topic
- Guessing meaning of new words through context clues and identifying suffixes

A ESCRIBIR

- Communicating personal feelings and giving suggestions

ENFOQUE CULTURAL

- La familia hispana
- Colombia

ENFOQUE INTERACTIVO

WWW

VIDEO

CD ROM

A primera vista

Las familias

Una foto familiar de tres generaciones: abuelos, hijos y nietos.

Practice activities for each vocabulary section are provided on the CD-ROM and website (www.prenhall.com/mosaicos)

Una familia colombiana celebra el bautizo de su hija. Las relaciones entre los padrinos, los ahijados y sus padres son muy importantes en la cultura hispana.

La familia de Pablo

Pablo habla de su familia

Me llamo Pablo Méndez Sánchez y vivo con mis padres, mi hermana y mis abuelos en un apartamento en Bogotá, la capital de Colombia.
Mi madre tiene un hermano, mi tío Jorge. Su esposa es mi tía María. Tienen tres hijos y viven también en Bogotá. Mi primo Jorgito es el menor. Mis primas Elenita y Ana son gemelas. Mis primos son muy simpáticos y pasamos mucho tiempo juntos.

Mis tíos sólo tienen dos sobrinos en Bogotá, mi hermana Inés y yo. Su otra sobrina, la hija de mi tía Lola, vive en Cartagena, al norte del país.

La nieta favorita de mis abuelos es mi hermanita Inés. Sólo tiene tres años y es la menor de todos sus nietos.

¿Qué dice usted?

4-1 Asociación. Asocie la descripción a la izquierda con la expresión correcta.

1. ____ La esposa de mi papá	a. mi primo
2. ____ El hermano de mi prima	b. mi nieto
3. ____ Los padres de mi papá	c. mi madre
4. ____ El hijo de mi hijo	d. mis abuelos
5. ____ El hermano de mi mamá	e. mi tío

4-2 La familia de Pablo. Complete las siguientes oraciones de acuerdo con el árbol genealógico *(family tree)* de Pablo.

1. La hermana de Pablo se llama ________.
2. Don José y doña Olga son los ________ de Pablo. Ellos tienen ________ hijas y ________ hijo.
3. Pablo es el ________ de Jaime.
4. Jaime es el ________ de Pablo, y Elena es su ________.
5. Inés y Ana son ________. Elenita y Ana son __________.
6. Don José y doña Olga tienen ________ nietos y ________ nietas en Bogotá.
7. Elena es la ________ de Jorgito, Elenita y Ana.
8. Lola es la ________ de Jorge y Elena.

4-3 ¿Quién es y cómo es? Escoja (*Choose*) a un miembro de la familia de Pablo. Su compañero/a debe decir cuál es su relación familiar con Pablo y usar la imaginación para dar información adicional.

MODELO: E1: ¿Quién es Elenita?
E2: Es la prima de Pablo. Tiene dieciocho años y estudia psicología. Es muy simpática y tiene muchos amigos.

Cultura

The ending **-ito/a** (**Jorge → Jorgito**) is very common in Hispanic countries; it is particularly used to differentiate parents from children of the same name. The ending **ito/a** also expresses smallness (**hermanito/a, sillita**) or affection (**mi abuelita**).
Hispanics are often given more than one name (**Carlos Alberto, María del Carmen**). These names are often combined (**Mariví,** from **María Victoria**). The name **María** may also be used as part of a man's name: **José María**.

Otros miembros de la familia de Pablo

La única hermana de mi mamá es mi tía Lola. Lola y Sergio están divorciados pero tienen una hija, mi prima Petra. Ahora tía Lola está casada con Osvaldo, el padrastro de Petra. Sergio está casado con Paula y tienen un hijo, Roberto. Paula es la madrastra de Petra, y Roberto es su medio hermano.

A INVESTIGAR

- ¿Sabe Ud. que el apellido Fernández viene del nombre Fernando?
- Asocie cada apellido con el nombre correspondiente.

—Hernández	1. Ramiro
—Álvarez	2. Martín
—Martínez	3. Hernán
—González	4. Álvaro
—Ramírez	5. Gonzalo

- ¿Hay apellidos en inglés que tienen origen en un nombre? ¿Cuáles?
- ¿Dónde va el apellido de la madre en español?

¿Qué dice usted?

4-4 **¿Cierto o falso?** Marque la columna adecuada de acuerdo con la información sobre la familia de Lola.

	CIERTO	FALSO
1. La tía Lola está casada con Sergio.	_____	_____
2. Osvaldo es el papá de Roberto.	_____	_____
3. Paula es la madrastra de Roberto.	_____	_____
4. Lola es la madre de Petra.	_____	_____
5. Petra tiene un medio hermano.	_____	_____

4-5 Mi familia. Prepare su árbol genealógico. Luego, intercambie su árbol con el de un/a compañero/a. Hágale preguntas a su compañero/a para obtener la siguiente información.

- Nombre del/de los abuelo(s) vivo(s) (*alive*): ____________________
- Nombre de los padres (padrastro/madrastra): ____________________
- Número y nombre(s) de (medio/a) hermano/a(s): ____________________
- Número y nombre(s) de primo/a(s): ____________________
- Descripción de dos familiares: ____________________

4-6 Encuesta. Primera fase. En parejas intercambien preguntas para obtener los siguientes datos.

1. tener cuatro abuelos vivos
2. ser hijo/a único/a
3. tener dos hermanos/as
4. vivir con los padres
5. vivir con los abuelos
6. número de primos/as
7. tener madrastra/padrastro
8. número de medio/a hermanos/as

Segunda fase. En pequeños grupos, van a clasificar la familia de cada miembro del grupo en estas categorías:

a. familia típica/tradicional norteamericana
b. familia norteamericana atípica
c. . . .

Escojan a un/a secretario/a para tomar notas. Lean las expresiones más abajo para dar *(give)* y defender su opinión.

Expresiones útiles para defender una opinión:

- En mi/nuestra opinión, . . . porque. . .
  En nuestra opinión, la familia norteamericana típica es pequeña.
- Yo pienso/Nosotros pensamos que. . . porque. . .
  Yo pienso que no existe una familia norteamericana típica.

¿Qué hacen los parientes?

Mis abuelos viven en una casa junto al parque. Normalmente, ellos pasean por las mañanas y almuerzan muy temprano. Después duermen la siesta y por la tarde visitan a sus parientes.

Jorgito es mi primo favorito. Es un poco menor que yo, pero corremos y jugamos mucho juntos. También nos gusta ver el fútbol en la televisión y montar en bicicleta los domingos.

Mi prima Ana hace dos años que tiene novio y frecuentemente dice que quiere casarse muy pronto. Elenita, su hermana gemela, piensa que Ana no debe casarse porque es muy joven.

Mi tío Jorge es un hombre muy ocupado. Todos los días sale de casa muy temprano y vuelve tarde. Mi tía María, su esposa, dice que él prefiere el trabajo a su familia. Pienso que en todas las familias hay problemas. En la mía también, pero me gusta mi familia.

¿Qué dice usted?

4-7 ¿Cierto o falso? Conteste de acuerdo con la información adicional sobre la familia de Pablo.

	CIERTO	FALSO
1. Normalmente los abuelos están muy ocupados.	_____	_____
2. El tío Jorge cree que Elenita tiene problemas.	_____	_____
3. Elenita piensa que su hermana es muy joven para casarse.	_____	_____
4. Jorgito y Pablo montan en bicicleta frecuentemente.	_____	_____
5. El tío Jorge trabaja mucho.	_____	_____
6. A Pablo no le gusta su familia.	_____	_____

4-8 Entrevista. Hágale preguntas a su compañero/a para obtener más información sobre su familia, basándose en los siguientes puntos:

1. Número de personas en la casa, edad y relación
2. Ocupación y descripción (física y de personalidad)
3. Actividades de estas personas por la noche
4. Nombre del pariente favorito, relación familiar y razón de la preferencia

A ESCUCHAR

Las familias. You will hear descriptions of four families. For each description mark the appropriate column to indicate whether the family is big or small.

	GRANDE	PEQUENA		GRANDE	PEQUENA
1.	_____	_____	3.	_____	_____
2.	_____	_____	4.	_____	_____

Explicación y expansión

1. Present tense of stem-changing verbs (e → ie, o → ue, e → i)

PENSAR (E → IE) (*to think*)			
yo	pienso	nosotros/as	pensamos
tú	piensas	vosotros/as	pensáis
Ud., él, ella	piensa	Uds., ellos/as	piensan

Practice activities for each numbered grammar point are provided on the CD-ROM and website (www.prenhall.com/ mosaicos)

VOLVER (O → UE) (*to return*)			
yo	vuelvo	nosotros/as	volvemos
tú	vuelves	vosotros/as	volvéis
Ud., él, ella	vuelve	Uds., ellos/as	vuelven

PEDIR (E → I) (*to ask for, to order*)			
yo	pido	nosotros/as	pedimos
tú	pides	vosotros/as	pedís
Ud., él, ella	pide	Uds., ellos/as	piden

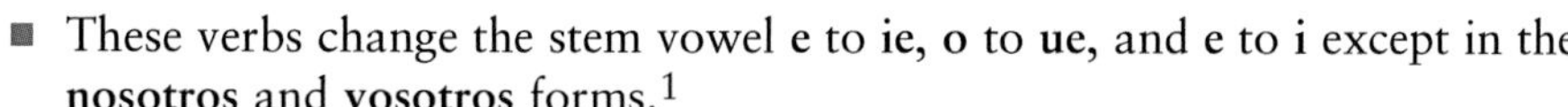

- These verbs change the stem vowel **e** to **ie**, **o** to **ue**, and **e** to **i** except in the **nosotros** and **vosotros** forms.[1]

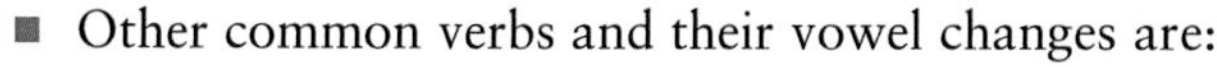

- Other common verbs and their vowel changes are:

e → ie	o → ue	e → i
cerrar (*to close*)	**almorzar** (*to have lunch*)	**servir** (*to serve*)
empezar (*to begin*)	**costar** (*to cost*)	**repetir** (*to repeat*)
entender (*to understand*)	**dormir** (*to sleep*)	
pensar (*to think*)	**poder** (*to be able to, can*)	
preferir (*to prefer*)		
querer (*to want, to love*)		

- Use **pensar** + *infinitive* to express what you or someone else is planning to do.

Pienso estudiar esta noche. — *I plan to study tonight.*
Pensamos comer a las ocho. — *We're planning to eat at 8:00.*

[1]Stem-changing verbs are identified in vocabulary lists as follows: **pensar (ie); volver (ue); pedir (i).**

• The Spanish equivalent for *to think of /about* someone or something is **pensar en.**

¿**Piensas en** tu familia cuando estás fuera de casa?
Do you think of your family when you are away from home?

Sí, **pienso** mucho **en** ellos. Y también **pienso en** mi casa
Yes, I think about them a lot. And I also think of my home.

• **Pensar de** is used to inquire for an opinion about someone or something. **Pensar que** is normally used to answer these questions.

¿Qué **piensas de** los planes de ayuda familiar?
What do you think of the plans to help families?

Pienso que son excelentes.
I think they are excellent.

- Note the irregular yo form in the following e → ie and e → i stem-changing verbs.

tener (*to have*)	**tengo,** tienes, tiene, tenemos, tenéis, tienen
venir (*to come*)	**vengo,** vienes, viene, venimos, venís, vienen
decir (*to say, tell*)	**digo,** dices, dice, decimos, decís, dicen
seguir (*to follow*)	**sigo,** sigues, sigue, seguimos, seguís, siguen

- The verb **jugar** (*to play* a game or a sport) changes **u** to **ue.**

Mario **juega** muy bien, pero nosotros **jugamos** regular.

¿Qué dice usted?

4-9 Preferencias de la familia. Dígale a su compañero/a qué prefieren tomar o comer usted y otro miembro de su familia en las situaciones indicadas. Después pregúntele a su compañero/a cuáles son sus preferencias.

MODELO: Por la mañana: jugo, café o té
E1: Yo prefiero tomar té, pero mi hermano prefiere tomar café. ¿Y tú?
E2: Pues yo prefiero té.

1. En el almuerzo: leche, chocolate o café
2. Después de correr: jugo, refresco o agua mineral
3. Para celebrar un cumpleaños: vino, cerveza o champaña
4. Los domingos: comida mexicana, comida italiana o comida española

4-10 ¿Qué piensan hacer estas personas? Túrnese con su compañero/a para decir qué piensa hacer cada persona en las situaciones siguientes. Cada uno debe dar una respuesta diferente.

MODELO: Mi hermano desea estar delgado.
E1: Él piensa correr mucho.
E2: Él piensa empezar una dieta.

1. Mi hermana tiene un examen de matemáticas mañana.
2. Ella no entiende muchos de los problemas.
3. Mi tía está muy enferma.
4. Mis abuelos están de vacaciones en Colombia.
5. Yo voy a ir a Cartagena para visitar a mis abuelos.

4-11 Comidas y bebidas. Pregúntele a su compañero/a qué pide para comer y beber en estos lugares. Él/Ella debe hacerle las mismas preguntas.

MODELO: en un partido de béisbol
E1: ¿Qué pides en un partido de béisbol?
E2: Pido un perro caliente y un refresco.

1. en un restaurante español muy elegante
2. en un McDonald's si quieres estar delgado/a
3. durante un partido de fútbol americano
4. en un restaurante de una playa de Colombia
5. en una pizzería

4-12 Entrevista. Entreviste a su compañero/a. Después su compañero/a debe entrevistarlo/la a usted.

1. ¿A qué hora almuerzas? ¿Dónde? ¿Con quién?
2. ¿Qué prefieres almorzar?
3. ¿Qué bebes a la hora del almuerzo?
4. ¿Duermes la siesta después del almuerzo?
5. ¿Vuelves a la universidad después del almuerzo?
6. ¿Qué haces en tu casa por la tarde?

4-13 ¿Cuándo y con quién? Usted debe hacerle preguntas a su compañero/a para obtener la siguiente información:

Durante la semana: a. hora del almuerzo y con quién(es) b. hora de la cena y con quién(es) c. actividades favoritas

Un fin de semana: a. hora del almuerzo y con quién(es) b. hora de la cena y con quién(es) c. actividades favoritas

4-14 Una reunión. En grupos pequeños, imagínense que todos son miembros de una misma familia y determinen cuál es la relación entre ustedes (hermanos, primos, tíos, etc.). Van a organizar una reunión familiar. Deben decidir:

1. lugar y hora de la reunión
2. número de niños y adultos que participan (especifiquen la relación familiar)
3. obligaciones de los adultos antes de la reunión
4. comida y bebida que van a servir
5. actividades y diversiones para los niños y para los adultos

1. You and a/some member(s) of your family are planning to take a trip abroad. Your partner should find out a) when you are planning to go, b) with whom you are going, c) what country and cities you prefer to visit, d) why, and e) if the other family member(s) prefer(s) to go to other places.
2. **Role A:** You have just turned 18 and your grandfather has invited you for the first time to one of the most expensive restaurants in town. First a) ask your grandfather what the specialties **(especialidades)** of the house are, b) tell him what you want to eat (just salad, no main course, and no dessert) and drink (mineral water), c) listen to your grandfather's recommendations and politely explain that you want to keep fit **(estar en forma)**, and d) finally, accept to eat vanilla ice cream **(helado de vainilla)** for dessert.

   Role B: Your grandson/granddaughter has just turned 18 and you have decided to invite him/her out for dinner at one of the most expensive restaurants in town. First, a) answer his/her questions regarding the specialties of the house (fish, all kinds of meats, etc.) and b) ask him/her what he/she is planning to order. You notice that he/she orders extremely healthy food, so c) recommend fancier and more expensive food, and d) insist that he/she order at least dessert.

2. Adverbs

- Adverbs are used to describe when, where or how an action/event is done/takes place. You have used Spanish adverbs when expressing time (**mañana, siempre, después**) and place (**detrás, debajo**). You have also used adverbs when expressing how you feel (**bien, muy mal, regular**). These same adverbs can be used when expressing how things are done.

Rafael nada **muy bien.**	*Rafael swims very well.*

- Spanish also uses adverbs ending in **-mente**, which corresponds to the English *-ly*, to qualify how things are done. To form these adverbs, add **-mente** to the feminine form of the adjective. With adjectives that do not have a special feminine form, simply add **-mente.**

Cantan **alegremente.**	*They sing happily.*
María lee **lentamente.**	*María reads slowly.*

Adjectives with a written accent retain it when forming adverbs ending in **-mente: difícil → difícilmente.**

- Some commonly used adverbs ending in **-mente** are:

generalmente	normalmente	frecuentemente
realmente	básicamente	simplemente
tranquilamente	regularmente	perfectamente
relativamente	tradicionalmente	lógicamente

¿Qué dice usted?

4-15 ¿Lenta o rápidamente? ¿Qué hace usted rápidamente y qué hace usted lentamente? Prepare una lista y compárela con la de un/a compañero/a. Puede usar los verbos que aparecen más abajo o usar otros verbos.

MODELO: Nado lentamente pero corro rápidamente.

almorzar	beber	estudiar
bailar	caminar	nadar
hablar español	tomar apuntes	leer el periódico
escribir composiciones		

4-16 ¿Está de acuerdo o no? Indique si está de acuerdo (**Sí**) o no (**No**) con las siguientes afirmaciones. Después usted y su compañero/a deben comparar sus respuestas y decir por qué están o no están de acuerdo.

1. ____ Los padres deben hablar frecuentemente con sus hijos adolescentes.
2. ____ Los nietos deben visitar regularmente a sus abuelos.
3. ____ Normalmente los hijos solteros viven con sus padres.
4. ____ Los padres siempre hablan lentamente cuando están enojados con sus hijos.
5. ____ Generalmente las familias grandes son más felices que las familias pequeñas.
6. ____ Los padres deben tener reuniones con los profesores de sus hijos regularmente.

4-17 Entrevista. Hágale estas preguntas a su compañero/a. Después él/ella le debe hacer las mismas preguntas a usted.

1. ¿Qué haces normalmente por la tarde?
2. ¿A qué lugares vas regularmente y con quién?
3. Generalmente, ¿adónde vas por la noche?
4. ¿Adónde vas para conversar tranquilamente con tus amigos?
5. ¿A quiénes llamas por teléfono más frecuentemente, a tus amigos o a tu familia?

1. Your class is conducting a survey regarding students' movie habits. Ask a classmate a) how many times a month he/she goes to the movies; b) with whom he/she generally goes; c) the type of movies he/she normally prefers (romantic, dramas, science fiction, etc.); d) if he/she eats or drinks at the movies, and what; e) the name of his/her favorite movie theater.

3. Present tense of *hacer*, *poner*, *salir*, *traer*, and *oír*

El padre pone la mesa.

La madre oye música y las noticias.

La hija trae las tostadas a la mesa.

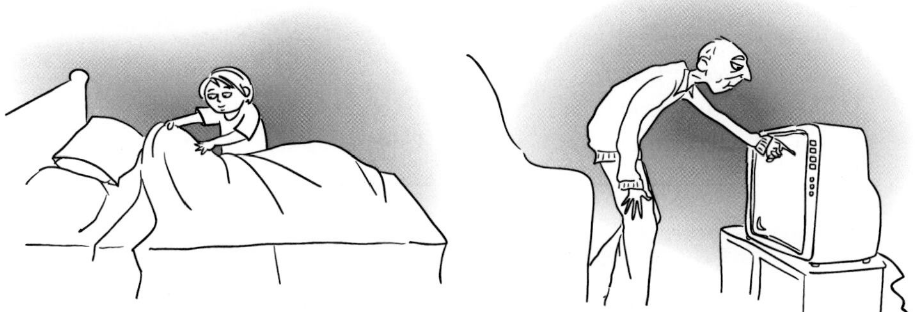

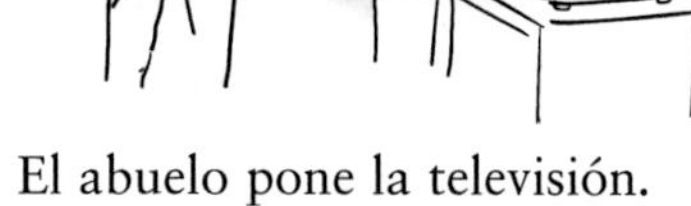

El hijo hace la cama.

El abuelo pone la televisión.

La familia desayuna y sale.

HACER (*to make, to do*)			
yo	**hago**	nosotros/as	**hacemos**
tú	**haces**	vosotros/as	**hacéis**
Ud., él, ella	**hace**	Uds., ellos/as	**hacen**

PONER (*to put*)			
yo	**pongo**	nosotros/as	**ponemos**
tú	**pones**	vosotros/as	**ponéis**
Ud., él, ella	**pone**	Uds., ellos/as	**ponen**

- **Poner** normally means *to put*. However, with some electrical appliances, **poner** means *to turn on*.

  Yo **pongo** los platos y los vasos en la mesa y mi abuelo **pone** la televisión. — *I put the plates and the glasses on the table and my grandfather turns on the T.V.*

SALIR (*to leave*)			
yo	**salgo**	nosotros/as	**salimos**
tú	**sales**	vosotros/as	**salís**
Ud., él, ella	**sale**	Uds., ellos/as	**salen**

- **Salir** can be used with several different prepositions: to express that you are leaving a place, use **salir de**; to express the place of your destination, use **salir para**; to express with whom you go out or the person you date, use **salir con**; to express what you are going to do, use **salir a**.

  Yo **salgo de** mi cuarto ahora. — *I'm leaving my room now.*
  Mi hermana **sale con** Mauricio. — *My sister goes out with Mauricio.*
  Ellos **salen** a bailar los sábados. — *They go out to dance on Saturdays.*

TRAER (*to bring*)			
yo	**traigo**	nosotros/as	**traemos**
tú	**traes**	vosotros/as	**traéis**
Ud., él, ella	**trae**	Uds., ellos/as	**traen**

OÍR (*to hear*)			
yo	**oigo**	nosotros/as	**oímos**
tú	**oyes**	vosotros/as	**oís**
Ud., él, ella	**oye**	Uds., ellos/as	**oyen**

¿Qué dice usted?

4-18 ¿Quién hace estas cosas en su casa? Primera fase. Marquen sus respuestas en la tabla y después, en pequeños grupos, comparen sus respuestas. Determinen cuál de las familias es la más tradicional y cuál es la menos tradicional. ¿Por qué?

MODELO: E1: ¿Quién compra la comida en tu casa?
E2: Yo compro la comida en mi casa.

ACTIVIDADES	MAMA	PAPA	YO	?
comprar la comida				
poner la mesa				
hacer el desayuno				
hacer las camas				
oír las noticias por la tarde				

4-19 Intercambio. Hoy la familia de su compañero/a está muy ocupada. Hágale preguntas a su compañero/a para saber a qué hora salen y para dónde van las personas que aparecen en la tabla.

MODELO: E1: ¿A qué hora sale Juan?
E2: (Sale) a las 8 de la mañana.

E1: ¿Para dónde va Juan?
E2: Va para el gimnasio.

NOMBRE	HORA	LUGAR
Juan	8:00 a.m.	gimnasio
Alicia	9:30 a.m.	estación de autobuses
tu sobrino	2:00 p.m.	aeropuerto
tú	. . .	. . .

4 -20 Las clases de español de mi hermano. Hable con su compañero/a sobre las actividades escolares de su hermano. Después, pregúntele sobre sus actividades.

MODELO: tener la clase de español por la mañana
E1: Mi hermano tiene la clase de español por la mañana. ¿Y tú?
E2: Yo tengo la clase por la tarde. *o* Yo también tengo la clase por la mañana.

1. hacer la tarea por la noche
2. salir para la universidad a las nueve frecuentemente
3. poner la tarea sobre el escritorio del profesor generalmente
4. traer los libros a la casa
5. salir de la clase a las diez normalmente

4-21 Entrevista. Usted quiere saber qué hace su compañero/a en su tiempo libre y él/ella quiere saber qué hace usted. Háganse preguntas para averiguar lo siguiente:

1. hora de salida de la universidad
2. lugares para donde va
3. actividades en esos lugares
4. actividades en su casa por las noches
5. programas de televisión favoritos

4-22 ¿De dónde salen, con quién y para dónde? Mire el dibujo y complete el siguiente párrafo con la forma correcta de **salir + de, salir + para** o **salir + con.**

1. Javier y Marcelo son amigos. Ellos ________ la casa de Javier. ________ el cine. Javier siempre ________ Marcelo los domingos por la tarde.

Ahora complete el siguiente párrafo de acuerdo con sus propias actividades y su propio horario. Compare sus respuestas con las de su compañero/a.

2. Yo ________ casa a las ________ de la mañana. ________ la universidad. Llego a la universidad a las ________. Las clases terminan a las ________. A esa hora ________ casa. Por las noches ________ mi novio/a.

1. Find out the following information about your partner's family: a) who sets the table, b) who prepares breakfast, c) who makes the beds, and d) what time each family member leaves the house.
2. **Role A:** You are Cinderella **(Cenicienta)** and decide to see a family counselor. Answer in detail all the counselor's questions regarding your family and your relationship with the different family members. Tell him/her: a) that you have two step sisters and describe their different personalities, b) that your step mother is not nice to you and explain why, and c) that your father is dead **(está muerto)**. Then, d) inform him/her of all the work you do at home and e) about your plans for the future.

   Role B: You are a family counselor. Cinderella has come to ask for advice. To help, you must gather the following information from her: a) the number of family members, b) what they are like, d) the things she does at home, and d) her plans for the future.

4. *Hace* with expressions of time

- To say that an action/state began in the past and continues into the present, use **hace** + *length of time* + **que** + present tense.

  Hace dos horas que juegan. *They've been playing for two hours.*

- If you begin the sentence with the present tense of the verb, do not use **que**.

  Trabajan hace dos horas. *They've been working for two hours.*

- To find out how long an action/state has been taking place, use **cuánto tiempo** + **hace que** + *present tense.*

  ¿Cuánto tiempo hace que juegan? *How long have they been playing?*

¿Qué dice usted?

4-23 Para conocernos mejor. Complete las siguientes oraciones según sus experiencias personales. Después compare sus respuestas con las de su compañero/a.

1. Estudio español hace. . .
2. Mi programa favorito de televisión es. . .
   Veo ese programa hace. . .
3. Hace. . . que tengo un gato/perro
4. Tengo un auto/bicicleta/motocicleta hace. . .
   Mi auto/bicicleta/motocicleta es. . .

4-24 Entrevista. Hágale las siguientes preguntas a su compañero/a. Comparta la información con la clase.

1. ¿Dónde vives? ¿Cuánto tiempo hace que vives allí?
2. ¿Dónde trabaja tu padre/madre? ¿Cuánto tiempo hace que trabaja allí?
3. ¿Cuánto tiempo hace que estudias en esta universidad?
   ¿Y por qué estudias español?
4. ¿Practicas algún deporte *(sport)*? ¿Cuánto tiempo hace que juegas al. . . ?
   ¿Juegas bien?

You are a new student at the university and your parents are coming to visit you. Since you are not familiar with the area, ask your friend about the good Colombian restaurant where he/she usually goes. Ask a) how long he/she has been going to this restaurant, b) what Columbian dishes they serve (**ajiaco de pollo, papas chorreadas, arroz con coco**) and how much they cost, and c) thank him/her for the information. Your friend will answer giving as much information as possible.

ALGO MÁS

Some reflexive verbs and pronouns

REFLEXIVES		
yo	**me lavo**	*I wash myself*
tú	**te lavas**	*you wash yourself*
Ud.	**se lava**	*you wash yourself*
él/ella	**se lava**	*he/she washes himself/herself*

- Reflexive verbs are those that express what people do to or for themselves.

REFLEXIVE

Mi hermana **se lava**. — *My sister washes herself.* (She is the doer and the receiver.)

NON-REFLEXIVE

Mi hermana **lava** el auto. — *My sister washes the car.* (She is the doer and the car is the receiver.)

- A reflexive pronoun refers back to the subject of the sentence. In English this may be expressed by pronouns ending in *-self* or *-selves*; in many cases, Spanish uses reflexives where English does not.

Yo **me levanto, me baño, me seco** y **me visto** rápidamente. — *I get up, take a shower, dry myself, and get dressed quickly*

- Place reflexive pronouns after the word **no** in negative constructions.

Tú **no te peinas** por la mañana. — *You don't comb your hair in the morning.*

- The pronoun **se** attached to the end of an infinitive shows that the verb is reflexive:

lavar — *to wash*
lavarse — *to wash oneself*

¿Qué dice usted?

4-25 **La rutina diaria de mi compañero/a.** Indique con un número (1, 2, 3, . . .) el orden en que usted cree que su compañero/a hace las siguientes acciones. Después verifique el orden con él/ella.

_____ desayuna
_____ se peina
_____ se seca
_____ se levanta
_____ sale
_____ se baña
_____ se viste

4-26 **¿Qué hace?** Cada uno escoja un miembro de su familia de quién le gustaría (*would like*) hablar. Luego, intercambien preguntas sobre las actividades de este pariente y llenen la tabla.

Miembro de la familia ________________

SE LEVANTA	7:00 A.M.	8:00 A.M.	?
DESAYUNA	HORA	COMIDA	BEBIDA
SE BANA	MANANA	TARDE	NOCHE
ACTIVIDADES	LAVAR EL COCHE	HACER LA CAMA	PONER LA MESA
SALE PARA	TRABAJO	UNIVERSIDAD	?

mosaicos

A ESCUCHAR

A. Un bautizo. Look at the following christening announcement. Answer the questions that you hear based on the announcement.

1. ______________________
2. ______________________
3. ______________________
4. ______________________
5. ______________________
6. ______________________

Raquel María

Nació en Santafé de Bogotá
el día 11 de octubre de 1999.

Padres:

Mónica Caicedo Torres
Rafael Mejía Jaramillo

Padrinos:

Ana María Ordóñez Montoya
Álvaro Morales Restrepo

Bautizada por el

Rev. Padre Miguel Urrutia
en la Capilla del Liceo de Cervantes
el día 6 de noviembre de 1999

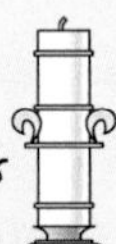

B. Un mensaje telefónico. Listen to the message Pedro left on Julio's answering machine. First, read the questions. You may wish to take notes of key information as you listen. Do not worry if you don't understand every word.

1. La fiesta va a ser en casa de
   a. Ana María.
   b. Pedro.
   c. un amigo de Pedro.
2. La fiesta va a empezar
   a. a las siete y media.
   b. a las nueve, más o menos.
   c. después de las diez.
3. Según el mensaje, Julio debe llevar *(take)* a la fiesta
   a. unos discos.
   b. algo para la comida.
   c. los refrescos.
4. Pedro dice en su mensaje que Julio
   a. no debe llegar temprano a la fiesta.
   b. debe comprar los refrescos.
   c. no debe hablar con Ana María sobre la fiesta.
5. La fiesta va a ser en la calle
   a. 157.
   b. 12.
   c. Real.

4-27 Entrevista. Pregúntele a su compañero/a a qué miembro de su familia asocia con los siguientes comentarios.

MODELO: Bebe cerveza frecuentemente después del trabajo.
E1: ¿Quién en tu familia bebe cerveza frecuentemente después del trabajo?
E2: Mi tío Ramón.

1. Es fanático/a del trabajo.
2. Es muy tranquilo/a.
3. Prefiere salir con amigos y no estar en casa.
4. Juega mucho con los niños.
5. Hace ejercicio (*exercises*) tres o cuatro veces a la semana.
6. Oye música a todas horas.

4-28 ¿Familias semejantes o familias diferentes? Primera fase. Háganse preguntas para averiguar lo siguiente:

- actividades típicas de sus padres durante los fines de semana
- actividades usuales de sus hermanos/as durante los fines de semana
- planes de la familia para las próximas vacaciones o día feriado (*holiday*)

Segunda fase. Escoja un/a compañero/a diferente y comparta la información obtenida en la **Primera fase.**

- Semejanzas y diferencias entre sus familias con respecto a las actividades del fin de semana.
- Semejanzas y diferencias entre sus familias sobre cómo pasan las vacaciones o celebran los días feriados.
- Clasificación de sus familias con respecto a la forma en que usan su tiempo libre: (muy/un poco) tranquila, tradicional, divertida, etc. ¿Son semejantes o diferentes?

4-29 Adivina, adivinador. Piense en una familia famosa de una serie de televisión. Descríbale a su compañero/a los miembros de la familia y qué hacen en un episodio típico del programa. Su compañero/a debe adivinar qué familia es.

A LEER

4-30 Preparación. Mire esta fotografía y responda a las preguntas con un/a compañero/a.

1. ¿Es buena o mala la relación entre este niño y su padre? ¿Por qué?
2. ¿Dónde están el niño y su padre?
3. Probablemente, ¿de qué conversan?
4. ¿Cuántos años tienen los padres del niño probablemente?
5. ¿Describa al niño y a su padre ?

4-31 Asociación. Indique con cuáles de las siguientes palabras asocia usted el arte en general (A), la música en particular (M), o ambos (AM).

1. ___ la inspiración
2. ___ la partitura (*score*)
3. ___ los colores
4. ___ la imaginación
5. ___ la perseverancia
6. ___ la armonía
7. ___ el prodigio

4-32 Preparación. Observe la fotografía y conteste a las siguientes preguntas.

1. ¿Cuántos años tiene esta niña probablemente?
2. ¿Qué instrumento toca?
3. ¿Qué parte de su cuerpo (*body*) necesita ella para tocar este instrumento?
4. ¿Qué lee la niña para tocar el piano?
5. En su opinión, ¿es fácil o difícil tocar el piano?

4-33 Anticipación. Lea el título del siguiente texto y responda a estas preguntas.

1. ¿Qué tema se presenta en el siguiente texto probablemente?
2. ¿Qué palabra(s) del título indica(n) el tema?
3. ¿Cuál es la diferencia entre las palabras "sí"y "si"?

Métodos de enseñanza importados de Japón convierten la música en un juego para los más pequeños.

por R.M.E.

No son niños prodigios, ni superdotados, pero a los tres años ya comienzan a tocar un instrumento, a formar parte de una orquesta y a sentir el ritmo. Con la ayuda de sus padres que son sus profesores más cercanos, utilizando el mismo sistema del lenguaje materno, estos pequeños aprenden con toda espontaneidad a leer las partituras. De este modo, cada clase se convierte en un juego apasionante y el mundo entero se transforma en una maravillosa lección de armonía.

4-34 Primera etapa. Indique. . .

1. **dos características** que *no* tienen los niños que toman estas clases.
2. **dos maneras** (*ways*) en que la vida de estos niños cambia *(changes)* cuando tocan un instrumento.
3. **dos palabras** que demuestran la fascinación de los niños por sus clases de música.

Los bebés de ocho meses observan con maravillosa sorpresa la evolución de los sonidos que bailan en una melodía de cascabeles[1]. Viven inmersos en un mundo dominado por la armonía y en la alegría de este inmenso juego adquieren un lenguaje musical preciso, mientras se configura su sensibilidad y capacidad de concentración.

Todos estos niños van a desarrollar el oído[2] al cien por cien y los resultados obtenidos a lo largo de estos años se pueden calificar de revolucionarios. A los tres años ya empiezan a tocar distintos instrumentos y aprenden a leer las partituras con total espontaneidad.

1. *rattle* 2. *ear*

4-35 Segunda etapa. Subraye (*underline*) la respuesta correcta, de acuerdo con el contenido de la lectura.

1. Los niños empiezan el contacto con la música: cuando son bebés/ cuando tienen tres años.
2. Dos aspectos de la vida de estos niños que se desarrollan con la música son: las matemáticas y el baile/ la sensibilidad y la concentración.
3. Dos actividades que estos niños pueden realizar a los tres años son: tocar instrumentos y leer música/ bailar y escribir partituras.

Disciplina y constancia

"Este método también se llama 'de la lengua materna'", explica Keka Cano, Presidenta de la Asociación del Método Suzuki de la Comunidad de Madrid. Nació en Japón y su creador fue el doctor Suzuki un violinista japonés que estudió en Alemania.

Está probado que este método de enseñanza les proporciona una serie de capacidades que les ayudará a lo largo de la vida. "Sin duda, podemos hacer referencia a la concentración, la memoria o el oído musical", manifiesta esta joven profesora con diez años de experiencia. "Además, en la práctica de un instrumento, es fundamental la disciplina, la constancia y esto les servirá siempre."

4-36 Tercera etapa. Complete la información según la lectura.

1. El creador del método es de origen __________.
2. El método Suzuki ayuda al desarrollo de las siguientes capacidades: __________, _________ o ______________.
3. Dos características muy importantes para aprender a tocar un instrumento son _________ y ____________.

Padres en crisis

Al principio, las clases se destinan principalmente al padre y, según empieza a estar preparado, el niño adquiere un rol mayor. Pero cuando los pequeños crecen y pueden asistir a clases solos, muchos padres pasan por una crisis. "¡Es que lo hemos hecho todo juntos!"

Los niños y los instrumentos crecen al mismo tiempo y dan lugar a una divertida compraventa[3] de violines en un improvisado mercadillo[4] musical. El primer violín, poco más grande que la palma de la mano, se conserva como un pequeño tesoro de la infancia.

Valorar la creatividad

"Los padres asisten también a clase y se plantea la enseñanza de la música de un modo divertido. Los niños se lo pasan tan bien[5] que cuando están enfermos tienen verdaderas peleas[6] porque no quieren estar ausentes. Asisten un día por semana y la clase es un grupo, porque los padres y niños se hacen amigos entre ellos, y el ambiente es muy agradable".

3. sales 4. small (open-air) market 5. have such a great time 6. arguments

4-37 Cuarta etapa. Indique si lo siguiente es cierto (**C**) o falso (**F**). Si es falso, indique cuál es la información correcta.

1. ____ Los padres pasan por una crisis al comienzo porque sus hijos se hacen (*become*) más independientes con el tiempo.
2. ____ Los niños usan otros instrumentos cuando son más grandes.
3. ____ Los niños venden su primer instrumento musical porque necesitan dinero.
4. ____ Sólo los niños pueden ir a clases de música.
5. ____ Las clases son aburridas y por eso los niños prefieren no ir.
6. ____ El ambiente de la clase de música es muy bueno.

4-38 Identificación. Encuentre en el texto los sustantivos *(nouns)* asociados con los siguientes verbos. Luego subraye la terminación.

VERBO	SUSTANTIVO	VERBO	SUSTANTIVO
1. enseñar	__________	5. oír	__________
2. jugar	__________	6. crear	__________
3. evolucionar	__________	7. practicar	__________
4. concentrar(se)	__________	8. pelear	__________

A ESCRIBIR

4-39 Preparación. Primera fase. Lea la siguiente carta que le escribe Julián, un alumno universitario colombiano, a su madre.

Querida mamá:

¿Qué tal están tú y papá? ¿Cómo está Mario? Espero que bien.

Bueno, te escribo estas líneas para comunicarte algunos de mis planes. Como tú sabes, estamos casi a fin de semestre, con toneladas de exámenes y trabajos de investigación. Como estoy nervioso, como mucho y estoy un poco gordo. También me siento super cansado, por eso necesito tomar unas vacaciones antes de los exámenes finales.

Bueno, todo no puede ser negativo en la vida, ¿no crees? Tengo una nueva amiga, Alicia. Paso mucho tiempo con ella cada día; vamos al cine juntos, paseamos por el parque de la universidad, salimos a los bares por las noches, etc. Me gusta mucho Alicia, por eso pienso ir a Cartagena con ella por unos días, pero no tengo dinero. Tú sabes que los hoteles son caros allí. ¿Puedes enviarme un cheque por 100.000 pesos para cubrir nuestra comida y el hotel?

Otro favor: en la playa hace mucho calor en este momento, por eso necesito ropa para la playa. Por favor, cómprame ropa informal pero elegante. ¡Quiero impresionar a Alicia! Es una chica fascinante y quiero ser su novio en el futuro. ¡Por favor no olvides mi perfume favorito!

Te prometo que voy a estudiar en Cartagena. Si hay problemas en alguno de mis exámenes, puedo estudiar durante el verano y tomar los exámenes nuevamente el próximo semestre, ¿no crees?

Un beso para ti, papá y Mario. Pienso llamarte por teléfono desde Cartagena, si puedo.

Abrazos,
Julián

Segunda fase. Piense que usted es la madre de Julián. Después de leer la carta de su hijo, usted está muy enojada con él. Identifique por lo menos cuatro problemas que tiene Julián. Escriba dos recomendaciones para cada problema.

MODELO: Mi hijo es irresponsable. Debe pensar en sus estudios primero. Debe dedicar más tiempo a sus clases y menos tiempo a Alicia.

4-40 Manos a la obra. Responda a la carta de Julián. Incorpore las notas de la **Segunda fase.**

Vocabulario útil para comenzar una carta a un familiar:

- Querido/a (nombre):
- Querido hijo/a:
- Mi amor:

Vocabulario útil para despedirse cariñosamente *(affectionately)* de un familiar:

- Con mucho cariño,
- Abrazos y besos,
- Te recuerdo (*I remember you* [familiar]) con cariño,

4-41 Revisión. Antes de darle su carta a su compañero/a editor/a, revise:

- primero, la coherencia de sus ideas y la cantidad de información que el lector necesita de usted.
- luego, la precisión gramatical (el vocabulario apropiado al contexto, la estructura de las oraciones, la concordancia).
- finalmente, la ortografía y la acentuación.

Vocabulario*

La familia

la abuela	*grandmother*
el abuelo	*grandfather*
el/la ahijado/a	*godchild*
la esposa	*wife*
el esposo	*husband*
la hermana	*sister*
el hermano	*brother*
la hija	*daughter*
el hijo	*son*
hijo/a único/a	*only child*
la madrastra	*stepmother*
la madre	*mother*
la madrina	*godmother*
la mamá	*mom*
la media hermana	*half sister*
el medio hermano	*half brother*
la nieta	*granddaughter*
el nieto	*grandson*
la novia	*fiancée, girlfriend*
el novio	*fiancé, boyfriend*
el padrastro	*stepfather*
el padre	*father*
los padres	*parents*
el padrino	*godfather*
el papá	*dad*
los parientes	*relatives*
el/la primo/a	*cousin*
la sobrina	*niece*
el sobrino	*nephew*
la tía	*aunt*
el tío	*uncle*

Verbos

almorzar (ue)	*to have lunch*
bañar(se)	*to take a bath, to bathe*
casarse	*to get married*
cerrar (ie)	*to close*
correr	*to run*
costar (ue)	*to cost*
decir (g, i)	*to say, tell*
desayunar	*to have breakfast*
dormir (ue)	*to sleep*
dormir la siesta	*to take a nap*
empezar (ie)	*to begin, start*
entender (ie)	*to understand*
hacer (g)	*to do, to make*
hacer la cama	*to make the bed*
jugar (ue)	*to play* (game, sport)
lavar(se)	*to wash* (oneself)
levantarse	*to get up*
oír (g)	*to hear*
pasar	*to spend* (time)
pasear	*to take a walk, to stroll*
pedir (i)	*to ask for*
peinar(se)	*to comb*
pensar (ie)	*to think*
pensar + inf.	*to plan to* + verb
poder (ue)	*to be able to, can*
poner (g)	*to put, to turn on*
poner la mesa	*to set the table*
preferir (ie)	*to prefer*
querer (ie)	*to want*
repetir (i)	*to repeat*
salir (g)	*to leave*
secar(se)	*to dry* (oneself)
seguir (i)	*to follow, to go on*
servir (i)	*to serve*
tener (g, ie)	*to have*
traer (g)	*to bring*
venir (g, ie)	*to come*
vestir(se) (i)	*to dress, to get dressed*
visitar	*to visit*
volver (ue)	*to return*

Descripciones

divorciado/a	*divorced*
gemelo/a	*twin*
ocupado/a	*busy*

Palabras y expresiones útiles

el bautizo	*baptism, christening*
la foto (grafía)	*photo*
junto a	*next to*
juntos/as	*together*
el/la mayor	*the oldest*
el/la menor	*the youngest*
la noticia	*news*
tarde	*late*
temprano	*early*
un poco	*a little*

* A list of adverbs can be found on page 136.

The following words appear in the directions of the various activities in this lesson. They are listed here for recognition only. You should become familiar with them since they will appear in activity directions from now on.

Palabras generales

cada	*each*
la cosa	*thing*
derecha	*right*
el dibujo	*drawing*
izquierda	*left*
mismo/a	*same*
la oración	*sentence*
el párrafo	*paragraph*
la pregunta	*question*
propio/a	*own*
la respuesta	*answer*
siguiente	*following*
la tabla	*chart*

Verbos

asociar	*to associate*
averiguar	*to find out*
completar	*to complete*
compartir	*to share*
contestar	*to answer*
entrevistar	*to interview*
escoger	*to choose*
explicar	*to explain*
intercambiar	*to exchange*
preguntar	*to ask a question*
responder	*to answer*
saber	*to know*
subrayar	*to underline*
turnarse	*to take turns*

La familia hispana

Para pensar

¿Tiene Ud. una familia grande o pequeña? ¿Quiénes forman parte de su familia? ¿Dónde viven? ¿Con qué frecuencia se ven? ¿Quiénes trabajan fuera de la casa? ¿Quiénes se ocupan de los quehaceres domésticos?

La familia es una de las instituciones sociales más importantes en el mundo hispano. La mayor parte de las actividades sociales, almuerzos, paseos, fiestas, etc., se realizan siempre con la familia. Antes, la familia nuclear era grande y estaba formada por los padres y tres o cuatro hijos. Además, la familia también incluía los abuelos, tíos y sobrinos y muchas veces todos vivían en la misma casa. Ahora, la familia hispana es más pequeña y aunque todavía muchas familias viven con los abuelos, tíos y sobrinos, esto ya no es tan común como antes. Hoy en día, debido a la mayor frecuencia de los divorcios o a la separación de los padres, también hay muchas familias donde existe la figura del padrastro o madrastra.

En la familia tradicional del pasado sólo los hombres trabajaban fuera de la casa y las mujeres tenían la responsabilidad de los quehaceres domésticos y de la crianza (*upbringing*) de los niños. En la actualidad, en muchas familias las mujeres también trabajan fuera de la casa, y además deben hacer las labores domésticas; sin embargo, entre las parejas jóvenes es cada vez más frecuente compartir las tareas. En las familias hispanoamericanas de clase media y clase media alta, es común tener un/a empleado/a, o más, que ayuda con la cocina, la limpieza de la casa y el cuidado de los niños.

Además de los abuelos, tíos y primos hay otras personas que forman parte de la familia hispana. Éstas son los padrinos, los amigos íntimos de los padres, a quienes se les llama cariñosamente "tíos", y los hijos de éstos, a quienes se les llama "primos" en algunos lugares. La vida social en los países hispanos es generalmente una vida en familia, con abuelos, nietos, padrinos, tíos y primos, todos en las mismas reuniones y las mismas fiestas. La familia hispana tiene una larga tradición de ser numerosa y unida.

Para contestar

Las familias. Con su compañero/a haga las siguientes actividades.

1. Compare la familia hispana tradicional y la moderna en cuanto a tamaño, miembros de la familia, división del trabajo, etc.
2. Compare la familia hispana moderna y la familia norteamericana en cuanto a tamaño, miembros, división del trabajo, etc.
3. Aparte del núcleo familiar, ¿qué otras personas forman parte de la 'familia' hispana?

Una reunión familiar

ENFOQUE CULTURAL

The *Enfoque cultural* is available in an interactive online format at *www.prenhall.com/mosaicos*

Riqueza cultural. En grupos pequeños mencionen tres ventajas y tres desventajas de vivir con los abuelos, tíos y primos en una misma casa.

Para investigar en la WWW

1. Vaya a la página de Mosaicos en la Internet *www.prenhall.com/mosaicos*. Busque anuncios de bautizos, matrimonios o avisos fúnebres. Haga una lista de los miembros de la familia que se mencionan. Imprima los anuncios más interesantes para compartir con sus compañeros de clase.
2. Compare esos anuncios con los que aparecen en el periódico de su comunidad. Puede basarse en lo siguiente:
   - familiares que se mencionan
   - orden de presentación de los familiares
   - tono de los anuncios (¿formal/informal?) Subraye las palabras que denotan el tono.

El barrio de la Candelaria en Bogotá, Colombia

Colombia

Ciudades importantes y lugares de interés:

Bogotá, la capital, con seis millones de habitantes, es una hermosa ciudad de muchos contrastes: tiene zonas de gran riqueza y otras de gran pobreza, zonas muy modernas y zonas antiguas. Un barrio muy interesante es el barrio de La Candelaria, donde se pueden ver muchas casas e iglesias coloniales. Entre los museos, el más famoso es el Museo del Oro, que tiene la colección más grande del mundo de objetos de oro de la época precolombina. Cerca de Bogotá están las minas de sal de Zipaquirá, y allí se encuentra, dentro de una montaña, una de las catedrales más grandes del mundo, con la peculiaridad de que sus columnas, paredes y estatuas son de sal. Medellín, en la parte occidental de Colombia, es un importante centro industrial y comercial. Cartagena, en la costa del Caribe, es una ciudad de gran belleza colonial y también un lugar donde jóvenes y adultos pueden disfrutar de hermosas playas y diversiones.

Un componente muy importante en todas las fiestas y celebraciones colombianas es su maravillosa música donde se aprecia la mezcla de tres culturas: la indígena, la africana y la española. La cumbia, por ejemplo, es uno de los géneros musicales más importantes que se asocian con Colombia. Tradicionalmente la mujer sostiene una vela en la mano derecha y lleva una falda larga que mueve al compás de la música, mientras el hombre baila alrededor de ella. Otro género musical colombiano es el vallenato que, como la cumbia, surgió en la costa del Atlántico y es también muy popular en el mundo hispano. Si quiere saber más sobre música colombiana y festivales musicales en los Estados Unidos y en América Latina, visite *www.prenhall.com/mosaicos*.

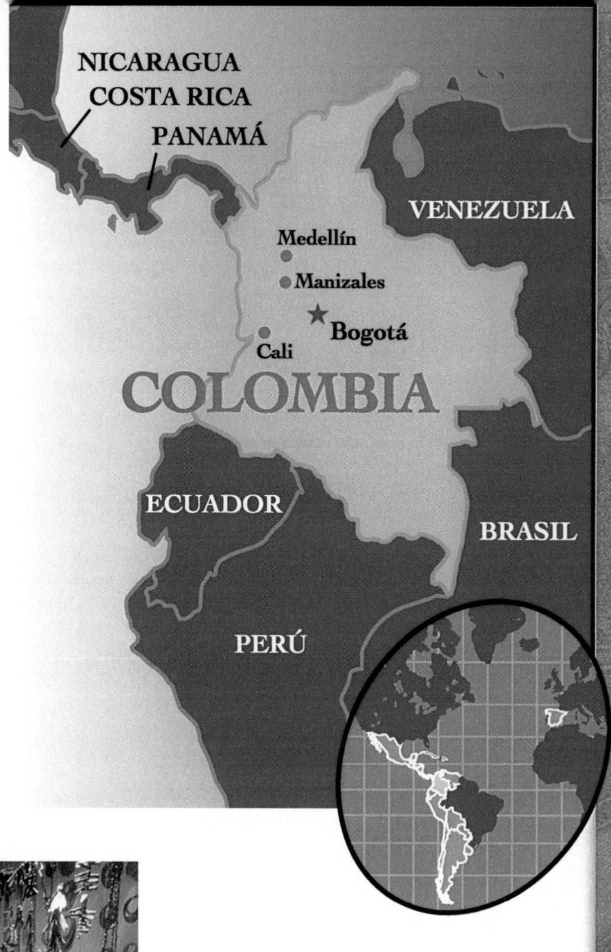

El Museo del Oro, Bogotá, Colombia

Expresiones colombianas:

No puedo ir al cine. Tengo mucho camello.	*I can't go to the movies. I have a lot of work.*
Te voy a poner un pereque.	*I'm going to ask you a favor.*
Él no tiene afán (no está de afán).	*He is in no hurry.*
Sacar una A en español es difícil. Eso no es soplar y hacer botellas.	*To get an A in Spanish is hard. It is not as easy as it looks.*

ENFOQUE INTERACTIVO

A MIRAR EL VIDEO 5:00

Watch the *Fortunas* video segment for *Lección 4* in class or on your CD-ROM. Why are Sabrina and Efraín looking at Tito's video camera? Do they have an alliance of their own?

Now complete the accompanying video activities on the CD-ROM. This is your chance to interact with the video characters! **25:00**

Sabrina y Efraín

El concurso

The first *misterio* has been solved, and now the contestants are searching for the second. Don't worry if your favorite character is behind. There are still six *misterios* and three *fortunas* to be found. The contestants' goal is to win and your goal is to have fun along with them, using the clues to solve each *misterio*. Remember, all of the *misterios* and *fortunas* relate to the culture and history of Mexico and the New World, and are located in Mexico City.

PISTAS

Distribución

For the initial *misterio* each contestant will receive one *pista.* The contestant who solves the first *misterio* will receive an additional *pista* for the next *misterio.* If an alliance is formed between two or three contestants to solve a *misterio,* they will receive a total of three *pistas* for the next *misterio.* Contestants who fail to solve a *misterio* will only receive one *pista.*

LA BÚSQUEDA 5:00

Because they solved the first *misterio*, Katie and Carlos now have three *pistas* (*1*, *3*, and *4*) for the second *misterio*. They also have momentum and, perhaps, a bit of chemistry on their side. How did you do in the first *misterio*? Had you already figured out that each clue alluded to one of the four acts of creation in the Aztec creation myth, and that "*Cinco es suficiente*" referred to the fifth and final act? Go to the *Fortunas* module and see if you can solve the second *misterio* before the contestants do.

Misterio Nº 2: La cuna de las culturas

Pistas

1. *Peregrinaje*
2. *Éxodo*
3. *Comenzar de nuevo*
4. *Águila y serpiente*

¿QUÉ OPINA USTED? 5:00

The points have been awarded for the first *misterio* and the first three viewer polls. Remember, your vote each week helps determine the outcome of the contest. Please go to the *Fortunas* module and click on *¿Qué opina usted?* to answer this episode's viewer poll and to help your favorite contestant move up in the standings.

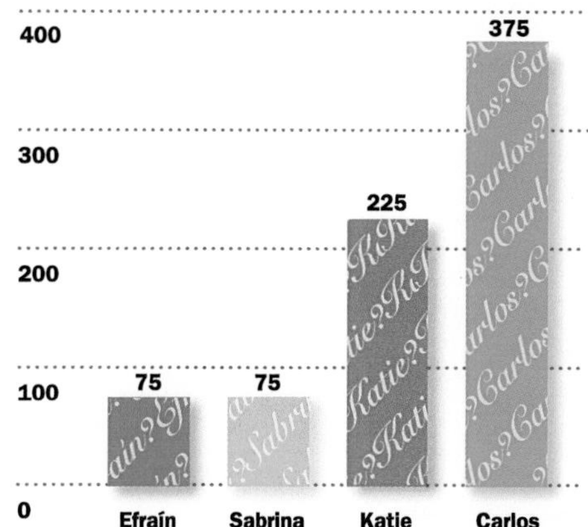

PARA NAVEGAR 10:00

COLOMBIA

Colombia es un país de ricas tradiciones artísticas. En particular, en el país hay una larga y profunda tradición literaria y musical. El colombiano Gabriel García Márquez, autor de *Cien años de soledad*, ganó el Premio Nobel de Literatura en 1982.

Gabriel García Márquez

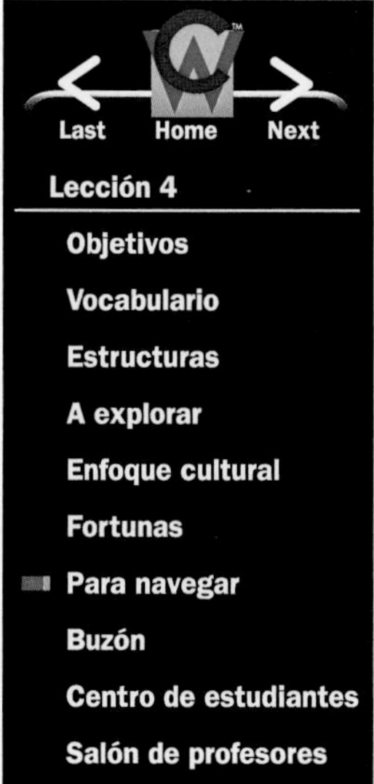

Go to the *Mosaicos Website* and click on the *Para navegar* module to explore links to Colombia. Read about the country's rich artistic tradition and history, and explore some of its exciting dimensions.

Lección 5

La casa y los muebles

COMUNICACION

- Asking about and describing housing and household items
- Discussing daily activities in the home
- Asking about and discussing daily schedules
- Expressing ongoing actions
- Describing physical and emotional states
- Expressing obligation

ESTRUCTURAS

- Present progressive
- Expressions with **tener**
- Direct object nouns and pronouns
- Demonstrative adjectives and pronouns
- **Saber** and **conocer**
- ALGO MAS: More on adjectives

MOSAICOS

A ESCUCHAR

A CONVERSAR

A LEER

- Recognizing nouns derived from verbs
- Associating visuals and written descriptions
- Determining meaning of new words by identifying their parts

A ESCRIBIR

- Reporting factual data to a friend

ENFOQUE CULTURAL

- Las casas y la arquitectura
- Nicaragua, El Salvador y Honduras

ENFOQUE INTERACTIVO

A primera vista

En casa

Una casa de estilo colonial en Guatemala. Algunas personas prefieren vivir cerca del centro, generalmente en edificios de apartamentos. Creen que los barrios de las afueras están muy lejos del trabajo y de los centros de diversión.

Practice activities for each vocabulary section are provided on the CD-ROM and website (www.prenhall.com/mosaicos)

Alquilo

Apartamento Edificio Venecia, Lomas de Miraflores Sur, sala-comedor, cocina con mueble, dos dormitorios, dos baños, dormitorio y baño para empleada, portón eléctrico, estacionamiento, TV cable, L. 6,500.00. Tel. 239-3367

Bienes Raíces Su Casa

En Altos de Castaños,
moderna residencia
con piscina, vista, jardín y terraza con bar,
sala, comedor, estudio, baño visitas,
3 habitaciones, 3 baños,
cocina completa,
garaje para 2 autos,
400 mts. de construcción,
$300.000.00 o su equivalente
en lempiras.

TEL. 232-3277, 232-5551 • FAX 232-5154

Cultura

Notice that the first floor is normally called **la planta baja** in most Hispanic countries. The second floor is called **el primer piso**.

RICARDO: ¿Aló?

XIOMARA: Hola, Ricardo, ¿qué estás haciendo?

RICARDO: ¡Ay, Xiomara! Estoy trabajando en la casa, limpiando todo, el baño, la cocina, mi cuarto.

XIOMARA: Pero, ¿no tienes que estudiar para el examen de matemáticas?

RICARDO: ¡Claro que tengo que estudiar! Pero mañana mis padres regresan de sus vacaciones y tengo que tener la casa limpia y ordenada. Todo está sucio y tú sabes que mi madre es maniática con la limpieza.

XIOMARA: Sí, ya lo sé, pero es muy tarde. ¿No tienes sueño?

RICARDO: Sí, pero todavía tengo que ordenar la cocina, pasear al perro, regar las plantas. ¡Uf, para qué hablar!

Cultura

In general, Hispanic homes tend to be smaller and built more closely together than homes in the United States, but spacious homes can be found in affluent neighborhoods. Living quarters for domestic help are especially characteristic of upper middle class homes, although this has begun to disappear in new constructions.

el aire acondicionado
el dormitorio
el espejo
el armario/el clóset
la calefacción
la lámpara
la cómoda
la almohada
las sábanas
el radio
la manta
la cama
el cuarto
el pasillo
el baño
la ducha
la toalla
el inodoro
el lavabo
la bañera/bañadera
el garaje
el cuadro
el televisor
la butaca
la chimenea
el sofá
la sala
las cortinas
la silla
la mesa
la alfombra
el comedor
la escalera
el refrigerador
la estufa
el fregadero
el horno
la cocina
el jardín
la barbacoa
la terraza

¿Qué dice usted?

5-1 ¿En qué parte de la casa están? Marque con una X el lugar correcto. Después, con un/a compañero/a describa qué actividades ocurren normalmente allí.

	TERRAZA	COCINA	BANO	SALA	DORMITORIO	COMEDOR	JARDIN
estufa y lavaplatos							
barbacoa							
sofá y butacas							
mesa de comer							
toallas y jabón *(soap)*							
cama y cómoda							
televisor							
almohadas y sábanas							

5-2 El curioso. Intercambie preguntas con un/a compañero/a para averiguar cómo son los cuartos de su casa/apartamento. Traten de obtener la mayor información posible.

MODELO: E1: ¿Cómo es la sala de tu casa?
E2: Es pequeña. La alfombra es verde y hay un sofá grande, dos sillas modernas y una mesa con una lámpara. ¿Y tu dormitorio?

5-3 Entrevista. Primera fase. Intercambie preguntas con su compañero/a para averiguar los siguientes detalles sobre su casa o apartamento. Traten de obtener la mayor información posible.

1. Tipo de casa/apartamento
2. Localización de la casa/el apartamento en relación a la universidad
3. Color de la casa/el apartamento; número de cuartos y color(es)
4. Localización de los diferentes cuartos
5. Cuarto favorito de su compañero/a y por qué
6. Dos características adicionales de la casa/el apartamento

Segunda fase Cambie de pareja y comparta la información obtenida en la Primera fase. Indique las semejanzas y diferencias entre el apartamento o casa de su compañero/a y el/la suyo/a (*your own*).

5-4 Encuesta. Primera fase. En pequeños grupos intercambien las siguientes preguntas. Todos los que contestan afirmativamente, deben firmar su nombre en la columna de la derecha.

MODELO: tener un sofá en la sala
E1: ¿Tienes un sofá en la sala?
E2: Sí.
E1: Firma aquí, por favor.

1. vivir en un condominio/apartamento ________
2. ser grande la casa/el apartamento ________
3. tener aire acondicionado/calefacción central ________
4. tener terraza ________
5. tener jardín/barbacoa ________

Segunda fase. Informen al resto de la clase de los resultados obtenidos y, entre todos, discutan lo siguiente: A. Número de personas o porcentaje de la clase que vive en un condominio. B. Tres ventajas/desventajas (*advantages/disadvantages*) de vivir en un condominio.

Las tareas domésticas

Gustavo lava los platos.

Beatriz seca los platos.

Beatriz cocina. Ella usa mucho los electrodomésticos.

Gustavo limpia el baño y pasa la aspiradora.

Gustavo saca la basura.

Gustavo barre la terraza.

Beatriz tiende la ropa.

Después la dobla cuando está seca.

Beatriz plancha la ropa.

¿Qué dice usted?

5-5 Por la mañana. ¿En qué orden hace usted estas cosas? Indíquelo con un número. Luego, compare sus respuestas con las de su compañero/a.

____ lavar los platos
____ preparar el café
____ salir para la universidad
____ desayunar
____ secar los platos
____ hacer la cama

5-6 Actividades en la casa. Pregúntele a su compañero/a dónde hace estas cosas normalmente.

MODELO: E1: ¿Dónde ves televisión?
E2: Veo televisión en mi cuarto. ¿Y tú? *o*
No veo televisión.

1. dormir la siesta
2. escuchar música
3. planchar
4. estudiar para un examen
5. almorzar durante la semana
6. desayunar el fin de semana
7. vestirse
8. hablar por teléfono con su amigo/a

5-7 Preparativos. Primera fase. Usted se va a casar pronto y tiene que comprar muchos muebles y accesorios para su nueva casa. Con un/a compañero/a, haga una lista de lo que necesita. Su compañero/a le va a recordar (*to remind you*) otras cosas que tiene que comprar.

MODELO: E1: Tengo que comprar una cama nueva para el dormitorio.
E2: ¿Y no tienes que comprar sábanas y mantas?

Segunda fase. Escoja a otro/a compañero/a. Ahora usted va a ser el/la comprador/a; su compañero/a va a ser un/una dependiente/a de la mueblería. Pregúntele a su compañero/a dónde están los objetos y muebles que necesita comprar. Él/Ella le va a contestar de acuerdo con el directorio de la mueblería La Mejor en la página siguiente.

MODELO: E1: Perdón, ¿en qué piso están las lámparas?
E2: Están en el primer piso.

BIENVENIDOS A LA MEJOR

4º	• Muebles para: salitas, dormitorios juveniles de estilo clásico y moderno, muebles convertibles, sofás-cama.
3º	• Salones, comedores, dormitorios de matrimonio, muebles auxiliares de estilo moderno. Alta calidad.
2º	• Mobiliario estilo chino, muebles auxiliares de estilo clásico y provenzal.
1º	• Electrodomésticos, T.V. y equipos musicales, lámparas, muebles de cocina, galería de cuadros. Muebles para entradas de estilo clásico y moderno. Artículos de regalo. Accesorios de baño.
Planta Baja	• Salones, comedores y dormitorios de estilo clásico y moderno. Muebles para oficina y despacho.
SÓTANO	• Terraza y jardín. Muebles rústicos y coloniales, sofás-cama, muebles de caña y mimbre. Comedores ECONÓMICOS.

A ESCUCHAR

¿Dónde vivir? You will hear a conversation between a couple and a real estate agent in San Salvador. Before listening to the dialog, you may read the questions below to familiarize yourself with them. Circle the letter next to the correct information.

1. La Sra. Mena dice que la primera casa
   a. es demasiado pequeña
   b. no está en una zona buena
2. El Sr. Mena desea comprar
   a. un apartamento
   b. una casa
3. La propiedad que van a ver los Sres. Mena está cerca
   a. del trabajo
   b. de un parque
4. Esta propiedad tiene
   a. dos cuartos
   b. tres cuartos
5. El agente dice que la propiedad tiene
   a. dos baños
   b. tres baños
6. Según el agente, la propiedad cuesta
   a. 1.200.000 colones
   b. 1.300.000 colones

Explicación y expansión

1. Present progressive

	ESTAR (*to be*)	PRESENT PARTICIPLE (*-ando/-iendo*)
yo	estoy	
tú	estás	habl**ando**
Ud., él, ella	está	com**iendo**
nosotros/as	estamos	escrib**iendo**
vosotros/as	estáis	
Uds., ellos/as	están	

Practice Activities for each numbered grammar point are provided on the CD-ROM and website (www.prenhall.com/mosaicos)

- Use the present progressive to emphasize an action in progress at the moment of speaking, as opposed to a habitual action.

  Marcela **está limpiando** la casa. *Marcela is cleaning the house.* (at this moment)
  Marcela **limpia** la casa. *Marcela cleans the house.* (normally)

- Spanish does not use the present progressive to express future time, as English does; Spanish uses the present tense instead.

  Salgo mañana. *I'm leaving tomorrow.*

- Form the present progressive with the present of **estar** + *the present participle.* To form the present participle, add **-ando** to the stem of **-ar** verbs and **-iendo** to the stem of **-er** and **-ir** verbs.

  hablar → **hablando**
  comer → **comiendo**
  escribir → **escribiendo**

- When the verb stem of an **-er** or an **-ir** verb ends in a vowel, add **-yendo.**

  leer → **leyendo**
  oír → **oyendo**

- Stem-changing **-ir** verbs (**ou** → e, e → ie, e → i) change **o** → **u** and e → **i** in the present participle.

  dormir (duermo) → **durmiendo**
  sentir (siento) → **sintiendo**
  pedir (pido) → **pidiendo**

¿Qué dice usted?

5-8 La vida activa. Túrnese con un/a compañero/a para decir qué están haciendo las personas en los dibujos y lo que ustedes creen que van a hacer después.

MODELO: E1: Ellos están cantando en una fiesta.
E2: Después van a bailar y a conversar con sus amigos.

5-9 Lugares y actividades. Piense en un lugar hispano y describa cuatro cosas que están ocurriendo allí. Su compañero/a debe adivinar qué lugar es.

1. It's s the beginning of the semester and you are renting an apartment with a classmate. Your partner, playing the role of your mother/father, is on the phone with you. He/She wants to know a) how is everything at the apartment, b) who does the cooking, c) if you are eating well, d) if you are studying a lot, e) what you are doing right now, and f) other questions related to school and your social life.
2. You cannot attend a big reunion that your family is having and you feel homesick. You call home; your partner is the family member who answers the phone. a) Greet him/her, b) excuse yourself for not being there, c) find out who is at the reunion and how everyone is, and d) ask what each family member is doing right now.

2. Expressions with *tener*

- You have already seen the expression **tener... años**. Spanish uses **tener** + *noun* in many cases where English uses *to be* + *adjective*. These expressions always refer to people or animals but never to things.

	hambre		*hungry*
	sed		*thirsty*
	sueño		*sleepy*
	miedo		*afraid*
tener	**calor**	*to be*	*hot*
	frío		*cold*
	suerte		*lucky*
	cuidado		*careful*
	prisa		*in a hurry/rush*
	razón		*right, correct*

- With these expressions use **mucho(a)** to indicate very.

Tengo **mucho** calor.	*I am very hot.*
(frío, miedo, sueño, cuidado)	*(cold, afraid, sleepy, careful)*
Tienen **mucha** hambre.	*They are very hungry.*
(sed, suerte)	*(thirsty, lucky)*

- Use **tener** + **que** + *infinitive* to express obligation.

Tengo que terminar hoy.	*I have to finish today.*

- Use **hay que** + *infinitive* to express obligation without emphasizing the subject.

Hay que terminar hoy.	*It's necessary to finish today.*

¿Qué dice usted?

5-10 Asociaciones. Asocie las oraciones de la izquierda con las expresiones de la derecha.

1. ___ Mi hermano va a comer mucho.	a. Tienen sed.
2. ___ Mi hermana duerme 10 horas.	b. Tengo prisa.
3. ___ Mis primos están en el Polo Norte.	c. Tiene mucha suerte.
4. ___ Mis abuelos toman mucha agua.	d. Tiene sueño.
5. ___ Mi mamá siempre gana cuando juega a la lotería.	e. Tienen mucho frío.
6. ___ Son las 8:00 y necesito estar en casa a las 8:10.	f. Tiene hambre.

5-11 ¿Cómo están estas personas?

MODELO: Pablo tiene frío.

Pablo

Lázaro

Sixto y Daniel

Josefina

Julio

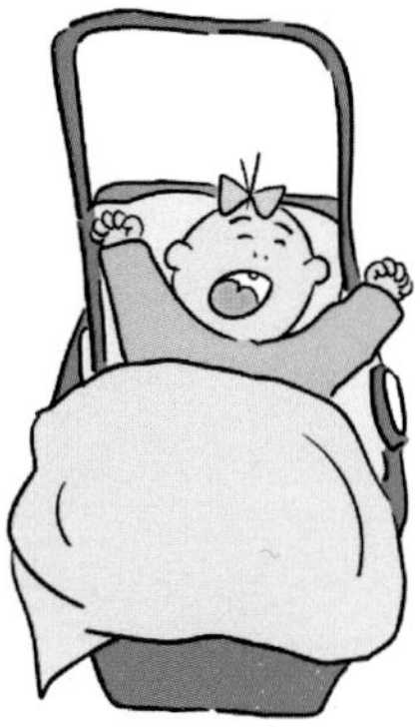

Aida

5-12 Agenda. Haga una lista de todas las cosas que tiene que hacer cada día de la semana próxima. Después intercambie información con un/a compañero/a.

MODELO: E1: ¿Qué tienes que hacer el lunes?
E2: Tengo que estudiar para el examen de matemáticas. ¿Y tú?

1. **Role A:** You share an apartment with a messy friend who is not tidy. Tell your friend that you don't like the fact that a) his/her books, backpack, etc. are always all over the living room, b) he/she leaves **(dejar)** dirty dishes in the sink, clothes in the washer, etc., and c) you have to do that extra work.

   Role B: a) Apologize by saying that you will be more careful in the future and explain how, b) suggest to your friend making a list of house chores, and c) say for which chores you will be responsible.

3. Direct object nouns and pronouns

¿Qué hacen estas personas?

¿Quién lava el **auto**?
Juan **lo** lava.

¿Quién saca **la basura**?
Alicia **la** saca.

Miguel corta el césped y su hija recoge las hojas.
¿Quién ayuda **a Miguel**?
Su hija **lo** ayuda.

- Direct object nouns and pronouns answer the question **what?** or **whom?** in relation to the verb.

¿Qué lava Pedro?	*What does Pedro wash?*
(Pedro lava) **los platos.**	*(Pedro washes) the dishes.*

- When direct object nouns refer to a specific person, a group of persons, or to a pet, the word **a** precedes the direct object. This **a** is called the personal **a** and has no equivalent in English. The personal **a** + **el** contracts to **al.**

Amanda seca **los platos.**	*Amanda dries the dishes.*
Amanda seca **a la niña.**	*Amanda dries off the girl.*
¿Ves la piscina?	*Do you see the swimming pool?*
¿Ves **al** niño en la piscina?	*Do you see the child in the swimming pool?*

- Direct object pronouns replace direct object nouns. These pronouns refer to people, animals, or things already mentioned, and are used to avoid repeating the noun.

DIRECT OBJECT PRONOUNS	
me	*me*
te	*you* (familiar, singular)
lo	*you* (formal, singular), *him, it* (masculine)
la	*you (formal, singular), her, it* (feminine)
nos	*us*
os	*you* (familiar plural, Spain)
los	*you* (formal and familiar, plural), *them* (masculine)
las	*you* (formal and familiar, plural), *them* (feminine)

- Place the direct object pronoun before the conjugated verb form.

¿Limpia Mirta **el baño**?	*Does Mirta clean the bathroom?*
No, no **lo** limpia.	*No, she doesn't clean it.*
¿Quieres mucho **a tu perro**?	*Do you love your dog a lot?*
Sí, **lo** quiero mucho.	*Yes, I love him a lot.*

- With compound verb forms, composed of a conjugated verb and an infinitive or present participle, a direct object pronoun may be placed before the conjugated verb, or be attached to the accompanying infinitive or present participle. When a direct object pronoun is attached to a present participle, a written accent is needed over the stressed vowel (the vowel before **-ndo**) of the participle.

¿Vas a ver **a Rafael**?	*Are you going to see Rafael?*
Sí, **lo** voy a ver./Sí, voy a ver**lo**.	*Yes, I'm going to see him.*
¿Están limpiando **la casa**?	*Are they cleaning the house?*
Sí, **la** están limpiando.	*Yes, they're cleaning it.*
Sí, están limpiándo**la**.	

- Since the question word **quién**(**es**) refers to people, use the personal **a** when **quién**(**es**) is used as a direct object.

¿**A quién**(**es**) vas a ver?	*Whom are you going to see?*
Voy a ver **a** Pedro.	*I'm going to see Pedro.*

ACENTOS

You have learned that words that stress the next-to the last syllable do not have a written accent if they end in a vowel: **lavando**. If we attach a direct object pronoun, the stress falls on the third syllable from the end and a written accent is needed: **lavándolo**.

¿Qué dice usted?

5-13 Mis responsabilidades en casa. Averigüe si su compañero/a es responsable de las siguientes tareas domésticas en su casa. Comparen después sus respuestas.

MODELO: sacar la basura
E1: ¿Sacas la basura?
E2: Sí, la saco./No, no la saco. ¿Y tú?

1. limpiar la cocina
2. lavar los platos
3. secar los platos
4. tender las camas
5. lavar la ropa
6. pasar la aspiradora

5-14 El apartamento de mi compañero/a. Usted va a cuidar el apartamento de su compañero/a por una semana y quiere saber cuáles son sus responsabilidades y lo que puede o no puede hacer allí.

MODELO: E1: ¿Debo sacar la basura?
E2: Sí, la debes sacar/debes sacarla todos los días.
E1: ¿Puedo usar tu estéreo?
E2: Claro que lo puedes usar.

¿DEBO O NO DEBO?	SI	NO	¿PUEDO O NO PUEDO?	SI	NO
regar las plantas	____	____	nadar en la piscina	____	____
pasear al perro	____	____	usar los electrodomésticos	____	____
limpiar el apartamento	____	____	invitar a un/a amigo/a	____	____
poner la alarma	____	____	hacer la tarea en la computadora	____	____
. . .	____	____	. . .	____	____

5-15 Los preparativos para la visita. La familia Granados está muy ocupada porque espera la visita de unos parientes. Conteste las preguntas de su compañero/a sobre lo que está haciendo cada miembro de la familia.

MODELO: E1: ¿Quién está preparando la comida?
E2: La abuela la está preparando/está preparándola.

5-16 Una mano amiga. Primera fase. Conteste las preguntas de su compañero/a sobre sus relaciones con otras personas y lo que hacen por usted.

MODELO: ayudar económicamente mis padres
E1: ¿Quién te ayuda económicamente?
E2: Mis padres me ayudan económicamente.

1. querer mucho
2. escuchar en todo momento
3. llamar por teléfono con frecuencia
4. ayudar con los problemas
5. aconsejar (*advise*) cuando estás indeciso/a
6. entender siempre

a. mi padre
b. mi madre
c. mi mejor amigo/a
d. mi novio/a
e. . . .

Segunda fase. Usted y su compañero/a deben decir ahora qué hacen por las siguientes personas. Indiquen en qué circunstancias.

MODELO: su esposo/a
E1: Lo/La ayudo cuando está cansado/a.
E2: Y yo lo/la escucho cuando tiene problemas en el trabajo.

1. su papá
2. su mamá
3. su mejor amigo/a
4. su novio/a
5. sus vecinos *(neighbors)*

SITUACIONES

Role A. You are at a furniture store buying a sofa. Tell the salesperson which sofa you want and ask him/her when they can deliver (**entregar**) it. Tell the salesperson you are not going to be home at that time, but that you can be home in the afternoon. Agree to the time and thank the salesperson.

Role B. You are a salesperson at a furniture store. Tell the customer that the sofa he/she wants is a very good one and that you can deliver it next Monday morning. Since the convenient time for the customer is the afternoon, tell him/her that you can deliver it between three and five.

4. Demonstrative adjectives and pronouns

Demonstrative adjectives

Esta silla tiene que estar aquí y esa mesa allí.

Los otros muebles están allá, en aquel edificio.

- Demonstrative adjectives agree in gender and number with the noun they modify. English has two sets of demonstratives (*this*, *these* and *that*, *those*), but Spanish has three sets.

this	**este** cuadro **esta** butaca	*these*	**estos** cuadros **estas** butacas
that	**ese** horno **esa** casa	*those*	**esos** hornos **esas** casas
that (over there)	**aquel** edificio **aquella** casa	*those* (over there)	**aquellos** edificios **aquellas** casas

LENGUA

Some Spanish speakers also use the word **este** or **pues** as pause fillers when trying to remember a word while speaking. **Voy a ver la película en el cine . . . este . . . Riviera.** What word do English speakers use in this situation?

- Use **este, esta, estos,** and **estas** when referring to people or things that are close to you in space or time.

Este escritorio es nuevo.	*This desk is new.*
Traen el sofá **esta** semana.	*They'll bring the sofa this week.*

- Use **ese, esa, esos,** and **esas** when referring to people or things that are not relatively close to you. Sometimes they are close to the person you are addressing.

Esa lámpara es muy bonita.	*That lamp is very pretty.*

- Use **aquel, aquella, aquellos,** and **aquellas** when referring to people or things that are more distant.

Aquel edificio es muy alto.	*That building (over there) is very tall.*

Demonstrative pronouns

- Demonstratives can be used as pronouns. A written accent mark may be placed on the stressed vowel to distinguish demonstrative pronouns from demonstrative adjectives.

Compran este espejo y **ése**.	*They are buying this mirror and that one.*

- To refer to a general idea or concept, or to ask for the identification of an object, use **esto, eso,** or **aquello.**

Trabajan mucho y **eso** es muy bueno.	*They work a lot and that is very good.*
¿Qué es **esto**?	*What is this?*
Es un espejo.	*It's a mirror.*

¿Qué dice usted?

5-17 En una mueblería en Managua. Usted y su compañero/a van a hacer los papeles de cliente/a y dependiente/a. El/La cliente pregunta los precios de algunos muebles y accesorios (usando los demostrativos correctos). El/La dependiente/a le hace preguntas para saber a qué se refiere.

MODELO:
CLIENTE/A: ¿Cuánto cuesta esa mesa?
DEPENDIENTE/A: ¿Cuál? ¿La mesa que está al lado de la silla?
CLIENTE/A: No, la mesa que está entre la butaca y la silla pequeña. *o* Sí, ésa.
DEPENDIENTE/A: Cuesta 750 córdobas. *o* Cuesta 2.150 córdobas.

A INVESTIGAR

¿Managua es la capital de qué país? ¿Cuál es la unidad monetaria de ese país? ¿A cuánto está el cambio (*rate of exchange*) en estos momentos?

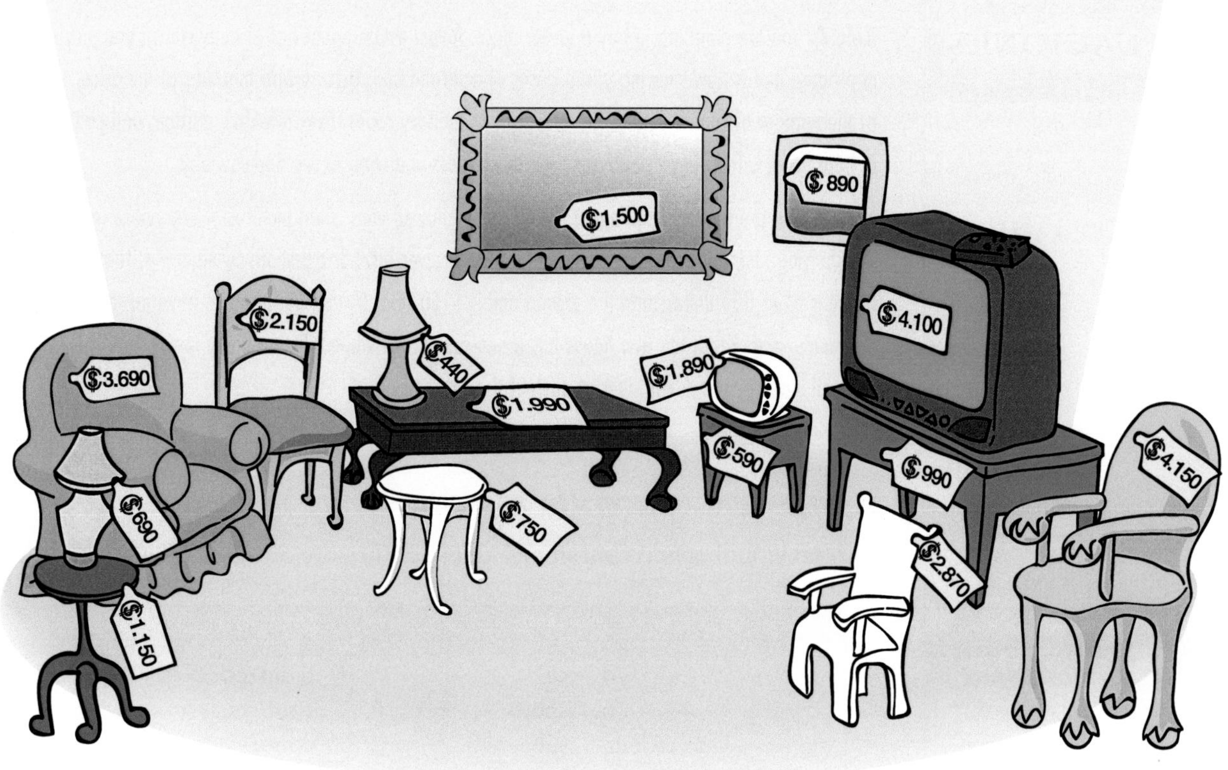

5-18 ¿De quién es? En su tiempo libre, usted y un/a compañero/a están trabajando de asistentes en una escuela primaria. Al final del día ustedes revisan el salón de clase y notan que los niños dejaron *(left)* varios objetos en diferentes lugares. Con su compañero/a, pregúntense *(ask each other)* de quién es cada objeto.

MODELO: E1: ¿De quién es este/ese/aquel bolígrafo?
E2: Éste/ése/aquél es de David. *o* Es de Miguel.

un cuaderno	unos lentes	una mochila azul	una grabadora
un libro	unos apuntes	una calculadora	unos lápices

5-19 Descripciones. Piense en un objeto o mueble y diga en qué parte de la casa está. Su compañero/a va a hacerle preguntas para adivinar qué es. Cada uno/a debe pensar en tres objetos.

MODELO: E1: Este mueble está generalmente en el comedor.
E2: ¿Es grande?
E1: Puede ser grande o pequeño.
E2: ¿Lo usamos para comer?
E1: Sí.
E2: Es la mesa.

SITUACIONES

Role A. You are planning to buy a larger place. A real estate agent has already shown you pictures of a house and is now showing you pictures of a second one. Discuss with him/her a) the price, b) the number of rooms, and c) facilities such as laundry room **(lavandería)**, garage, and pool, of both houses. Tell him/her which of the two houses you want to see and say why.

Role B. You are a real estate agent. You already showed your client pictures of one house and now are showing him/her pictures of a second house. Answer his/her questions by saying a) that the first house is $145,000 dollars and the second one is $150,000, b) that both houses have three bedrooms, and c) that the first house has a one-car garage while this one has a two-car garage. Also tell him/her the advantages of each of the two houses.

5. *Saber* and *conocer* (*to know*)

Both **saber** and **conocer** mean *to know*, but they are not used interchangeably.

ACENTOS

Sé, the **yo** form of the verb **saber,** has a written accent to distinguish it from the pronoun **se.**
Yo **sé** que su hermano **se** llama José.

	SABER	CONOCER
yo	**sé**	**conozco**
tú	**sabes**	**conoces**
Ud., él, ella	**sabe**	**conoce**
nosotros/as	**sabemos**	**conocemos**
vosotros/as	**sabéis**	**conocéis**
Uds., ellos/as	**saben**	**conocen**

- Use **saber** to express knowledge of facts or pieces of information.

  Él **sabe** dónde está el edificio. — *He knows where the building is.*

- Use **saber** + *infinitive* to express that you know how to do something.

  Yo **sé** jugar al tenis. — *I know how to play tennis.*

- Use **conocer** to express acquaintance with someone or something. **Conocer** also means *to meet.* Remember to use the personal **a** when referring to people.

  Conozco a mis vecinos. — *I know my neighbors.*
  Conozco bien ese libro. — *I am very familiar with that book.*
  Ella quiere **conocer a** Luis. — *She wants to meet Luis.*

¿Qué dice usted?

5-20 ¿Sabes quién es. . . ? Pregúntele a su compañero/a si sabe quién es la persona mencionada y si la conoce.

MODELO: el actor principal de *Misión Imposible 2*
E1: ¿Sabes quién es el actor principal de *Misión Imposible 2*?
E2: Sí, sé quién es. Es Tom Cruise.
E1: ¿Lo conoces?
E2: No, no lo conozco. *o* Sí, lo conozco.

1. tu representante en el congreso
2. el rector de la universidad
3. el/la jefe/a (*boss*) de tu papá o de tu mamá
4. el rey de España
5. el/la presidente/a de Nicaragua
6. . . .

5-21 Adivina, adivinador. En grupos pequeños, túrnense para leer las siguientes descripciones y adivinar quién es.

MODELO: E1: Es una chica muy pobre que va a un baile. Allí conoce a un príncipe, pero a las 12:00 de la noche ella debe volver a su casa.
E2: Sí, sé quién es. Es Cenicienta *(Cinderella)*.

1. Es un gorila gigante con sentimientos (*feelings*) humanos. En una película aparece en el edificio *Empire State* de Nueva York.
2. Es una cantante cubanoamericana que vive en Miami. Es joven, bonita y canta ritmos hispanos. Su marido trabaja con ella. Cantó en las Olimpiadas de 1996 en Atlanta. Actuó en una película con Meryl Streep.
3. Es una diseñadora de ropa y joyas, hija de un famoso pintor español. Su perfume más famoso lleva su nombre.
4. Es un hombre de otro planeta con doble personalidad. Trabaja en un periódico, pero cuando se pone una ropa azul especial, puede volar (*to fly*).
5. Es un hombre joven y fuerte, educado por los gorilas en la jungla. Nada muy bien y su compañera se llama Jane.
6. Es española y juega muy bien al tenis. En su familia hay otros tenistas famosos. Participa en muchos campeonatos internacionales.

5-22 ¿Qué sabes hacer? Pregúntele a su compañero/a si sabe hacer las siguientes cosas.

MODELO: bailar música rock
E1: ¿Sabes bailar música rock?
E2: Sí, sé bailar música rock. *o* No, no sé bailar música rock. ¿Y tú?

1. tocar la guitarra
2. jugar al tenis
3. nadar
4. hacer tacos
5. cocinar platos exóticos
6. trabajar con computadoras
7. usar el microondas
8. . . .

5-23 Bingo. Para ganar el Bingo, usted debe llenar vertical, horizontal o diagonalmente tres casilleros (*boxes*) con los nombres de los/las compañeros/as que contestan afirmativamente a las preguntas y dan la respuesta correcta.

¿Sabes dónde está la ciudad de Tegucigalpa?	¿Sabes cuál es la capital de El Salvador?	¿Sabes dónde está la ciudad de Managua?
¿Conoces a un estudiante de Centroamérica?	¿Sabes cuál es la unidad monetaria de Nicaragua?	¿Sabes el nombre de un lago importante en Nicaragua?
¿Sabes preparar un plato centroamericano?	¿Conoces algún país hispano?	¿Sabes dónde están las ruinas mayas de Copán?

5-24 Saber y conocer. Con su compañero/a, complete el siguiente diálogo con las formas correctas de **saber** y **conocer**.

E1: ¿_____ a esa chica?
E2: Sí, yo _____ a todas las chicas aquí.
E1: Entonces, ¿_____ dónde vive?
E2: No, no lo _____.
E1: Pero _____ su número de teléfono, ¿verdad?
E2: No, tampoco lo _____.
E1: Y. . . ¿_____ cómo se llama?
E2: Pues, la verdad es que no lo _____.
E1: ¿Cómo dices que la _____? Tú no _____ dónde vive, tú no _____ su nombre.
E2: Es que yo tengo muy mala memoria.

SITUACIONES

Your partner wants to set a blind date for you with a friend from Honduras but you want to have some information about his/her friend before agreeing on a date. Using **saber** or **conocer**, ask your partner if he/she knows a) his/her friend's family, b) how old his/her friend is, and c) how long has he/she known this friend, d) from what part of Honduras he/she comes, and e) if he/she speaks English. Also, find out if your date knows how to play tennis, and if he/she likes to dance.

ALGO MÁS

More on adjectives

- Ordinal numbers are adjectives and agree in gender and number with the noun they modify (e.g., **la segunda casa, el cuarto edificio**). **Primero** and **tercero** drop the final **o** when used before a masculine singular noun.

  el **primer** cuarto el **tercer** piso

- When **bueno** and **malo** precede masculine singular nouns, they are shortened to **buen** and **mal.**

  Es un **buen** edificio. *It's a good building.*
  Es un **mal** momento para comprar. *It's a bad time to buy.*

- **Grande** shortens to **gran** when it precedes any singular noun. Note the meaning associated with each position.

  Es una casa **grande**. *It's a big house.*
  Es una **gran** casa. *It's a great house.*

¿Qué dice usted?

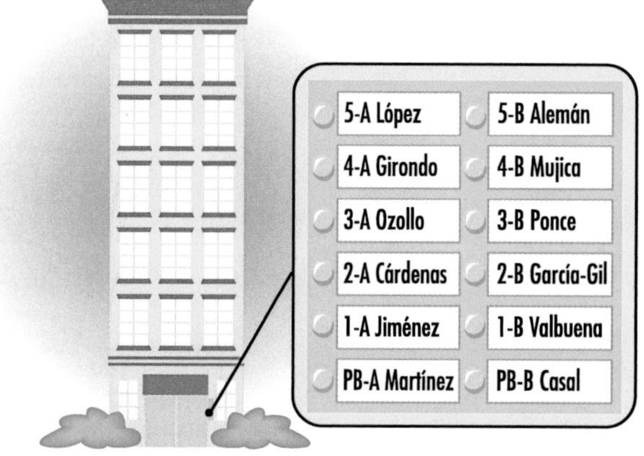

5-25 **¿En qué piso viven?** Pregúntele a su compañero/a dónde viven las diferentes personas. Su compañero/a debe contestarle de acuerdo con el dibujo.

MODELO: E1: ¿Dónde viven los Girondo?
E2: Viven en el cuarto piso, en el apartamento 4-A.

5-26 **Opiniones.** Usted y su compañero/a deben turnarse para explicar qué son o quiénes son las siguientes personas y lugares. Después deben dar su opinión sobre ellos. Usen algunas de las palabras siguientes.

buen bueno/a gran grande mal malo/a primer primero/a

MODELO: el Parque El Imposible
Es una gran reserva natural donde hay muchos animales en peligro de extinción. El Parque El Imposible está en El Salvador. Es muy grande y es una reserva natural muy importante de América Central.

1. el Parque Central
2. Antonio Banderas
3.
4. Violeta Chamorro
5. el lago Nicaragua

mosaicos

3. la Casa Blanca

A ESCUCHAR

A. ¿Lógico o ilógico? Listen to the following statements and indicate whether each is **Lógico** or **Ilógico.**

	LOGICO	ILOGICO		LOGICO	ILOGICO
1.	_____	_____	5.	_____	_____
2.	_____	_____	6.	_____	_____
3.	_____	_____	7.	_____	_____
4.	_____	_____	8.	_____	_____

B. La casa de los Pérez Esquivel. Based on the drawing below, determine whether each of the following statements is **Cierto** or **Falso.**

	CIERTO	FALSO		CIERTO	FALSO
1.	_____	_____	5.	_____	_____
2.	_____	_____	6.	_____	_____
3.	_____	_____	7.	_____	_____
4.	_____	_____	8.	_____	_____

5-27 El apartamento de mis vecinos. Usted tiene curiosidad por saber cómo es el apartamento de sus vecinos. Cubra (*Cover*) el plano y hágale preguntas a su compañero/a para obtener la siguiente información. Su compañero/a le va a contestar de acuerdo con el plano.

1. número y localización de los baños
2. localización de la cocina
3. número, tamaño y localización de los closets
4. si tiene terraza o balcón
5. . . .

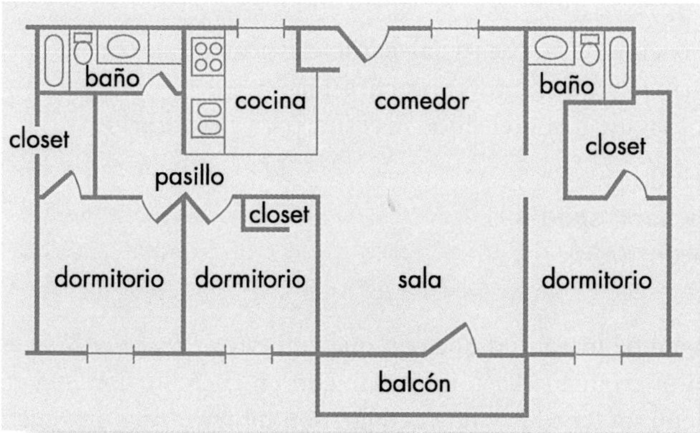

5-28 Estoy buscando apartamento. Usted necesita alquilar un apartamento. Un/a compañero/a lee los siguientes anuncios en un periódico. Hágale preguntas a su compañero/a para obtener la siguiente información:

1. alquiler
2. localización
3. piso
4. número de habitaciones
5. número de baños
6. con muebles o sin muebles
7. aire acondicionado
8. otras características
9. número de teléfono o dirección de contacto

ALQUILERES
Se alquila apartamento en zona céntrica, cuarto piso: amueblado, 2 habitaciones, 2 baños, 5.000 colones mensuales. Tfno. 2 33 14 78
Se arrienda apartamento espacioso para familia: quinto piso, ascensor, excelente ubicación, cerca de centros comerciales, sin muebles, 3 dormitorios, dos baños, aire acondicionado, jardín, garaje para dos autos. 6.500 colones. Tfno. 2 54 22 83

5-29 La casa o apartamento ideal. Describan cada uno/a de ustedes su casa o apartamento ideal. Incluyan los siguientes datos en su descripción:

- la ciudad o pueblo (*town*) donde va a tener este apartamento o casa
- los cuartos y/o comodidades (*comforts*) que va a tener
- los muebles y accesorios
- la(s) persona(s) que va(n) a vivir con usted

¿Tienen usted y su compañero/a gustos similares o diferentes? Expliquen.

A LEER

5-30 Preparación. Entreviste a un/a compañero/a y averigüe lo siguiente:

1. si le gusta la cocina de su casa y las características de su cocina
2. si le gusta cocinar y qué plato(s) prepara bien
3. cuál(es) de los siguientes utensilios necesita para prepararlo:

   _____ un cuchillo (*knife*)
   _____ una cuchara (*spoon*)
   _____ un tenedor (*fork*)

5-31 Etiqueta de mesa. Indique con qué cubiertos *(silverware)* se comen los siguientes platos en una situación formal: con un cuchillo, con una cuchara, con un tenedor, con un tenedor y un cuchillo, con un tenedor y una cuchara. Compare sus respuestas con las de su compañero/a.

1. el pollo: ______________________
2. la ensalada de tomate: ______________________
3. la sopa: ______________________
4. las enchiladas: ______________________
5. el arroz: ______________________
6. el mango: ______________________
7. las quesadillas: ______________________
8. los espaguetis: ______________________

5-32 Primera mirada. Observe la fotografía y luego escriba el número del utensilio al lado de su descripción.

_____ **Embudo.** Es muy útil para pasar líquidos de un recipiente a otro.

_____ **Rallador.** De metal es mejor. Sirve para rallar el queso que ponemos sobre los espaguetis. También sirve para rallar pan, cebolla, etc.

_____ **Sacacorchos.** Un poquito de vino da más sabor a sus platos. Antes de servir vino es necesario sacar el corcho de la botella con este utensilio.

_____ **Cuencos.** Es conveniente tener pequeños, medianos y grandes, especialmente para preparar y servir ensaladas.

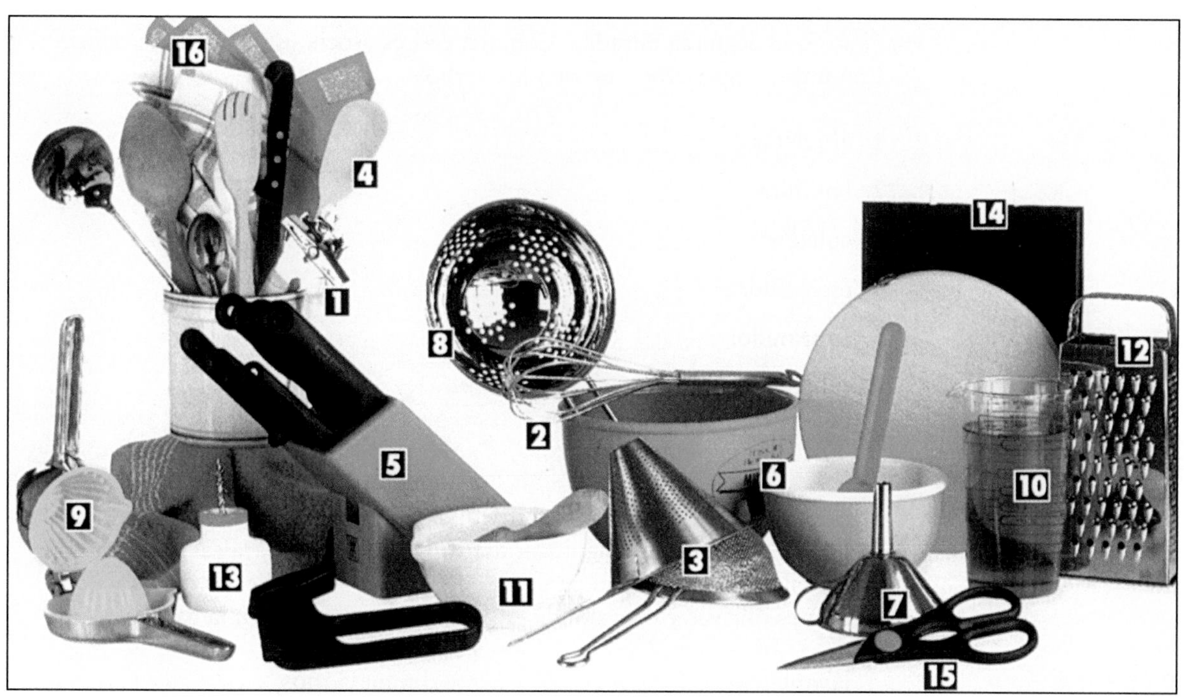

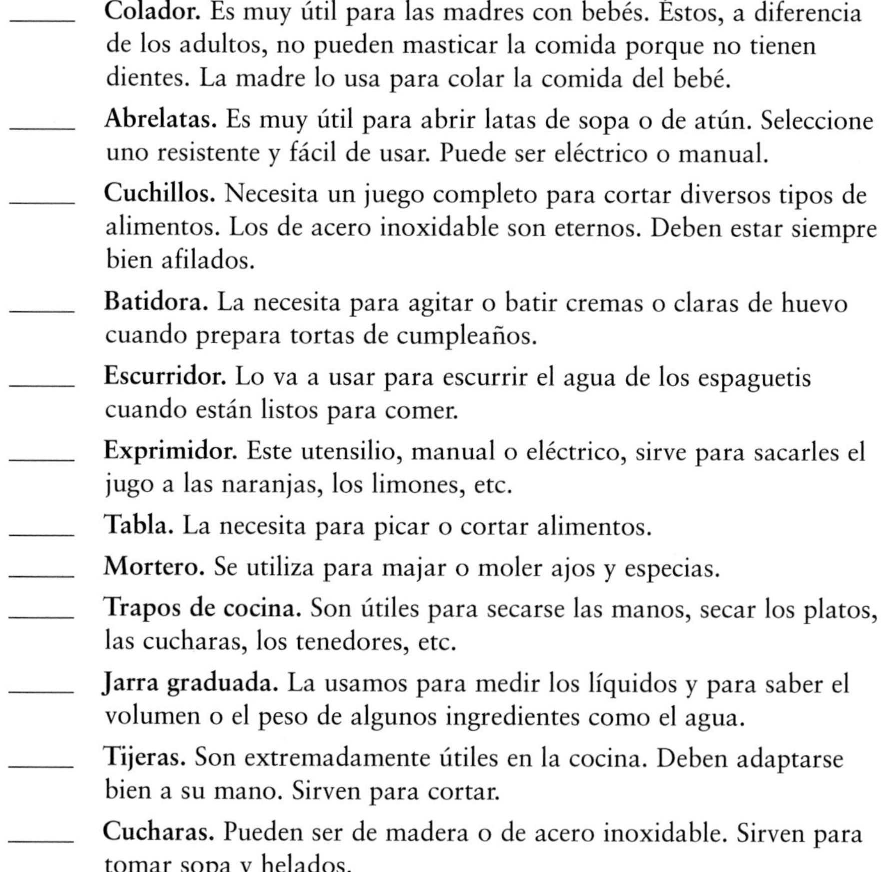

_____ **Colador.** Es muy útil para las madres con bebés. Éstos, a diferencia de los adultos, no pueden masticar la comida porque no tienen dientes. La madre lo usa para colar la comida del bebé.

_____ **Abrelatas.** Es muy útil para abrir latas de sopa o de atún. Seleccione uno resistente y fácil de usar. Puede ser eléctrico o manual.

_____ **Cuchillos.** Necesita un juego completo para cortar diversos tipos de alimentos. Los de acero inoxidable son eternos. Deben estar siempre bien afilados.

_____ **Batidora.** La necesita para agitar o batir cremas o claras de huevo cuando prepara tortas de cumpleaños.

_____ **Escurridor.** Lo va a usar para escurrir el agua de los espaguetis cuando están listos para comer.

_____ **Exprimidor.** Este utensilio, manual o eléctrico, sirve para sacarles el jugo a las naranjas, los limones, etc.

_____ **Tabla.** La necesita para picar o cortar alimentos.

_____ **Mortero.** Se utiliza para majar o moler ajos y especias.

_____ **Trapos de cocina.** Son útiles para secarse las manos, secar los platos, las cucharas, los tenedores, etc.

_____ **Jarra graduada.** La usamos para medir los líquidos y para saber el volumen o el peso de algunos ingredientes como el agua.

_____ **Tijeras.** Son extremadamente útiles en la cocina. Deben adaptarse bien a su mano. Sirven para cortar.

_____ **Cucharas.** Pueden ser de madera o de acero inoxidable. Sirven para tomar sopa y helados.

5-33 Segunda mirada. ¿Con qué verbos asocia usted estos utensilios? Con un/a compañero/a, escriba los verbos.

1. abrelatas ________
2. batidora ________
3. colador ________
4. escurridor ________
5. exprimidor ________
6. rallador ________
7. sacacorchos ________

5-34 Ampliación. En la Actividad 5-32 usted descubrió que la palabra compuesta **sacacorchos** significa: utensilio que se usa para sacar corchos de las botellas. Con un/a compañero/a, determine el significado de los siguientes objetos y diga dónde es posible encontrarlos en la casa.

lavaplatos	limpiavidrios
guardarropa	quitasol
portadocumentos	cortavientos
tocadiscos	paraguas

A ESCRIBIR

5-35 Preparación. Antes de hacer la Actividad 5-36, lea la siguiente carta que Elba, una socióloga hondureña, le escribe a su amiga Rosa, una socióloga nicaragüense.

Querida Rosa:

¿Qué tal están tú y tu familia? Mi familia y yo estamos muy bien. En este momento mi marido y yo estamos disfrutando de nuestras vacaciones. Por eso estamos pensando ir a la playa unos días con los niños. Allí podremos relajarnos juntos y olvidarnos del trabajo y de la casa por un tiempo. ¡Qué maravilloso!

Bueno, te escribo estas líneas para compartir contigo un artículo super interesante, "El trabajo peor pagado", que leí en un periódico de mi país. Habla del inmenso trabajo que nosotras, las amas de casa, hacemos. Me imagino que va a interesarte para tus investigaciones.

El autor afirma que la mayoría de las mujeres hondureñas se dedica a trabajos del hogar como limpiar la casa, lavar y planchar la ropa, coser, cuidar a los hijos, atender al marido, etc., pero también dice que la realidad de la mujer está cambiando. En años recientes, según el autor, se ve un aumento de mujeres en las diferentes áreas del mundo laboral—en la industria, el comercio, incluso en la política—, y como es natural reciben un salario por su trabajo.

Sin embargo, el gran problema para las mujeres que todavía trabajan en casa persiste: no reciben salario ni recompensa por las interminables horas de dedicación al hogar. De acuerdo con el autor del artículo, esto es totalmente injusto y dice que la mujer debe recibir compensación monetaria por su trabajo. Además, cree que antes del matrimonio, los futuros esposos deben llegar a un acuerdo sobre cuál debe ser la cantidad que va a recibir la mujer.

También dice que lo peor es la actitud de los hombres que piensan que la mujer debe quedarse en casa y cumplir con su rol de esposa y madre, que el hombre tiene la obligación de sustentar el hogar económicamente, y por lo tanto, él sí debe trabajar fuera de casa y recibir un sueldo suficiente para cubrir las necesidades del hogar. Según ellos, los quehaceres de la casa son la absoluta responsabilidad de la mujer; él hombre sólo cumple con sus horas de trabajo fuera de la casa, y en el hogar, espera atenciones de la esposa y los hijos y no quiere responsabilidades domésticas. ¡Qué horror!

Como tú sabes, yo me siento muy afortunada porque tengo un esposo excepcional. Raúl y yo tenemos un compromiso que nos hace muy felices: él, nuestros hijos y yo somos responsables de las tareas de casa. De hecho, él cocina más que yo porque sale de su trabajo más temprano; generalmente prepara la cena por lo menos tres veces a la semana. Los niños y yo ayudamos poniendo la mesa, lavando y secando los platos, etc. Así la vida es más fácil porque todos colaboramos. Eso me parece justo. Seguramente va a pasar algún tiempo antes de que la mujer reciba el reconocimiento de la sociedad por el trabajo que hace en casa. Tenemos que luchar más, ¿no crees?

Bueno Rosa, espero que mi próxima carta sea aún más positiva con respecto a la vida de nuestras mujeres. Por favor, mándame tus artículos para informarme más sobre este tema.

Te deseo un muy buen año junto a tu familia. Espero verte en la Conferencia de la Mujer que va a realizarse en Antigua, Guatemala. Allí vamos a hablar más.

Cariños a tu esposo y a Javier y Rita.

Besos de tu amiga,
Elba

5-36 Manos a la obra: fase preliminar. En grupos pequeños, respondan a la siguiente encuesta. La columna **lo hace más** va a presentar los resultados del grupo:

¿QUIEN?	USTED	MAMA	PAPA	HERMANO/A	NADIE	OTRA PERSONA	FRECUENCIA POR SEMANA	LO HACE MAS
1. cocina								
2. compra la comida								
3. limpia la casa								
4. lava la ropa								
5. cose (*sews, mends*)								
6. plancha la ropa								
7. cuida el jardín								
8. cuida a los niños								

5-37 Manos a la obra. Rosa le escribe a usted para saber si la realidad de la vida de la mujer norteamericana de la clase media (*middle class*) es similar o diferente a la de la mujer hondureña, según el artículo "El trabajo peor pagado" que menciona Elba en su carta. Utilice la información obtenida en su clase en la Actividad 5-36 e incluya ejemplos de su propia familia, si desea, para escribirle una carta a Rosa con la siguiente información.

- división de responsabilidades del trabajo de casa
- labores típicas de la mujer y del hombre en la casa norteamericana y en su familia
- cantidad de tiempo y frecuencia con que los miembros de la familia realizan estas tareas domésticas

5-38 Revisión. Su compañero/a editor/a va a ayudarle a expresar sus ideas bien para que Rosa comprenda su carta.

Vocabulario*

En una casa

el aire acondicionado — *air conditioning*
el armario — *closet, armoire*
el baño — *bathroom*
la barbacoa — *barbecue*
la basura — *garbage, trash*
la calefacción — *heating*
el césped — *lawn*
la chimenea — *fireplace*
la cocina — *kitchen*
el comedor — *dining room*
el cuarto/dormitorio — *bedroom*
el garaje — *garage*
el jardín — *backyard, garden*
la piscina — *swimming pool*
el piso — *floor*
la planta baja — *first floor*
la sala — *living room*
la terraza — *terrace*

Muebles y accesorios

la alfombra — *carpet, rug*
la butaca — *armchair*
la cama — *bed*
la cómoda — *dresser*
la cortina — *curtain*
el cuadro — *picture*
el espejo — *mirror*
la lámpara — *lamp*
la mesa de noche — *night stand*
el sofá — *sofa*

Electrodomésticos

la aspiradora — *vacuum cleaner*
la lavadora — *washer*
el lavaplatos — *dishwasher*
el (horno) microondas — *microwave oven*
el/la radio — *radio*
el refrigerador — *refrigerator*
la secadora — *drier*

Para la cama

la almohada — *pillow*
la manta — *blanket*
la sábana — *sheet*

En el baño

la bañadera — *tub*
la ducha — *shower*
el inodoro — *toilet*
el lavabo — *washbowl, bathroom sink*
la toalla — *towel*

En la cocina

la estufa — *stove*
el fregadero — *kitchen sink*
el plato — *dish, plate*

Lugares

las afueras — *outskirts*
allá — *over there*
allí — *there*
el apartamento — *apartment*
aquí — *here*
el barrio — *neighborhood*
el centro — *downtown, center*
cerca (de) — *near (*close to*)*
el edificio — *building*
lejos (de) — *far (*from*)*

Descripciones

limpio/a — *clean*
ordenado/a — *tidy*
seco/a — *dry*
sucio/a — *dirty*

Verbos

ayudar	*to help*
barrer	*to sweep*
cocinar	*to cook*
conocer (zc)	*to know, to meet*
cortar	*to cut*
creer	*to believe*
doblar	*to fold*
limpiar	*to clean*
ordenar	*to tidy up*
pasar la aspiradora	*to vacuum*
planchar	*to iron*
preparar	*to prepare*
recoger	*to pick up*
regar	*to water*
regresar	*to come back*
saber	*to know*
secar	*to dry*
sentir (ie, i)	*to feel*
tender (ie)	*to hang (clothes); to make (a bed)*

Palabras útiles

¡Claro!	*of course*
la diversión	*entertainment, fun*
el perro	*dog*
todavía	*still*
ya	*already*

* For expressions with *tener* see page 168
For direct object pronouns see page 170
For demonstrative adjectives and pronouns see page 173
For ordinal numbers see page 179

Las casas y la arquitectura

Para pensar

¿Vive Ud. en un apartamento o en una casa? ¿Cómo es, grande o pequeño/a? ¿moderno/a o antiguo/a? ¿Hay apartamentos/casas parecidos/as al/a la suyo/a en su vecindario? ¿Dónde está situado/a, cerca del centro de la ciudad o en las afueras?

Hay mucha variedad en las viviendas en los países hispanos. En realidad, una de las cosas que más llama la atención del visitante extranjero es la variedad que existe entre las casas. Cada casa tiene su sello, su estilo personal que la diferencia de todas las otras a su alrededor.

Las casas/apartamentos pueden estar cerca del centro de la ciudad o en las afueras. Algunas personas prefieren vivir cerca del centro de la ciudad para poder disfrutar de todos sus beneficios, teatros, centros comerciales, bancos, medios de transporte, etc. Otras prefieren vivir lejos del centro para tener más tranquilidad y seguridad. Generalmente, en el centro o cerca del centro de la ciudad hay más edificios de apartamentos, y en las afueras hay más casas.

El tipo de casas y apartamentos varía de acuerdo con la ciudad o pueblo donde están situados. En algunos lugares la influencia de las culturas precolombinas (maya, azteca o inca), es evidente. Si quiere aprender algo más sobre estas culturas precolombinas, puede visitar *www.prenhall.com/mosaicos*. En otros lugares se puede apreciar la influencia de la época colonial y se pueden admirar casas con hermosos balcones de madera, grandes patios interiores, azulejos (*tiles*) en los pisos o paredes y bellas rejas exteriores.

El tipo de construcción también depende del clima de la ciudad o país. Donde el clima es generalmente templado, la mayor parte de las casas no tiene aire acondicionado ni calefacción. En San Salvador y otras ciudades centroamericanas, por ejemplo, es común ver casas o apartamentos de amplios ventanales y balcones adornados con variedad de plantas y flores. En zonas más frías, sin embargo, esto no siempre es posible y muchas veces las puertas y ventanas permanecen cerradas.

Generalmente en las casas hispanas no hay la gran variedad de electrodomésticos que hay en una casa en los Estados Unidos, debido principalmente a su alto costo y también a la posibilidad de tener empleados que ayudan en los quehaceres domésticos.

En resumen, ¡las casas hispanas tienen mucha personalidad!

Para contestar

A. Las casas. Con su compañero/a responda a las siguientes preguntas:

1. Ustedes van a mudarse a un país hispano. ¿Dónde prefieren vivir? ¿En el centro o en las afueras? ¿Por qué?
2. ¿Cómo son las casas coloniales? ¿En qué ciudades creen ustedes que se pueden ver casas de este estilo? ¿Por qué? ¿Hay casas de estilo colonial en su vecindario?
3. ¿Qué electrodomésticos hay en su casa? ¿Cuáles cree que se encuentran o que no se encuentran en la mayoría de las casas hispanas? ¿Por qué?

B. Riqueza cultural. En grupos de tres, usando la información de más arriba, describan cómo es su casa ideal.

The *Enfoque cultural* is available in an interactive online format at *www.prenhall.com/mosaicos*

Para investigar en la WWW

Vaya a la página de Mosaicos en la Internet *www.prenhall.com/mosaicos*.

1. Busque anuncios de agencias de bienes raíces (*real estate*) en Managua, Tegucigalpa y San Salvador. Traiga esta información a clase y, si es posible, una ilustración de diferentes tipos de vivienda. Luego, en grupos pequeños comparta esta información con sus compañeros/as: diga qué tipo de viviendas anuncian, en qué zona de la ciudad están, cómo son, qué precio tienen, etc. Decidan cuál es la casa favorita del grupo y por qué.

Casa de estilo colonial

2. Busque información acerca de viviendas de estilo colonial en diferentes ciudades hispanoamericanas (descripción, situación, estado en el que se encuentran — bien conservada/ necesita mejoras, etc.) Traiga algunas ilustraciones, si es posible, y compártalas con sus compañeros/as. Describan entre todos las diferentes viviendas y escojan su favorita.

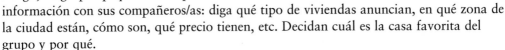

Nicaragua

Datos y lugares de interés:
Nicaragua, llamada la tierra de los lagos y volcanes, es un hermoso país con una larga historia de problemas económicos y sociales. Sin embargo, en 1990 Violeta Chamorro ganó unas elecciones democráticas y el país empezó un período de recuperación.

Hay muchos lugares de interés en Nicaragua. La capital, Managua, es una ciudad de un millón de habitantes. Está situada en la costa sur del Lago Managua y es el principal centro administrativo y comercial del país.

Cerca de Managua está Granada, la ciudad más antigua de Nicaragua, muy conocida por su arquitectura colonial. Otro lugar de interés es el Lago Nicaragua, el lago más grande de América Central.

Expresiones nicaragüenses:

ñeque	Él es ñeque.	*He is strong/vigorous.*
jalar	Ella está jalando con Luis.	*She is Luis' girlfriend.*
chavalo/a	Ese chavalo es terrible.	*That kid is terrible.*

El Salvador

Datos y lugares de interés:

El Salvador, cuya capital es San Salvador, es un pequeño país de Centro América en la costa del Pacífico. Como Nicaragua, El Salvador tiene una larga historia de problemas políticos y económicos, pero en 1992 un tratado de paz terminó con más de diez años de guerra civil. Durante esos años, muchos salvadoreños vinieron a los Estados Unidos, especialmente al área de Washington, D.C., donde hoy en día hay una importante comunidad salvadoreña.

Hay muchas cosas que usted puede hacer en El Salvador: visitar hermosas playas, lagos, interesantes ruinas mayas y bosques tropicales como el Parque El Imposible, donde existen unas 400 especies diferentes de árboles y una gran variedad de animales en peligro de extinción.

Expresiones salvadoreñas:

chinear	**María chinea a su hijo continuamente.**	*María holds her child in her arms continuously.*
cipote	**Sólo es un cipote.**	*He is only a child.*
primero Dios	**—Vas a la playa mañana?** **—Primero Dios.**	*—Are you going to the beach tomorrow?* *—God willing.*

Honduras

Datos y lugares de interés:

Honduras es un país con hermosas playas tanto en la costa del Océano Pacífico como en el Mar Caribe. Como el resto de Centroamérica, tiene una población en su mayoría mestiza, sin embargo, una gran parte del pueblo hondureño es de origen africano, y la influencia africana se nota en la música, los bailes y el folclor del país.

La capital de Honduras es Tegucigalpa. En su catedral, construida en el siglo XVI, se pueden admirar numerosas obras de arte, y en el Museo Nacional se encuentran piezas precolombinas de gran valor. Si le interesan las culturas precolombinas, debe visitar las ruinas de Copán, una de las ciudades más importantes de la civilización maya.

Expresiones hondureñas:

agarrar a uno de ojo de gallo	**Parece que José me agarró de ojo de gallo.**	*It looks like Jose has ill will towards me.*
güirro	**¿Qué está haciendo ese güirro?**	*What is that child doing?*

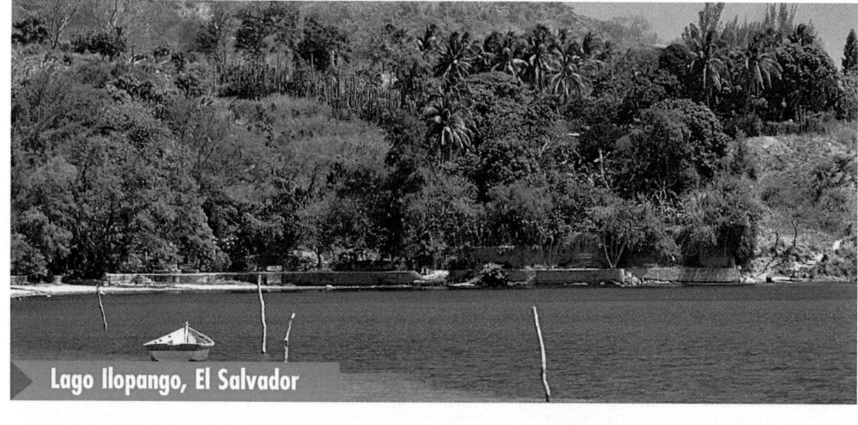

Lago Ilopango, El Salvador

ENFOQUE INTERACTIVO

A MIRAR EL VIDEO 5:00

Watch the *Fortunas* video segment for *Lección 5* in class or on your CD-ROM. Is there a romance developing between Katie and Carlos? Were you surprised by the winners of the second *misterio*?

Now complete the accompanying video activities on the CD-ROM. This is your chance to interact with the video characters! **25:00**

¿El romance?

El concurso

The second *misterio* has been solved at *La Plaza de las Tres Culturas* in Mexico City. Now the contestants are searching for the third *misterio,* where they will find the first *fortuna*. What were your feelings for the losers of the second *misterio*? When contestants lose, they receive fewer *pistas* for the next *misterio*. What would your strategy be to level the playing field if you had fewer clues than your opponents had?

Misterio Nº3: Tiempo viejo

Pistas
1. *Mira el sol*
2. *Piedra grande*
3. *Muy viejo*
4. *¿Qué hora es?*

LA BÚSQUEDA 5:00

Because they solved the second *misterio,* Sabrina and Efraín have received three *pistas* (*1*, *2*, and *3*) for the third *misterio*. They seem to have an advantage, but everything may not be exactly as it appears. Think about how the contestants are working together. What's going on beneath the surface? Where do you think the clues for the third *misterio* are pointing to? Go to the *Fortunas* module to investigate the possibilities. Be sure to review the first and second misterios as well—they may help you find the first *fortuna*.

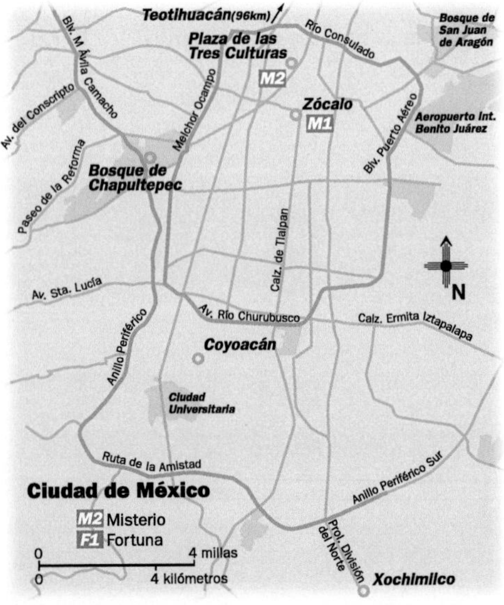

¿QUÉ OPINA USTED? 5:00

The points are in for the second *misterio* and the latest viewer polls. Katie and Carlos are still in front but, evidently, viewers have been impressed by Sabrina and Efraín as well. This week we're voting on possible and best alliances. Your vote counts in determining the winner of the contest, so go to the *Fortunas* module and click on *¿Qué opina usted?* to vote in this episode's poll. Be sure to read the contestants' diaries before you vote!

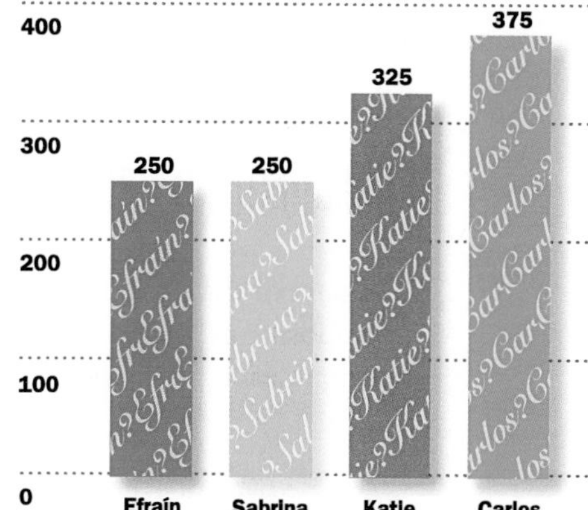

PARA NAVEGAR 10:00

LA DESTRUCCIÓN CAUSADA POR EL MAR

Normalmente, cuando pensamos en la arquitectura de Centroamérica, pensamos en casas de brillantes colores, iglesias bonitas e influencia indígena. En 1998, sin embargo, estas imágenes cambiaron por la destrucción masiva causada por el huracán Mitch. En Honduras murieron más de 6.000 personas. Esta destrucción afectó a todos los países centroamericanos, en particular a Honduras y Nicaragua.

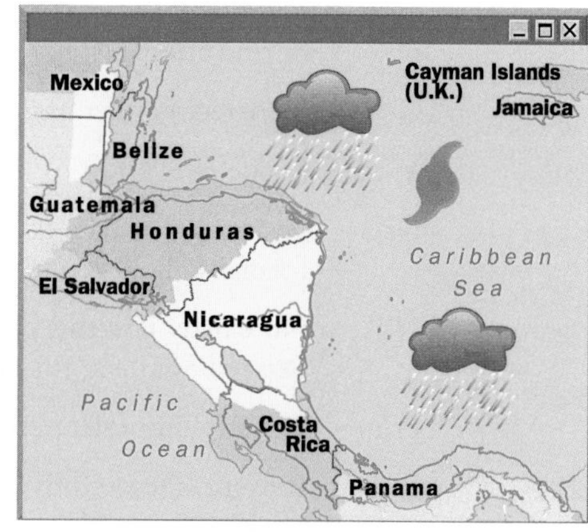

La destrucción causada por el mar

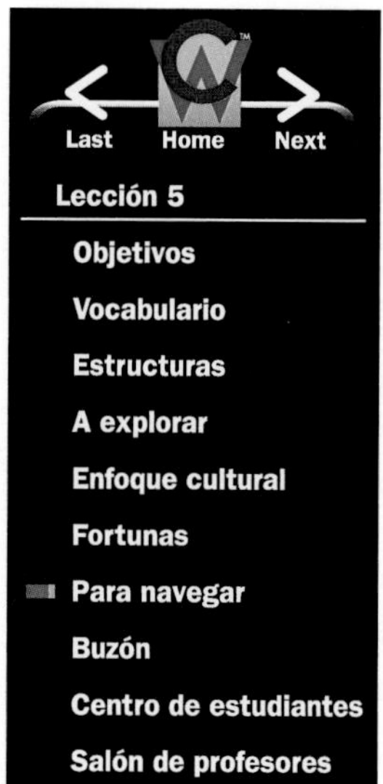

Go to the *Mosaicos Website* and click on the *Para navegar* module to explore links to Honduras, Nicaragua, and El Salvador. Read about these countries' history and rich artistic traditions, and explore some of their exciting dimensions.

Apéndice 1

Composition correction codes

As part of the process of developing good writing skills in Spanish, you will be exchanging compositions with a classmate. The following correction codes can be very helpful as you critique each other's work.

Code	Interpretation
C	Conjugation of a verb, or an error in some derived verb form, for example **la puerta estaba *abrida.**
Cog	False cognate, for example **sopa** for **jabón,** or **ropa** for **soga.**
D	Dictionary error, for example **banco** for **orilla,** or even **morderse las uñas** for **comerse las uñas.**
F	Form (often a "regularized" adjective, such as **una niña muy *jóvena**).
G	Incorrect gender assignment to a noun, for example **la programa** for **el programa.**
Mode	Mode confusion (if subjunctive, change to indicative and vice versa).
Nag	Noun agreements (gender, number) with adjectives and other noun-centered forms such as pronouns, demonstratives, possessives.
NE	**No existe.** Use this code to signal a made-up word or expression that does not exist in Spanish, for example ***en facto** for **en realidad.**
Prim	Preterite/imperfect confusion (if preterite, change to imperfect and vice versa).
R	Rewrite successfully completed.
Ref	Reflexive. Use this code to signal that a reflexive verb/construction is needed.
Sag	Subject-verb agreement error, for example ***Juan querías salir.**
S/E	**Ser/estar** confusion (if **ser,** change to **estar** and vice versa).
Sp	Spelling error. Use this code to signal errors in spelling. Note that written accent marks are considered part of a word's spelling in Spanish.
T	Tense. Use this code to signal any non-Prim (see above) tense error.
X	Any basic grammatical error not covered by some other symbol, but which the student should reasonably know, such as **después de *yendo** for **después de ir.**
Wo	Word order error, for example, ***es no grande** for **no es grande.**
+	Use this code to signal any especially nice touch in the student's writing.
?	Use this code to signal that the reader could not make any sense of the word, clause, sentence, or paragraph.

Adapted from Higgs, 1979

Word formation in Spanish

Recognizing certain patterns in Spanish word formation can be a big help in deciphering meaning. Use the following information about word formation to help you as you read.

- **Prefixes.** Spanish and English share a number of prefixes that shade the meaning of the word to which they are attached: **inter-** (between, among); **intro/a-** (within); **ex-** (former, toward the outside); **en-/em-** (the state of becoming); **in-/a-** (not, without), among others.

inter-	interdisciplinario, interacción
intro/a-	introvertido, introspección
ex-	ex-esposo, exponer *(expose)*
en-/em-	enrojecer *(to turn red),* empobrecer *(to become poor)*
in-/a-	inmoral, incompleto, amoral, asexual

- **Suffixes.** Suffixes and, in general, word endings will help you identify various aspects of words such as part of speech, gender, meaning, degree, etc. Common Spanish suffixes are **-ría, -za, -miento, -dad/tad, -ura, -oso/a, -izo/a, -(c)ito/a,** and **-mente.**

-ría	place where something is made and/or bought: **panadería, zapatería** *(shoe store),* **librería.**
-za	feminine, abstract noun: **pobreza** *(poverty),* **riqueza** *(wealth, richness).*
-miento	masculine, abstract noun: **empobrecimiento** *(impoverishment),* **entrenamiento** *(training).*
-dad/tad	feminine noun: **ciudad** *(city),* **libertad** *(liberty, freedom)*
-ura	feminine noun: **verdura, locura** *(craziness).*
-oso/a	adjective meaning having the characteristics of the noun to which it's attached: **montañoso, lluvioso** *(rainy).*
-izo/a	adjective meaning having the characteristics of the noun to which it's attached: **rojizo** *(reddish),* **enfermizo** *(sickly).*
-(c)ito/a	diminutive form of noun or adjective: **Juanito, mesita** *(little table),* **Carmencita.**
-mente	attached to the feminine form of adjective to form an adverb: **rápidamente, felizmente** *(happily).*

- **Compounds.** Compounds are made up of two words (e. g. *mailman*), each of which has meaning in and of itself: **tocadiscos** *(record player)* from **tocar** and **disco; sacacorchos** *(cork screw)* from **sacar** and **corcho.** Your knowledge of the root words will help you recognize the compound; and likewise, learning compounds can help you to learn the root words. What do you think **sacar** means?

- **Spanish-English associations.** Learning to associate aspects of word formation in Spanish with aspects of word formation in English can be very helpful. Look at the associations below.

SPANISH	ENGLISH
es/ex. + consonant	*s* + consonant
esclerosis, extraño	*sclerosis, strange*
gu-	*w-*
guerra, Guillermo	*war, William*
-tad/dad	*-ty*
libertad, calidad	*liberty, quality*
-sión/-ción	*-sion/-tion*
tensión, emoción	*tension, emotion*

Stress and written accents in Spanish

In Spanish, normal word stress falls on the second-to-last syllable of words ending in a vowel, **-n,** or **-s,** and on the last syllable of words ending in other consonants.

hablo	**clase**	**amiga**	**libros**
escuchan	**comer**	**universidad**	**venir**

When a word does not follow this pattern, a written accent is used to signal where the word is stressed. Below are examples of words that do not follow the pattern.

1. Words accented on the third-to-last syllable:

física	**sábado**	**simpático**
catástrofe	**gramática**	**matemáticas**

2. Words that are accented on the last syllable despite ending in a vowel, **-n** or **-s.**

hablé	**comí**	**están**	**estás**
alemán	**Belén**	**inglés**	**conversación**

3. Words that are accented on the second-to-last syllable despite ending in a consonant other than **-n** or **-s.**

lápiz	**útil**	**débil**	**mártir**
Félix	**cárcel**	**módem**	**fácil**

Diphthongs

The combination of an unstressed **i** or **u** with another vowel forms a single syllable which is called a diphthong. When the diphthong is in the accented syllable of a word and a written accent is required, it is written over the other vowel, not over the **i** or **u**.

Dios	**adiós**	**bien**	**también**
seis	**dieciséis**	**continuo**	**continuó**

When a stressed **i** or **u** appears with another vowel, two syllables are formed, and a written accent mark is used over the **i** or **u**.

cafetería	**país**	**Raúl**	**frío**
continúa	**río**	**leíste**	**economía**

Interrogative and monosyllabic words

Some words in Spanish follow normal stress patterns but use written accents for other reasons. For example, interrogative and exclamatory words always use a written accent on the stressed vowel: **¿Dónde viven ellos?**, **¿Cuántas clases tienes?**, **¡Qué bueno!** Many one-syllable (monosyllabic) words carry a written accent to distinguish them from other words with the same spelling but different meanings.

dé	*give* (formal command)	**de**	*of*
él	*he*	**el**	*the*
más	*more*	**mas**	*but*
mí	*me*	**mi**	*my*
sé	*I know, be* (formal command)	**se**	*him/herself, (to)him/her/them*
sí	*yes*	**si**	*if*
té	*tea*	**te**	*(to) you*
tú	*you*	**tu**	*your*

Apéndice 2

Verb Charts

REGULAR VERBS: SIMPLE TENSES

Infinitive Present Participle Past Participle	Indicative					Subjunctive		Imperative
	Present	Imperfect	Preterite	Future	Conditional	Present	Imperfect	
hablar hablando hablado	hablo hablas habla hablamos habláis hablan	hablaba hablabas hablaba hablábamos hablabais hablaban	hablé hablaste habló hablamos hablasteis hablaron	hablaré hablarás hablará hablaremos hablaréis hablarán	hablaría hablarías hablaría hablaríamos hablaríais hablarían	hable hables hable hablemos habléis hablen	hablara hablaras hablara habláramos hablarais hablaran	habla tú, no hables hable usted hablemos hablen Uds.
comer comiendo comido	como comes come comemos coméis comen	comía comías comía comíamos comíais comían	comí comiste comió comimos comisteis comieron	comeré comerás comerá comeremos comeréis comerán	comería comerías comería comeríamos comeríais comerían	coma comas coma comamos comáis coman	comiera comieras comiera comiéramos comierais comieran	come tú, no comas coma usted comamos coman Uds.
vivir viviendo vivido	vivo vives vive vivimos vivís viven	vivía vivías vivía vivíamos vivíais vivían	viví viviste vivió vivimos vivisteis vivieron	viviré vivirás vivirá viviremos viviréis vivirán	viviría vivirías viviría viviríamos viviríais vivirían	viva vivas viva vivamos viváis vivan	viviera vivieras viviera viviéramos vivierais vivieran	vive tú, no vivas viva usted vivamos vivan Uds.

***Vosotros* commands**		
hablar hablad no habléis	comer comed no comáis	vivir vivid no viváis

REGULAR VERBS: PERFECT TENSES

Indicative										Subjunctive			
Present Perfect		Past Perfect		Preterite Perfect		Future Perfect		Conditional Perfect		Present Perfect		Past Perfect	
he		había		hube		habré		habría		haya		hubiera	
has	hablado	habías	hablado	hubiste	hablado	habrás	hablado	habrías	hablado	hayas	hablado	hubieras	hablado
ha	comido	había	comido	hubo	comido	habrá	comido	habría	comido	haya	comido	hubiera	comido
hemos	vivido	habíamos	vivido	hubimos	vivido	habremos	vivido	habríamos	vivido	hayamos	vivido	hubiéramos	vivido
habéis		habíais		hubisteis		habréis		habríais		hayáis		hubierais	
han		habían		hubieron		habrán		habrían		hayan		hubieran	

IRREGULAR VERBS

Infinitive Present Participle Past Participle	Indicative					Subjunctive		Imperative
	Present	Imperfect	Preterite	Future	Conditional	Present	Imperfect	
andar	ando	andaba	anduve	andaré	andaría	ande	anduviera	anda tú,
andando	andas	andabas	anduviste	andarás	andarías	andes	anduvieras	no andes
andado	anda	andaba	anduvo	andará	andaría	ande	anduviera	ande usted
	andamos	andábamos	anduvimos	andaremos	andaríamos	andemos	anduviéramos	andemos
	andáis	andabais	anduvisteis	andaréis	andaríais	andéis	anduvierais	anden Uds.
	andan	andaban	anduvieron	andarán	andarían	anden	anduvieran	
caer	caigo	caía	caí	caeré	caería	caiga	cayera	cae tú,
cayendo	caes	caías	caíste	caerás	caerías	caigas	cayeras	no caigas
caído	cae	caía	cayó	caerá	caería	caiga	cayera	caiga usted
	caemos	caíamos	caímos	caeremos	caeríamos	caigamos	cayéramos	caigamos
	caéis	caíais	caísteis	caeréis	caeríais	caigáis	cayerais	caigan Uds.
	caen	caían	cayeron	caerán	caerían	caigan	cayeran	
dar	doy	daba	di	daré	daría	dé	diera	da tú,
dando	das	dabas	diste	darás	darías	des	dieras	no des
dado	da	daba	dio	dará	daría	dé	diera	dé usted
	damos	dábamos	dimos	daremos	daríamos	demos	diéramos	demos
	dais	dabais	disteis	daréis	daríais	deis	dierais	den Uds.
	dan	daban	dieron	darán	darían	den	dieran	

IRREGULAR VERBS (CONTINUED)

Infinitive Present Participle Past Participle	Indicative					Subjunctive		Imperative
	Present	Imperfect	Preterite	Future	Conditional	Present	Imperfect	
decir	digo	decía	dije	diré	diría	diga	dijera	di tú,
diciendo	dices	decías	dijiste	dirás	dirías	digas	dijeras	no digas
dicho	dice	decía	dijo	dirá	diría	diga	dijera	diga usted
	decimos	decíamos	dijimos	diremos	diríamos	digamos	dijéramos	digamos
	decís	decíais	dijisteis	diréis	diríais	digáis	dijerais	digan Uds.
	dicen	decían	dijeron	dirán	dirían	digan	dijeran	
estar	estoy	estaba	estuve	estaré	estaría	esté	estuviera	está tú,
estando	estás	estabas	estuviste	estarás	estarías	estés	estuvieras	no estés
estado	está	estaba	estuvo	estará	estaría	esté	estuviera	esté usted
	estamos	estábamos	estuvimos	estaremos	estaríamos	estemos	estuviéramos	estemos
	estáis	estabais	estuvisteis	estaréis	estaríais	estéis	estuvierais	estén Uds.
	están	estaban	estuvieron	estarán	estarían	estén	estuvieran	
haber	he	había	hube	habré	habría	haya	hubiera	
habiendo	has	habías	hubiste	habrás	habrías	hayas	hubieras	
habido	ha	había	hubo	habrá	habría	haya	hubiera	
	hemos	habíamos	hubimos	habremos	habríamos	hayamos	hubiéramos	
	habéis	habíais	hubisteis	habréis	habríais	hayáis	hubierais	
	han	habían	hubieron	habrán	habrían	hayan	hubieran	
hacer	hago	hacía	hice	haré	haría	haga	hiciera	haz tú,
haciendo	haces	hacías	hiciste	harás	harías	hagas	hicieras	no hagas
hecho	hace	hacía	hizo	hará	haría	haga	hiciera	haga usted
	hacemos	hacíamos	hicimos	haremos	haríamos	hagamos	hiciéramos	hagamos
	hacéis	hacíais	hicisteis	haréis	haríais	hagáis	hicierais	hagan Uds.
	hacen	hacían	hicieron	harán	harían	hagan	hicieran	
ir	voy	iba	fui	iré	iría	vaya	fuera	ve tú,
yendo	vas	ibas	fuiste	irás	irías	vayas	fueras	no vayas
ido	va	iba	fue	irá	iría	vaya	fuera	vaya usted
	vamos	íbamos	fuimos	iremos	iríamos	vayamos	fuéramos	vamos
	vais	ibais	fuisteis	iréis	iríais	vayáis	fuerais	(no vayamos)
	van	iban	fueron	irán	irían	vayan	fueran	vayan Uds.

Infinitive Present Participle Past Participle	Indicative					Subjunctive		Imperative
	Present	Imperfect	Preterite	Future	Conditional	Present	Imperfect	
oír oyendo oído	oigo oyes oye oímos oís oyen	oía oías oía oíamos oíais oían	oí oíste oyó oímos oísteis oyeron	oiré oirás oirá oiremos oiréis oirán	oiría oirías oiría oiríamos oiríais oirían	oiga oigas oiga oigamos oigáis oigan	oyera oyeras oyera oyéramos oyerais oyeran	oye tú, no oigas oiga usted oigamos oigan Uds.
poder pudiendo podido	puedo puedes puede podemos podéis pueden	podía podías podía podíamos podíais podían	pude pudiste pudo pudimos pudisteis pudieron	podré podrás podrá podremos podréis podrán	podría podrías podría podríamos podríais podrían	pueda puedas pueda podamos podáis puedan	pudiera pudieras pudiera pudiéramos pudierais pudieran	
poner poniendo puesto	pongo pones pone ponemos ponéis ponen	ponía ponías ponía poníamos poníais ponían	puse pusiste puso pusimos pusisteis pusieron	pondré pondrás pondrá pondremos pondréis pondrán	pondría pondrías pondría pondríamos pondríais pondrían	ponga pongas ponga pongamos pongáis pongan	pusiera pusieras pusiera pusiéramos pusierais pusieran	pon tú, no pongas ponga usted pongamos pongan Uds.
querer queriendo querido	quiero quieres quiere queremos queréis quieren	quería querías quería queríamos queríais querían	quise quisiste quiso quisimos quisisteis quisieron	querré querrás querrá querremos querréis querrán	querría querrías querría querríamos querríais querrían	quiera quieras quiera queramos queráis quieran	quisiera quisieras quisiera quisiéramos quisierais quisieran	quiere tú, no quieras quiera usted queramos quieran Uds.
saber sabiendo sabido	sé sabes sabe sabemos sabéis saben	sabía sabías sabía sabíamos sabíais sabían	supe supiste supo supimos supisteis supieron	sabré sabrás sabrá sabremos sabréis sabrán	sabría sabrías sabría sabríamos sabríais sabrían	sepa sepas sepa sepamos sepáis sepan	supiera supieras supiera supiéramos supierais supieran	sabe tú, no sepas sepa usted sepamos sepan Uds.
salir saliendo salido	salgo sales sale salimos salís salen	salía salías salía salíamos salíais salían	salí saliste salió salimos salisteis salieron	saldré saldrás saldrá saldremos saldréis saldrán	saldría saldrías saldría saldríamos saldríais saldrían	salga salgas salga salgamos salgáis salgan	saliera salieras saliera saliéramos salierais salieran	sal tú, no salgas salga usted salgamos salgan Uds.

IRREGULAR VERBS (CONTINUED)

Infinitive Present Participle Past Participle	Indicative					Subjunctive		Imperative
	Present	Imperfect	Preterite	Future	Conditional	Present	Imperfect	
ser siendo sido	soy eres es somos sois son	era eras era éramos erais eran	fui fuiste fue fuimos fuisteis fueron	seré serás será seremos seréis serán	sería serías sería seríamos seríais serían	sea seas sea seamos seáis sean	fuera fueras fuera fuéramos fuerais fueran	sé tú, no seas sea usted seamos sean Uds.
tener teniendo tenido	tengo tienes tiene tenemos tenéis tienen	tenía tenías tenía teníamos teníais tenían	tuve tuviste tuvo tuvimos tuvisteis tuvieron	tendré tendrás tendrá tendremos tendréis tendrán	tendría tendrías tendría tendríamos tendríais tendrían	tenga tengas tenga tengamos tengáis tengan	tuviera tuvieras tuviera tuviéramos tuvierais tuvieran	ten tú, no tengas tenga usted tengamos tengan Uds.
traer trayendo traído	traigo traes trae traemos traéis traen	traía traías traía traíamos traíais traían	traje trajiste trajo trajimos trajisteis trajeron	traeré traerás traerá traeremos traeréis traerán	traería traerías traería traeríamos traeríais traerían	traiga traigas traiga traigamos traigáis traigan	trajera trajeras trajera trajéramos trajerais trajeran	trae tú, no traigas traiga usted traigamos traigan Uds.
venir viniendo venido	vengo vienes viene venimos venís vienen	venía venías venía veníamos veníais venían	vine viniste vino vinimos vinisteis vinieron	vendré vendrás vendrá vendremos vendréis vendrán	vendría vendrías vendría vendríamos vendríais vendrían	venga vengas venga vengamos vengáis vengan	viniera vinieras viniera viniéramos vinierais vinieran	ven tú, no vengas venga usted vengamos vengan Uds.
ver viendo visto	veo ves ve vemos veis ven	veía veías veía veíamos veíais veían	vi viste vio vimos visteis vieron	veré verás verá veremos veréis verán	vería verías vería veríamos veríais verían	vea veas vea veamos veáis vean	viera vieras viera viéramos vierais vieran	ve tú, no veas vea usted veamos vean Uds.

STEM-CHANGING AND ORTHOGRAPHIC-CHANGING VERBS

Infinitive Present Participle Past Participle	Indicative					Subjunctive		Imperative
	Present	Imperfect	Preterite	Future	Conditional	Present	Imperfect	
incluir (y) incluyendo incluido	incluyo incluyes incluye incluimos incluís incluyen	incluía incluías incluía incluíamos incluíais incluían	incluí incluiste incluyó incluimos incluisteis incluyeron	incluiré incluirás incluirá incluiremos incluiréis incluirán	incluiría incluirías incluiría incluiríamos incluiríais incluirían	incluya incluyas incluya incluyamos incluyáis incluyan	incluyera incluyeras incluyera incluyéramos incluyerais incluyeran	incluye tú, no incluyas incluya usted incluyamos incluyan Uds.
dormir (ue, u) durmiendo dormido	duermo duermes duerme dormimos dormís duermen	dormía dormías dormía dormíamos dormíais dormían	dormí dormiste durmió dormimos dormisteis durmieron	dormiré dormirás dormirá dormiremos dormiréis dormirán	dormiría dormirías dormiría dormiríamos dormiríais dormirían	duerma duermas duerma durmamos durmáis duerman	durmiera durmieras durmiera durmiéramos durmierais durmieran	duerme tú, no duermas duerma usted durmamos duerman Uds.
pedir (i, i) pidiendo pedido	pido pides pide pedimos pedís piden	pedía pedías pedía pedíamos pedíais pedían	pedí pediste pidió pedimos pedisteis pidieron	pediré pedirás pedirá pediremos pediréis pedirán	pediría pedirías pediría pediríamos pediríais pedirían	pida pidas pida pidamos pidáis pidan	pidiera pidieras pidiera pidiéramos pidierais pidieran	pide tú, no pidas pida usted pidamos pidan Uds.
pensar (ie) pensando pensado	pienso piensas piensa pensamos pensáis piensan	pensaba pensabas pensaba pensábamos pensabais pensaban	pensé pensaste pensó pensamos pensasteis pensaron	pensaré pensarás pensará pensaremos pensaréis pensarán	pensaría pensarías pensaría pensaríamos pensaríais pensarían	piense pienses piense pensemos penséis piensen	pensara pensaras pensara pensáramos pensarais pensaran	piensa tú, no pienses piense usted pensemos piensen Uds.

STEM-CHANGING AND ORTHOGRAPHIC-CHANGING VERBS (CONTINUED)

Infinitive Present Participle Past Participle	Indicative					Subjunctive		Imperative
	Present	Imperfect	Preterite	Future	Conditional	Present	Imperfect	
producir (zc) produciendo producido	produzco produces produce producimos producís producen	producía producías producía producíamos producíais producían	produje produjiste produjo produjimos produjisteis produjeron	produciré producirás producirá produciremos produciréis producirán	produciría producirías produciría produciríamos produciríais producirían	produzca produzcas produzca produzcamos produzcáis produzcan	produjera produjeras produjera produjéramos produjerais produjeran	produce tú, no produzcas produzca usted produzcamos produzcan Uds.
reír (i, i) riendo reído	río ríes ríe reímos reís ríen	reía reías reía reíamos reíais reían	reí reíste rio reímos reísteis rieron	reiré reirás reirá reiremos reiréis reirán	reiría reirías reiría reiríamos reiríais reirían	ría rías ría riamos riáis rían	riera rieras riera riéramos rierais rieran	ríe tú, no rías ría usted riamos rían Uds.
seguir (i, i) (ga) siguiendo seguido	sigo sigues sigue seguimos seguís siguen	seguía seguías seguía seguíamos seguíais seguían	seguí seguiste siguió seguimos seguisteis siguieron	seguiré seguirás seguirá seguiremos seguiréis seguirán	seguiría seguirías seguiría seguiríamos seguiríais seguirían	siga sigas siga sigamos sigáis sigan	siguiera siguieras siguiera siguiéramos siguierais siguieran	sigue tú, no sigas siga usted sigamos sigan Uds.
sentir (ie, i) sintiendo sentido	siento sientes siente sentimos sentís sienten	sentía sentías sentía sentíamos sentíais sentían	sentí sentiste sintió sentimos sentisteis sintieron	sentiré sentirás sentirá sentiremos sentiréis sentirán	sentiría sentirías sentiría sentiríamos sentiríais sentirían	sienta sientas sienta sintamos sintáis sientan	sintiera sintieras sintiera sintiéramos sintierais sintieran	siente tú, no sientas sienta usted sintamos sientan Uds.
volver (ue) volviendo vuelto	vuelvo vuelves vuelve volvemos volvéis vuelven	volvía volvías volvía volvíamos volvíais volvían	volví volviste volvió volvimos volvisteis volvieron	volveré volverás volverá volveremos volveréis volverán	volvería volverías volvería volveríamos volveríais volverían	vuelva vuelvas vuelva volvamos volváis vuelvan	volviera volvieras volviera volviéramos volvierais volvieran	vuelve tú, no vuelvas vuelva usted volvamos vuelvan Uds.

Apéndice 3

Spanish to English Vocabulary

This vocabulary includes all words presented in the text, except for proper nouns spelled the same in English and Spanish, diminutives with a literal meaning, typical expressions of the Hispanic countries presented in the **Enfoque cultural**, and cardinal numbers (found on pages 14 and 15). Other cognates and words easily recognized because of the context, which are presented after lesson 11, are not included either.

The number following each entry corresponds to the **lección** in which the word was first introduced. Numbers in italics followed by *r* signal that the item was presented for recognition rather than as active vocabulary.

A

a *at, to* B; **es a las** *it's at* B; **a veces** *sometimes* 1
abajo *below 4r*
abierto *open 10r,* 13; *opened* 13
el/la abogado/a *lawyer* 9
abrazar(se) (c) *to embrace* 13
el abrazo *embrace, hug 1r*
el abrelatas *can opener 5r*
el abrigo *coat* 6
abril *April* B
abrir *to open* Br, 11
abrupto/a *abrupt 10r*
absoluto/a *absolute 5r*
la abuela *grandmother* 4
el abuelo *grandfather* 4
los abuelos *grandparents* 4
abundar *abound, to be plentiful 13r*
aburrido/a *boring* 1; *bored* 2
aburrirse *to be bored 7r*
acabar *to finish, to end* 13; **acabar de + inf.** *to have just + past. part. 2r,* 13
académico/a *academic 3r*
acampar *to camp 10r*
acceder *to agree 10r; to access 14r*
el acceso *access 9r*
el accesorio *accessory* 5
el accidente *accident 9r*
la acción *action 8r*
el aceite *oil* 10
la aceituna *olive 10r*
el acento *accent 3r*
la acentuación *accentuation 2r*
aceptar *to accept* 8*r,* 13
acerca de *about 1r*
el acero *steel 5r*
aclarar *to clarify 8r*
aclaratorio/a *clarifying 14r*
acogedor/a *friendly 6r*
acompañar *to accompany 2r,* 8
aconsejable *advisable 12r*
aconsejar *to give advice 5r,* 10
el acontecimiento *event 1r*
el acorazado *battleship 3r*
acortar *to shorten* 13
acostar *to put to bed* 7; **acostarse (ue)** , *to go to bed* 7
acostumbrado/a *used to 10r; accustomed 14r*
acreditar *to accredit 12r*
la actitud *attitude 5r*
la actividad *activity 1r*
activo/a *active* B
el actor *actor 3r,* 9
la actriz *actress* 9
la actuación *performance 9r*
actual *present, current* 14
la actualidad *present time 4r,* 13
actualmente *at the present time* 9
actuar *to act 5r,* 13
acuático/a adj. *water 7r*
el acuerdo *agreement 5r;* **estar de acuerdo** *to agree 2r,* 3; **de acuerdo con/a** *according to 4r*
el acumulador *battery* 12
acumular *to accumulate 9r*
acusar *to accuse 9r*
la adaptación *adaptation 3r*
adaptar(se) *to adapt 5r*
adecuado/a *appropriate 4r*
adelante *forward 9r;* **más adelante** *later on 11r;*
el adelanto *advance 14r*
adelgazar (c) *to lose weight 10r*
el ademán *gesture 15r*
además adv. *besides 1r*
adepto/a *follower 7r*
el aderezo *salad dressing* 10
adicional *additional 4r*
adicto/a *addicted 10r*
adiós *good-bye* B
el/la adivinador/a *fortune teller 4r*
la adivinanza *riddle 2r*
adivinar *to guess, to figure out* 1*r*
la administración *management* 1r
administrativo/a *administrative 5r*
la admiración *admiration 2r*
admirar *to admire 2r*
la admisión *admission 1r*
admitido/a *admitted 1r*
el/la adolescente *adolescent 4r*
adonde *where (to) 1r*
adónde *where (to)* 3
adoptar *to adopt 10r*
adornado/a *decorated 8r*
el adorno *decoration 10r*
adquirir *to acquire 4r*
la aduana *customs* 12
adulto/a *adult 3r,* 14
la adversidad *adversity 9r*
advertir (ie, i) *to observe, to warn 14r*
aéreo/a adj. air *3r*
aeróbico/a *aerobic 5r*
la aerolínea *airline* 12
el aeropuerto *airport 4r, 12*
afectar *to affect 8r*
afeitar(se) *to shave* 7
el/la aficionado/a *fan 7*
afilado/a *sharp 5r*
la afirmación *statement 8r*
afirmar *to assure 5r*
afirmativamente *in the affirmative 5r*
afortunado/a *fortunate 5r*

africano/a *African 2r*
las afueras *outskirts 5*
la agencia *agency;* agencia de viajes *travel agency* 12
la agenda *agenda 3r*
el/la agente *agent 5r,* 12; agente de viajes *travel agent* 12
agitar *to shake 5r*
agosto *August* B
agradable *nice* 2
agradecer (zc) *to thank 8r*
el agradecimiento *gratitude 8r*
el agregado *addition 2r*
agregar *to add 10r*
agresivo/a *aggressive Br*
agrícola *agricultural 9r*
agrio/a *sour* 10
agrupar *to group together 8r*
el agua *water* 3; agua con gas *carbonated water* 3
el aguacate *avocado* 10
el agujero *hole 14r*
el/la ahijado/a *godchild* 4
ahí *there 1r*
ahora adv. *now 1r,* 2
ahorrar *to save 6r*
el aire *air, flair 2r,* 3*;* aire acondicionado *air conditioning 3r,* 5; al aire libre *outdoors 3*
el ají *pepper 10r*
el ajiaco *type of soup 4r*
el ajo *garlic 5r, 10*
al *to the* (contraction of *a + el*) *1r,* 3; al lado (de) *next to* B
la alarma *alarm 5r*
el albergue *lodgings 8r*
el/la alcalde/sa *mayor 10r*
alcalino *alkaline 10r*
alcanzar (c) *to reach 11r,* 13
alcohólico/a *alcoholic 10r*
la aldea *village 9r*
alegrarse (de) *to be glad (about)* 11
alegre *happy, glad 2*
la alegría *joy 1r, 8*
alemán/alemana *German 1r*
la alergia *allergy 3r*
el alfabeto *alphabet Br*
el alfiler *pin 15r*
la alfombra *carpet, rug 5*
el alga *seaweed 10r*
algo *something 1; anything 12*
el algodón *cotton 6*
alguien *someone, anyone, somebody* 12
algún *some 1r,* 12; *any 12*
alguno/a *some 1r,* 2; *any Br,* 12
algunos/as *any, some 5r,* 12
la alimentación *diet 10r*
alimentar *to feed 10r*
el alimento *food 5r, 10*
alineado/a *lined-up 6r*
el aliño *seasoning* 10
allá *over there 3r*
allí *there 1r, 3r, 5*
el almacén *department store* 6
almacenar *to keep, to sore 2r*
la almohada *pillow 5*
almorzar (ue) *to have lunch* 4
el almuerzo *lunch Br,* 3
aló *hello* 3
el alojamiento *lodging 12r*
alquilar *to rent* 3
el alquiler *rent 5r*
alrededor *around 1r*
el altar *altar 8r*
alternar *to alternate 12r*
alto/a *tall,* 2; *high 1r,* 2; más alto *louder Br*
altruista *altruistic 9r*
la altura *height 7r*
el/la alumno/a *student* 1
la alusión *reference 9r*
el ama de casa *housewife, homemaker 5r, 9*
amable *nice 2r*
el/la amante *lover 8r*
amar *to love 14r*
amarillo/a *yellow* 2
amasar *to knead 10r*
amazónico/a *Amazonian 6r*
la ambición *ambition 2r*
ambicioso/a *ambitious* Br
ambiental *environmental 8r*
el ambiente *atmosphere, environment 4r*
el ámbito *scope, world 9r*
ambos/as *both 2r*
ambulante: vendedor/a ambulante *street vendor 8r*
amenazar (c) *to threaten, to menace* 15
americano/a *American 3r*
amigable *friendly 2r*
el/la amigo/a *friend* B
la amistad *friendship 2r,* 8
el amor *love* 3
la ampliación *enlargement, expansion 1r*
ampliar *to expand 14r*
amplio/a *wide 1r*
amueblado/a *furnished 5r*
el amuleto *amulet 10r*
el analfabetismo *illiteracy 14r*
el análisis *analysis 11*
analizar (c) *to analyze 6r*
anaranjado/a *orange* 2
ancho/a *wide 6*
el anda *platform to place an image 8r*
el andinismo *mountaineering 9r*
andino/a *Andean 6r*
la angustia *anguish 12r*
el anillo ring 6
el/la animador/a *host, hostess 9r*
la animación *animation 9r*
animado/a *animated, lively 9r*
el/la animador/a *host (of a program) 9r*
el animal *animal 1r,* 2
animar *to entertain, to host 9r*
el anisado *anisette (licor) 3r*
el aniversario *anniversary Br*
anoche *last night 6*
anotar *to jot down 6r*
la ansiedad *anxiety 11r*
ante(a)noche *night before last 6*
anteayer *day before yesterday* 6
el/la antepasado/a *ancestor 8*
anterior adj. *previous, prior 1r*
anterioridad: con anterioridad *in advance 8r*
antes adv. *in advance, before 1r, 8*
el antibiótico *antibiotic 11r*
la anticipación *anticipation, in advance* 1r
la antigüedad *antique 9r*
antiguo/a *old 1r,* 8; *former* 8
antipático/a *unpleasant* 2
la antropología *anthropology 1*
anual *annual 7r*
anunciar *to advertise 5r; to announce, to tell 8r,* 14
el anuncio *ad (advertisement), announcement 3r, 9*
añadir to add *6r,* 10
el año *year* B; el año pasado *last year* 6*;* el año próximo *next year* 3; Año Nuevo *New Year's Day* 8
apagar (gu) *to extinguish, to put out* 9; *to turn off (the light)* 15
el aparato *instrument, set 10r*
aparecer (zc) *to appear, to show up 4r*
la aparición *appearance 9r*
la apariencia *appearance 2r*
el apartado postal (de correos) *P.O. box 9r*
el apartamento *apartment* 1r, 5
aparte (de) *besides 2r*
apasionante *exciting 4r*
el apellido *last name 2r,* 14
el aperitivo *appetizer, apéritif 3r*
el apetito *appetite 10r*
aplaudir *to applaud* 7
apoyar *to support, to back up 7r*

el apoyo *support 9r*
apreciar *to appreciate 4r*
aprender *to learn* 1r
apretar (ie) *to press 15r*
la aprobación *approval 14r*
apropiado/a *appropriate 4r*
aprovechar *to take advantage* 7
aproximadamente *approximately 6r*
apuntes: tomar apuntes *to take notes* 1
aquel/aquella adj. *that 3r,* 5; aquél/aquélla pron. *that one 2r,* 5
aquellos/aquellas adj. *those* 5; aquéllos/aquéllas pron. *those* 5
aquí *here* 5
el árabe *Arab 10r; Arabian 1r*
arbitrar *to referee 7r*
el árbitro *umpire, referee* 7
el árbol *tree 4r,* 7
el archivo *file cabinet* 2r
la ardilla *squirrel 2r*
el área *area 5r,* 13
la arena *sand 7r*
arenoso/a *sandy 7r*
el arete *earring* 6
argentino/a *Argentinian* 2
el argumento *argument 12r*
el arma *arm 14r*
el armario *closet, armoire* 5
la armonía *harmony 4r*
armonioso/a *harmonious 10r*
la arqueología *archaeology 8r*
arqueológico/a *archaelogical 8r*
el/la arquitecto/a *architect* 9
la arquitectura *architecture* 1
arreglar *to fix, to repair 9r*
arrendar (ie) *to rent 5r*
arriba *above 5r*
arriesgar *to risk 13r*
arrogante *arrogant* Br
el arroz *rice* 3
el arte *art* Br; bellas artes *fine arts 9r*
el artefacto *artifact 9r*
artesanal adj. *handicrafts 10r*
la artesanía *handicrafts 4r,* 10
el/la artesano/a *craftsman/woman 2r*
el artículo *article 1r*
el/la artista *artist 2r*
artístico/a *artistic 6r*
la arveja *pea 10r*
asado/a *baked 3r; roast 6r*
la asamblea *assembly 9r*
la ascendencia *ancestry, origin 2r*
ascender *to ascend, to advance (in business) 14r*
el ascenso *promotion 13r, 14*
el ascensor *elevator 5r*
asegurar *assure 9r*

el aserrín *sawdust 8r*
el asesinato *assassination, murder 12r*
la asfixia *asphyxia 12r*
así *so 1r; this way* 6; así como *as well as 2r*
asiático/a *Asian 2r*
el asiento *seat* 12; asiento de pasillo *aisle seat* 12
asimilar/se *to assimilate, to incorporate 12r*
asimismo *likewise 10r*
la asistencia *attendance 7r*; *asistencia social welfare 14*
el/la asistente *assistant 5r, 13*
asistir *to attend 4r*
la asociación *association 1r*
asociado/a *associated 7r*
asociar *to associate 4r*
el aspecto *aspect 2r; appearance 8r*
la aspiradora *vacuum cleaner* 5
la aspirina *aspirin* 11
el/la astronauta *astronaut 9r*
el/la astrónomo *astronomer 3r*
asumir *to assume (responsibilities)* 13
el asunto *subject, matter, issue* 15
la atención *attention, service 3r*
atender (ie) *to take care of 5r; to attend, to answer (telephone)* 9
atendido/a *attended 6r*
atentamente *sincerely 2r*
aterrizar (c) *to land 15r*
aterrorizar (c) *to terrorize 9r*
atípico/a *atypical 4r*
atlántico/a adj *Atlantic 2r*
el/la atleta *athlete 7r*
atlético/a *athletic* Br
la atmósfera *atmosphere* 7
la atracción *attraction 12r*
el atractivo *attraction 8r*; adj. *attractive* Br
atragantar *to choke 12r*
atrapar *to catch 14r*
atrasado/a *late 12r*
el atún *tuna 3r*
el auditorio *auditorium 3r*
el aula *classroom 13r*
aumentar *to increase 6r*
el aumento *increase 5r; raise 9r*
aun *even 9r*
aún *still 9r*
aunque *although 2r,* 14
la ausencia *absence 9r*
ausentarse *to be absent 14r*
ausente adj. *absent* Br
auténtico/a *authentic 8r*
auto(móvil) *car* 2
autobiográfico/a *autobiographic 2r*

el autobús *bus 4r,* 12
la autopista *freeway* 12
el/la autor/a *author 5r*
la autoría *authorship 9r*
la autoridad *authority 7r*
autoritario/a *authoritarian 9r*
el/la auxiliar: auxiliar de vuelo *steward, stewardess* 12
el avance *advance 9r*
avanzado/a *advanced 1r*
el ave *fowl, bird (poultry) 8r, 10*
la avenida *avenue Br*
la aventura *adventure 9r*
averiguar *to find out 1r*
el avión *airplane 3r,* 12
avisar *to let (someone) know 14r*
el aviso *advertisement, notice 4r, sign 14r*
ayer *yesterday* 6
la ayuda *help 4r*
el/la ayudante *assistant 13*
ayudar *to help 4*
azar: el azar *at random 12r*
azteca *Aztec 5r*
el/la azúcar *sugar 9r,* 10
azul *blue* 2
el azulejo *tile 5r*

B

bailar *to dance 1*
el bailarín/la bailarina *dancer 2r*
el baile *dance 1r*
la bajada *slope 7r*
bajar *to get off, to come down 7r;* bajar de peso *to lose weight 3r*
bajo/a *short 2;* prep. *under 3r*
el balboa *monetary unit of Panamá 1r*
el balcón *balcony 5r*
el balneario *(seaside) resort 2r*
el baloncesto *basketball 7*
bancario adj. *bank 14r*
el banco *bank 5r*
la banda *band 8r*
la bandeja *tray 10*
el banquete *banquet Br*
la bañadera/bañera *tub 5*
bañar(se) *to bathe, to take a bath* 4; bañarse en la playa *to go swimming 3r*
el baño *bathroom 2r, 5*
el bar *bar 4r*
barato/a *inexpensive, cheap* 6
la barbacoa *barbecue 5*
el barco *ship, boat 3r,* 2
barrer *to sweep 5*
el barrio *neighborhood Br, 5*

el barro *mud, clay 3r*
basar(se) *to base 4r*
la base *base 2r*
básicamente *basically 4r*
básico/a *basic 1r*
el basquetbol *basketball 2r, 7*
bastante adv. *enough* 1; bastante bien *pretty well, rather well* B; *a lot 10r*
bastar *to be enough 15r*
la basura *garbage 5*
la bata *robe* 6
batallar *to fight 4r*
el bate *baseball bat 7*
la batería *battery* 12
el batido *shake 3r*
la batidora *beater 5r*
batir *to beat 5r, 10*
el bautizo *baptism, christening* 4
el/la bebé *baby 4r*
beber *to drink* 3
la bebida *drink* 3
la beca *scholarship 13r*
el béisbol *baseball 2r, 6*
la belleza *beauty 1r*
bello/a *beautiful 1r*
la bendición *blessing 8r*
la beneficiencia *charity 9r*
el beneficio *benefit 5r*
besar *to kiss* 13
el beso *kiss 1r*
la biblioteca *library* 1
el/la bibliotecario/a *librarian 9*
la bicicleta *bicycle* 1
bien adv. *well* B; ¡Qué bien! *That's great* 3
los bienes *goods 9r;* bienes raíces *real estate 5r*
el bienestar *well-being, welfare* 15
bienvenido/a *welcome B*
bilingüe *bilingual 2r*
el billete *ticket 3r*
la billetera *wallet* 6
la biología *biology* 1r
la biosfera *biosphere 15*
el bistec *steak 3*
blanco/a *white* 1
bloquear *to block* 15
la blusa *blouse* 6
la boca *mouth 11*
el bocado *bite 10r*
la boda *wedding 8*
la boletería *ticket office 3r*
el boleto *ticket 3r, 12;* boleto de ida y vuelta *roundtrip ticket* 12
el bolígrafo *ball-point pen* B
el bolívar *monetary unit of Venezuela 1r*
el boliviano *monetary unit of Bolivia 1r; Bolivian 2r*
los bolos *bowling 7*
la bolsa/el bolso *purse, bag 6*
bolsa de valores *stock market 15r*
el/la bombero/a *firefighter 9*
bonito/a *pretty 2*
el bono *bonus 9r*
el borde *edge 10r*
el borrador *eraser B*
el bosque *forest 5r, 15;* bosque tropical *rain forest 5r, 15*
la bota *boot* 6
el bote *boat 10r*
la botella *bottle 5r, 10*
el botones *bellhop* 12
el boxeador *boxer 7r*
boxear *to box 7r*
la brasa: a la brasa *barbecued 6r*
brasileño/a *Brazilian 7r*
el brazo *arm* 11
brillante *brilliant 5r*
el brote *outbreak 11r*
el/la bruto/a *brute, stupid 9r*
el buceo *skin diving 7r*
buen *good 2r, 5*
bueno/a *good* 1; *well 1r*
la bufanda *scarf* 6
el bulevar *boulevard 2r*
el bus *bus* 12
busca: en busca de *in search of 9r,* 15
el buscapersonas *beeper 11r*
buscar (qu) *to look for* 1
la búsqueda *search 1r*
la butaca *armchair 5*
el buzón *mailbox 1r, 12*

C

el caballero *gentleman 2r*
el caballo *horse 3r*
el cabello *hair* 11
la cabeza *head* 11
la cabina *cabin, cockpit 15r*
cada adj. *each, every 1r, 7*
la cadera *hip 11*
caer(se) *to fall* 11; caer bien *to like 6r*
café *brown* 2
el café *coffe house* 1; *coffee 1r,* 3; plus café *after dinner drink 3r*
la cafeína *caffeine 10r*
la cafetería *cafeteria 1*
la caída *drop 6r*
la caja *cash register 9r box 12r;* caja fuerte *safe* 12
el/la cajero/a *cashier* 9; el cajero automático *ATM (machine) 6r*
el calcetín *sock* 6
el calcio *calcium 10r*
la calculadora *calculator* B
calcular *to calculate 7r*
el cálculo *calculus* 1r
la calefacción *heater 5*
el calentamiento *warming 15r*
calentar (ie) *to warm up, to heat up 12r*
la calidad *quality 5r,* 14
cálido/a *warm 3r*
caliente *hot* 3
la calificación *qualification 2r, rating 14r*
calificar (qu) *to qualify, to describe 4r*
callado/a *quiet* 2
callarse *to be quiet 2r*
la calle *street* B
el calor: tener calor *to be hot* 5; hacer calor *to be hot (weather) 4r, 7*
la caloría *calorie 10r*
el calzado *footwear 7r*
los calzoncillos *boxer shorts* 6
la cama *bed 5*
la cámara *camera 9r, chamber 13r*
la camarera *waitress 3*
el camarero *waiter* 3
el camarón *shrimp* 3
el camarote *cabin (on boat)* 12r
cambiar *to change, to exchange* 2r, 6; cambiar de papel *switch roles Br*
el cambio *change 2r*
el camello *camel 8r*
el/la caminante *walker 3r*
caminar *to walk* 1
la caminata *walk 10r*
el camino *road, way 8*
el camión *truck 9r*
la camisa *shirt 6*
la camiseta *T-shirt 6*
el camisón *nightgown* 6
el campamento *camp 6r*
la campaña *campaign 9r*
el/la campeón/a *champion* 7
el campeonato *championship 5r, 7*
el/la campesino/a *peasant 15*
el campo *field* 7; *countryside 13*
el canal *channel 7r; canal 12r*
canalizar (c) *to channel 7r*
cancelar *to cancel* 12
el cáncer *cancer 3r*
la cancha *court 7*
la canción *song 2r,* 3
el/la candidato/a *candidate 2r*
cansado/a *tired* 2
el cansancio *fatigue 10r*
cansar(se) *to get tired* 10
cantado/a *sung 8r*

el/la cantante *singer 3r*
cantar *to sing* 3
la cantidad *quantity, amount 4r*
la cantina *bar 9r*
cantonés/cantonesa *Cantonese 3r*
la caña *rattan 5r*
la capacidad capacity *4r*
la capacitación *training 9r*
la capa *layer 15r*
capaz *capable 12r*
la capilla *chapel 4r*
la capital *capital* 1r
el capitán/la capitana *captain 7r*
el capó *car hood* 12
la cara *face* 11
el carácter *character 8r*
la característica *characteristic 1r*
el caramelo *candy 8r*
el carbón *coal 15r*
el/la cardiólogo/a *cardiologist 9r*
carecer (zc) *to lack 2r,* 14
cargar *to load 8r*
el cargo *position 9r,* 13
caribeño/a *from the Caribbean 6r*
el cariño *affection, love 5r, 14r*
cariñosamente *affectionately 4r*
cariñoso/a *affectionate 2r*
carmelita *brown 2r*
el Carnaval *Mardi Gras* 8
la carne *meat 6r,* 10; carne molida/picada *ground meat* 10; carne de res *beef* 10
caro/a *expensive 4r, 6*
la carrera *career 1r; race 2r, 6*
la carreta *cart, wagon* 8
la carretera *highway* 12
el carro *car* 12
la carroza *float 8*
la carta *letter 2r,* 12; *menu 3r*
el cartero *mailman* 12
el cartón: de cartón *(made of) cardboard* 15
la casa *home, house* 1
casado/a *married* 2
casarse *to get married 4r, 14*
el cascabel *bell 4r*
el casco *helmet 13r*
casero/a adj *house 11r*
el casete *cassette* 1
casi adv. *almost 8r*
el casillero *pigeonhole 5r*
el caso *case 9r*
castaño *brown 2*
el castellano *Castillian (Spanish) language 1r*
el/la catador/a *wine taster 9r*
catalán *Catalonian 1r*
el catálogo *catalogue 7r*
la catarata *cataract, fall 2r*
el catarro *chest cold* 11
catastrófico/a *catastrophic 12r*
la catedral *cathedral 1r*
la categoría *category 4r*
católico/a *Catholic 8r*
el caudillo *strong man, dictator 14r*
la causa: *cause 12r;* a causa de *because of* 12
causar *to cause* 15
el cayo *key 12r*
la cebolla *onion 5r, 10*
la cédula *identification card 2r*
la ceja *eyebrow* 11
la celebración *celebration 1r, 8*
celebrar *to celebrate* 3
celta *Celt 2r*
la célula *cell 15r*
el celular *cellular phone 10r*
el cementerio *cemetery 8*
la cena *dinner, supper* 3
cenar *to have dinner* 3
el censo *census 13r, 14*
la censura *censorship 8r*
centenario/a *hundred-year old 8r*
centrar(se) *to center 10r*
céntrico/a adj. *central 5r*
el centro *center 1r,* 5; *downtown* 5; centro comercial *shopping center 5r,* 6
centroamericano/a *Central American 2r*
la cepa *roostalk 9r*
cerca (de) *near 2r, 5*
cercano/a *close, near by 4r*
el cerdo *pork 10*
el cereal *cereal* 3
el cerebro *brain* 11
la ceremonia *ceremony 6r*
la cereza *cherry* 10
cerrado/a *closed 5r*
cerrar (ie) *to close* Br, 4
certificado/a *certified 9r*
la cerveza *beer* 3
el cesto *wastepaper basket* B; el cesto/la cesta *basket, hoop* 7
el ceviche *raw fish dish* 3
el champaña *champagne 4r*
chao/chau *good-bye* B
la chaqueta *jacket* 6
la charcutería *delicatessen 6r*
la charla *talk, chat 1r*
charlar *to chat 14r*
el cheque *check 6r;* cheque de viajero *traveller's check* 12
la chica *girl* B
el chico *boy B*
chileno/a *Chilean* 2
la chimenea *fireplace* 5
chino/a *Chinese 5r*
el chiste *joke 8r*
chocar (qu) *to crash 12r*
el chocolate chocolate *3r*
el chofer *driver 9*
la chuleta *chop* 10
el churro *batter deep fried 10r*
el ciberespacio *cyberspace 15r*
el ciclismo *cycling 7*
el/la ciclista *cyclist 7*
ciego/a *blind 15r*
el cielo *sky 12r,* 15
la ciencia *science* 1; ciencia-ficción *science-fiction 2r*
el/la científico/*a scientist 9*
cierto adv. *true, certain 1r,* 10; por cierto *by the way 9*
la cifra *figure 14r*
la cima *summit, top 8r*
el cine *movies* Br, 3
cinematográfico/a adj. *movie 3r*
el/la cineasta *film director 9r*
la cinta *movie 9r*
la cintura *waist 11*
el cinturón *belt* 6; cinturón de seguridad *safety belt* 12
circular *to circulate 11r*
el círculo *circle 8r*
la circunstancia *circumstance 5r*
la cirugía *surgery 9r*
el/la cirujano/a *surgeon 11r*
la cita *date 2r*; cita a ciegas *blind date 2r*; cita (textual) *quote 7r*
la ciudad *city 1r,* 3
el/la ciudadano/a *citizen 13*
civil *civil, civilian 2r*
la civilización *civilization 4r*
la clara (de huevo) *egg white 5r*
claro/a *light, clear 2r; of course 5*
la clase *class* B
clásico/a *classic 1r*
clasificado/a *classified 1r*
clasificar (qu) *to classify 4r*
clasificatorio/a *preliminary 7r*
el/la cliente *client 6r,* 9
el clima *climate 3r*
climatizado/a *air conditioned 15r*
la clínica *clinic, hospital 11r*
el club *club 2r*
el cobre *copper 9r*
la cocaína *cocaine 14r*
el coche *car 4r, 12*
la cocina *kitchen,* 5; *cooking, cuisine Br*
cocinado/a *cooked 10r*
cocinar *to cook* 5
el/la cocinero/a *cook 2r*
el coco *coconut 4r*
el código: código postal *zip code 3r*

el codo *elbow 11*
el cognado *cognate Br*
la coherencia *coherence 4r*
el cohete *rocket* 15
coincidir *to coincide 6r*
colaborar *to collaborate 5r*
el colador *colander, strainer 5r*
colar *to strain 5r*
la colección *collection 4r*
el/la coleccionista *collector 9r*
colectivo/a *collective 8r*
el/la colega *colleague 4r*
el colibrí *hummingbird 8r*
la colina *hill 9r*
el collar *necklace* 6
colocar (qu) *to place 13r*
colombiano/a *Colombian 2*
el colón *monetary unit of Costa Rica and El Salvador 1r*
colonial *colonial 2r*
el color *color* 2; de color entero *solid color* 6
colorado/a *red 10r*
el colorante *colouring 10r*
el colorido *color 8r; colorful 8r*
la columna *column 4r*
la coma *comma 3r*
el comandante *commander, major 12r*
combatir *to fight 14r*
combinar *combine 3r*
la comedia *comedy 3r*
el comedor *dining room 5*
comentar *to comment, to discuss 6r*
el comentario *comment, commentary 3r*
comenzar (ie, c) *to begin 1r,* 8
comer *to eat 1r, 3*
comercial *commercial 2r*; centro comercial *shopping center* 6
la comercialización *commercialization 6r*
el/la comerciante *business person, trading 13r*
el comercio *commerce, business 5r*, 13
cómico/a *comic, funny* Br
la comida *dinner, supper* 3; *food* 10
el comienzo *beginning* 8
el comino *cumin 10r*
la comisión *commission 7r*
el comité *committee 6r*
como adv. *as, like 1r,* 8
cómo *how, what* B; *as 8;* ¿cómo te va? *How is it going?* 1; cómo no of course 9
la cómoda *dresser 5*
la comodidad *comfort 5r*
cómodo/a *comfortable 3r*
compacto/a *compact 2r*

el/la compañero/a *partner, classmate Br, 1*
la compañía *company, corporation 2r,* 9
comparar *to compare 4r*
la comparación *comparison 8r*
la comparsa *costumed group* 8
compartir *to share 1r*
el compás *rhythm 4r*
la compensación *compensation 5r*
la competencia *competition 1r*
competente *competent Br*
competir (i) *to compete* 7
el complejo *complex 14r*
complementar *to complement 10r*
complementario/a *complementary 1r*
completar *to complete* Br
completo/a *complete* 1r
la complicación *complication 11r*
complicado/a *complex 10r*
el componente *component 4r*
el comportamiento *behavior 9r*
composición *composition 1r*
el/la compositor/a *composer 9r*
la compra *shopping* 6; ir de compras *to go shopping 3r,* 6
el/la comprador/a *buyer 6r*
comprar *to buy* 1
la compraventa *buying and selling 4r*
comprender *to understand Br*
comprobar (ue) *to check, to confirm 9r*
comprometidola *committed 14r*
el compromiso *obligation, commitment 2r*
compuesto/a *compound 5r*
la computadora *computer* B
común *common 1r*
la comunicación *communication 2r*
comunicar(se) (qu) to communicate *3r, 9*
la comunidad *community 4r*
con *with* B; con permiso *excuse me* B
la concentración *concentration 4r*
concentrar *to concentrate 7r*
la concepción *conception 8r*
el concepto *concept 6r*
el concierto *concert Br*
conciliar: conciliar el sueño *to get to sleep 10r*
la concordancia *agreement 4r*
el concurso *contest* 1r
la condición *condition 10r*
el condimento *condiment 10r*
el condominio *condominium* 1r
el/la conductor/a *driver 12r*
la conducta *behaviour 10r*
la confección *making 8r*
confeccionar *to make 8r*
la conferencia *lecture 1r; conference 2r*

la confiabilidad *trust 14r*
la confianza *trust* 14
configurar *to shape, to form 4r*
confiscar (qu) *to confiscate 14r*
confundido/a *confused 11r*
confundir(se) *to mix up, to confuse, to be confused 13r*
congelado/a *frozen 10r*
congelar(se) *to freeze* 7
congénito/a *congenital 15r*
el/la congresista *congressman-woman 13r*
el congreso *congress, convention 5r*
conjugar *to conjugate 4r*
el conjunto *set, group 12r;* adj. *joint 9r*
conmemorar *to commemorate 8r*
conmigo *with me 2r,* 7
el/la conocedor/a *expert 9r*
conocer (zc) *to know, to meet* 1r, 5
conocido/a *known, famous 2r; acquaintance 2r*
la conquista *conquest 7r*
el/la conquistador/a *conqueror 8r*
conquistar *to conquer 13r*
consagrado/a *recognized 9r*
la consecuencia *consequence 2r*
conseguir *to obtain, to get 2r; to accomplish 12r*
el/la consejero/a *counselor, adviser 9r*
el consejo *advise 11r*
el/la conserje *concierge* 12
la conservación *preservation 15*
conservado/a *kept, preserved 5r*
el/la conservador/a *conservative 2r*
el conservante *preservative 10r*
conservar(se) *to keep, preserve 4r*
considerablemente *considerably 7r*
considerar(se) *to consider 2r*
consistir *to consist of, to be composed of 6r*
la constancia *perseverance 4r*
constante *constant 1r*
constar *to consist 10r*
constituir *constitute 2r*
la construcción *construction 5r*
construido/a *built 5r*
construir (y) *to build 1r,* 15
el cónsul *consul 2r*
el consulado *consulate 2r*
consultar *to consult* 1r, 14
el consultorio *doctor's office* 9
consumado/a *accomplished 9r*
el/la consumidor/a *consumer 6r*
consumir *to consume, to eat 3r*
la contabilidad *accounting* 1r
contactar *to contact 9r*
el contacto *contact 1r*

el/la contador/a *accountant* 9
contagiar(se) *to give or spread/to get a desease by contagion* 11
el contagio *contagion, spreading of a desease* 11r
la contaminación *contamination* 8r, 15
contaminado/a *contaminated* 3r, 7
contar (ue) *to tell* 8r, 13
contemporáneo/a contemporary 1r
contener (g, ie) *to contain* 10r
el contenido *contents* 4r, 11; *contenido controlled* 11r
contento/a happy, glad 2
la contestación *answer* Br
el contestador: *el contestador automático answering machine* 15
contestar *to answer* Br, 6
el contexto *context* 3r
contigo *with you* 5r, 7
continuación: a continuación *below* 10r
continuamente *continuously* 10r
continuar *to continue* 8r, 14
contra *against* 7r, 15
contraer (g) *to contract* 11r
contrario/a *opposite, contrary* 7
el contraste *contrast* 4r
contratar *to hire* 14r
el contrato *contract* 9r
la contribución *contribution* 13r
contribuir *to contribute* 2r
controlar *to control* 7r
conveniente *convenient* 5r
convenir (g, ie) *to suit, to be convenient* 6r
el convento *convent* 8r
la conversación *conversation* Br
conversar *to talk, to converse* 1
convertir(se) (ie, i) *to make, to become* 4r, 13
cooperar *to cooperate* 4r
la cooperativa *cooperative society* 9r
la coorporación *corporation* 3r
la copa *stemmed glass* 10; *drink* 3r; la Copa Mundial *World Cup* 7
la copia *copy* 6r
copiar *to copy* 1r
el coraje *courage* 12r
el corazón *heart* 11
la corbata *tie* 6
el corcho *cork* 5r
el córdoba *monetary unit of Nicaragua* 1r
correcto/a *correct* 4r
el corredor/a *runner, cyclist* 6
el correo *mail, post office* 9; el correo electrónico *e-mail* 2r, 15; por correo *by mail* 9r
correr *to run* 4; correr el riesgo *run the risk* 15
la correspondencia *correspondence, mail* 2r
corresponder *to correspond* 2r
correspondiente *corresponding* 7r
la corrida (de toros) *bullfight* 1r, 8
el cortado *coffee with a small amount of milk or cream* 2r; adj. *cut up*
cortar *to cut* 5r, 10
el cortavientos *windbreaker* 7r
la cortesía *courtesy* Br
la cortina *curtain* 5
corto/a *short* 2
la cosa *thing* 1r
la cosecha *harvest* 15
coser *to sew* 5r
el cosmético *cosmetic* 6r
cosmopolita *cosmopolitan* 6r
la costa *coast* 2r
costar (ue) *to cost* 4; ¿cuánto cuesta? *How much is it?* 1
la costilla *rib* 10
el costo *cost* 1r
la costumbre *custom, use* 8
la creación *creation* 8r
el/la creador/a *inventor, creator* 4r
crear *to create* 4r
la creatividad *creativity* 4r
creativo/a creative Br
crecer (zc) *to grow up* 4r
el crecimiento *growth* 15r
el crédito *credit* 3r
la creencia *belief* 14
creer *to believe, to think* 3r, 5
la crema *cream* 3r, 10
el/la creyente *believer* 8r
la crianza *upbringing* 4r
criarse *to be brought up* 13
el crimen *crime* 8r, 14
criollo/a adj. *Spanish American* 3r
la crisis *crisis* 14r
cristiano/a *christian* 8r
Cristo *Christ* 8r
criticar (qu) *to criticize* 13r
el/la crítico/a *critic* 14r
la crónica *chronicle* 8r
el crucero *cruise* 6r, 12
el crucigrama *crossword puzzle* 6r
cruzar (c) *to cross* 2r
el cuaderno *notebook* B
la cuadra *city block* 3r, 12
cuadrado/a *square* 15r
el cuadrilátero *boxing ring* 7r
el cuadro *picture* 5; de cuadros *plaid* 6
cuál/es *what* B; *which (one)* 1
el/la/los/las cual(es) *which* 8r
cualquier/a *any* 1r
cuándo interrog. *when* B
cuando adv. *when* 1r, 2
cuanto: en cuanto *as soon as* 14
cuánto/a/os/as interrog *how much, how many* 1
la Cuaresma *Lent* 8
el cuarto quarter B; *room, bedroom* 2r, 5; *fourth* 5
cubano/a *Cuban* 2
cubanoamericano/a *Cuban American* 5r
los cubiertos *silverware* 5r
el cubo: en cubitos *in cubes* 10r
cubrir *to cover* 5r, 13
la cuchara spoon 5r, 10
la cucharada *spoon(full)* 10r
la cucharadita *teaspoon* 10r
la cucharita teaspoon 10
el cuchillo *knife* 5r, 10
la cueca *typical Chilean music* 12r
el cuello *neck* 11
la cuenca *river basin* 15
el cuenco *bowl* 5r
la cuenta: cuenta corriente *checking account* 9r
el cuento *story* 3r
el cuero *leather*; de cuero *(made of) leather* 6
el cuerpo *body* 4r, 11
la cueva *cave* 10r
el cuidado *care* 4r, 5; tener cuidado *to be careful* 5
cuidar(se) *to take care of* 5r, 11
la culpa *guilt* 14r
culpable *guilty* 11r
el cultivo *cultivation* 15r
la cultura *culture* 2r
cultural *cultural* 1r
la cumbia *Colombian music and dance* 4r
el cumpleaños *birthday* Br, 3
el cumplimiento *fulfillment* 14r
cumplir *fulfill, to keep* 5r
la cura *cure* 9r
el/la curandero/a *quack doctor* 11r
curar(se) *to cure, to get well* 10r
curativo/a *curative* 10r
la curiosidad *curiosity* 1r
curioso/a *curious* 5r
el currículum *résumé* 9
el cursillo *short course of studies* 12r
el curso *course* 1r
cuyo/a *whose* 5r

D

la dama *lady* 2r
la danza *dance* 1r

dañar *to damage, to harm* 15
el daño *damage, harm* 15
dar *to give 1r,* 6 **dar por sentado** *to take for granted 14r*
el dato *piece of information, data 3r,* 14
de about 2; *of, from* 2; **de nada** *you're welcome* B
debajo (de) adv. *under B*
deber *ought to, should* 3; **el deber** *duty* 14
debido: debido a *due to 4r,* 15
débil *weak* 2
decidir *to decide 3*
décimo/a *tenth 5*
decir (g, i) *to say, to tell Br,* 4; **es decir** *that is to say 2r*
la decisión *decision 6r*
decisivo/a *decisive 6r*
la declaración *declaration 9r*
declarado/a *declared 8r*
declarar *to declare 9r*
la decoración *decoration 6r*
el décuplo *decuple, tenfold* 15r
la dedicación *dedication 5r*
dedicar (qu) *to dedicate 4r*
el dedo finger *11*
defender (ie) *to defend 4r,*
la defensa *defense 11r*
el/la defensor/a *defender 13r*
la deficiencia *deficiency 10r*
la deforestación *deforestation 15*
la degustación *tasting 9r*
dejar *to leave (behind) 5r,* 9; *to let, to allow 9*
del *of the* (contraction of de + el) *1r,* 2
delante de *in front of 9r*
delgado/a *thin* 2
delicioso/a *delicious 2r*
la delincuencia *delinquency 8r*
la demanda *demand, claim 9r*
demás: los demás *the rest, others* 14
demasiado *too, excessively 5r*
democrático/a *democratic 5r*
demostrar (ue) *to show, to demonstrate 4r*
el demostrativo *demonstrative 5r*
la denominación *denomination 14r*
denotar *to denote, to indicate 4r*
denso/a *dense 15r*
el/la dentista *dentist 11r*
dentro *inside, in 4r*
el departamento *department* 1r
depender *to depend 5r*
el/la dependiente/dependienta *salesperson* 1
el deporte *sport* Br, 7
el/la deportista *sportsman/woman 7r*
deportivo/a adj. *sport 1r,* 6
deprimido/a *depressed 10r, 11*
la derecha *right 4r,* 12
el derecho *law 1r;* adv. *right 14r, straight* 12
el desacuerdo *disagreement 13r*
el/la desamparado/a *homeless 14r*
desaparecido/a *missing 2r*
desapercibido/a *unnoticed 9r*
desarrollar(se) *to develop 3r,* 15
el desarrollo *development 8r*
desayunar *to have breakfast 3r,* 4
el desayuno *breakfast 3*
descansar *to rest* 3
el descanso *rest 7r*
el/la descendiente *descendant, offspring 13r*
descomponer *to breakdown* 15
desconocido/a *unknown 9r*
el descontento *discontent 9r*
descremado/a *skim (milk) 10r*
describir *describe 1r*
la descripción *description Br*
descubrir to discover *5r*
el descuento *discount 6r*
desde *from 2r, since* 13; **desde luego** *of course 7r*
desear *to wish, to want 1r,* 2
desempleado/a *unemployed 9r*
el deseo *wish 9r*
desesperado/a *desperate 11r*
el desfile *parade* 8; **desfile de modas** *fashion show 6r*
el deshielo *thaw 15r*
el desierto *desert 3r*
la desigualdad *inequality 14r*
desmontar *to dismantle, dismount 12r*
desordenar *to disarrange 4r*
desorganizado/a *disorganized 9r*
el despacho *study, office 5r*
despacio *slowly* Br
la despedida *farewell* Br
despedir (i) *to fire, to terminate 9r;* **despedirse** *to say good-bye 3r*
despegar *to take off 15r*
despejado/a *clear (weather)* 7
desperdiciar *to waste* 15
el despertador *alarm clock 7r*
despertarse (ie) *to wake up* 7
después *after, later 1r,* 3; *then 4r*
destacado/a *outstanding, distinguished* 15
destacar (qu) *to stand out 7r*
destinar(se) *to address 4r; to destine 9r*
el destino *destination 3r,* 12
destruir (y) *to destroy 15r*
la desventaja *disadvantage* 1r, 14
la desventura *misfortune 9r*
el detalle *detail 5r*
el detective *detective* Br
detener (g, ie) *to stop 7r*
el deterioro *damage 7r*
determinad/a *specific 6r*
determinar *to determine 1r*
detestar(se) *to detest 11r*
detrás (de) *behind* B
la devoción *devotion 8r*
devolver (ue) *to return, to give back* 6r
el día *day* B; **buenos días** *good morning* B; **todos los días** *every day* 1; **el Día de Acción de Gracias** *Thanksgiving* 8; **el Día de las Brujas** *Halloween* 8
el/la diabético/a *diabetic 10r*
la Diablada *Hispanoamerican folkloric festival* 8
el diablo *devil 8r*
el dialecto *dialect 1r*
el diálogo *dialog 5r*
el diámetro *diameter 10r*
diariamente *daily 10r*
diario/a *daily 3r*
el dibujo *drawing 4r*
el diccionario *dictionary* 1
diciembre *December* B
la dicotomía *dichotomy 10r*
el dictador *dictator 14r*
la dictadura *dictatorship 13r*
dictar *to give (classes) 9r*
el diente *tooth 5r, 11*
la dieta *diet 3*
la diferencia *difference 3r*
diferenciar *to differenciate 3r*
diferente *different 1r*
difícil *difficult* 1
la difficultad *difficulty 13r*
difunto/a *dead, deceased* 8; *Día de los Difuntos All Souls Day* 8
digerir (ie) *to digest 10r*
la digestión *digestion 10r*
dinámico/a *dynamic* Br
el dinero *money 3r,* 6
Dios *God 8r*
la diplomacia *diplomacy 2r*
diplomático/a *diplomatic 2r*
la dirección *address B; direction 12r*
la directiva *board of directors 14r*
directo/a *direct 10r*
el/la director/a *director, manager 2r*
el directorio *directory 5r*
dirigido/a *addressed 6r, managed 14r*
dirigir (j) *to send, to address 2r*
la disciplina *discipline 4r*
el disco *disk, record 2r*
la discoteca *discotheque 1*

la discriminación *discrimination 14r*
disculpar *to excuse 8r*
discutir *to argue, to discuss 2r, 7*
el/la diseñador/a *designer 5r*
diseñar *to design 9r, 15*
el diseño *design 1r*
el disfraz *costume 8r*
disfrazarse (c) *to wear a costume* 8
disfrutar *to enjoy 1r*
disminuir *to decrease 13r*
disparar *to fire 15r*
disponible *available 2r, 12*
la disposición *disposal 6r*
dispuesto/a *ready, determined to* 15
disputado/a *played, disputed 7r*
el disquete *disquette* Br, 1
la distancia *distance 12r*
distintivo/a *distinctive 2r*
distinto/a *different 4r*
distraido/a *absent minded 15r*
la distribución *distribution 9r*
la distribuidora *distributor 13r*
distribuir *to distribute 8r*
el distrito *district 8r*
disuelto/a *dissolved 10r*
la diversidad *diversity 2r*
la diversión *entertainment 3r, 5*
diverso *diverse, different 5r*
divertido/a *funny, amusing 2*
divertirse (ie, i) *to have a good time/fun 3r,* 8
dividir *to divide 9r*
división *division 4r*
divorciado/a *divorced 2r,* 4
divorciarse *to divorce 9r*
el divorcio *divorce 8r, 14*
doblado/a *dubbed 3r*
doblar *to fold* 5; *to bend 11r; to turn 12*
doble *double 5r,* 12
el/la doctor/a *doctor* Br, 11
la doctrina *doctrine 10r*
el documental *documentary Br*
el documento *document Br*
el dólar *dollar* 1
doler (ue) *to hurt* 11
el dolor *pain, ache 8r,* 10
doméstico/a *domestic 4r*
el domicilio *residence, home 2r*
domingo *Sunday* B; Domingo de Resurrección *Easter Sunday* 8
el/la dominicano/a *Dominican 11r*
el dominio *control, knowledge 9r*
don *title of respect* m. B
donar *to donate 9r*
dónde interrog. *where 1r; wherever, 14*
doña *title of respect* f. B
dormir (ue, u) *to sleep* 4; dormir la siesta *to take a nap* 4;
dormirse (ue, u) *to fall asleep* 7
el dormitorio *bedroom 5*
dramatizar (c) *to dramatize 8r*
el/la dramaturgo/a *playwright 9r*
la droga *drug 8*
la ducha *shower 5*
ducharse *to take a shower 10r*
la duda *doubt 4r*
dudar *to doubt* 10
dudoso/a *doubtful* 10
el/la dueño/a *owner 10r*
dulce adj. *sweet 3r,* 10; *candy 8r,* 10
duplicar *duplicate 15r*
la duración *duration 1r*
durante *during 1r, 3*
durar *to last 1r, 7*
el durazno *peach 15r*
duro/a *hard 10r*

E

e *and 2r*
ecológico/a *ecological 7r*
el/la ecólogo/a *ecologist 15r*
la economía *economics* 1; *economy 13r*
económico/a *economic 2r; inexpensive 5r*
economista *economist 2r*
ecuatoriano/a *Ecuadorian 10r*
la edad *age 2r, 13*; tercera edad *senior citizen 3r,* 14
la edición *edition 8r*
el edificio *building 1r, 5*
la educación *education 1r*
educado/a *educated 5r*
efectivo/a *effective15r;* en effectivo *cash 6*
el efecto *effect 10r*
efectuar (se) *to take place, to carry out 15r*
la eficiencia *efficiency* 14
eficiente *efficient* Br
el/la ejecutivo/a *executive* 9
el ejemplo *example 1r,* 3
el ejercicio *exercise 4r,* 11
el *the* B
él *he* B
la elaboración *making 8r*
elaborar *to make 8r*
la elección *election 5r*
el/la electricista *electrician 9*
eléctrico/a *electric 3r*
el electrodoméstico *electrical appliance 5*
electromagnético/a *electromagnetic 10r*
electrónico/a *electronic 3r,* 15
el elefante *elephant 3r*
elegante *elegant Br*
elegir (i, j) *to select, to choose* 11r
el elemento *element 8r*
eliminar *to eliminate 10r*
ella *she* B
ellos/as *they 1*
el elote *corn (on the cob)* 10
embarazada *pregnant 11r*
embargo: sin embargo *nevertheless 1r*
el embudo *funnel 5r*
la emergencia *emergency 9r*
el/la emigrante *emigrant* 13
emigrar *to emigrate* 13
emisor/a adj. *issuing, transmitting 10r*
emocionado/a *excited* 7
emocional *emotional 12r*
empacar (qu) *to pack 12r*
la empanada *small meat pie 10r;* empanadas salteñas *typical Bolivian meat pies 10r*
empezar (ie, c) *to begin, start 3r, 4*
el/la empleado/a *employee 2r, 12*
la empresa *company, corporation 9*
en *in, at* B; en punto *sharp, on the dot* B; en cuanto a *in regards to* 12; en la actualidad *at the present time* 13; en busca de *in search of* 15
enamorado/a *in love* 13
enamorarse *to fall in love 11r*
encantado/a *delighted* B
encantar *to delight, to love* 6
el/la encargado/a *person in charge 8r*
el encanto *charm 1r*
encargarse *to be in charge 9r*
encender (ie) *to turn on 13r*
encerrado/a *locked up 12r*
encerrar (ie) *to lock up* 8
la enchilada *Mexican dish 5r*
el encierro (de los toros) *penning (of bulls) 8r*
encima *on top 10r*
encontrar (ue) *to find 1r,* 6; encontrarse *to be 5r*; *to meet, to encounter* 15
el encuentro *encounter, meeting Br*
la encuesta *survey 3r,* 14
la energía *energy 1r*
enérgico/a *energetic* 14
enero *January* B
enfermar(se) *to get sick 8r*
la enfermedad *sickness 11*
el/la enfermero/a *nurse 9*
enfermo/a *adj. sick 3r,* 11
enfrentar *to confront* 12r
enfrente (de) *in front of* B

enfriar *to cool down 10r*
engordar *to gain weight 10r*
enharinado/a *lightly covered with flour 10r*
el enlace *link* 14
enlatado/a *canned 10r*
enmendar (ie) *to correct 11r*
la enmienda *correction 2r*
enojado/a *angry, mad* 2
enorme *enornous, huge 2r*
enriquecer (zc) *to enrich 1r*
la ensalada *salad* 3
el ensayo: el ensayo nuclear *nuclear test* 15
enseguida *immediately* 6
la enseñanza *teaching 4r*
enseñar *to teach* 1r
entender (ie) *to understand* 4
entero/a *whole 4r;* de color entero *solid color* 6
entonces *then 2r,* 8
el entorno *sorrounding 7r*
la entrada *appetizer 3r; ticket for admission 3r,* 8; *entrance 5r*
entrar *to go in, to enter* 6
entre *between, among* B
entregar *to deliver 5r*
el/la entrenador/a *coach* 7
el entrenamiento *training 10r*
entrenar *to train 10r*
entretenido/a *entertaining 10r*
el entretenimiento *entertainment 3r*
entrevista *interview 2r,* 9
el/la entrevistador/a *interviewer 9r*
entrevistar *to interview 4r*
entusiasmado/a *enthusiastic 9r*
el entusiasmo *enthusiasm 10r*
envejecer (zc) *to get old 10r*
enviar *to send 2r,* 9
envolver (ue) *to wrap 10r*
el episodio *episode 4r*
la época *time 2r*
la equidad *equity 14r*
equilibrar *to balance 10r*
el equilibrio *equilibrium, balance 10r*
el equipaje *luggage* 12
el equipo *team 2r,* 7; el equipo deportivo *equipment* 7
equivalente *equivalent 5r*
equivocado/a *wrong 2r*
erguido/a *erect 10r*
la escala *stopping point 12r*
escalar *to climb 10r*
la escalera *stairs, stairway* 5
el escáner *scanner 6r*
escapar *to escape, to flee* 13
el escaparate *shop window 6r*
la escasez *lack, scarcity 7r*
la escena *scene 8r*
escencial *essential 10r*
escoger (j) *to choose 1r*
escolar adj. *school 4r*
escribir *to write* Br, 3
escrito/a *written 2r*
el/la escritor/a *writer 2r,* 13
el escritorio *desk* B
escuchar *to listen Br,* 1
la escuela *school* 1r
la escultura *sculpture 3r*
el escurridor *colander 5r*
escurrir *to drain 5r*
ese/a adj. *that* B; ése/a pron. *that one* 5
esforzarse (ue) *to strive 6r*
eso pron. *that* 5; por eso *that, that's why* 3
esos/as adj. *those* 5; ésos/as pron. *those* 5
espacial adj. *space 9r*
el espacio *space 7r*
espacioso/a *spacious 5r*
el espagueti *spaghetti* 3
la espalda *back* 11
el español *Spanish* Br, 1; español/a adj. *Spanish 1r,* 2
la especia *spice 5r*
especial *special 3r*; en especial *especially 8r*
la especialidad *specialty 1r*
el/la especialista *specialist 2r*
especializado/a *specialized 6r*
especializarse (c) *to specialize 6r*
especialmente *specially 2r*
la especie *species 3r*
específicamente *specifically 3r*
especificar (qu) *to specify, to point out 4r*
espectacular *spectacular 8r*
el espectáculo *show 3r*
el/la espectador/a *spectator 7r*
el espejo *mirror 5;* el espejo retrovisor *rearview mirror* 12
la esperanza *hope 10r*
esperar *to hope, to expect 4r,* 10; *to wait for 2r,* 9
la espinaca *spinach* 10
el espíritu *spirit, disposition 7r;* joven de espíritu *young at heart 2r*
la espontaneidad *spontaneity 4r*
la esposa *wife* 4
el esposo *husband* 4
el esqueleto *skeleton 8r*
el esquí *skiing, ski* 7
el/la esquiador/a *skier* 7
esquiar *to ski 2r,* 7
la esquina *corner 11r,* 12
la estabilidad stability 14r
establecer(se) (zc) *to establish, to settle 11r,* 13
la estación *season 6r,* 7; *station 4r,* 12
estacionar *to park* 14r
el estacionamiento *parking 5r*
el estadio *stadium 3r*
la estadística statistic; adj. *statistical 8r,* 14
el estado *state 1r; status 2r; condition 7r*
estadounidense *U.S.A. citizen 13r*
el estancamiento *stagnation 13r*
estándar *standard 10r*
estar *to be Br,* 1; estar bien/mal *to be well/not well* B; estar a cargo *to be in charge 9r;* estar a dieta *to be on a diet* 3; estar de acuerdo *to agree 2r,* 3; estar de moda *to be fashionable* 6; estar enamorado/a *to be in love* 13; estar en forma *to keep fit 4r;* estar seguro/a *to be sure* 7
la estatua *statue 4r*
estatura *height 14r*
el estatuto *law 14r*
el este *east 1r*
este/a adj. *this* 1; éste/a pron. *this one* 5; esta noche *tonight* 3
el estéreo *stereo 5r*
estereotipado/a *stereotyped* 14r
el estilo *style 5r*
estimado/a *estimated, dear 2r*
el estímulo *stimulant 1r*
estirar *to stretch 11r*
esto *this 4r,* 5
el estómago *stomach 3r,* 11
estornudar *to sneeze* 11
estos/as adj. *these* 5; éstos/as pron. *these* 5
la estrategia *strategy 7r*
estrecho/a *narrow, tight* 6
la estrella *star 3r*
el estreno *première 9r*
el estrés *stress 12r*
estricto/a *strict 11r*
la estructura *structure 4r*
el/la estudiante *student* B
estudiantil adj *student 1r*
estudiar *to study* 1
el estudio *study 1r; studying 9r*
estudioso/a *studious* 1
la estufa *stove* 5
la etapa *stage 4r*
eterno/a eternal *5r*
la etiqueta *etiquette 5r*
étnico/a *ethnic 2r*
euro *monetary unit of Spain* 1
europeo/a *European 2r*

el euskara *Basque language 1r*
el evento *event 1r*
la evidencia *evidence 12r*
evidente *evident 2r*
evitar *to avoid 10r*
la evolución *evolution 4r*
evolucionar *to evolve 4r*
exacto/a *exact 8r*
el examen *examination* 1
examinar *to examine 11*
excelente *excellent* 1
la excepción *exception 13r*
excepcional *exceptional 5r*
excepto *except 7*
excesiva *excessive 10r*
el exceso *excess 9r*
exclusivo/a *exclusive 12r*
la excursión *excursion 3r*
la excusa *excuse 10r*
exhaustivamente *exhaustingly 12r*
exhibir *to exhibit 2r*
existente *existent 3r*
existir *to exist 2r*
el éxito *success 7r, 13;* tener éxito *to be successful* 13
exótico/a *exotic 5r*
la expectativa *expectation 12r*
la experiencia *experience 1r, 9*
experimentar *to experience 12r*
el experimento *experiment 15r*
el/la experto/a *expert 7r*
la explicación *explanation 9r*
explicar (qu) *to explain 1r*
la exploración *exploration 9r*
explorar *to explore 1r*
el explorador *explorer* Br
la exportación *export 9r*
exportador/a adj. *exporting 9r*
la exposición *exhibit 1r*
expresar *to express 10r*
la expresión *expression Br*
el exprimidor *fruit-squeezer 5r*
exquisito/a *delicious, exquisite 3r*
extender(se) (ie) *to extend, to expand 13r; to spread out, to extend* 13
la extensión *extension 2r*
la extinción *extinction 5r*
extranjero/a adj *foreign 1r; foreigner 2r*
extrañar *to miss 13r*
extraordinario/a *extraordinary 6r*
extraterrestre adj *extraterrestrial Br*
extremadamente *extremely 5r*
extrovertido/a *extrovert Br*

F

la fábrica *factory 15r*
fabricar *to make 8r*
fabuloso *fabulous* 3
fácil *easy* 1
fácilmente *easily 9r*
factible *feasible 13r*
facturar *to check (luggage)* 12
la facultad *college, school of* 1
la falda *skirt 4r,* 6
fallecido/a *dead 8r*
falso/a *false 1r*
falta: hacer falta *to need 14r*
la fama *fame* 13
la familia *family Br, 4*
el familiar *relative 2r*; adj *family 2r*
famoso/a *famous 1r*
fanático/a *fanatic 4r*
la fantasía *fantasy 3r*
fantástico/a *fantastic 3r*
el/la farmacéutico/a *pharmacist 11*
la farmacia *pharmacy* 11
la fascinación *fascination 2r*
fascinante *fascinating 4r*
fascinar *to fascinate 3r*
la fase *phase 1r*
el fastidio *annoyance 4r*
la fatiga *fatigue 10r*
fatigado/a *fatigued, tired 10r*
favorecer (zc) *to favour, to help 7r*
favorito/a *favorite* Br, 1
febrero *February* B
la fecha *date* B
la federación *federation 7r*
la felicidad *happiness 14*
felicitar *to congratulate 7r*
feliz *happy* 2
el fenómeno *phenomenon 14r*
feo/a *ugly* 2
la feria *fair 1r*
el feriado: día feriado *holiday 3r*
la ferretería *hardware shop 6r*
el ferrocarril *railroad* 12
fértil *fertile 2r*
el festival *festival 7r*
la festividad *festivity 8r*
festivo *festive 8r*
fiable *trustworthy* 14
la fibra *fiber 10r*
la fiebre *fever 11*
fielmente *faithfully 7r*
la fiesta *party Br,* 3
fijarse *to pay attention 11r*
fijo/a *fixed 6r*
la filmoteca *film society, film club 3r*
la filosofía *philosophy 1r*
el fin: *end 1,* 7; fin de semana *weekend* 1; *objective 9r*
el final *end 5r*
final adj *final 2r*
finalista *finalist 7r*
finalmente *finally 1r*
financiado/a *financed 11r*
financiero/a *financial 6r,* 14
financiar *to finance 15r*
fino/a *fine 3r*
la firma *signature* 1r
firmar *to sign 1r*
la física *physics Br*
físicamente *physically 7r*
físico/a *physical 2r*
el/la fisioterapista *physiotherapist 11r*
la flexibilidad *flexibility 9r*
flexible *flexible 2r*
la flor *flower 5r, 7*
el flujo *flow 14r*
la fobia *phobia 12r*
el folclor *folklore 1r*
folclórico/a *folkloric 2r*
el folleto *pamphlet, brochure 3r*
fomentar *to foment* 14
los fondos *money 9r; fund 11r*
la fonoventa *phone sale 3r*
forma *form 2r*
la formación *formation 7r*
formar *to form 2r*
la fórmula *formula 15r*
el formulario *form 1r*
la fortaleza *fortress 3r*
la fortuna *fortune 1r*
la fotocopiadora *photocopier 9r*
la foto(grafía) *photography 2r*
fracturar(se) *to fracture, to break* 11
el francés/francesa *French 2r*
la frase *phrase 8r*
la frecuencia *frequency* 1r
frecuentemente *frequently 1r*, 4
el fregadero sink *5*
freír(i) *to fry* 10
el frenesí *frenzy 11r*
la frente *forehead* 11
la fresa *strawberry* 10
fresco/a *cool* 7; *fresh 10r*
los frijoles *beans 3r*
el frío adj. *cold* 3; tener frío *to be cold 5*
la frontera *frontier, border 2r*
la fruta *fruit* 3
la fuente *fountain 1r; source 8r,* 14
fuera *out, outside* 3
fuerte *strong 1r, 2*
la fuerza *force 10r,* 14
fuerza laboral *work force 14*
fumar *to smoke* 11
la función *show, function 2r*
el funcionamiento *functioning 14r*
funcionar *to function 6r*

fundamental *fundamental, basic 4r*
fundar *to found 1r,*13
furioso/a *furious 6r*
la fusión *fusion 8r*
el fútbol soccer *2r, 7*
el/la futbolista *football player 7r*
el futuro *future 4r*

G

la gabardina *raincoat 7r*
el gabinete *cabinet (presidential) 13r*
las gafas: gafas de sol *sun glasses* 6
la galería *gallery 3r*
el gallego *Galician 1r*
la galleta *cookie* 10
la gamba *shrimp (in Spain) 10r*
el/la ganador/a *winner 7r*
ganar *to win 4r,* 7 ; *to earn, to make 6r*
ganas: tener ganas de *to feel like 10r*
el garaje *garage 5*
la garganta *throat* 11
el gas: agua con gas *carbonated water* 3
la gasolina *gasoline 12r*
gastar *to spend 4r,* 6
la gastronomía *gastronomy 9r*
el/la gato/a *cat* 2
la gelatina *gelatin 9r, 10*
el/la gemelo/a *twin* 4
genealógico/a *genealogical 4r*
la generación *generation 4r*
generalmente *generally* 4
generar *to generate 10r*
el género *type 4r*
generoso/a *generous Br*
genético/a *genetic 15r*
la generosidad *generosity 9r*
genial *great 2r*
la gente *people 6r,* 8
la geografía *geography* 1
geográfico/a *geographic 2r*
el gerente *manager* 9; gerente de ventas *sales manager 9*
la gestión *matter, business 9r*
el gesto *gesture 4r*
gigante adj. *giant 5r*
el gimnasio *gymnasium* 1
el glaciar *glacier 2r*
el gobierno *government 6r,* 13
el golf *golf* 7
la golondrina *sparrow 15r*
el golpe: golpe militar *military coup* 13
gordo/a *fat* 2
la gorra *cap* 6
gozar (c) *to enjoy 8r*
la grabación *recording* 3r
la grabadora *taperecorder, cassette player* B
gracias *thank you* B; Día de Acción de Gracias *Thanksgiving Day* 8
gracioso/a *funny 2r*
el grado *degree 7r; grade 8r*
la graduación *graduation Br*
graduado/a *graduated 5r*
gradualmente *gradually 15r*
graduarse *to graduate 14r*
gráfico/a *graphic 1r*
gramatical *grammatical 4r*
gran *great 1r, 5*
grande *big* 1
el grano *grain* 10r
la grasa *fat 10r*
gratis *free 3r*
la gratitud *gratitude 10r*
gratuito/a *gratuitous, free of charge 11r*
grave *seriously ill, serious 14r*
la gravedad *seriousness 15r*
el griego *Greek 10r*
la gripe *flu 11*
gris *gray* 2
gritar *to shout, scream 8r*
grueso/a *coarse 7r*
el grupo *group 1r*
el/la guacamayo/a *macaw 8r*
el guajolote *turkey 10r*
el guante *glove* 6; *baseball mit* 7
guapo/a *good-looking, handsome* 2
el guaraní *monetary unit of Paraguay 1r; language spoken in Paraguay 10r*
guardar *to keep* 12
el guardarropa wardrobe *5r*
la guardería *nursery 6r*
guatemalteco/a *Guatemalan* 2
la guayabera *loose-fitting men's shirt 6r*
gubernamental adj. *government 6r*
la guerra *war 5r*
el gueto *ghetto 15r*
el/la guía *guide 3r*
guiar *to guide 9r*
la guitarra *guitar 1r, 3*
gustar *to like 2; to be pleasing to* 6; me gustaría *I would like 2r,* 6
el gusto *liking, taste 6r;* mucho gusto *pleased to meet you* B

H

haber *to have* 13
había *there was, there were* 8
la habitación *room 5r,* 12; habitación doble/sencilla *double/single room* 12
el/la habitante *inhabitant, resident 2r*
el hábito *habit 6r*
hablador/a *talkative* 2
hablar *to speak* 1
hace *ago* 7
hacer (g) *to do, make 1r,* 4; hacer cola *to stand in line* 12; hacer escala to *make a stopover* 12; hacer la maleta *to pack 12r;* hacer preguntas *to ask questions 4r;* hacerse *to become 4r;* hacer el papel *play the part 6r;* ¿Qué tiempo hace? *What's the weather like?* 7
hacia *towards, near 8r*
el hambre: tener hambre *to be hungry 5*
la hamburguesa *hamburger 1r, 3*
la hamburguesería *hamburger place 3r*
la harina *flour* 10
hasta *until* B; hasta luego, hasta pronto *see you later* B; hasta la vista *see you later* 1; hasta que *until 14*
hay *there is, there are* B; hay que + inf. *it's necessary to + verb* 5
el hebreo *Hebrew 2r*
el hecho *fact 9r*; de hecho *in fact 5r;* adj. *made 8r*
el helado *ice cream* 3
el helecho *fern 13r*
la hermana *sister* 4
el hemisferio *hemisphere 10r*
la hermanastra *stepsister 4*
el hermanastro *stepbrother* 4
el hermano *brother* 4
hermoso/a *beautiful 1r*
el héroe *hero 10r*
hervir (ie, i) *to boil* 10
el hielo *ice 7*
la hierba/yerba *herb 3r*
la hija *daughter* 4; hija única *only daughter* 4
el hijo *son 2r,* 4; hijo único *only son* 4
hiperactivo/a *hyperactive 1r*
el hipermercado *large market 6r*
hípico/a adj. *horse 7r*
hipocondríaco/a *hypodondriac 1r*
el hipódromo *race track 3r*
el hipopótamo *hippopotamus* 2
hispánico *Hispanic 8r*
hispano/a *Hispanic 1r*
hispanoamericano/a *Spanish American 2r*
hispanohablante *Spanish speaker 13r*
la historia *history* 1
histórico/a *historic 4r*

el hogar *home 5r, 14*
hola *hello, hi* B
el hombre *man 4r,* 4; **hombre de negocios** *businessman 9*
el hombro *shoulder* 11
el homenaje *homage 10r*
homogéneo/a *homogenous 2r*
hondureño/a *Honduran 5r*
la honestidad *honesty* 14
honrado/a *honoured 8r*
la hora *time, hour* B; **hora americana//inglesa** *precise time Br*
el horario *schedule* Br; **horario corrido** *uninterrupted schedule*
hornear *to bake 10r*
el horno *oven* 5; **horno microondas** *microwave oven* 5
el hospital *hospital 1r, 11*
el hotel *hotel 4r,* 12
hoy *today B;* **hoy en día** *nowadays 4r,* 8
hubo *there was, there were* (pret, of haber) *14r*
el hueso *bone* 11
el/la huésped *guest 1r,* 12
el huevo egg *3;* **huevo duro** *hard-boiled egg 10r*
huir *to flee, to escape 13r*
las humanidades *humanities* 1
humano/a *human 5r,* 11; **ser humano** *human being* 15
húmedo/a *humid, damp 10r*

I

la ida: ida y vuelta *round trip 3r, 12*
la idea *idea 2r*
ideal *ideal 2r*
idealista adj, *idealistic* Br
la identidad *identity 2r*
la identificación *identification* Br
identificar (qu) *to identify 4r*
el idioma *langugage 1r,* 13
la iglesia *church 1r,* 8
igual adj. *the same 1r; alike, equal 2r*; **al igual que** *like, same as 1r*
la igualdad *equality* 14
igualmente *likewise* B
ilógico/a *illogical 5r*
la ilustración *illustration 5r*
ilustre *illustrious 3r*
la imagen *image, statue 8r*
la imaginación *imagination 6r*
imaginar(se) *to imagine 4r*
imaginario/a *imaginary 12r*
imitar *to imitate 5r*
el impacto *impact 10r*
imparcial *impartial Br*
impartir (la bendición) *to give 8r*
impedir (i) *to prevent 7r*
el imperio *empire 3r*
el impermeable *raincoat 6*
el implante *implant 15r*
implicar (qu) *to involve, implicate 10r*
la importación *import 10r*
importado/a *imported 4r*
la importancia *importance 2r*
importante *important Br,* 9
importar *to import 10r*
la imprenta *printing 15r*
imprescindible *essential 9r*
impresionante *impressive 1r*
impresionar *to impress 2r*
la impresora *printer 2r*
imprimir *to print 4r*
el impuesto *tax 12r*
impulsivo/a *impulsive Br*
impulso *impulse 7r*
inapropiado/a *inappropriate 9r*
inaugurar *to inaugurate 6r*
la inauguración *inauguration 9r*
el/la inca *Inca 3r*
el incendio *fire 9*
incentivar *to encourage, to incite 7r*
el incentivo *incentive 13r*
el incienso *incense 8r*
la iniciativa *initiative 9r*
incluido/a *including 10r*
incluir (y) *to include 3r*
incluso *including 5r; even 7r*
inconcluso/a *unfinished 12r*
incorporar *to incorporate 4r*
incorrecto/a *incorrect 14r*
increíble *incredible 2r*
incrementar *increment 10r*
indeciso/a *undecided 5r*
independencia *independence 3r,* 8
independiente *independent Br*
independizarse (c) *to become independent/liberated* 14
indicado/a *indicated, recommended 8r*
indicar (qu) *to indicate 2r,* 9
el índice *index, percentage 9r*
el/la indígena *indigenous, native 2r*
el/la indio/a *Indian 12r*
indiscutible *indisputable 8r*
el individuo *individual 6r*
la industria *industry 5r*
inesperado *unexpected 8r*
la infancia *childhood 4r*
infantil adj. *children's 3r*
la infección *infection* 11
infeccioso/a *infectious 11r*
infectado/a infected 11
infectar *to infect 11r*
la inflación *inflation 9r*
la inflamación *inflammation 11r*
la influencia *influence 5r*
influenciar *to influence 10r*
influir *to influence 15r*
la información *information 1r*
informal *informal Br*
informar(se) *to inform, to become informed 2r*
la informática *computer science* 1
el informe *report 2r*
el/la ingeniero/a *engineer 9*
ingerir (ie) *to ingest 10r*
el inglés *English 1r*
el ingrediente *ingredient 5r*
ingresar *to be admitted 1r*
el ingreso *income 9r*
iniciar *to begin 8r*
injusto/a *unjust 5r*
inmaculado/a *immaculate 8r*
inmediatamente *immediately 2r*
inmenso/a *immense, vast 4r*
la inmersión *immersion 1Br*
inmerso/a *immerse 4r*
la inmigración *immigration 2r*
el/la inmigrante *immigrant* 13
inmigrar *immigrate 13r*
innegable *undeniable 13r*
innovador/a *innovatory 6r*
el inodoro *toilet 5*
inolvidable *unforgettable 1r*
inoxidable *stainless 5r*
inquieto/a *restless 7r*
inscribir *to register 14r*
el/la inspector/a *inspector 12*
la inspiración *inspiration 4r*
la institución *institution 9r*
el instituto *institute 9r*
la instrucción *instruction 9r*
el instrumento *instrument 3r*
insultar(se) *to insult 13r*
el/la integrante *member 11r*
intelectual *intelectual 2r*
inteligente *intelligent Br,* 2
la intención *intention 15r*
intenso/a *intense 1r*
intercambiar *to exchange 2r*
el intercambio *exchange 1r*
interceptar *to intercept 14r*
el interés *interest 1r*
el/la interesado/a *interested (person), applicant 9r*
interesado/a *interested 1r*
interesante *interesting Br*
interesar *to interest 2r,* 6

interminable *endless 5r*
internacional *international 1r*
el/la internauta *Internet user 14r*
el/la intérprete *interpreter 9*
interrogativo/a *interrogative Br*
interrumpir *to interrupt 9r*
intervenido *intercepted 14r*
intervenir (g, ie) *to intervene 9r*
íntimo/a *intimate, close 1r*
intrigante *intriguing 3r*
intrínseco/a *intrinsic 2r*
introducir (zc) *to introduce 7r*
introvertido/a *introvert Br*
inusual *unusual 3r*
inventar *to invent 7r*
invertir (ie, i) *to invest 11r*
la investigación *investigation, research 3r*
investigar (gu) *to investigate 8r*
integral
el invierno *winter 6*
la invitación *invitation 2r, 8*
el/la invitado/a *guest 3r*
invitar *to invite 3r, 8*
la inyección *injection 11*
ir *to go Br, 3;* **ir a +** *inf.* *to go to + verb* 3; **irse** *to go away, to leave* 7; **ir de compras** *to go shopping 3r,* 6
irónico/a *ironic 9r*
irracional *irrational 12r*
irradiado/a *irradiated 10r*
irresponsable *irresponsible 4r*
irritado/a *irritated* 11
irse *to go away, to leave* 7
la isla *island 6r*
italiano/a *Italian 2r*
el itinerario *itinerary 12r*
la izquierda *left 4r,* 12

J

el jabón *soap 5r, 15*
jamás *never 3r,* 12; **por siempre jamás** *forever and ever 3r*
el jamón *ham* 3
Janucá *Hanukka 3r*
japonés/a *Japanese 4r*
el jardín *backyard, garden* 5
la jarra *jar, pitcher 5r*
la jaula *(bird) cage 14r*
el/la jefe/a *manager, boss 2r,* 9
el jesuita *Jesuit 10r*
Jesús *Jesus 8r*
el joropo *typical Venezuelan music 12r*
el/la joven *young man/woman* 3; **joven** adj. *young* 2
la joya *jewel, jewelry 5r*
la joyería *jewelry 3r*
judío/a *Jewish 2r*
el juego game *3r, 7; set 5r;*
jueves *Thursday* B
el/la juez/a *judge 9*
el/la jugador/a *player* 7
jugar (ue) *to play (game, sport)* 4; **jugar a los bolos** *to bowl* 7
el jugo *juice* 3
el juguete *toy 6r*
la jugetería *toy store 6r*
julio *July* B
la jungla *jungle 5r*
junio *June* B
junto a *next to* 4
juntos *together 2r,* 15
el jurado *jury 9r*
la justicia *justice* 15r
justo/a *right Br*
juvenil adj. *young 5r*
la juventud *youth* 13

K

el kilómetro *kilometer 6r*

L

la art. *the* 1; pron. *you, her, it*
el labio *lip* 11
la labor *labor, work 4r*
laboral adj. *labor 5r*
el laboratorio *lab* 1
lacrimógeno/a *tear-producing* 15
lácteo/a *dairy (product) 6r, 10*
lado: al lado de *next to* B
el ladrón *thief 13r*
el lago *lake 2r,* 7
lamentar *to be sorry 10r*
la lámpara *lamp* 5
la lana *wool* 6; **de lana** *wool (made of)* 6
la langosta *lobster* 10
el/la lanzador/a *pitcher* 13
lanzar (c) *to throw 7r,* 13
el lápiz *pencil B*
largo/a *long 2;* **a lo largo** *throughout, along 4r*
las art. *the*; pron. *you, them*
lástima: ¡Qué lástima! *What a pity!* 1
la lata *can 5r*
latinoamericano/a *Latin-American 7r*
el lavabo *washbowl* 5
la lavadora *washing machine* 5
la lavandería *laundry room 5r*
el lavaplatos *dishwasher* 5
lavar(se) *to wash* 4; **lavarse los dientes** *to brush one's teeth* 7
la leche *milk* 3
la lechuga *lettuce 3*
el/la lector/a *reader 2r*
la lectura *reading 4r*
leer *to read* Br, 3
la legumbre *legume, vegetable 10r*
lejano/a *distant, remote 13r*
lejos (de) adv. *far 2r, 5*
el lempira *monetary unit of Honduras 5r*
la lencería *linen 6r*
la lengua *language* 1; *tongue* 11
el lenguaje *language 4r*
lentamente *slowly* 4
los lentes *glasses* 2; **lentes de contacto** *contact lenses* 2
el león *lion 3r*
la letra *letter 9r*
el letrero *sign 14r*
levantar *to raise, to lift Br,* 7; **levantarse** *to get up, to stand up Br,* 4
la ley *law 14r*
la leyenda *legend 3r*
liberado/a *released 15r*
liberal *liberal* Br
liberar *to release 10r; to liberate 12r*
la libra *pound 10r*
libre *free 1r, 3*
la librería *bookstore* 1
el libro *book B*
el liceo *school 4r*
el licor *alcoholic beverage 10r*
la liga *league 13r*
ligero/a *light 15r*
limitar *to limit 7r*
el limón *lemon* 5r
el limpiaparabrisas *windshield wiper* 12
limpiar *to clean* 5
el limpiavidrios *window cleaner 5r*
la limpieza *cleaning 4r*
limpio/a *clean* 5
la línea *line 2r*
el líquido *liquid* 5r
lírico/a *lyric 9r*
la lista *roll, list* B; **la lista de espera** *waiting list* 12
listo/a *smart, ready* 2
la literatura *literature* 1
literario/a *literary 4r*
la llamada *call* 9
llamar *to call 3r*; **llamarse** *to be called, to be named* B
llano/a *flat 2r*

la llanta *tire 12*
la llave *key* 12
la llegada *arrival 8r, 12*
llegar *to arrive* 1
llenar *to fill out 1r, 9*
lleno/a *full 2r, 12*
llevar *to wear, to carry 3r,* 6; llevar a cabo *to carry out 8r;* llevarse bien *to get along well 9r, 13;* llevarse mal *not to get along 13r*
llorar to cry *9r*
llover (ue) *to rain 6r,* 7
la lluvia *rain* 7; la lluvia ácida *acid rain* 15r; lluvia de ideas *brainstorm 2r*
lo pron. *you, him, it;* lo + adj.) *the 1r*; lo que *what, that which 1r*
el local *site, place 6r*
la localización *location 5r*
localizado/a *situated 5r*
localizar (c) *to locate 8r, 14*
loco/a *crazy 6r*
el/la locutor/a *radio announcer 9*
lógicamente *logically* 4
lógico/a *logic Br*
lograr *to achieve 10r*
el logro *accomplishment 8r*
la loma *hill 5r*
la longitud *length 7r*
los art. *the* 1; pron. *you, them 5*
la lotería *lottery 5r*
luchar *to fight 5r*
luego *then 1r,* 3; *after 6r*
el lugar *place Br,* 1; tener lugar *to take place 8r*
lujo: con lujo de *with great*
lujoso/a *luxurious 6r*
la luna *moon;* luna de miel *honeymoon 7r*
lunar: de lunares polka-dotted 6
lunes *Monday* B
la luz *light 6r*

M

el machismo *machismo* 14
la macrobiótica *macrobiotics 10r*
la madera *wood 5r*
la madrastra stepmother 4
la madre *mother* 4
el/la madrileño/a *person from Madrid 1r*
la madrina *godmother* 4
la madrugada *early morning, dawn 1r*
la madurez *maturity* 14r
mágico/a *magic 10r*
magnífico/a *great, magnificent 6*

el maíz *corn* 10; palomita de maiz *pop corn*
majar *to crush, to pound 5r*
mal *not well, sick* B; *bad 5*
la maleta *suitcase* 12
el maletero *trunk (in a car)* 12
el maletín *briefcase* 12
el mallorquín *Majorcan language 1r*
malo/a *bad* 1; ser malo/a *to be bad* 2; estar malo/a *to be ill* 2
la mamá *mom 1r, 4*
la mancha *spot 11r*
mandar *to send 5r, 9*
el mandato *order, command 9r*
mandón/mandona *bossy 9r*
manejar *to drive 3r,* 12; *to manage, to handle 15*
el manejo *working knowledge 9r; handling 14r*
la manera *way 4r*
el mango *mango* 10r
maniático/a *fussy, finical 5r*
manifestar (ie) *to express 4r*
la mano *hand Br,* 11; manos a la obra *let's get down to work 1r*
la manta *blanket 5*
la manteca *lard* 10
el mantel *tablecloth* 10
mantener(se) (g, ie) *to mantain 2r,* 8
el mantenimiento *maintenance 5r*
la mantequilla *butter 3r,* 10
el manual *manual 5r*
manufacturero/a *manufacturing 9r*
la manzana *apple 2r, 10*
la manzanilla *camomile 11r*
mañana adv. *tomorrow* B; hasta mañana *until tomorrow* B
la mañana *morning* B; de la mañana *A.M.* B
el mapa *map* 1
maquillarse *to put on makeup* 7
máquina *machine 15r*; la máquina fotográfica *camera 6r*; máquina de escribir *typewriter 9r*
el mar sea *1r,* 3
la maravilla *marvel 2r*
maravilloso/a *marvelous 4r,* 8
la marca *brand name 6r*
el marcapasos *pacemaker 15r*
marcar (qu) *to mark 4r; to score 7r*
la marcha *march 1r*
la margarina *margarine* 10
el mariachi *Mexican band 8r*
el marido *husband* 4
la marinera *typical Peruvian music 12r*
marino/a adj *sea 10r*
el marisco *seafood 3r,* 10
marrón *brown* 2

martes *Tuesday* B
marzo *March* B
más *more* B; más o menos *more or less* B; más... que *more...than* 8
la masa *dough* 10
masticar (qu) *to chew 5r*
matar *to kill* 8
el mate *tealike beverage 2r*
las matemáticas *mathematics Br*
la materia *subject of study 9r*
el material *material 8r*
materialista *materialist Br*
materno/a *maternal 2r;* adj. *mother, 4r*
matricularse *to register 1r*
el matrimonio *marriage, wedding 4r*
el mausoleo *mausoleum 10r*
máximo/a *maximum 7r*
mayo *May* B
la mayonesa *mayonnaise* 10
mayor *old 2;* el/la mayor *the oldest* 4; *greater 4r;* la mayor parte *most 1r*
la mayoría *the majority 5r,* 14
mayoritario/a *majority 13r*
me *me 5* ; me llamo *my name is* B
la medalla *medal 7r*
el médano *slope 7r*
la media *half* B; *stocking, sock* 6; *average 12r, 14*; adj. *middle 4r*
mediano; a mediados *in the middle 13r*
la medialuna *type of croissant 2r*
mediano/a *average, medium* 2
la medianoche *midnight* B
mediante *through 10r*
la medicina *medicine* 1; *medication 11r*
el/la médico/a *medical doctor 4r, 9*
la medida *meassurement 10r;* en la medida posible *as much as possible 10r;* a medida que *at the same time as 10r;*
el medio *means 2r, 12;* medio ambiente *environment 15;* medio/a hermano/a *half-brother/sister* 4
el mediodía *noon* B
medir (i) *to measure 5r*
meditar *to meditate 10r*
la megatienda *superstore 6r*
la mejilla *cheek* 11
mejor *best 1r, 7; better, 2r, 8*
la mejora *improvement 5r*
mejorar *to improve 9*
melancólico/a *melancholic 12r*
la melodía *melody 4r, 8*
la memoria *memory 4r*
mencionar *to mention 1r*
el/la menor *the youngest* 4; *younger* 8
menos *minus (for telling time)* B;

más o menos *more or less* B; menos... que *less/fewer than* 8; a menos que *unless* 14; por lo menos *at least 1r*
el mensaje *message 4r*
la menta *mint 3r*
la mentira *lie 13r*
el/la mentiroso/a *liar 4*
el menú *menu 3r*
el mercadillo *small open-air market 4r*
el mercado *market 6r*
la mercancía *merchandise, goods 6r, 13*
merecer (zc) *to deserve 14r*
el merengue *typical music of the Dominican Republic 11r*
el mes *month B;* mes pasado *last month* 6; mes próximo *next month* 3
la mesa *table*; mesa de noche *night stand 5*
el mestizaje *mestization 2r*
mestizo/a *mestizo 2r*
la meta *goal 11r*
metabolizar (c) *metabolize 10r*
el metal *metal 5r*
metódico/a *methodical 10r*
el método *method* 1r
el metro *subway 6r, 12; meter 6r*
la metrópoli *metropolis 2r*
metropolitano/a *metropolitan 13r*
mexicano/a *Mexican 2*
mexicoamericano/a *Mexican American 13r*
la mezcla *mixture, blend 4r*
mezclar *to blend, to mix 10r*
mi/s *my* B, 2
mí *me, 2r, 3*
el micrófono *microphone 9r*
el microondas *microwave 5*
el microscopio *microscope 9r*
el miedo: tener miedo *to be afraid 5*
el miembro *member 1r*
mientras *while, meanwhile 2r, 3*
miércoles *Wednesday* B
el milagro *miracle 8r*
milenario/a *millenary 10r*
el milenio *millennium 7r*
militar *military 8r*
la milla *mile 3r*
el millón *million* 3
el mimbre *wicker 5r*
la mímica *mimicry, imitation 9r*
la mina *mine 4r*
minero/a adj. *mining 9r*
la minería *mining 15r*
el minibus *small bus 2r*
mínimo/a *minimum 2r*
el ministerio (de) *ministry (government) 2r,* 14
el ministro *minister (government) 15r*
la minoría *minority 8r*
minoritario/a *minority 13r*
el minuto *minute 2r*
mió (-a, -os, -as) *my (of) mine* 12
la mirada *look 1r*
mirar *to look (at)* 1
la misión *mission 11r*
el/la misionero/a *missionary 10r*
mismo/a *same 2r;* lo mismo *the same thing 7r*
el misterio *mystery 1r*
misterioso/a *mysterious 3r*
la mitad *half 8r, 13*
el mobiliario *furniture 5r*
la mochila *backpack* B
la moda *fashion* 6; desfile de moda *fashion show 6r*
el/la modelo *model 3r*
el módem *modem 9r*
moderno/a *modern Br*
modesto/a *modest 2r*
modificar (qu) *to modify 15r*
el modo *way 4r*
el molde *mould 8r*
moler (ue) *to grind 5r*
molestar *to bother, to be bothered by* 11
molido/a *ground 10r*
el momento *moment 2r*
monetario/a *monetary 5r*
el/la monitor/a *camp counselor 7r*
el monstruo *monster 9r*
la montaña *mountain 4r*
el montañismo *mountaineering 9r*
montar *to ride* 1
el monumento *monument 1r*
morado/a *purple* 2
moreno/a *brunet* 2
morir *to die 10r, 13*
el/la moro/a *Moor 1r*
el mortero *mortar 5r*
la mostaza *mustard 10*
el mostrador *counter 12*
mostrar (ue) *to show 3r,* 6
motivado/a *motivitaed 9r*
motivar *to motivate 9r*
el motivo motive *8r*
la moto(cicleta) *motorcycle 4r, 12*
el motor *motor 12*
mover (ue) *to move 4r,* 8
la movilidad *mobility 8r*
el movimiento *movement 1r*
la muchacha *girl, young woman* 3
el muchacho *boy, young man* 3
mucho/a *much, lot 1r, 2;* mucho gusto *pleased to meet you* B
muchos/as *many 1r;* muchas veces *often* 1
la mudanza *move 14r*
mudarse *to move 5r*
el mueble *furniture 5*
el muelle *dock 14r*
la mueblería *furniture store 5r*
la muerte *death 10r*
muerto/a *dead 4r, 8;* Día de los muertos *All Saints/All Souls Day* 8
la muestra *sample 3r*
la mujer *woman 2r, 9;* mujer de negocios *business woman* 9
multiplicar (qu) *multiply 7*
la multa *ticket (fine) 13r*
la multitud *crowd 14r*
mundial *world-wide 3r, 7*
el mundo *world* Br, 15
la muñeca *wrist 11*
el músculo *muscle* 11
el museo *museum 1r, 12*
la música *music 1r, 3;* música ambiental *background music 4r*
el/la músico/a *musician 9r*
el muslo *thigh 9r*
muy *very* B

N

nacer (zc) *to be born 4r, 13*
el nacimiento *birth 2r*
la nación *nation 3r*
nacional *national 1r*
la nacionalidad *nationality 2r*
nacionalizado/a *nationalized 9r*
nada adv. *nothing* 12; de nada *you're welcome* B
nadar *to swim* 3
nadie *no one, nobody* 12
la naranja *orange* 3; adj *orange 2r*
el narcotráfico *drug traffic 14r*
la nariz *nose* 11
la narración *narration 6r*
el/la narrador/a *narrator* 15r
narrar *to narrate 2r*
la natación *swimming 7r*
la natalidad *birth 14r*
nativo/a *native* 1r
la naturaleza *nature 7r*
la náusea *nausea 11r*
la nave espacial *space ship 9r,* 15
navegable *navigable 10r*
la navegación *navegation 14r*
navegar *to navigate 1r*
la Navidad *Christmas 3r,* 8
naviero/a *shipping 15r*
Nazareno *Nazarene 8r*

necesario/a *necessary 1r,* 10
la necesidad *need, necessity 5r, 14*
necesitar *to need* 1
negativo/a *negative 4r*
el negocio *business 9*
negro/a *black* 2
la nena *baby, infant girl 14r*
el nene *baby, infant boy 14r*
el nervio *nerve* 11
nervioso/a *nervous* 2
la neurosis *neurosis 10r*
neutro *neuter 10r*
nevar (ie) *to snow* 7
ni *neither, nor* 2; ni... ni *neither... nor* 2; ni siquiera *not even 15r*
nicaragüense *Nicaraguan* 2
la nieta *granddaughter* 4
el nieto *grandson* 4
la nieve *snow* 7
ningún *not, not any 10r, 12*
ninguno/a *not any, none 7r, 12*
la niñera *nanny 9r*
la niñez *childhood 7r*
el/la niño/a *child 1r, 4*
el nivel *level 1r, 14*
no *no, not B;* no sé *I don't know Br*
la noche *evening, night* B; de la noche *P.M.* B; esta noche *tonight 3;* por la noche *at night* 1
la Nochebuena *Christmas Eve* 8
la Nochevieja *New Year's Eve* 8
nocturno/a adj. *night 8r*
nombrar *to name 13r*
el nombre *name* Br
nominado/a *nominated 8r*
normalmente *normally* 4
el noreste *northeast 1r*
el noroeste *northwest 1r*
el norte *north 1r*
Norteamérica *North America 3r*
norteamericano/a *North American* 1
nos *us*
nosotros/as *we* 1
la nota *grade* 1; tomar notas *take notes* 1r
notable *notable, noteworthy* 14
notablemente *notably 9r*
notar *to notice 5r*
la noticia *news* 4
novedoso/a *novel, new 6r*
la novela *novel 1r*
el/la novelista *novelist* 13
noveno/a *ninth 5*
la novia *girlfriend, fiancée 2r, 4*
noviembre *November* B
el novio *boyfriend, fiancé 2r, 4*
nublado/a *cloudy 7*
el núcleo *nucleus 4r*
nuestro/a(s) *our 1r, 2*
nuevamente *newly, again 4r*
nuevo/a *new 1r, 2;* nuevo sol *monetary unit of Peru 1r*
la nuez *nut 2r*
el número *number B*
numeroso/a *numerous 2r, 3r*
nunca *never* 1
la nutrición *nutrition 10r*
nutrido/a *full, busy 14r*

O

o *or* B
el objetivo *objective 1r*
el objeto *object 3r*
la obligación *obligation, duty 4r*
obligar *to force, to oblige 12r*
obligatorio/a *obligatory 8r*
la obra *work 1r,* 13*;* obra de teatro *play 3r*
el/la obrero/a *worker 9*
la observación *observation 2r*
el/la observador/a *observer 2r*
observar *to observe 4r*
obtener (g, ie) *to obtain, to get 3r*
obtenido/a *obtained 4r*
obvio *obvious* 10
ocasionar *to cause 7r*
octavo/a *eighth 5*
octubre *October* B
oculto/a adj *hidden Br*
la ocupación *occupation 2r,*
ocupado/a *busy, occupied* 4
ocupar *to occupy 10r,* 13; ocuparse *to be in charge of 4r*
ocurrir *to happen, to occur 3r*
odiar *to hate* 13
el odio *hate* 14
el oeste *west 10r*
la oferta *offer 6r*
oficial *official 1r*
la oficina *office* 1
el oficio *occupation 9*
ofrecer (zc) *to offer 1r, 9*
el oído *(inner) ear 4r, 11*
oír (g) *to hear 4*
ojalá *I/we hope* 10
el ojo *eye* 2
la ola *wave 7r*
las Olimpiadas *Olympic Games 5r*
oliva: de oliva *olive 10r*
olvidar *to forget 4r, 15*
la opción *option 7r*
la ópera *opera 3r*
la operación *operation 11r*
operar *to operate 11r*
opinar *to think 2r*
la opinión *opinion* 1r
opíparamente *in grand style 11r*
la oportunidad *opportunity 9*
optativo/a *optional 15r*
óptico/a *optician 2r*
el optimismo *optimism 2r*
optimista adj. *optimistic* Br
óptimo/a *optimum 10r*
opuesto/a *opposite 2r*
la oración *sentence 4r*
el orden *order 4r;* el orden público *law and order 9r;* la orden *order, command 9r;* a sus órdenes *at your service* 12
ordenado/a *tidy 5*
el ordenador *computer 1r*
ordenar *to tidy up 5*
la oreja *(outer) ear* 11
el organismo *organism 9r*
organizado/a *organized 12r*
el/la organizador/a *organizer 10r*
organizar (c) *to organize 1r*
el órgano *organ 15r*
oriental *eastern 2r*
el origen *origin 2r*
originar *to originate, to start 13r*
la orilla; a orillas de *on the coast, beside 2r*
el oro *gold 3r*
la orquesta *orchestra 4r, 8*
la ortografía *orthography 4r*
os *you*
oscuro/a *dark, obscure 2r*
el/la oso/a *bear* 2
otavaleño/a *from Otavalo, Ecuador 10r*
el otoño *autumn, fall* 6
otro/a *other, another 1r;* otra vez *again* Br
oxígeno *oxigen 11r*

P

el/la paciente *patient 9r;* adj. *patient Br*
pacifista *pacifist 15r*
el padrastro *stepfather* 4
el padre *father 3r, 4*
los padres *parents* 4
el padrino *godfather* 4
pagado/a *paid 5r*
pagar *to pay 3r,* 6
la página *page Br*
el pago *payment 6r*
el país *country 1r,* 3
el pájaro *bird 14r*
la palabra *word Br*

el palacio *palace 1r*
la palma *palm 4r*
el palo *golf club* 7
la paloma *dove 14r*
palpable *tangible 13r*
la pampa *pampa 2r*
el pan *bread* 3
la panadería *bakery 6r*
panameño/a *Panamanian* 2
la pandilla *gang 14r*
el pánico *panic 12r*
la pantalla *screen 13r*
los pantalones *pants 6;*
pantalones cortos *shorts* 6
el panteón *pantheon 10r*
las pantimedias *pantyhose* 6
el pañuelo *handkerchief* 6
la papa *potato* 3;
papas fritas *French fries* 3; papa a la huancaína *Peruvian typical dish;* papas chorreadas *Colombian typical dish 4r*
el papá *dad 1r, 4*
la papada *double chin 9r*
la papaya *papaya 10r*
el papel *paper 1r*; cambiar de papel *switch roles Br*; hacer el papel *play the part 6r*
la papelería *stationery shop 6r*
el paquete *package* 12
el par *pair 7r;* sin par *without equal 1r*
para *for, to 1;* para mí *for me* 3; *towards, in order to* 11; para que *so that* 14
el parabrisas *windshield* 12
el paracaídas *parachute 15*
el parachoques *bumper* 12
la parada *parade* 8; *stop* 12
el paraguas *umbrella* 6
paraguayo/a *Paraguayan 10r*
parar *to stop 6r*
parcial *partial Br*
pardo *brown 2r*
parecer (zc) *to seem 1r,* 6
parecido/a *similar 5r*
la pared *wall 4r*
la pareja *partner/couple 2r*
el parentesco *kinship 4r*
el pariente *relative* 4
el parque *park 1r, 5*
el párrafo *paragraph 4r*
la parte *part 1r;* por otra parte *on the other hand 3r,* 14; en todas partes *everywhere 8r*
la participación *participation 8r*
el/la participante *participant* 8r
participar *to participate 1r*, 7
particular: en particular *especially 3r*
el partido *game Br*, 7
partir: a partir de *beginning in 10r*
la partitura *musical score 4r*
la pasa *raisin 10r*
el pasado *past 4r;* adj. *last 6;*
pasado mañana *the day after tomorrow* 3
el pasaje ticket 3r, 12; *passage 9r;*
pasaje de ida y vuelta *round trip* 12
el/la pasajero/a *passenger 12*
el pasaporte *passport 2r,* 12
pasar *to spend (time) 2r,* 4; *to go through 4r; pour 5r; to happen 6r; to come in 9r;* pasarlo bien *to have fun 3r*; pasar la aspiradora *to vacuum* 5; pasar lista *to call roll* Br; ¿Qué pasa? *What's going on? 9r;* ¿Qué te/le(s) pasa? *What's wrong with you?* 11
el pasatiempo *pastime 15r*
la Pascua *Easter* 8
pasear *to stroll 1r, 4*
el paseo *walk 4r*
el pasillo *hall 5;* asiento de pasillo *aile seat* 12
la pasión *passion* Br
pasional *passional 9r*
pasivo/a *passive Br*
el paso *step 1r; passing 8r*
el pastel *pie, cake 8r*
la pastelería *pastry shop* 10
la pastilla *pill 3r, 11*
patear *to kick 7r*
paterno/a *paternal* 2r
patinar *to skate* 7
el patrimonio *patrimony 8r*
paulatinamente *gradually 15r*
el pavo *turkey* 10
la paz *peace 5r*
el pecho *chest* 11
la peculiaridad *peculiarity 4r*
el/la pediatra *pediatrician 11r*
pedir (i) *to ask for* 4
peinar (se) *to comb* 4
pelado/a *peeled 10r*
la pelea *argument 4r*
pelear *to fight* 13
la película *film* 3
el peligro *danger 5r*
peligroso/a *dangerous 10r*
el pelo *hair* 2
la pelota *ball* 7
la peluquería *beauty salon, barbershop 9r*
el/la peluquero/a *hairdresser 9*
pena: ¡Qué pena! *What a pity!* 8
pendiente *pending 10r*
la península *peninsula 7r*
pensar (ie) *to think 1r, 4;* pensar + *inf. to plan to + verb* 4
peor *worse, worst 6r,* 8
el pepino *cucumber* 10
pequeño/a *small* 1
peor *worse, worst 5r*
la pepa *seed 10r*
la pera *pear 10*
el/la perdedor/a *loser 7r*
perder (ie) *to loose* 7; perderse *to get lost* 12
la pérdida *loss 11r, 15*
perdido/a *lost 12r*
perdón *excuse me* B
el peregrinaje *peregrination 8r*
perezoso/a *lazy* 2
perfeccionista *perfectionist* Br
perfectamente *perfectly 4*
el perfil *profile* 14
el perfume *perfume 4r*
el periódico *newspaper* 3
el/la periodista *journalist, newspaperman/woman 7r, 9*
el período *period 5r*
permanecer (zc) *to stay 1r*
permanente *permanent 13r*
permitir *to permit, to allow 9r, 10*
pero *but 1*
el/la perro/a *dog 4r,* 5
perseguir *to chase 8r*
la perseverancia *perseverance 4r*
persistir *to persist 5r*
la persona *person Br,* 2
el personaje *character 8r; person 9r*
el personal *personnel 2r*
la personalidad *personality 2r*
la perspectiva *perspective 9r*
pertenecer (zc) *to belong 2r*
peruano/a *Peruvian* 2
pesar; a pesar de *in spite of 12r*
la pesca *fishing 15r*
el pescado *fish 3:* harina de pescado *fishmeal 15r*
pescar (qu) *to fish 10r*
la peseta *monetary unit of Spain until 2001 1r*
pesimista *pessimist* Br
el peso *weight 3r*
pesquero/a *fishing 15r*
la pestaña *eyelash* 11
el petróleo *petroleum, oil 6r*
petrolero/a adj. *petroleum 6r*
el/la pianista *pianist 8r*
picado/a *chopped, ground 10r*
picar (qu) *to chop 5r*
el pie *foot 10r, 11;* a pie *on foot 10r*
la piedra *stone 6r*
la piel *skin 11r*

la pierna *leg 3r, 11*
la pieza *piece, object 5r*
pilotear *to pilot, to fly 12r*
el/la piloto *pilot 9r*
la pimienta *pepper* 10
el pimiento *green pepper* 10
el pino *pine 8r*
pintado/a *painted 12r*
el pintor *painter 5r*
pintoresco/a *colourful, picturesque 8r*
la pintura *painting 9r*
la piña *pineapple* 10
la piñata *pottery filled with candies 8r*
la pirámide *pyramid* 12
pisar *to step on 14r*
la piscina *swimming pool 5*
el piso *floor, apartment (in Spain)* 5
la pista *clue 1r; slope, court, track* 7
el/la piyama *pajama 6r*
la pizarra *chalkboard B*
la pizzería *pizza place 4r*
la placa *license plate* 12
el placer *pleasure* 8r, *14*
el plan *plan 3r*
planchar *to iron 5*
planear *to plan 12r*
el planeta *planet 5r,* 15
el planetario *planetarium 3r*
planificar (qu) *to plan 3r*
el plano/a *plan 5r; level 10r*
la planta *plant* 5; planta baja *first floor 5*
plantear *to plan out 4r*
plástico/a *plastic 9r*
la plata *silver 10r*
el plátano *banana* 10
el plato *dish, 2r 5*; plato principal *main dish* 3; *plate* 10
la playa *beach* 1
la plaza *plaza 1;* plaza de toros *bullring 3r, 8*
el pliegue *fold 10r*
el/la plomero/a *plumber 9*
el plomo *lead 15r*
la pluma *feather 8r*
poblado/a *inhabited 8r*
el/la poblador/a *settler* 13
la población *population, people 2r, 13*
pobre *poor* 2
la pobreza *poverty 4r*
poco/a: un poco *a little 2r, 4;* pocos/as *few 1r*
poder (ue) *to be able to, can 1r, 4;* el poder *power* 14
poderoso/a powerful *14r*
el poema *poem 1r*
el/la poeta *poet 9r*
la polémica *polemic 7r*

el policía *policeman 9;* la mujer policía *policewoman* 9; la policía *police 2r*
el poliéster: de poliéster *polyester (made of)* 6
la política *politics 2r, 13*
el/la político/a *politician 13r; political* adj. *1r*
la pollera *typical Panamanian dress 12r*
el pollo *chicken* 3
el polo *pole 5r*
el pomelo *grapefruit* 10
poner (g) *to put, to turn on 4;* ponerse *to put on 5r,7;* poner la mesa *to set the table* 4; poner una inyección *to give a shot/injection* 11; ponerse al día *to keep up to date 9r*
popular *popular Br*
popularidad *popularity 7r*
por *by, 1r; for 2r; about, through* 3; *because of 2r,* 6; por favor *please B;* por eso *that's why 1r, 3;* por fin *finally, at last* 3; por lo menos *at least* 3; por supuesto *of course* 3; por ciento *per cent* 3; por cierto *by the way* 9; por ejemplo *for instance 1r, 3;* por correo *by mail* 9; por la mañana/tarde *in the morning/ afternoon* 1; por la noche *at night* 1; por lo menos *at least 1r*; por lo tanto *therefore 10r;* por otra parte *on the other hand* 14; por qué *why 1*
el porcentaje *percentage 5r, 14*
la porción *portion 10r*
porque *because* 1
la portada *cover (magazine)* 13
el portadocumentos *briefcase 5r*
portador: al portador *cash (in checks) 9r*
el portal *website 13r*
portátil *portable 2r,* 15
el/a porteño/a *resident of Buenos Aires*
el portón *gate 5r*
portugués/a *Portuguese* 1r
el porvenir *future 9r*
las Posadas *Hispanic festivities 8r*
el/la posadero/a *participant in* las *Posadas*
la posesión *possession 12r*
el/la posgraduado/a *postgraduate 14r*
la posibilidad *possibility 1r*
posible *possible 2r,* 10
positivo/a *positive 5r*
el postre *dessert 3r, 10*
la postura *posture 10r*

el potasio *potassium 10r*
la práctica *practice 1r;* adj. *practical 9r*
practicar (qu) *to practice* 1
el precio *price* Br, 6
precioso/a *beautiful 6; precious 6r*
precisamente *precisely 7r*
la precisión *precision 4r*
precolombino/a *pre-Columbian 1r*
predilecto/a *favorite 7r*
predominar *to predominate 2r*
la preferencia *preference 2r*
preferir (ie) *to prefer 1r, 4*
la pregunta *question Br*
preguntar *to ask (a question) Br*
prehispánico/a *pre-Hispanic 8r*
la preinscripción *preregistration 1r*
preliminar *preliminary 3r*
el premio *award, prize 6r,* 13
preocupado/a *preoccupied*
preocupar(se) *to worry 10r*
la preparación *preparation 1r*
preparar *to prepare* 1r, 5
el preparativo *preparation 5r,* 8
prescindir *to do without 11r*
la presencia *aspect 9r, presence 13r*
la presentación *presentation* Br
presentar *to present 3r,*
presente *present, here Br*
la preservación *preservation 8r*
el/la presidente/a *president 2r*
la presión *pressure 10r*
prestar *to lend 6r*
la pretensión *pretension 9r*
preventivo/a *preventive 10r*
previo/a *prior, previous 2r*
primario/a *elementary 5r*
la primavera *spring* 6
primer *first 5*
primero/a *first 1r, 5;* primera clase *first class* 12
el/la primo/la prima *cousin* 4
la princesa *princess 2r*
principal *main, principal 1r*
principalmente *mainly 2r*
el príncipe *prince 5r*
el principio *beginning* 4r; a principios *at the beginning* 14
la prioridad *priority 7r*
la prisa: tener prisa *to be in a hurry 5*
privado/a *private* Br
privilegiado/a *exceptional 7r*
probablemente *probably 3r*
probado/a *proved 4r*
probar(se) (ue) *to try (on)* 6
el problema *problem* Br
procedente de *to come from 13r*
proceder *to come from* 14
procesado/a *processed 6r*

la procesión *procession* 8
el proceso *process 8r*
proclamar *to proclaim 10r*
el prodigio *prodigy 4r*
la producción *production 6r*
la productividad *productivity 15r*
el producto *product 2r*
el/la productor/a *producer 9r*
la profesión *profession 2r,* 9
el/la profesional *professional 2r*
el profesionalismo *professionalism 3r*
el/la profesor/a *professor* B
profundo/a *deep 14r*
el/la progenitor/a *progenitor, direct ancestor 4r*
el programa *program 1r*
el/la programador/a *programmer 9r*
programar *to program 12r*
la prohibición *prohibition 7r*
prohibido/a *forbidden* 1
prohibir *to prohibit, to forbid* 10
prolífico/a *prolific 9r*
prolongado/a *lengthy 10r*
el promedio *average 1r, 14*
la promesa *promise 7r*
prometor/a *promising 9r*
prometer *to promise 2r*
la promoción *promotion 9r*
promover (ue) *to promote 7r*
el pronombre *pronoun 1r*
el pronóstico *(weather) forecast* 7
la prontitud *promptness 2r*
pronto *soon* 1; tan pronto *as soon as 11r, 14*
la propaganda *publicity, advertising* 7r
la propiedad *property 5r*
propio/a *own 2r, 9*
proponer (g) *to propose 8r*
proporcionar *to provide 4r*
el propósito *purpose 2r*
la propuesta *proposition, suggestion 10r*
la protección *protection 15r*
proteger (j) *to protect 11r*
la proteína *protein 10r*
la protesta *protest 1r*
provenzal *Provance style 5r*
la provincia *province 8r*
provocar (qu) *to provoke 14r*
próximamente *soon, shortly 9r*
próximo/a *next, next to* 3
la proyección *projection 1r*
el proyecto *project 3r*
la prueba *test 9r*
el/la psicólogo/a *psychologist* 9
la psicología *psychology* 1
el/la psiquiatra *psychiatrist 9r*
la publicación *publication* 13r
publicar (qu) *to publish 6r*
la publicidad *advertisement 9r*
público/a *public 1r*
el pueblo *town* 3r, 8; *people 7r*
el puente *bridge 9r*
la puerta *door B;* puerta de salida *gate 12*
el puerto *port, harbor 9r*
el puré *purée 9r;* puré de papas *mashed potatoes*
puertorriqueño/a *Puerto Rican* 2
pues *well 3r*
el puesto *position 2r,* 9; *stall 6r*
el pulmón *lung* 11
la pulsera *bracelet* 6
el punto *period 3r; point 4r*; punto y coma *semi colon 3r;* en punto *sharp* (time)
la puntuación *punctuation 6r*
puntual *punctual 7r*
el pupitre *student's desk* B
la pureza *purity 10r*
la purificación *purification 8r*
purificar (qu) *to purify, to cleanse 10r*
puro/a *pure* 14

Q

que *that 1r*, 2; lo que *what* 1r
qué *what* B; ¿Qué tal? *How's it going?* B; ¡Qué lástima! *What a pity!* 1; ¡Qué pena! *What a pity!* 8; ¡Qué va! *nothing of the sort, no way* 11
quedar *to be left over* 6; *to be 3r;* quedar bien *to fit* 6; quedarse *to stay* 5r; queda de usted *I remain 2r*
el quehacer *chore 4r*
la queja *complaint 14r*
quejarse *to complain* 14
la quema *burning 8r*
querer (ie) *to want 1r,* 4; Quisiera ... *I would like ...* 6
querido/a *dear 1r*
la quesadilla *Mexican dish 5r*
el queso *cheese* 3
quién interrog. *who B;* de quién/es *whose* 2
la química *chemistry* 1r
químico/a *chemical 9r*
quinto/a *fifth* 5
quitar *to take away, to remove* 7; quitarse *to take off* 7
el quitasol *sunshade, parasol 5r*
quizá(s) *maybe* 10

R

el radiador *radiator* 12r
el/la radio *radio* 5
la raíz *root 1r*
el rallador *kitchen grater 5r*
rallar *to grate 5r*
el Ramadán *Ramadan 3r*
rápidamente *rapidly, fast* 4
rápido/a *fast* 3
la raqueta *racket 6r,* 7
raro/a *odd 7r*
el rascacielos *skyscraper 2r*
el rasgo *trait, feature 3r*
la raspadura *scratching 2r*
el rato *time 3r*
el ratón *mouse* 15
la raya: de rayas *striped* 6
la raza *race 2r*
la razón *reason 4r;* tener razón *to be right 2r, 5*
la reacción *reaction 1r*
reaccionar *to react 11r*
reactivar *to reactivate 15r*
real *royal 1r*
la realidad *reality, truth 5r*; en realidad *in fact, really* 9
realista *realistic 13r*
la realización *realization 7r*
realizar (c) *to carry out 4r, 14r; to take place 5r*
realmente *really 4r,* 9
la rebaja *sale, reduction* 6
rebajado/a *marked down* 6
rebelde *rebellious* Br
recaudar *to raise, to collect 10r*
la recepción *reception 6r; front desk* 12
el/la recepcionista *receptionist 9r*
el receso *recess* Br
la receta *recipe* 10; *prescription* 11
recetar *to prescribe* 11
el rechazo *rebuff 14r*
recibir *to receive 5r*
el recibo *receipt 9r*
reciclar *recycle 14r*
recién adv. *recently 11r*
reciente adj. *recent 5r*
el recipiente *receptacle 5r*
reclamar *to claim 2r*
recolectar *to gather, collect 13r*
recomendable *advisable 10r*
la recomendación *recommendation 4r*
recomendar (ie) *to recommend 6r,* 10
la recompensa *reward 5r*
el reconocimiento *recognition 5r*
recopilar *to gather* 14

recordar (ue) *to remember 1r,* 8
recorrer *to travel 7r*
el/la rector/a *president (of a university) 5r*
el recuerdo *memory 8r*
la recuperación *recuperation 5r*
el recurso *resource 6r,* 15
la red *net* 7; *web 7r*
redondo/a *round Br*
reducido/a *reduced 10r*
reducir (zc) *to reduce 10r*
la referencia *reference 4r*
referir(se) (ie, i) *to refer 5r*
refinado/a *refined 10r*
reflejar *reflect 2r*
el refrán *proverb, saying 3r*
el refresco *soda, refreshment 3*
el refrigerador *refrigerator 5*
regalar *to give (a present) 6*
el regalo *present 5r, 6*
regar (ie) *to water 5*
regatear *to bargain 6r*
el régimen *regimen, diet 10r*
la región *region 1r*
la regla *rule 6r*
regresar *to come back 5*
regular *so so, not so good (well)* B
regularidad: con regularidad *regularly 10r*
regularmente *regularly 4*
la reina *queen 8*
reinar *to reign, to prevail 8r*
el reino *kingdom Br*
la reja *iron grill 5r*
rejuvenecer (zc) *to rejuvenate 10r*
la relación *relation 2r; relationship 4r;* **relaciones** *exteriores foreign affairs 2r*
relacionado/a *related 1r*
relacionar *to relate 1r*
relajante *relaxing 3r*
relajarse *to relax 5r*
relatar *to recount 6r*
relativamente *relatively 2r*
religioso/a adj. *religious* Br
el relleno *filling 10r*
el reloj *clock, watch* B
rematar *to auction 9r*
el remedio *remedy 11r*
rendir (i) *to render, to pay 10r*
la reparación *reparation, repair 7r*
reparar *to repair 9r*
repartir *to distribute 12r*
repente: de repente *suddently 8r*
repetir (i) *to repeat* Br, 4
la réplica *copy 11r*
el/la reportero/a *reporter 7r*
el reposo *rest 11r*
el/la representante *representative 5r*
representar *to represent 7*
la reproducción *reproduction 15r*
la república *republic 2r*
el repuesto *part 15r*
requerido/a *required 13r*
requerir (ie) *to require 7r*
el requisito *requirement 2r*
la res: carne de res *beef 10*
la reserva *reserve 3r, 15*
la reservación *reservation 3r,* 12
reservado/a *reserved 12r*
reservar *to make a reservation 8r,* 12
la residencia *residence 1r*
el/la residente *resident 5r*
resistente *resistant 5r*
la resolución *resolution 11r*
resolver (ue) *to solve 6r*
respectivamente *respectively 10r*
respecto: con respecto a *in relation to 4r*
respetar(se) *to respect* 8
respirar *to breathe* 11
responder *to answer 1r*
la responsabilidad *responsibility 2r*
responsable *responsible* Br, 1
la respuesta *answer 2r*
el restaurante *restaurant 2r, 3*
el resto *rest 4r;* **restos** *ruins*
la restricción *restriction 10r*
el resultado *result, outcome 4r*
resultar *to result, to be 8r, come about 14r*
resumen: el resumen *summary 14r*
en resumen *to summarize 4r*
la resurrección: Domingo de Resurrección *Easter Sunday* 8
retirar *to remove 10r;* **el retiro** *retirement 14r*
la reunión *reunion, meeting* Br, 3
reunirse *to get together, to meet 1r,* 8
la revelación *revelation 13r*
el reverso *back 2r*
revisar *to revise, to go over* 1; *to inspect* 12
la revisión *revision, inspection 1r*
la revista *magazine 1r,* 3
la revolución *revolution 13r*
revolucionario/a *revolutionary 4r*
el rey *king 3r,* 8; **Reyes Magos** Wise Men 6r, 8
rezar (c) *to pray 8r*
rico/a *rich, wealthy* 2; *good tasting* 10
el riel *rail 15r*
el riesgo *risk, danger 9r*
el rincón *corner 7r*
el rió *river 15r*
la riqueza *wealth 1r*
el ritmo *rhythm 1r*
el rito *rite 8r*
robar *to steal 8r*
el robot *robot 3r*
la roca *rock 7r*
la rodilla *knee* 11; **de rodillas** *kneeling 8r*
rojo/a *red* 2
el rol *role 6r*
romano/a *Roman 2r*
romántico/a *romantic* B
romper *to break* 13; *to tear* 15
la ropa *clothing 5r,* 6; **ropa interior** *underwear 6r*
rosa *pink 2r*
rosado/a *pink* 2
rubio/a *blonde* 2
el ruego *plead 14r*
el ruido *noise* 8
las ruinas *ruins 3r, 12*
el ruso *Russian 13r*
rústico/a *rustic 5r*
la ruta *route, road 3r*
la rutina *routine 3r*

S

sábado *Saturday B*
la sabana *savanna, plain 10r*
la sábana *sheet 5*
saber *to know (facts)* Br, 5
el sabor *flavor 5r*
sabroso/a *delicious 3r*
el sacacorchos *corkscrew 5r*
sacar (qu) *to get, to take (out) 1; sacar fotos to take photos 12r*
la sacarina *saccharine 11r*
el sacerdote *priest 8r*
el saco *blazer* 6
sacrificar(se) (qu) *to sacrifice*
el sacrificio *sacrifice 8r*
la sal *salt 4r,* 10
la sala *living room* 5; **sala de espera** *waiting room* 12
el salario *salary 5r*
la salida *departure, exit* 12; **hora de salida** *dismissal time 4r, departure time* 12
salir (g) *to leave 3r,* 4
el salón *room* B
la salsa *sauce* 10; **salsa de tomate** *tomato sauce* 10; *type of music 2r*
la salsateca *salsa discotheque 10r*
saltar *to jump* 14
la salud *health 7r, 11*
saludable *healthy 10r*
saludar(se) *to greet* 13

el saludo *greeting* Br
la salvación *salvation 15r*
salvadoreño/a *Salvadoran 5r*
salvar *to save (from danger), to rescue 15r*
sanar *to cure 10r*
la sanción *sanction 14r*
la sandalia *sandal* 6
el sándwich *sandwich* 3
sangrar *to bleed 11r*
la sangre *blood 2r,* 11
sano/a *healthy 10r;* **sano/a y salvo/a** *safe and sound* 15
el/la santo/a *saint Br;* **Semana Santa** *Holy Week* 8
la sardana *typical Catalonian dance 1r*
satírico/a *satiric 2r*
satisfacer (g) *to satisfy 6r*
sazonar *to season* 10
el secador *hairdryer 9r*
la secadora *drier 5*
secar(se) (qu) *to dry* 4
la sección *section 3r*
seco/a *dry 5*
el/la secretario/a *secretary 2r*
secundario/a *secondary 1r*
la sed: tener sed *to be thirsty 5*
la seda: de seda *silk (made of)* 6
sedentario/a *sedentary 10r*
la segregación *segregation* 15r
segregar *to secrete 11r*
seguido/a *followed 8r*
seguidor/a *follower 10r*
seguir (i) *to follow, to go on* 4; **seguir derecho** *to go straight ahead* 12
según *according to 1r,* 13
segundo/a *second 1r, 5*
seguramente *for sure, for certain 5r*
la seguridad *safety, security 5r,* 8
el seguro *insurance 6r;* adj. *sure 5r;* n. *safe 12r,*
la selección *selection 7r*
seleccionado/a *selected 7r*
seleccionar *to select 1r*
el sello stamp 5r, 12
la selva *jungle 6r,* 15
selvático/a *of the jungle* 15
la semana *week* B; **Semana Santa** *Holy Week 1r,* 8
semejante *similar 4r*
la semejanza *similarity* 4r
el semestre *semester* 1
la semilla *seed 8r*
el seminario *seminar 12r*
el/la senador/a *senator 1r*
la sencillez *simplicity 10r*
sencillo/a *simple 9r*
sendero *path 13r*
la sensibilidad *sensibility 4r*
sentarse (ie) *to sit down Br,* 7
sentimental *sentimental* Br
el sentimiento *feeling 5r*
sentir(se) (ie, i) *to feel 2r,* 11; *to be sorry* 11; **lo siento** *I'm sorry* B
la señal *signal 9*
el señor (Sr.) *Mr.* B; *lord 8r*
la señora (Sra.) *Mrs.* B
señorial *aristocratic, stately 13r*
la señorita *Miss* B
la separación *separation 4r,* 14
separado/a *separated 2r*
septiembre *September* B
séptimo/a *seventh 5*
sepultado/a *buried 8r*
ser *to be* Br, 2; **el ser humano** *human being* 15
la serenata *serenade 1r*
la serie *series 4r*
serio/a *serious* Br, 11
la serpiente *snake* 2
el servicio service *3r*
la servilleta *napkin* 10
servir (i) *to serve 3r,* 4; **¿en que puedo servirle?** *How may I help you? 6*
severo/a *severe, serious 12r*
la sevillana *typical dance of Andalusia 12r*
el sexo *sex 2r, 8*
sexto/a *sixth 5*
sí *yes B*
si *if 1r,* 3
el sida AIDS *11r,* 14
siempre *always* 1
la siesta *nap* 4
el siglo *century 1r*
el significado *meaning 7r*
significar (qu) *to mean 1r; to signify 3r*
significativamente *significantly 9r*
siguiente adj. *following 1r*
la silla *chair B*
el sillón *armchair 5r*
simbolizar *to symbolize 8r*
el símbolo *symbol 8r*
simpático/a *nice, charming* 2
simplemente *simply 4r*
simultáneamente *simultaneously9r*
sin *without 2r,* 7; **sin embargo** *nevertheless 1r,* 9; **sin que,** *without* 14
la sinagoga *sinagogue 8r*
sincero/a *sincere* Br
el sinfín *an endless number 6r*
sino *but 1r*
el sinónimo *synonym 3r*
el síntoma *symptom* 11
la sirena *siren 9r*
el sistema *system 4r*
el sitio *place 2r*
la situación *situation, location 4r*
situado/a *located 1r*
situar *to place 15r*
el sobre *envelope* 12
sobre *on, above* B; *about 2r*
la sobrina *niece* 4
el sobrino *nephew 4*
sociable *sociable 2r*
la sociedad *society 5r,* 13
la sociología *sociology* 1
el/la sociólogo/a *sociologist 5r*
el sodio *sodium 10r*
el sofá *sofa 5*
el sol *sun 7*
solamente *only 1r*
la soledad *solitude 8r; loneliness 14r*
solemne *solemn 8r*
la solemnidad *solemnity 8r*
soler (ue) *use to + inf. 9r*
el/la solicitante *solicitant, applicant 2r*
solicitar *to request, to apply for 2r,* 9
la solicitud *application 9*
sólo adv. *only 1r,* 3, 4
solo/a adj. *alone 2r,* 14; *one 6r;* **de un solo color** *solid color* 6
soltar *to let go 14r*
el/la soltero/a *single, bachelor* 2
la solución *solution 6r*
el sombrero *hat 6*
el somnífero *sleeping pill 11r*
sonar (ue) *to ring 7r*
el sonido *sound 4r*
la sopa *soup 3*
sordo/a *deaf 15r*
sorprendido/a *surprised 9r*
la sorpresa *surprise 2r*
sopresivo/a *surprising 8r*
sospechar *to suspect 14r*
el sostén *brassiere* 6
sostener (g, ie) *to hold 4r*
su(s) *your* (formal), *his, her, its* B; *theirs* 2
suave *soft 8*
subir *to go up 8r,* 12; *to increase 10r;* **subir de peso** *gain weight 3r*
subrayar *to underline 4r*
el subtítulo *subtitle 3r*
el suburbio *suburb* 5r
la sucursal *branch 14r*
sucio/a *dirty 5*
la sudadera *jogging suit, sweat shirt* 6
sudamericano/a *South-American 7r*
sueco/a *Swede 3r*
el sueldo *salary 9*

el sueño *dream 2r;* tener sueño *to be sleepy 5*
la suerte *luck* 1; tener suerte *to be lucky* 5; a la suerte *at random 12r*
el suéter *sweater 6*
suficiente *enough 3r*
la sugerencia *suggestion 3r*
sugerir (ie, i) *to suggest 6r*
suma adj. *much 10r*
sumar *to add 1r*
la superación *improvement 9r overcoming 13r*
superar *to surpass 9r; to overcome 12r*
superdotado/a *gifted*
el supermercado *supermarket 6r, 10*
la súplica *plead 14r*
el sur *south 1r*
suramericano/a *South American 2r*
el sureste *southeast 7r*
el/la surfista *surfer 7r*
el surgimiento *breakout 14r*
surgir (j) *to appear, to arise 14r*
suroeste *southwest 13r*
el surtido *selection 6r*
la suscripción *subscription 6r*
la sustancia *substance 10r*
el sustantivo *noun 10r*
sustentar *to support 5r*
suyo (-a, -os, -as) *(of) yours, his, hers, theirs 5r,* 12

T

la tabla *chart 4r; cutting board 5r*
tal *such* 10; ¿Qué tal? *How's it going?* B; *tal como such as 8r;* tal vez *maybe* 10; con tal (de) que *provided that* 14
el talento *talent 8r*
la talla *size 6*
tallado/a *carved 10r*
el tamaño *size 4r*
también adv. *also, too* 1
tampoco adv. *neither, nor, either 5r,* 12
tan adv. *so 1r*; *as 1r,* 8
el tango *type of music and dance 2r*
tanto/a *as much* 1r, 8; en tanto *meanwhile 9r;* por lo tanto *therefore 10r*
tantos/as *as many* 8
tardar *to take (time) 15r*
tarde *late 1r,* 4; más tarde *later* 3; n. *afternoon* B
la tarea *assignment, homework* Br, 1
la tarjeta *card 2r, 6;* tarjeta de crédito *credit card 3r,* 6; tarjeta de embarque *boarding pass* 12; tarjeta postal *post card 2r,* 12
la tasa *rate, interest 14r*
la taza *cup* 10
te *you 5*; te llamas *your name is* B
el té *tea* 3
el teatro *theater 3r,* 8
el techo *roof 8r*
la técnica *technique 12r*
el tecnicismo *technicality 9r*
el/la técnico/a *technician* 9; adj. *technical 9r*
la tecnología *technology 8r*
el tejido *weaving 8r*
la tela *fabric 6r*
telefónico/a adj. *telephone 9r*
el teléfono *telephone Br,* 3
la telenovela *soap opera 11r*
la telepatía *telepathy 3r*
el/la televidente *TV viewer* 13
el televisor *TV set* B
la tele(visión) *television* 1
el tema *topic 2r*
temer *to fear* 11
el temor *fear 7r*
el temperamento *temperament 9r*
la temperatura *temperature 3r*
templado/a *moderate 5r*
temporal *temporary 13r*
temprano *early* 4
tender (ie) *to hang (clothes)* 5; tender la cama *to make the bed 5r*
el tenedor *fork 5r,* 10
tener (g, ie) *to have* Br, 4; tener años *to be...years old* 2; tener deseos de + inf. *to feel like + pres. part.* 8; tener dolor de... *to have a(n)... ache* 11; tener éxito *to be successful* 13; tener mala cara *to look terrible* 11; tener que + inf. *to have to + verb* 1r, 5; tener lugar *to take place 8r*
el tenis *tennis Br,* 7
el/la tenista *tennis player 2r,* 7
la tensión *pressure* 11; tensión arterial *blood pressure* 11
el teñido *dyeing 8r*
la teocracia *theocracy 8r*
el tequila *Mexican liqueur 8r*
la terapia *therapy 12r*
tercer *third 5*
tercero/a *third 5*
la terminación *ending 10r*
terminar *to finish* 3
el termómetro *thermometer 2r, 11*
la terraza *terrace 1r, 5*
el terreno *terrain 14r*
terrestre adj. *land 3r*
terrible *terrible* Br
el territorio *territory 15r*
el/la testigo *witness 13r*
el testimonio *testimony 8r*
el texto *text 1r*
la tía *aunt* 4
tibio/a *lukewarm 10r*
el tiempo *time* Br, 3; *weather* 7; tiempo libre *free time 1r*; 3; a tiempo *on time* 12
la tienda *store 6*
la Tierra *Earth 15;* tierra *land, soil 2r,* 15
el tigre *tiger 3r*
las tijeras scissors *5r*
tímido/a *timid* Br
el tinte *shade, overtone 9r*
la tintoreriá *dry cleaner's 14r*
el tío *uncle* 4
típico/a *typical 1r,* 3
el tipo *type, style, 3r; kind 10r*
titulado/a *entitled 9r*
el/la titular *holder 2r*
el título *title 4r*
la tiza *chalk* B
la toalla *towel 5*
el tobillo *ankle* 11
el tocadiscos *record player 5r*
tocar (qu) *to play an instrument, to touch 3*
todavía adv. *still, yet 4r,* 13
todo *all, everything* 12; todos *everybody, all 12;* todos los días *every day* 1
tolerante *tolerant* 1r
tomar *to take, to drink* 1; tomar el sol *to sunbathe* 3
el tomate *tomato 3*
la tonelada *ton 4r*
el tono *tone 2r*
tonto/a *silly, foolish* 2
torcer(se), (ue, z) *to twist* 11
el torneo *tournament 7r*
la toronja *grapefruit* 10
la torta *cake 5r*
la tortura *torture 10r*
la tos *cough* 11
toser *to cough* 11
la tostada *toast* 3
totalmente *totally 5r*
la totora *cattail (plant) 10r*
trabajador/a *hard working* 2
trabajar *to work* 1
el trabajo *work 1r,* 9
la tradición *tradition 2r,* 8
tradicional *traditional* Br
tradicionalmente *traditionally* 4

traducir (zc) *to translate* 7
traer (g) *to bring 3r,* 4
el tráfico *traffic 12r*
trágico/a *tragic 8r*
el traje *suit* 6; traje de baño *bathing suit* 6; traje pantalón *pant suit* 6
tranquilamente *quietly* 4
la tranquilidad *tranquility 5r*
tranquilizante *tranquilizer 12r*
tranquilo/a *calm, tranquil* Br, 2
el transbordador espacial *space shuttle* 15
transformar *to transform 4r*
la transición *transition 14r*
transmitir *transmit 11r*
la transmutación *transmutation 10r*
la transparencia *transparency 11r*
transparente *transparent 9r*
transplantar *to transplant 11r*
el transporte *transportation 5r*
el trapo *cloth, kitchen cloth 5r*
trasladar(se) *to move, to transfer* 13
el tratado *treaty 5r*
el tratamiento *treatment 10r*
tratar *to try 5r; to deal, to discuss 9r*
través: a través de adv. *through* 13
tremendo/a *tremendous 9r*
el tren *train 11r,* 12
el trigo *wheat 15r*
el/la tripulante *crew member* 14
triste *sad* 2
la tristeza *sadness* 13
el triunfo *victory 7r*
el trofeo *trophy 7r*
tropezar (ie) *to stumble 15r*
tropical *tropical 10r*
el trueque *exchange 9r*
tu/s adj. *your* B, 2
tú pron. *you* (familiar) B
la tumba *tomb 10r*
la tuna *group of student minstrels 1r*
el túnel *tunnel 3r*
la túnica *tunic 8r*
el turismo *tourism 9r*
el/la turista *tourist 1r;* clase turista *economy class* 12
turístico/a adj. *tourist 7r*
turnarse *to take turns 4r*
el turno *turn, shift 11r*
tuyo (-a, -os, -as) *(of) yours, his, hers, theirs* 12

U

la ubicación *location 5r*
ubicar (qu) *to place, to locate 14r*
la úlcera *ulcer 11r*
último/a *last 6r,* 8
un/a *a, an, one* B; unos cuantos *some 1r*
único/a *only, unique* 4; hijo/a único/a *only child* 4
la unidad *unity 5r*
unido/a *united 1r*
el uniforme *uniform 3r*
la unión *union 7r*
unir *to unite, to join (together) 2r*
la universidad *university* 1
universitario/a adj. *university 1r*
el universo *universe* B, 15
unos/as *some* 1
urbano/a *urban 12r*
urgente *urgent 1r*
urgentemente *urgently 9r*
uruguayo/a *Uruguayan 7r*
usar *to use* 1r, 2; *to wear* 3
el uso *use 2r*
usted *you* (formal sing.) B
ustedes you (formal pl.) 1
usualmente *usually 8r*
el/la usuario/a *user 7r*
el utensilio *utensil 5r*
útil *useful Br*
utilizar (c) *to use, utilize 4r*
la uva *grape 10*

V

las vacaciones *vacation 1r,* 3
vacante *vacant, opening 9*
vacío/a *empty* 12
la vacuna *vaccination 15r*
la vainilla *vanilla 4r, 10*
el valenciano *Valencian language*; adj. *from Valencia*
valer *to be worth* 6
la validez *validity 2r*
valiente *brave* Br
valioso/a *valuable 13r*
el valle *valley 9r*
el vallenato *typical Colombian music 4r*
el valor *value, price 3r*
valorar *to value 4r*
vanagloriarse *to boast 6r*
el vaquero *cowboy 7r*; los vaqueros/jeans *jeans 6;*
variable *variable, changeable 9r*
variado/a *varied 2r*
la variante *variant 7r*
variar *to vary 5r*
la variedad *variety 2r*
varios/as *various, several 1r*
el varón *male* 14
el vascuence *Basque language 1r*
el vaso *glass 3r, 10*
el vecindario *neighborhood 5r*
el/la vecino/a *neighbor 5r,* 14
la vegetación *vegetation 15r*
el vegetal *vegetable* 3
vegetariano/a *vegetarian 3r*
la vela *candle 4r*
la velada *evening 9r*
el velero *sailboat 3r*
la velocidad *speed* 12
la vena *vein* 11
el vencimiento *expiration 3r*
el/la vendedor/a *salesman, saleswoman 6r,* 9
vender *to sell 4r,* 6
venerar *venerate 8r*
venezolano/a *Venezuelan* 2
venir (g, ie) *to come* 4
la venta *sale 3r, 9*
la ventaja *advantage 2r,* 14
la ventana *window* B
ventanilla *window (car, plane, etc.)* 12
el ventanal *large window 5r*
ver *to see 1r,* 3
el verano *summer 2r,* 6
el verbo *verb 1r*
la verdad: ¿verdad? *truth, right?* 1
verde *green, not ripe* 2
la verdura *vegetable* 3
verificar (qu) *to verify 4r*
versátil *versatile 7r*
el vestido *dress 3r,* 6
vestir(se) (i) *to dress, to get dressed* 4
el vestuario *dressing room 7r*
la vez: a veces *sometimes* 1; dos veces *twice* 4; una vez *once* 12; muchas veces *often, many times* 1; alguna vez *sometimes, on occasions* 12; otra vez *again 7r;* una vez *once* 12; de vez en cuando *now and then 10r*
viajar *to travel 2r,* 12
el viaje *trip 3r, 12;* viaje espacial *space trip* 15
el/la viajero/a *traveller*
la víctima *victim* 8r
la vida *life* 1r, 15
el video *video 1r*
el videocasete *videocassette 3r*
la videocasetera *VCR* B
viejo/a *old* 2
el viento *wind* 7
viernes *Friday* B
vigilar *to watch 12r*
el villancico *Christmas carol 8r*

el vinagre *vinegar* 10
la vinificación *fermentation 9r*
el vino *wine* 3; **vino tinto** *red wine* 10
el viñedo *vineyard 9r*
la violencia *violence* 8
violeta adj. *violet, 2r*
el violín *violin 4r*
el/la violinista *violinist 8r*
la virgen *virgin 8r*
virtual *virtual 3r*
el virus *virus* 15r
la visa *visa 3r*
la visita *guest 5r*
el/la visitante *visitor 5r*
visitar *to visit 1r*, 4
la vista *view 5r*
la vitalidad *vitality 1r*
la vitamina *vitamin 10r*
la viuda *widow* 14
el viudo *widower* 14
los víveres *food supplies 6r*
la vivienda *housing 13r*
vivir *to live 1r*, 3
vivo/a *alive, living 4r*
el vocabulario *vocabulary* Br
la vocal *vowel* Br
el vocero *spokesman 15r*
volador *flying 15r*
el volante *steering wheel* 12
volar (ue) *to fly 5r*, 12
el volcán *volcano 5r*
el voleibol volleyball 7
el volumen *volume 5r*
la voluntad *will, will power 13r*
el/la voluntario/a *volunteer 14r*
volver (ue) *to return* 4
vos *you (familiar) 2r*
vosotros/as pron. *you (familiar plu.)* 1
votar *to vote 12r*
la voz *voice 14r*
el vuelo *flight 3r*, 12
la vuelta: viaje de ida y vuelta *round trip* 12
vuestro/a adj. *your (familiar plural)* 2

Y

y *and B*
ya *already 3r*, 5; **ya que** *since 8r;* **ya sea** *whether 9r*
yacente *lying, recumbent 8r*
la yema *egg yolk 10r*
la yerba/hierba *herb 9r*
yo *I* B
el yogur *yogurt* 10
yugoslavo/a *Yugoslavian 2r*

Z

la zanahoria *carrot* 10
la zapatilla *slipper* 6
el zapato *shoe* 6
la zarzuela *Spanish operetta 3r*
la zona *2r*
el zoológico *zoo 3r*

Apéndice 4

English to Spanish Vocabulary

A

a (an) un/a
above sobre
absence la ausencia
absent ausente
academic académico/a
accent el acento
accept aceptar
accessory el accesorio
accident el accidente
accompany acompañar
according según
account: checking account la cuenta: cuenta corriente
accountant el/la contador/a, el/la contable
accounting la contabilidad
accredit acreditar
ache el dolor
act actuar
active activo/a
activity la actividad
actress la actriz
adapt adaptar(se)
add añadir, sumar
address la dirección
adequate adecuado/a
admiration la admiración
admire admirar
adult adulto/a
advance el adelanto
advantage la ventaja
advertisement el aviso, el anuncio
advertising la publicidad
advice el consejo
advisable recomendable
advise aconsejar
aerobic aeróbico/a
affect afectar
affection el cariño
affiliation la afiliación
affirmatively afirmativamente
African africano/a
after después
afraid: to be afraid (of) tener miedo (de)
against contra
age la edad
agency: travel agency la agencia: agencia de viajes
agenda la agenda
aggressive agresivo/a
AIDS el sida
air el aire
air conditioning el aire acondicionado
airline la aerolínea
airplane el avión
airport el aeropuerto
aisle: aisle seat el pasillo: asiento de pasillo
alcoholic alcohólico/a
all todo/a, todos/as
allergic alérgico/a
allergy la alergia
allow dejar, permitir
almost casi
alone solo/a
already ya
also también
altar el altar
alternate alternar
although aunque
always siempre
ambitious ambicioso/a
among entre
amusing divertido/a
analysis el análisis
analyst: systems analyst el/la analista: analista de sistemas
analyze analizar
ancestor el/la antepasado/a
and y
anguish la angustia
animal el animal
ankle el tobillo
anniversary el aniversario
announce anunciar
announcement el anuncio
annoyance el fastidio
another otro/a
answer *v.* contestar; *n.* la contestación, la respuesta
answering machine el contestador automático
anthropology la antropología
antibiotic el antibiótico
anticipation la anticipación
antiquity la antigüedad
any algún, alguno/a/s
anyone cualquier/a
apartment el apartamento
appear aparecer, surgir
appearance la apariencia
appetite el apetito
applaud aplaudir
apple la manzana

applicant el/la solicitante
application la solicitud
April abril
architect el/la arquitecto/a
architecture la arquitectura
area el área
Argentinian argentino/a
argue discutir
argument la discusión
arm el brazo (body); el arma (weapon)
armament el armamento
armchair la butaca, el sillón
around alrededor
arrest detener
arrival la llegada
arrive llegar
arrogant arrogante
article el artículo
artifact el artefacto
artist el/la artista
as como
as many tantos/as
as much tanto/a
ascend ascender
Asian asiático/a
ask (a question) preguntar: **ask for** pedir
aspect el aspecto
asphyxiation la asfixia
aspirin la aspirina
assault el asalto
assembly la asamblea
assignment la tarea
assimilate asimilar/se
assistant el/la asistente, ayudante
associate asociar
assume presumir, asumir
astronaut el/la astronauta
astronomer el/la astrónomo
at a; en
athlete el/la atleta
athletic atlético/a
atrophy atrofiar
attend asistir (a): **attend to** atender
attendance la asistencia
attention la atención
attraction la atracción
attractive atractivo/a
August agosto
aunt la tía
authoritarian autoritario/a
autobiographical autobiográfico/a
autumn el otoño
available disponible
avenue la avenida
average *n.* el promedio, *adj.* mediano/a
avocado el aguacate
avoid evitar
award el premio

B

baby el/la bebé, el/la nene/a
baby-sitter la niñera, el canguro
back la espalda
backpack la mochila
backyard el jardín
bacon el tocino
bad malo/a
bag el/la bolso/a
balance *v.* equilibrar; *n.* el equilibrio; el saldo, balance
ball la pelota
ball-point pen el bolígrafo
banana el plátano
band la banda
bank el banco
banquet el banquete
baptism el bautizo
barbecue la barbacoa
barbershop la peluquería, barbería
bargain *v.* regatear
baseball el béisbol
baseball bat el bate
basic básico/a
basically básicamente
basket el/la cesto/a
basketball el baloncesto, basquetbol
bathe bañar(se)
bathroom el baño
battery el acumulador, la batería
be estar; ser, resultar; **be a couple** formar pareja; **be able** poder; **be afraid** tener miedo; **be born** nacer; **be called** llamarse; **be careful** tener cuidado; **be cold** tener frío; **be hot** tener calor; **be hungry** tener hambre; **be in a hurry** tener prisa; **be in charge** estar a cargo; **be in love (with)** estar enamorado (de); **be left over** quedar (*like* gustar); **be lucky** tener suerte; **be missing** faltar (*like* gustar); **be necessary** hacer falta; **be part of** formar parte de; **be pleasing** gustar; **be right** tener razón; **be sleepy** tener sueño; **be sorry** sentir (ie, i); **be successful** tener éxito; **be sure** estar seguro/a; **be surprised** sorprenderse; **be thirsty** tener sed; **be used to** estar acostumbrado/a
beach la playa
beat batir
beater la batidora
beautiful bello/a, precioso/a
beauty salon la peluquería
because porque
because of a causa de, por
become convertirse (en), hacerse; **become independent** independizarse; **become impacient** impacientarse
bed la cama
beef la carne de res
beeper el buscapersonas
beer la cerveza
begin comenzar, empezar
beginning el principio
behind detrás (de)
belief la creencia
believe creer
belt el cinturón
benefit el beneficio
besides además

best el/la mejor
better mejor
between entre
bicycle la bicicleta
big grande
bilingual bilingüe
bill la cuenta; el billete (*currency*)
biology la biología
biosphere la biosfera (*alt.* biósfera)
birth el nacimiento
birthday el cumpleaños
black negro/a
blanket la manta
blazer el saco
bleed sangrar
blind ciego/a
block bloquear
block (of city street) la cuadra, la manzana (*Sp.*)
blond rubio/a
blood la sangre
blood pressure la tensión arterial
blouse la blusa
blue azul
boat bote, barco
body el cuerpo
boil hervir
bone el hueso
book el libro
bookstore la librería
boot la bota
border la frontera
bored aburrido
boring aburrido/a
both ambos/as
bother molestar
bottle la botella
boy el chico, el muchacho
bracelet la pulsera
brain el cerebro
bra (brassiere) el sostén
brave valiente
bread el pan
break romper
breakfast el desayuno
breathe respirar
bridge el puente
briefcase el maletín, el portadocumentos
bring traer
brother el hermano
brother-in-law el cuñado
brown café, castaño, marrón
brunet moreno/a
brush *v.* cepillar(se), *n.* el cepillo: **brush one's teeth** cepillarse/lavarse los dientes
build construir
building el edificio
bullfight la corrida de toros
bullfighter el torero/a
bullfighting el toreo
bumper el parachoques
bus el autobús, bus
business el negocio
businessman el hombre de negocios
businesswoman la mujer de negocios
busy ocupado/a
but pero
butter la mantequilla
buy comprar

C

cabin la cabina
cabin (on a boat) el camarote
cabinet (presidential) el gabinete
cafeteria la cafetería
caffeine la cafeína
cake el pastel, el bizcocho, la tarta (*Sp.*)
calculator la calculadora
calculus el cálculo
call llamar
calm tranquilo/a
calorie la caloría
camera la cámara
camouflage camuflar
can opener el abrelatas
cancel cancelar
cancer el cáncer
candidate el/la candidato/a
candy el caramelo, el dulce
cap la gorra
capacity la capacidad
capital la capital (*city*), el capital (*money*)
capture capturar
car el coche, carro, auto(móvil)
car hood el capó
cardboard el cartón
care el cuidado
career la carrera
carpenter el/la carpintero/a
carpet la alfombra
carrot la zanahoria
carry out llevar a cabo, realizar
cash el efectivo
cash register la caja
cashier el/la cajero/a
cassette el/la casete
Castilian el castellano
catalog el catálogo
catastrophic catastrófico/a
catch (an illness) contagiarse
category la categoría
cathedral la catedral
cause causar, ocasionar
celebrate celebrar
celebration la celebración
cell la célula
cemetery el cementerio
census el censo
center el centro
cereal el cereal
certain cierto/a
certified certificado/a
chair la silla
chalk la tiza
chalkboard la pizarra
champagne el champán, champaña
champion el/la campeón/a
championship el campeonato
change cambiar
charming encantador/a, simpático/a
chart la tabla
chat charlar

check (luggage) facturar
cheek la mejilla
cheese el queso
chemistry la química
cherry la cereza
chest el pecho
chest cold el catarro
chicken el pollo
child el/la niño/a
childhood la niñez
Chilean chileno/a
chocolate el chocolate
choose escoger
chop picar: **pork chop** la chuleta
Christmas la Navidad
Christmas Eve la Nochebuena
church la iglesia
citizen el/la ciudadano/a
city la ciudad
civil civil
claim reclamar
claro clear, of course
class la clase
classic clásico/a
classified clasificado/a
classify clasificar (qu)
classroom el aula, el salón de clase
clean *v.* limpiar; *adj.* limpio/a
cleaning la limpieza
clear claro/a, despejado/a (*weather*)
client el/la cliente/a
climate el clima
clinic la clínica
clock el reloj
close cerrar
closet el armario, el clóset
cloth el trapo
clothing la ropa
cloudy nublado/a
club el club
coach el/la entrenador/a
coat el abrigo
cocaine la cocaína
cockpit la cabina
coffee el café
cognate el cognado
coincide coincidir
colander el colador, escurridor
cold frío/a
collect recaudar
college universidad
Colombian colombiano/a
colonial colonial
color el color
column la columna
comb peinar(se)
combine combinar
come venir
come from *v.* proceder; *adv.* procedente de
come in pasar, entrar
comical cómico/a
comment el comentario
commerce el comercio
common común
communicate comunicar(se)
communication la comunicación
community la comunidad
company la compañía, empresa
compare comparar
competent competente
competition la competencia
complain quejarse
complaint la queja
complete *v.* completar; *adj.* completo/a
computer la computadora, el ordenador (*Sp.*)
computer science la informática
concert el concierto
concierge el/la conserje
conclusion la conclusión
condominium el condominio
conference la conferencia
confiscate confiscar
confront enfrentar
confuse confundir(se)
congenital congénito/a
congress el congreso
consequence la consecuencia
conservative conservador/a
consider considerar(se)
construct construir
construction la construcción
consul el/la cónsul
consulate el consulado
consult consultar
consume consumir
contact lenses lentes de contacto
contagion el contagio
contain contener
contamination la contaminación
contemporary contemporáneo/a
contents el contenido
contest el concurso
context el contexto
contraband el alijo, contrabando
contract *v.* contraer; *n.* el contrato
contribution la contribución
control controlar
convention el congreso
conversation la conversación
cook *v.* cocinar; *n.* el/la cocinero/a
cookie la galleta, galletita
cool fresco/a
cooperate cooperar
co-op (cooperative society) la cooperativa
copy la copia
cork el corcho
corkscrew el sacacorchos
corn el maíz, el elote (*on the cob*)
corner el rincón, la esquina (*street*)
correct correcto/a
correspondence la correspondencia
corresponding correspondiente
cost *v.* costar, *n.* el costo
cotton el algodón
cough la tos
cough toser
counselor el/la consejero/a
counter el mostrador
country el país
countryside el campo
course el curso
court la corte (*law*), la cancha (*sports*)

courtesy la cortesía
cousin el/la primo/a
cover cubrir
crash chocar
crazy loco/a
cream la crema
creation la creación
creative creativo/a
credit card la tarjeta (de crédito)
crew member el/la tripulante
crime el crimen, la delincuencia
crisis la crisis
critic el/la crítico/a
crowd la multitud
crucial crucial
crucifix el crucifijo
cruise el crucero
crumb la migaja
crush majar
cry llorar
Cuban cubano/a
cucumber el pepino
cultivate cultivar
cultivation el cultivo
culture la cultura
cup la taza
cure *v.* curar(se), *n.* la cura
currency la moneda
current actual
curtain la cortina
custom la costumbre
customs la aduana
cut *v.* cortar, *n.* el corte
cyberspace el ciberespacio
cycling el ciclismo
cyclist el/la ciclista

D

dad el papá
daily diariamente
daily diario/a
dairy (product), lácteo/a
damage *v.* dañar; *n.* el daño
dance bailar, el baile
dancer el bailarín/la bailarina
data el dato, la información
date la fecha
daughter la hija
daughter-in-law la nuera
dawn la madrugada
day el día
dead muerto/a
deaf sordo/a
death la muerte
deceased difunto/a, muerto
December diciembre
decide decidir
decision la decisión
decisive decisivo/a
declare declarar
decrease disminuir
dedicate dedicar
defend defender
defense la defensa
deforestation la deforestación
delight encantar
delighted encantado/a
deliver entregar
demand la demanda
demonstrate demostrar
demonstration la manifestación (*political*)
denomination la denominación
dense denso/a
dentist el/la dentista
department el departamento
department store el almacén
departure la salida
depend depender
depressed deprimido/a
descendant el/la descendiente
description la descripción
deserve merecer
design el diseño
designer el/la diseñador/a
desk el escritorio: **student desk** el pupitre
desperate desesperado/a
dessert el postre
destiny el destino
destroy destruir
detective el detective
detest detestar(se)
develop desarrollar
diabetic el/la diabético/a
dialog el diálogo
dictator el dictador
dictatorship la dictadura
dictionary el diccionario
diet la dieta
difficult difícil
digest digerir
digestion la digestión
dining room el comedor
dinner la cena
diplomacy la diplomacia
diplomatic diplomático/a
director el/la director/a
dirty ensuciar
disadvantage la desventaja
disarrange desordenar
discipline la disciplina
discotheque la discoteca
discover descubrir
discrimination la discriminación
dish el plato
dishwasher el lavaplatos
dismantle desmontar
disquette el disquete
distance la distancia
distant lejano/a
distribute repartir, distribuir
distribution la distribución
diverse diverso/a
diversity la diversidad
diving el buceo
divorce *v.* divorciarse, *n.* el divorcio
divorced divorciado/a
do hacer
doctor el/la doctor/a: **medical doctor** el/la médico/a
doctor's office el consultorio
document el documento
dollar el dólar
domestic doméstico/a

door la puerta
dormitory el dormitorio
double doble: **double/single room** la habitación doble/sencilla
doubt dudar
drain escurrir
drawing el dibujo
dress *v.* vestir(se); el *n.* vestido
dresser la cómoda
drink *v.* beber, *n.* la bebida
drive manejar, conducir
driver el chofer, conductor
drug la droga
drug traffic el narcotráfico
drug trafficker el narcotraficante
dry secar(se)
dryer la secadora
due debido a
duplicate duplicar
during durante
dynamic dinámico/a

E

e-mail el correo electrónico
each cada
early temprano
ear la oreja, el oído (*inner*)
earring el arete
earth la tierra
easy fácil
eat comer
ecologist el/la ecólogo/a
economic económico/a
economics la economía
economy class clase turista
educated educado/a
effect el efecto
efficient eficiente
egg el huevo
eighth octavo/a
elbow el codo
electric eléctrico/a
electrical appliance el electrodoméstico
electrician el/la electricista
electronic electrónico/a
elegant elegante
element el elemento
embassy la embajada
embrace abrazar(se)
emergency la emergencia
emigrant el/la emigrante
emigrate emigrar
emotional emocional
employee el/la empleado/a
empty vacío/a
encounter el encuentro
end el final
energy la energía
engineer el/la ingeniero/a
English el inglés
enjoy disfrutar
enough bastante
ensemble el conjunto
entertainment la diversión
envelope el sobre
equal igual
equality la igualdad
equilibrium el equilibrio
equipment el equipo
equivalent equivalente
eraser el borrador
error el error
eternal eterno/a
ethnic étnico/a
European europeo/a
evening la noche
event el evento, acontecimiento, suceso
every cada, todos/as
everything todo
evidence la evidencia
examination el examen
examine examinar
excellent excelente
except excepto
exception la excepción
exceptional excepcional
exchange *v.* cambiar, *n.* el intercambio: **stock exchange** la bolsa de valores
excited emocionado/a
exclusive exclusivo/a
Excuse me. Perdón.
executive el/la ejecutivo/a
exhaustive exhaustivo
expectation la expectativa
expensive caro/a
experience la experiencia
experiment el experimento
explain explicar
explosion la explosión
express expresar
expression la expresión
extension la extensión
exterior el exterior
extinction la extinción
extremely extremadamente
extrovert extrovertido/a
eye el ojo
eyebrow la ceja
eyelash la pestaña

F

fabric la tela
fabulous fabuloso/a
face la cara
fact el hecho
factual factual
fall caer(se)
false falso/a
fame la fama
family la familia
famous famoso/a, conocido/a
fan el abanico, el ventilador; el/la aficionado/a (*sports, etc.*)
fanatic fanático/a
fantasy la fantasía
far lejos (de)
farewell la despedida
fascinate fascinar
fashion la moda
fashion show el desfile de modas
fast rápido/a

fat gordo/a
father-in-law el suegro
fatigue el cansancio, la fatiga
fatigued cansado/a, fatigado/a
favorite favorito/a
fear *v.* temer; *n.* el miedo;
be afraid tener miedo
February febrero
feed alimentar
feel sentir(se)
festival el festival
festive festivo
fiancé/e el/la novio/a
fiber la fibra
fifth quinto/a
fight pelear, luchar
file el archivo
fill llenar
film la película
financed financiado/a
find encontrar: **find out** averiguar
finger el dedo
finish acabar, terminar
fire *n.* el incendio, el fuego; *v.* despedir (*an employee*), disparar (*a weapon*)
firefighter el/la bombero/a
fireplace la chimenea
first primer, primero/a
fish el pescado
fishing (boat) pesquero/a
fit caber, quedar(le) bien a uno (*clothing*)
fix arreglar
flat plano/a
flavor el sabor
flexible flexible
flight el vuelo
float (in a parade) la carroza
floor el piso: **first floor** la planta baja
flour la harina
flow *v.* fluir, *n.* el flujo
flower la flor
flu la gripe
fly volar
fold doblar
follow seguir
following siguiente
food la comida, el alimento
foot el pie
footwear el calzado
for por; para
forbidden prohibido/a
force obligar, forzar
forehead la frente
foreign extranjero/a: **foreign affairs** las relaciones exteriores
foreigner el/la extranjero/a
forget olvidar
fork el tenedor
form *v.* formar, *n.* la forma, el formulario (*to fill out*)
formal formal
formula la fórmula
found fundar
fowl (poultry) el ave
fracture fracturar(se)
free libre: **free of charge** gratis
frequency la frecuencia
frequently frecuentemente
Friday viernes
fried frito/a
friend el/la amigo/a
friendship la amistad
from de
front desk la recepción
fruit la fruta
fry freír
full lleno/a
function *v.* funcionar, *n.* el uso, la función
fund el fondo
funnel el embudo
furious furioso/a
furniture el mueble

G

game el juego, el partido
gang la pandilla
garage el garaje
garbage la basura
garden el jardín
garlic el ajo
gasoline la gasolina
gather recolectar
gelatin la gelatina
gene el gene (*alt.* el gen)
genealogical genealógico/a
generally generalmente
generation la generación
generous generoso/a
genetic genético/a
geography la geografía
German alemán
gesture el gesto, el ademán
get conseguir, obtener, adquirir, sacar (qu); **get dressed** vestirse; **get married** casarse: **get ready** arreglarse, prepararse; **get old** envejecer: **get together** reunirse; **get up** levantarse
together juntos/as
ghetto el gueto
giant gigante
girl la chica, la muchacha
give dar, regalar (*as a gift*)
glad contento/a
glass el cristal, el vaso; la copa (*stemmed glass*)
glove el guante
go ir
godchild el/la ahijado/a
godfather el padrino
godmother la madrina
golf-club el palo (*wood*), el hierro (*iron*)
good bueno/a
good-bye adiós
good-looking guapo/a
goods los bienes
government el gobierno
grade la nota
gradually gradualmente
graduate graduado/a
graduation la graduación
grain el grano
granddaughter la nieta
grandfather el abuelo

grandmother la abuela
grandson el nieto
grape la uva
grapefruit la toronja
grate rallar
grater el rallador
gray gris
green verde
greet saludar(se)
greeting el saludo
grind moler
ground molido/a
group el grupo
Guatemalan guatemalteco/a
guess adivinar
guitar la guitarra
gymnasium el gimnasio

H

habit el hábito
hair el cabello, el pelo
hairdresser el/la peluquero/a
hairdryer el secador
half la mitad, la media
hall el pasillo
ham el jamón
hamburger la hamburguesa
hand la mano
handicrafts la artesanía
handkerchief el pañuelo
hang tender, colgar
happen ocurrir
happiness la felicidad
happy feliz, alegre
hard duro/a: **hard-working** trabajador/a
harvest la cosecha
hat el sombrero
hate odiar, el odio
have tener (g) (ie), poseer, disponer de (g); haber (*aux.*); **have a good time** divertirse, pasarlo bien; **have breakfast** desayunar; **have dinner/supper** cenar; **have just +** ***past. part.*** acabar de + *inf.* **have lunch** almorzar; **have to +** ***verb*** tener que + *inf.*
he él
head la cabeza
health la salud
healthy sano/a
hear oír
heart el corazón
heat el calor
heater la calefacción
hello hola
helmet el casco
help *v.* ayudar, *n.* la ayuda
hemisphere el hemisferio
here aquí, acá
highway la carretera
hip la cadera
Hispanic hispano/a
home el hogar
homework la tarea
honeymoon la luna de miel
hope esperar; **I/We hope** ojalá
horizontal horizontal
hospital el hospital
host/hostess el/la anfitrión/a
hot caliente
hotel el hotel`
house la casa
housewife el ama de casa
housing la vivienda
human humano/a; **human being** ser humano
humanities las humanidades
humid húmedo/a
humidity la humedad
hurt doler (ue) (*like* gustar)
husband el marido, el esposo
hysteria la histeria

I

I yo
I/we hope ojalá
ice cream el helado
ideal ideal
idealist idealista
identification la identificación; **identification card** la cédula, el carnet
identify identificar
identity la identidad
if si
illiteracy el analfabetismo
illogical ilógico/a
imaginary imaginario/a
imagination la imaginación
imitate imitar
immediately enseguida, inmediatamente
immigrant el/la inmigrante
impartial imparcial
implant el implante
importance la importancia
important importante
improve mejorar
impulsive impulsivo/a
in en: **in front of** enfrente (de)
inauguration la inauguración
incentive el incentivo
include incluir
income el ingreso
incorrect incorrecto/a
increase *v.* aumentar, subir; *n.* el aumento (de sueldo, etc.)
independent independiente
index el índice
indicate indicar
indicated indicado/a
individual el individuo
inequality la desigualdad
inexpensive barato/a
infect infectar
infection la infección
infectious infeccioso/a
inflammation la inflamación
influence la influencia
inform *v.* informar; *n.* el informe
informal informal
information la información
ingredient el ingrediente
inhabitant el/la habitante
injection la inyección

inspector el/la inspector/a
insult insultar(se)
insurance el seguro
intelligent inteligente
intention la intención
intercept interceptar
intercepted intervenido
interest *v.* interesar; *n.* el interés
interested interesado/a
interesting interesante
interior el interior
international internacional
interpreter el/la intérprete
interrogative interrogativo/a
interrupt interrumpir
interview *v.* entrevistar; *n.* la entrevista
intervene intervenir
intimate íntimo/a
introvert introvertido/a
investigation la investigación
invitation la invitación
invite invitar
involve implicar
iron *v.* planchar; *n.* el hierro (*metal*); la plancha (*clothes*)
ironic irónico/a
irrational irracional
irreparable irreparable
irritated irritado/a
isolate aislar
Italian italiano/a
itinerary el itinerario

J

jacket la chaqueta
January enero
Japanese japonés/a
jar el tarro, la jarra
jeans los vaqueros/jeans
jewel, jewelry la joya
jogging suit la sudadera
journalist el/la periodista
joy la alegría
judge el/la juez/a
juice el jugo, el zumo (*Sp.*)
juice press el exprimidor
July julio
jump saltar
June junio
jungle la selva, la jungla
justice la justicia

K

keep guardar
key la llave
kick patear
kid el/la niño/a, el/la chaval/a
kill matar
kinship el parentesco
kitchen la cocina
knee la rodilla
knife el cuchillo
know conocer (zc), saber (*facts*)
knowledge el conocimiento

L

lab laboratorio
lack *n.* la falta; *v.* carecer (de), faltar (*like* gustar)
lamp la lámpara
language el idioma, la lengua: **language lab** el laboratorio de lenguas
lard la manteca
last *v.* durar; ; *adj.* último/a, pasado/a: **last night** anoche, **night before last** anteanoche
late tarde
law la ley
lawyer el/la abogado/a
lazy perezoso/a
learn aprender
leather el cuero
leave salir, irse
left izquierda
leg la pierna
lemon el limón
lend prestar
Lent la Cuaresma
let dejar
letter la carta
lettuce la lechuga
level el nivel
liar el/la mentiroso/a
liberal liberal
librarian el/la bibliotecario/a
library la biblioteca
lie la mentira
life la vida
likewise igualmente
lion el león
lip el labio
liquid el líquido
list la lista
listen escuchar
literature la literatura
live vivir
living room la sala
load cargar
loaded cargado/a
lobster la langosta
local local
locate localizar
location la localización, ubicación
lock up encerrar
locked up encerrado/a
logical lógico/a
logically lógicamente
loneliness la soledad
long largo/a
look (at) mirar
look for buscar
loose suelto/a
lose perder
loss la pérdida
lottery la lotería
love *v.* amar; *n.* el amor
luggage el equipaje
lunch el almuerzo
lung el pulmón

M

machine la máquina; **washing machine** la lavadora; **answering machine** el contestador automático
magazine la revista
magnificent magnífico/a
mail el correo
mailbox el buzón, el casillero (*in office*)
mailman el cartero
main principal
maintenance el mantenimiento
majority la mayoría
make hacer, fabricar; **make a bed** tender la cama; **make reservations** hacer reservas/reservaciones
malformation la malformación
manager el/la gerente, director/a
mango el mango
mantain mantener(se)
manual manual
many muchos/as
map el mapa
March marzo
Mardi Gras el Carnaval
margarine la margarina
mark marcar
marked down rebajado/a
marriage el matrimonio
married casado/a
marry casarse
mask la careta
material el material
materialist materialista
maternal materno/a
mathematics las matemáticas
matter *v.* importar (*like* gustar); *n.* el asunto, la gestión
maturity la madurez
maximum máximo/a
May mayo
maybe quizá(s)
mayonnaise la mayonesa
mayor el/la alcalde/sa
mean significar, querer decir
meaning el significado
means medios
meat la carne
mechanic el/la mecánico/a
medicine la medicina
meditate meditar
meet encontrar(se), conocer (*for the first time*)
meeting la reunión
melody la melodía
member el miembro
memory la memoria
mention mencionar
menu el menú
merchandise la mercancía
metabolize metabolizar
metal el metal
methodical metódico/a
metropolitan metropolitano/a
Mexican mexicano/a
microphone el micrófono
microscope el microscopio
microwave el microondas
midnight la medianoche
mile la milla
military militar: **military coup** el golpe militar
milk la leche
mineral el mineral
minibomb la minibomba
minimal mínimo/a
minimum el mínimo
minister (government) el ministro
ministry (government) el ministerio (de)
minus menos
mirror el espejo
Miss la señorita
mission la misión
mistake la equivocación
mistery el misterio
model el/la modelo
modem el módem
modern moderno/a
modify modificar
mom la mamá
Monday lunes
money dinero
month el mes
motorcycle la moto(cicleta)
more más
morning la mañana
mortal mortal
mortar el mortero
mother la madre
mother-in-law la suegra
motive el motivo
mouse el ratón
moustache el bigote
mouth la boca
move mover
movement el movimiento
movies el cine
Mr. el señor (Sr.)
Mrs. la señora (Sra.)
much mucho/a
murder el asesinato
murderer el/la asesino/a
muscle el músculo
museum el museo
music la música
musical musical
mustard la mostaza
mutual mutuo
my mi, mis

name *v.* nombrar; *n.* el nombre
napkin la servilleta
narrator el/la narrador/a
narrate narrar
narrow estrecho/a
natal (pertaining to birth) natal
nation la nación
national nacional

nationality la nacionalidad
native nativo/a
navegation la navegación
near cerca (de)
nearby cercano/a
neck el cuello
necessity la necesidad
necklace el collar
need *v.* necesitar; *n.* la necesidad
neighbor el/la vecino/a
neighborhood el vecindario, el barrio
neither tampoco
nephew el sobrino
nervous nervioso/a
net la red
network la cadena
neurosis la neurosis
never nunca
nevertheless sin embargo
new nuevo/a
New Year's Eve la Nochevieja
news la noticia
newspaper el periódico
next próximo/a, al lado
Nicaraguan nicaragüense
nice agradable
niece la sobrina
night la noche
nightgown el camisón
ninth noveno/a
nobody nadie
no no
noise el ruido
none ninguno/a
noon el mediodía
normally normalmente
North American norteamericano/a
nose la nariz
not no
not any ningún
notably notablemente
note la nota, el apunte
notebook el cuaderno
noteworthy notable
nothing nada
notice *v.* notar; *n.* el aviso
novel la novela
novelist el/la novelista
November noviembre
now ahora
nuclear nuclear
number el número
nurse el/la enfermero/a
nursery la guardería
nutrition la nutrición

O

obituary obituario
observation la observación
observe observar
obtain obtener
October octubre
occupation el oficio, la ocupación
occupy ocupar
of de: **of the** (*contraction of* de + el) del
offer *v.* ofrecer; *n.* la oferta
office la oficina
official oficial
offspring el/la descendiente
often a menudo
oil el aceite
old viejo/a
older mayor
Olympic Games las Olimpiadas (*alt.* las Olimpíadas)
on sobre
onion la cebolla
only sólo
only daughter la hija única
only son hijo único
open abrir
open air market el mercado al aire libre
operate operar
operation la operación
opinion la opinión
opportunity la oportunidad
opposite opuesto/a, contrario/a
optimist optimista
option la opción
orange *n.* la naranja, *adj.* anaranjado/a
orchestra la orquesta
order el/la orden
organ el órgano
organism el organismo
organize organizar
organized organizado/a
origen el origen
other otro/a
ought deber
our nuestro/a(s)
outbreak el brote
outcome el resultado
outdoors al aire libre
outskirts las afueras
outstanding destacado/a
overcome superar
own propio/a
oxygen el oxígeno

P

P.O. box el apartado de correos
pacemaker el marcapasos
pacifist pacifista
pack empacar
package el paquete
pain el dolor
painting el cuadro, la pintura
pajama el/la piyama
pamphlet el folleto
Panamanian panameño/a
panic el pánico
pants los pantalones
pantyhose las pantimedias
papaya la papaya
parachute el paracaídas
parade el desfile, la parada
paragraph el párrafo
parents los padres
park el parque

parking lot el estacionamiento
part la parte
partial parcial
participant el/la participante
participate participar
participation la participación
partner el/la compañero/a; la pareja
party la fiesta
passive pasivo/a
passenger el/la pasajero/a
passion la pasión
passport el pasaporte
pastime el pasatiempo
pastry shop la pastelería
paternal paterno/a
patient el/la paciente
pay pagar
peace la paz
pear la pera
peasant el/la campesino/a
peeled pelado/a
pencil el lápiz
people la gente
pepper la pimienta
percentage el porcentaje
perfectionist perfeccionista
perfectly perfectamente
performance la actuación
perfume el perfume
period el período
permanent permanente
permit permitir
person la persona
personal personal
personality la personalidad
Peruvian peruano/a
pessimist el/la pesimista: **pessimistic** pesimista
petroleum el petróleo
pharmacist el/la farmacéutico/a
pharmacy la farmacia
phase la fase
phenomenon el fenómeno
photography la fotografía
physical físico/a
physics la física
pill la pastilla
pillow la almohada
pilot el piloto
pin el alfiler
pineapple la piña
pink rosado/a
pinpoint destacar, señalar
place *v.* colocar; *n.* el lugar
plan *v.* planear, *n.* el plan
planet el planeta
plate el plato
play jugar (*game, sport*), tocar (*musical instrument*)
player el/la jugador/a
plaza la plaza
pleased complacido/a
pleasure el placer
plumber el/la plomero/a
poem el poema
poet el poeta
police la policía
police officer el policía, la (mujer) policía
politician el político
polkadotted de lunares
polyester el poliester
poor pobre
popular popular
population la población
pork el cerdo
port el puerto
portable portátil
Portuguese portugués/portuguesa
position el puesto
positive positivo/a
possession la posesión
postcard la tarjeta postal
post office el correo
posterior posterior
postgraduate el/la posgraduado/a
powerful poderoso/a
practical práctico/a
practice practicar
prefer preferir
preference la preferencia
preliminary preliminar
preparation la preparación
prepare preparar
prescribe recetar
prescription la receta
present *v.* presentar; *n.* el regalo; **at present** *adv.* actualmente, en la actualidad
presentation la presentación
preservation la conservación
president el/la presidente/a
pretty bonito/a
previous anterior
price el precio
prince el príncipe
principal el/la director/a (*of a school*); *adj.* principal
printing la imprenta
prior previo/a
private privado/a
prize el premio
probably probablemente
problem el problema
procession la procesión
product el producto
productivity la productividad
profession la profesión
professor el/la profesor/a
profile el perfil
progenitor el/la progenitor/a
program *v.* programar; *n.* el programa
programmer el/la programador/a
prohibit prohibir
project el proyecto
promote promover
promotion el ascenso
pronoun el pronombre
protect proteger
protection la protección
protein la proteína
protest la protesta
proverb el refrán

psychiatrist el/la psiquiatra
psychologist el/la psicólogo/a
psychology la psicología
public *n.* el público; *adj.* público/a
publication la publicación
publicity la publicidad, la propaganda
Puerto Rican puertorriqueño/a
pure puro/a
purple morado/a
purpose el propósito
purse el/la bolso/a
put poner
put in order ordenar
put on makeup maquillarse
pyramid la pirámide

Q

quantity la cantidad
quarter el cuarto
question la pregunta
quiet callado/a
quietly tranquilamente
quote la cita

R

race la carrera; la raza
racket la raqueta
radiator el radiador
radio el/la radio
radio announcer el/la locutor/a
railroad el ferrocarril
rain *v.* llover; *n.* la lluvia
rain forest el bosque tropical
raincoat el impermeable, la gabardina
raise levantar
rapidly rápidamente
rate la tasa
reaction la reacción
reactivate reactivar
read leer
reader el/la lector/a
ready listo/a, dispuesto/a
really realmente
rearview mirror el espejo retrovisor
rebellious rebelde
receipt el recibo
recent reciente
recently recién, recientemente
receptacle el recipiente
receptionist el/la recepcionista
recess el recreo
recipe la receta
recommend recomendar
recommendation recomendación
recording la grabación
recuperation la recuperación
recycle reciclar
red rojo/a
reduced reducido/a
referee el árbitro
reflect reflejar
refreshment el refresco
refrigerator el refrigerador
region la región
regional regional
regularly regularmente
relate relacionar
related relacionado/a
relation(ship) la relación
relative el familiar, el pariente
relatively relativamente
release liberar
released liberado/a
religious religioso/a
remedy el remedio
remember recordar
rent *v.* alquilar; *n.* el alquiler
repair *v.* reparar; *n.* la reparación
repeat repetir
reporter el/la reportero/a
represent representar
representative el/la representante
reprimand regañar
reproduction la reproducción
republic la república
reservation la reservación
reserve la reserva
residence la residencia, el domicilio
resident el/la residente
resolution la resolución
resource el recurso
respect respetar(se)
responsibility la responsabilidad
responsible responsable
rest *v.* descansar; *n.* el resto
restaurant el restaurante
restriction la restricción
result *v.* resultar; *n.* el resultado
résumé el currículum vitae
return volver, devolver
reunion la reunión
revelation la revelación
revise revisar
revision la revisión
revolution la revolución
rhythm el ritmo
rib la costilla
rice el arroz
rich rico/a
riddle la adivinanza
right derecho/a
ring el anillo
risk el riesgo
river el río
river basin la cuenca
robe la bata
rocket el cohete
roll la lista
romantic romántico/a
roof el techo
round redondo/a
round trip (el viaje) de ida y vuelta
routine la rutina
ruins las ruinas
rule la regla
run correr
runner el corredor/a

S

sad triste
sadness la tristeza
safe la caja fuerte
safety la seguridad
saint el/la santo/a
salad la ensalada
salad dressing el aderezo
salary el sueldo
same mismo/a
sale la venta; la rebaja
salesman el vendedor
salesperson el/la dependiente/dependienta
saleswoman la vendedora
salt la sal
salvation la salvación
sanction la sanción
sandal la sandalia
sandwich el sándwich
satiric satírico/a
Saturday sábado
sauce la salsa
save (from danger) salvar
say decir
scarf la bufanda
schedule el horario
School of ... la Facultad de ...
science la ciencia
scientist el/la científico/a
scissors las tijeras
scream gritar
screen la pantalla
sea el mar
seafood el marisco
season *v.* sazonar, aliñar; *n.* la estación, la temporada
seasoning el aderezo, el aliño
second segundo/a
secretary el/la secretario/a
secretion la secreción
section la sección
security la seguridad
sedentary sedentario/a
see ver
seed la semilla
seem parecer
segregate segregar
segregation la segregación
seize decomisar
seizure el decomiso
select seleccionar
selection la selección
sell vender
semester el semestre
seminar el seminario
send enviar, mandar
senior citizen la tercera edad
sentiment el sentimiento
sentimental sentimental
separation la separación
September septiembre
serious serio/a; grave
seriousness la gravedad
serve servir
service el servicio
settler el/la poblador/a
seventh séptimo/a
severe severo/a
several algunos
sew coser
sex el sexo
shake agitar
sharp afilado/a
shave afeitar(se)
she ella
sheet la sábana
ship *v.* enviar; *n.* la nave, el barco: **space ship** la nave espacial
shirt la camisa
shoe el zapato
shopping la compra
shopping center el centro comercial
short bajo/a; corto/a
shorten acortar
shoulder el hombro
shout gritar
show *v.* mostrar; *n.* la función
shower *v.* ducharse, bañarse; *n.* la ducha
shrimp el camarón
shuttle el transbordador
sick enfermo/a
sickness la enfermedad
sign el letrero
signal la señal
signature la firma
silk la seda
silly tonto
similarity la semejanza
simplicity la sencillez
simply simplemente
sincere sincero/a
sing cantar
singer el/la cantante
single (bachelor) soltero/a
sink el fregadero
sister la hermana
sister-in-law la cuñada
sit down sentarse
situation la situación
sixth sexto/a
size la talla
ski esquiar
skiing el esquí
skimmed descremado/a
skin la piel
skirt la falda
sky el cielo
sleep dormir: **fall asleep** dormirse
slipper la zapatilla
slope la pista
slowly lentamente
small pequeño/a
smart listo/a
smoke fumar
snow *v.* nevar; *n.* la nieve
so tan (*degree*), entonces, luego: **so long** hasta luego: **so-so** regular: **so that** para que
soap el jabón
soccer el fútbol
social social
society la sociedad
socioeconomic socioeconómico/a

sociology la sociología
sock el calcetín
soda el refresco
sofa el sofá
soft suave
solemn solemne
solicitant el/la solicitante
solid color de color entero
solution la solución
some alguno/a
somebody alguien
someone alguien
something algo
sometimes a veces
son el hijo
son-in-law el yerno
song la canción
soon pronto
soup la sopa
sour agrio/a
source la fuente
space el espacio
spaghetti el espagueti
Spanish *n.* el español; *adj.* español/a
speak hablar
specialized especializado/a
specially especialmente
speciality la especialidad
speed la velocidad
spend gastar
spice la especia
spinach las espinacas
spokesman el vocero
spoon la cuchara
sport el deporte
sportive deportivo/a
spot la mancha
stopping point la escala
spring la primavera
store la tienda
store window el escaparate
stability la estabilidad
stadium el estadio
stainless inoxidable
stairs la escalera
stamp el sello
start *v.* empezar, comenzar; *n.* el comienzo
state el estado
statistic la estadística
statue la estatua
steak el bistec
steal robar
steel el acero
steering wheel el volante
stemmed glass la copa
stepbrother el hermanastro
stepfather el padrastro
stepmother la madrastra
stepsister la hermanastra
stereotyped estereotipado/a
steward el auxiliar de vuelo
stewardess la auxiliar de vuelo
still todavía
stomach el estómago
strategy la estrategia
strawberry la fresa
street la calle
stress el estrés
stripe la raya
striped de rayas
strong fuerte
student el/la estudiante, el/la alumno/a
study estudiar
studying el estudio
subject of study la materia
suburb el suburbio
subway el metro
success el éxito
such tal
sugar el azúcar
suggest sugerir
suggestion la sugerencia
suit el traje
suitcase la maleta
summer el verano
sun el sol
sunglasses las gafas de sol
Sunday domingo
sunshade el quitasol
supermarket el supermercado
support apoyo
surprise la sorpresa
survey la encuesta
suspect sospechar
stove la estufa
sweat shirt la sudadera
sweater el suéter
sweep barrer
sweet shop la dulcería
sweet dulce
swim nadar
swimming la natación
swimming pool la piscina, la alberca (*Mex.*)
symptom el síntoma
synonym el sinónimo
system el sistema

T

T-shirt la camiseta
table la mesa
tablecloth el mantel
take place efectuar(se)
take tomar, llevar: **take a shower** ducharse: **take advantage of** aprovechar: **take a walk/stroll** pasear, salir de paseo: **take away** quitar: **take care of** cuidar: **take pictures** sacar fotos
talk conversar
talkative hablador/a
tall alto/a
tape recorder la grabadora
tardy retrasado/a, moroso/a (*in payment*)
tea el té
teach enseñar
team el equipo deportivo
tear-producing lacrimógeno/a
teaspoon la cucharita

technician el/la técnico/a
tecnocracy la tecnocracia
telephone el teléfono
television la televisión: **TV set** el televisor
tell decir
temperature la temperatura
tennis el tenis: **tennis player** el/la tenista
tenth décimo/a
term of office el mandato
terrace la terraza
terrible terrible
territory el territorio
terrorize aterrorizar
textual textual
thanks gracias
that ese, esa, eso, aquel, aquella, aquello (*dem.*); que (*rel.*); **that is** o sea; **that one** ése, ésa, aquél, aquélla; **that which** lo que
the el, la, los, las; lo
theater el teatro
then entonces
therapy la terapia
there is, there are hay: **there was, there were** había
thermometer el termómetro
they ellos/as
thin delgado/a
think pensar, creer
third tercer, tercero/a
this este/a
threaten amenazar
throat la garganta
through a través (de), por
throw lanzar
Thursday jueves
ticket el boleto, el billete, el pasaje: **ticket for admission** la entrada
tie la corbata
time el tiempo, la hora
timid tímido/a
tire cansar: **get tired** cansar(se)
tire la llanta
tired cansado/a
today hoy
toilet el inodoro
tomorrow mañana
tone el tono
tongue la lengua
too también, además
tooth el diente
torture la tortura
toy el juguete
trace el rastro
tradition la tradición
traditional tradicional
traditionally tradicionalmente
train *v.* entrenar; *n.* el tren
trait el rasgo
transfer trasladar(se)
transition la transición
translate traducir
translator traductor/a, intérprete
transmit transmitir
transmutation la transmutación
transparency la transparencia
transplant transplantar
transportation el transporte
travel *v.* viajar, recorrer; *n.* el turismo: **travel agent** el/la agente: de viajes
traveller's check el cheque de viajero
tray la bandeja
treatment el tratamiento
trip el viaje
tropical tropical
trunk el maletero, el baúl
try tratar
try on probarse
tub la bañadera
Tuesday martes
tuna el atún
tunic la túnica
tourist el/la turista; turístico/a
turkey el pavo, guajolote (*Mex.*)
turn doblar: **turn off** apagar(se)
TV viewer el/la televidente
twin el/la gemelo/a
twist torcer(se)
typewriter la máquina de escribir

U

ugly feo/a
ulcer la úlcera
umbrella el paraguas
umpire el árbitro
uncle el tío
under debajo (de)
underline subrayar
understand entender
underwear ropa interior
unexpected inesperado
unforgettable inolvidable
uniform el uniforme
universe el universo
university la universidad
unnoticed desapercibido/a
unpayable impagable
unpleasant antipático/a
until hasta (que)
urban urbano/a
urgent urgente
use utilizar, usar
utensil el utensilio

vacant vacante
vacation la vacación
vaccination la vacuna
vacuum cleaner la aspiradora
valid válido/a
valuable valioso/a
vanilla la vainilla
variable variable
VCR la videocasetera
vegetable el vegetal, la verdura
vegetarian vegetariano/a
vegetation la vegetación
vein la vena

Venezuelan venezolano/a
verb el verbo
verify verificar
vertical vertical
very muy
victory el triunfo
victim la víctima
vinegar el vinagre
violence la violencia
violinist el/la violinista
virus el virus
vitamine la vitamina
vocabulary el vocabulario
volleyball el voleibol
volume el volumen
volunteer el/la voluntario
vote votar
voucher el vale
vowel la vocal

W

waist la cintura
waiter el camarero
waitress la camarera
wake up despertarse
walk caminar
want querer
war la guerra
wardrobe el guardarropa, el vestuario
warn advertir
warning el aviso
wash lavar(se)
washbowl el lavabo
washing machine la lavadora
waste desperdiciar
watch *v.* mirar, vigilar; *n.* el reloj
water *v.* regar; *n.* el agua (f.)
way el camino
we nosotros/as
weak débil
wear llevar, usar
wear a costume disfrazarse
weather report el pronóstico, el tiempo
wedding la boda
Wednesday miércoles
week la semana
weight el peso
welcome *n.* la bienvenida, *v.* dar la bienvenida
welfare el bienestar, asistencia social
well bien
what qué
when *interrog.* cuándo; *adv.* cuando
where dónde
where (to) adónde
which (one) cuál/es
while mientras
white blanco/a
who quién
why por qué
wide ancho/a
widow la viuda
widower el viudo
wife la esposa
will la voluntad
win ganar
wind el viento
window la ventana, ventanilla
window cleaner el limpiavidrios
windshield el parabrisas
windshield wiper el limpiaparabrisas
wine el vino
winner el/la ganador/a
winter el invierno
Wise Men Reyes Magos
wish desear
with con
without sin
woman la mujer
wood la madera
wool la lana
word la palabra
work *v.* trabajar; *n.* el trabajo
worker el/la obrero/a
world el mundo
world-wide mundial, universal
worry preocupar(se)
wrist la muñeca
write escribir
writer el/la escritor/a

Y

year el año
yellow amarillo/a
yes sí
yesterday ayer: **day before yesterday** anteayer
yet todavía
yogurt el yogur
you tú; usted, Ud.; vosotros/as; ustedes, Uds.; te, os, lo, la, los, las; ti, le, les
young joven

Z

zone la zona
zoo el zoológico

Credits

TEXT CREDITS

p. 34: advertisement reprinted by permission of Centro Audiovisual; **p. 80:** *Mafalda* comic strip, reprinted by permission of Joaquín S. Lavado, QUINO, toda Mafalda, Ediciones de la Flor, 1997; **pp. 147-148:** excerpts from the article "El «Sí» de los Niños," reprinted by permission of *Blanco y Negro*; **p. 319:** excerpts from *¿Qué pasa?* Reprinted by permission of Vanidades; **pp. 385-386:** excerpts from the article "Dieta: buenos consejos" reprinted by permission of *Vanidades*; **p. 465** En Las altas esferasa, Socorro Ramirez, Reprinted by permission of Fempress; **p. 466:** "El 21% de los universitarios españoles usa Internet como fuente de noticias" reprinted by permission of Diario El País International, S.A.; **p. 494:** *Mafalda* comic strip, reprinted by permission of Joaquín S. Lavado, QUINO, toda Mafalda, Ediciones de la Flor, 1997; **p. 506:** "Apocalipsis I" by Marco Denevi, reprinted by permission of the author.

PHOTO CREDITS

p. 2 Robert Frerck/Odyssey Productions; p. 5 Robert Frerck/Odyssey Productions; p. 6 Robert Frerck/Odyssey Productions; p. 26 Robert Frerck/Odyssey Productions; p. 28 (top) A.G.E. FotoStock; P. 28 (bottom) Peter Menzel Photography; p. 32 Robert Frerck/Odyssey Productions; p. 50 (left and right) University of Salamanca; p. 55 Robert Frerck/Odyssey Productions; p. 57 Robert Frerck/Odyssey Productions; p. 59 Robert Frerck/Odyssey Productions; p. 61 Robert Frerck/Odyssey Productions; p. 62 (top) A.G.E. FotoStock; p. 62 (middle) Michael Keller/Corbis/Stock Market; p. 62 (bottom) Peter Menzel Photography; p. 63 (top) David Young-Wolff/ PhotoEdit; p. 63 (bottom) Getty Images Inc.; p. 84 (middle) Getty Images, Inc.; p. 87 David R. Frazier Photolibrary, Inc.; p. 89 Mula–Eshet/Corbis/Stock Market; p. 91 Reuters/Jeff Christensen/Archive Photos; p. 92 Robert Frerck/Odyssey Productions; p. 94 (top) SuperStock, Inc.; p. 94 (middle) Robert Frerck/Odyssey Productions, Inc.; p. 94 (bottom) Nik Wheeler; p. 95 Robert Fried/D. Donne Bryant Stock Photography; p. 97 Larry Luxner/Luxner News Inc.; p. 114 Bill Bachmann/Stock Boston; p. 121 Reuters/Silva Izquierdo/Archive Photos; p. 122 A.G.E. FotoStock; p. 123 Charles and Josette Lenar/Corbis; p. 125 (top) Miramax/Kobal Collection; p. 125 (bottom) Orion Classics/Shooting Star International Photo Agency; p. 126 Myrleen Ferguson/PhotoEdit; p. 128 (top) N. Frank/The Viesti Collection, Inc.; p. 128 (middle) K. McGlynn/The Image Works; p. 146 (top) Mary Kate Denny/PhotoEdit; p. 146 (bottom) Victor Englebert/Englebert Photography, Inc.; p. 153 Tony Freeman/PhotoEdit; p. 154 A.G.E. FotoStock; p. 155 Peter Menzel/Peter Menzel Photography; p. 157 Marcelo Salinas/Latin Focus Photo Agency; p. 158 German Meneses Photography; p. 160 (top) Robert Frerck/Odyssey Productions; p. 190 © Chip and Rosa Maria de la Cueva Peterson; p. 191 © Michael Everett/DDB Stock Photo. All rights Reserved; p. 194 Kathy Willens/AP/Wide World Photos; p. 296 Getty Images, Inc.; p. 198 Ulrike Welsch/PhotoEdit; p. 199 David J. Sams/Texas Inprint/Stock Boston; p. 222 Peter Menzel/Stock Boston; p. 223 A.G.E. FotoStock; p. 225 Barbara Bareto/ Latin Focus Photo Agency; 226 A.G.E. FotoStock; p. 228 (top) Joe Traver/ Liaison Agency, Inc.; p. 228 (middle) Bill Bachmann/PhotoEdit; p. 228 (bottom) Reuters/Sam Mircovich/Archive Photos; p. 256 Daniel Rivadamar/Odyssey Productions; p. 257 Russell Gordon/Odyssey Productions; p. 259 Shaun Botterill/Allsport Photography (USA), Inc.; p. 260 A. Ramey/PhotoEdit; p. p. 262 (top) Owen Franken/Stock Boston; p. 262 (middle) Robert Frerck/Odyssey Productions; p. 262 (bottom) Joe Viesti/The Viesti Collection, Inc.; p. 263 (top) Jeremy Horner/The Hutchison Library; p. 263 (middle) Robert Frerck/Odyssey Productions; p. 263 (bottom) Larry Mangino/The Image Works; p. 267 Spencer Grant/PhotoEdit; p. 290 Robert Frerck/Odyssey Productions; p. 291 Robert Frerck/Odyssey Productions; p. 293 Robert Frerck/Odyssey Productions; p. 294 Jose L. Pelaez/ Corbis/Stock Market; p. 296 (top) LeDuc/Monkmeyer Press; p. 296 (center) Dian/Monkmeyer Press; p. 296 (bottom) Getty Images, Inc.; p. 297 (top) Robert Frerck/Odyssey Productions; p. 297 (center right) Beryl Goldberg; p. 297 (bottom left) Rob Crandall/The Image Works; p. 297 (bottom right) Elena Rooraid/PhotoEdit; p. 301 Adam Smith/FPG International LLC; p. 324 Walter Bibikow/The Viesti Collection, Inc.; p. 325 Walter Bibikow/The Viesti Collection, Inc.; p. 328 Lars Bahl/Impact Visuals Photo & Graphics, Inc.; p. 334 (top) Robert Frerck/Odyssey Productions; p. 334 (center right) Robert Frerck/ Odyssey Productions; p. 334 (center left) Nik Wheeler; p. 334 (bottom) Richard Lord Enterprises, Inc.; p. 355 Robert Frerck/Odyssey Productions; p. 356 Hubert Stadler/Corbis; p. 357 Jeremy Horner/The Hutchison Library; p. 359 Jose Caruci/AP/Wide World Photos; p. 361 José L. Pelaez/Corbis/Stock Market; p. 368 (top) Rolando Pujol/ South American Pictures; p. 368 (middle) Paul Smith/Panos Pictures; p. 368 (bottom) SuperStock, Inc.; p. 390 Joe Viesti/The Viesti Collection, Inc.; p. 391 José Fuste Raga/Corbis/Stock Market; p. 393 Tony Arruza/CORBIS; p. 394 Tom McCarthy/PhotoEdit; p. 396 (top) Claudia Dhimitri/The Viesti Collection, Inc.; p. 396 (middle) John F. Mason/Corbis/Stock Market; p. 396 (bottom) Michele Burgess/Stock Boston; p. 426 J.G. Fuller/The Hutchison Library; p. 427 Wolfgang Kaehler/Liaison Agency, Inc; p. 429 Jeff Greenberg/ PhotoEdit; p. 430 Spencer Grant/Liaison Agency, Inc.; p. 432 (top) Stephen Jaffe/ AFP/Corbis; p. 432 (bottom) Ian Waldie/ Reuters New Media, Inc./Corbis; p. 433 (top) Peter Muhly/AFP/Corbis; p. 433 (middle) Prentice Hall High School; p. 433 (bottom) Michel Setboun/Corbis/ Sygma; p. 434 David R. Frazier/Photo Researchers, Inc.; p. 435 (top) Walter Bibikow/The Viesti Collection, Inc.; p. 435 (bottom) Ken Ross/The Viesti Collection, Inc.; p. 455 Peter Bennett/The Viesti Collection, Inc.; p. 456 The Viesti Collection, Inc.; p. 457 © Tony Arruza/ CORBIS; p. 459 © Robert Frerck/ Odyssey/Chicago; p. 460 Marc Pokempner/Stone; p. 464 (left) Ricardo Mazalan/AP/Wide World Photos; p. 464 (right) Tomas Van Houtryve/AP/Wide World Photos; p. 485 Dario Lopez–Mills/ AP/Wide World Photos; p. 487 Jimmy Dorantes/Latin Focus Photo Agency; p. 488 Nick Souza/Latin Focus Photo Agency; p. 491 Kevin Horan/Stock Boston; p. 494 NASA/Stock Boston; p. 495 NASA/Latin Focus Photo Agency; p. 495 NASA/Latin Focus Photo Agency; p. 510 Chris Sharp/South American Pictures; p. 511 Victor Englebert/ Englebert Photography, Inc.; p. 512 (top) Tony Morrison/South American Pictures; p. 512 (bottom) Russell Gordon/Odyssey Productions; p. 513 Bill Gleasner/The Viesti Collection, Inc.; p. 515 Michael Newman/PhotoEdit.

Index of Language Functions

Index